HEALTH POLICY
AND THE UNINSURED

Edited by
Catherine G. McLaughlin

HEALTH POLICY
AND THE UNINSURED

THE URBAN INSTITUTE PRESS
WASHINGTON, DC

THE URBAN INSTITUTE PRESS
2100 M Street, N.W.
Washington, D.C. 20037

Library of Congress Cataloging-in-Publication Data

Health policy and the uninsured / edited by Catherine G. McLaughlin.
        p. ; cm.
Includes bibliographical references and index.
    ISBN 0-87766-719-5 (alk. paper)
  1. Medically uninsured persons—United States. 2. Insurance, Health—United States. 3. Medical policy—United States.
    [DNLM: 1. Medically Uninsured—United States. 2. Health Policy—United States. 3. Insurance, Health—economics—United States. 4. Vulnerable Populations—United States. W 250 AA1 H434 2004] I. McLaughlin, Catherine G.
    RA413.7.U53H434 2004
    368.38'2'00973—dc22
                                                                    2003025092

ISBN 0-87766-719-5 (paper, alk. paper)

Printed in the United States of America
10 09 08 07 06 05 04   1 2 3 4 5

THE URBAN INSTITUTE is a nonprofit, nonpartisan policy research and educational organization established in Washington, D.C., in 1968. Its staff investigates the social, economic, and governance problems confronting the nation and evaluates the public and private means to alleviate them. The Institute disseminates its research findings through publications, its Web site, the media, seminars, and forums.

Through work that ranges from broad conceptual studies to administrative and technical assistance, Institute researchers contribute to the stock of knowledge available to guide decisionmaking in the public interest.

Conclusions or opinions expressed in Institute publications are those of the authors and do not necessarily reflect the views of officers or trustees of the Institute, advisory groups, or any organizations that provide financial support to the Institute.

Acknowledgments

This collection of papers was commissioned by the Economic Research Initiative on the Uninsured (ERIU), which was made possible through the generous funding of The Robert Wood Johnson Foundation. In addition to the financial support provided by the Foundation, the cooperation and encouragement of both David Colby and Linda Bilheimer at RWJF have been invaluable.

I also thank each of the authors for their willingness to take on these assignments and doing such a wonderful job of providing useful conceptual frameworks and comprehensive critical syntheses of the extant literature. Their papers benefited from the comments of participants at ERIU's 2001 Research Agenda Setting Conference, especially the discussants who challenged each author to make every finding just a little clearer. They are John Bound, Tom Buchmueller, David Card, Jose Escarce, Dana Goldman, Roger Feldman, Hilary Hoynes, Emmett Keeler, Susan Marquis, Alan Monheit, and Anne Polivka.

Virtually all members of the ERIU staff have made important contributions to this volume. Sarah Crow, Mary Harrington, and Hanns Kuttner not only wrote sections of the introductory chapter, they also helped shepherd all of the papers through the lengthy process of moving from drafts of conference papers to polished chapters in a unified volume. Chrissie Juliano provided critical assistance in the final stages of the publication process. Kristin Reiter and Karoline Mortensen supplied able research assistance to the authors. Brenette Logan efficiently coordinated the interaction of all of these contributors and the exchange of all communications.

The editorial and marketing staff at the Urban Institute Press has been supportive and attentive throughout this process, and I thank them for helping this book become a reality. Finally, I also thank the three anonymous reviewers of the original manuscript.

Contents

Preface

The purpose of *Health Policy and the Uninsured* is to improve our understanding about one of the nation's most pressing problems—lack of health insurance coverage for all Americans. This book was developed as part of the work of the Economic Research Initiative on the Uninsured, funded by The Robert Wood Johnson Foundation, to address some of the most perplexing questions about why people lack health insurance in the United States and to provide needed information to policymakers.

Since the early years of the twentieth century, the push for health insurance coverage has been a heated and perennial topic of political debate in the United States. Now, almost a century after the first discussions of government's role in promoting national health insurance, the debate continues as the number of people without coverage rises.

The United States is unique in the industrialized world in the proportion of people without health insurance. In 2002, nearly 44 million Americans (about 17 percent of the nonelderly population) did not have health insurance coverage. The fact that health insurance coverage is still not universal in this country is attributable, in part, to the unique way in which it has developed here. In contrast to most western countries, which adopted social insurance approaches, health coverage in the United States has developed incrementally along separate pathways. The majority of the population is enrolled in private, mostly employment-based health insurance plans. Since 1966, the public sector has sponsored parts of the health care financing system in the form of Medicare and Medicaid and, more recently, the State Children's Health Insurance Program (SCHIP). Medicare is a social insurance program for the elderly and disabled, financed primarily by federal taxes, with uniform benefits, premiums, and cost sharing. The Medicaid and SCHIP programs, by contrast, are intergovernmental grant-in-aid programs, financed by both the federal and state governments (and to a small extent by counties), which provide coverage to low-income families, children, and certain other low-income people who are generally elderly or disabled. The states maintain substantial discretion over who is eligible and what services are covered in these programs.

When The Robert Wood Johnson Foundation was established as a national organization in 1972, trustees and staff did not focus on health insurance coverage. They thought that universal coverage was just around the corner. The Nixon administration's health insurance proposal was one of several competing health insurance bills introduced at that time. But neither President Nixon's health insurance proposal nor the competing proposals were enacted. By the time Nixon's plan and the others were defeated, the Foundation had already embarked on the path of improving the delivery system, especially the noninsurance aspects of access to care.

From then until recently, while the Foundation addressed some aspects of the problem, its approach was opportunistic and piecemeal. In 1998, the Foundation moved to focus its grantmaking. As part of that effort, it decided on a three-element strategy to address coverage issues.

Raise Awareness. The first element of the strategy was to raise awareness. This effort started with what many refer to as the "strange bedfellows" effort, involving, among other groups, FamiliesUSA, the Health Insurance Association of America, the American Medical Association, the American Nurses Association, Catholic Health Association, Service Employees International Union, the U.S. Chamber of Commerce, and the AFL-CIO. They held Washington, D.C., regional, and town hall meetings, and most importantly, sponsored "Cover the Uninsured Week." The first "Cover the Uninsured Week" in March 2003, cochaired by former Presidents Gerald Ford and Jimmy Carter, was extremely successful. Over 800 events in every state and the District of Columbia generated much public interest and press coverage.

Max Out. The second element of the strategy was to increase participation of eligible individuals in public insurance opportunities. The

Covering Kids Initiative (and its successor, Covering Kids and Families) was established across the nation to encourage the enrollment of children and, later, eligible adults into Medicaid and SCHIP. It supported outreach to enroll eligible people, simplification of application procedures, and coordination of applications between Medicaid and SCHIP.

Provide Information. The third element was to develop objective information needed by key audiences about the issue, its causes, consequences, and the variety of solutions. One aspect of this was *Covering America: Real Remedies for the Uninsured*, which presented a series of policy options that represented different philosophical approaches to expanding coverage.

A second aspect of the information effort was to support needed research on this issue. Among other projects, the Foundation funded the Urban Institute to conduct the National Survey of America's Families to analyze coverage issues. It also funded the Institute of Medicine to examine why coverage matters. Finally, the Foundation sponsored the Economic Research Initiative on the Uninsured (ERIU).

Economic Research Initiative on the Uninsured

The formal purpose of the ERIU project is to investigate what we know and don't know about the characteristics of the uninsured, causes of being uninsured, and consequences of being uninsured. The project has a special focus on the interaction between the labor market and health insurance.

Why focus this project on the labor market? The answer is simple. Employer-sponsored health insurance has become one of our enduring institutions, although many think that it is dying or that it should be allowed to expire. Beginning in World War II, health insurance access for Americans became available through the workplace. Today, about 82 percent of those insured in the prime working ages (18 to 65) have employer-based health insurance. Our employment decisions, including the type of employment we choose and the organizations for which we work, affect and are affected by our need for insurance. As the labor market changes, with more contingent and temporary workers, our health insurance coverage will change.

The ERIU project also has several secondary purposes. First, because of changing research funding patterns, health services research had shifted away from coverage issues to other areas, such as quality of care. By offering new support, the project hoped to attract researchers back to examining coverage issues. Second, analysis of insurance coverage was somewhat moribund, with many of the same people asking similar questions, using the same analytical frameworks. To address this concern, the project tried to encourage non-health economists, including labor and public finance economists, and economists from economics departments as well as from business schools to conduct research on coverage.

To lower the entry costs for non-health economists, the project has developed several tools. First, this book provides a critical review of the literature. Second, ERIU has developed and maintained a searchable web-based literature database of over 1,500 journal articles, non-journal articles, and working papers on coverage produced since 1990. Third, ERIU has also created a directory that describes ways to access a dozen publicly available data sets that contain information about health insurance coverage and individual characteristics. The directory also provides information on the data collection methods and the samples used. All three of these resources are meant to jump-start new research efforts.

ERIU has been extremely successful. In addition to the resources mentioned above, it has held three research conferences. Many non-health economists participated in the research meetings and were funded to develop projects. These conferences and research solicitations energized the field. Being invited to the research meetings of ERIU became a hot ticket for researchers. New ideas were brought to bear on issues of insurance, such as a bargaining framework adopted from the Nobel Prize winner John Nash. The project also attracted new researchers, ensuring that this work will continue. To date, ERIU has funded 45 research projects across three waves of competitive proposal solicitations. Grantees were selected from schools of public health and public policy, economics departments, and medical schools at nearly 30 different universities and a half-dozen think tanks or independent research firms.

ERIU supports more basic research than The Robert Wood Johnson Foundation usually undertakes; most Foundation-supported research tends to be applied research. ERIU has asked hard and, sometimes, uncomfortable questions. It has challenged researchers to conduct more and better research. Indeed, this book presents challenges to those researchers who are analyzing health coverage.

David C. Colby
December 2003

Causes and Consequences of Lack of Health Insurance

Gaps in Our Knowledge

Catherine G. McLaughlin, Sarah E. Crow, Mary Harrington, and Hanns Kuttner

While questions related to the causes and consequences of being without health insurance are often debated in policy and research circles, relatively little research has been undertaken to develop and test theoretical and conceptual models of why observed patterns of coverage exist. Much of the standard wisdom on health insurance comes from studies that are descriptive or that present findings from regression analyses that have not been integrated into a careful methodological framework. Too little of the work takes into account challenges such as whether a cause was actually an effect.

The six chapters that make up this book were commissioned by the Economic Research Initiative on the Uninsured (ERIU) at the University of Michigan, Ann Arbor. The initiative is part of a multifaceted effort funded by the Robert Wood Johnson Foundation to increase the nation's collective understanding of the issues surrounding the lack of health insurance coverage in the United States. The goal of ERIU is to conduct and fund research that increases our understanding of the complex interactions among labor markets, health care markets, and health insurance coverage.

In an attempt to discover which questions related to the causes and consequences of health insurance have been answered with some authority and which remain unanswered, ERIU commissioned the six critical syntheses in this book. The studies were presented in July 2001 to a conference of about 60 economists. While published research articles often begin with an abbreviated review of the economics literature, critical syntheses of a body of work are less common. Until now, no one has pulled together the breadth of the literature on the lack of coverage. Many complicated connections link health status, labor market participation, and individual decisionmaking with respect to health insurance coverage. Conducting useful research and suggesting appropriate policy changes requires a more complete understanding of those connections.

The syntheses address *who* does not have health insurance, *why* they do not have health insurance, and *what* difference health insurance makes. Each discusses the methodological hurdles involved in researching these questions. This comprehensive and coordinated critique of the literature serves several purposes. First, it summarizes for policymakers what we know and do not know about the uninsured. Second, it provides a framework for the health policy research needed to fill the remaining gaps in our knowledge. And third, it serves as a useful primer for economists and other policy analysts who are new to the field, making it easier for them to conduct needed research and thus contribute to the debate.

This introduction presents some of the major findings and gaps from each of the chapters. It is not an attempt to summarize the chapters fully, but rather to give the reader a sense of what they offer collectively. In short: what can we say with some confidence about the uninsured, and what areas need more research?

Counting the Uninsured

Chapter 1 addresses the question, Who are the uninsured and how many are there in the United States? Pamela Farley Short adds several new insights into how the estimates of the uninsured are calculated and interpreted. In 1998, Lewis, Ellwood, and Czajka compared estimates from the Current Population Survey (CPS) and the Survey of Income and Program Participation (SIPP) and described estimates from the National Center for Health Statistics' National Health Interview Survey, the Agency for Healthcare Research and Quality's Medical Expenditure Panel Study (MEPS), the Center for Studying Health System Change's Community Tracking Study, and the *Assessing the New Federalism's* National Survey of America's Families. They pointed out some of the survey design and implementation issues that should be considered when counting how many people are uninsured and who they are. Chollet (2000) looked at the same six major, nationally representative surveys above and added a discussion of the role of different methodologies in influencing estimates of how many are without health insurance.

Short takes the next step, contrasting the picture of who is uninsured that emerges from cross-sectional analyses with the image that comes from looking at who is insured and uninsured over a period of time. From a longitudinal perspective, the dualism of "insured" and "uninsured" gives way to three categories: those who are always without health insurance, those who are sometimes without health insurance, and those who always have health insurance. Drawing on this more complicated picture of the uninsured, Short analyzes the extent of continuous and sporadic coverage for various population groups. Since Swartz and McBride (1990) first analyzed spells without health insurance, it has been known that over half of the new spells without insurance end within six months. Thus the most important feature of a survey is its ability to distinguish continuous lack of coverage from sporadic lack of coverage.

Estimates from the six surveys noted above identified approximately 40 million uninsured individuals in 1999, with a difference of 7 million between the smallest and largest estimates. However, as Short points out, a number of features about these commonly used data sets merit careful consideration. For example, in many of the nationally representative surveys that collect data on health insurance, there is no direct question that identifies the uninsured. Rather, the uninsured are those who do not give positive answers to questions about different types of coverage. Because data on the uninsured are residual, forgetfulness and underreporting of health insurance are likely to inflate estimates.

In addition, cross-sectional estimates understate the number of people who experience a spell without insurance. Longitudinal estimates capture all of the uninsured spells for a sample of people over time and produce higher counts of the uninsured. Moreover, counting the uninsured over longer periods (e.g., two years rather than one) produces a higher count. Because longitudinal data allow researchers to determine the length of spells, they are also better for assessing the welfare implications of being uninsured. Short's analysis challenges much of the research that relies on cross-sectional data, including repeated cross sections used as a pseudopanel (e.g., multiple years of data from the CPS). A gross count of the uninsured obscures very different social phenomena: a person who cycles back and forth between Medicaid and uninsurance is different from a person who never has health insurance. Cross-sectional surveys have no way of differentiating between them and thus blunt our ability to identify the effects of health insurance. Chapter 1 raises questions in the mind of anyone who reads research that relies on binary categories such as insured and not insured, with and without private coverage, and so on. What difference would it make if the duration of the spell without health insurance or the propensity to remain insured was known?

The failure of the literature on health insurance to take the Short critique to heart is less a failure on the part of researchers than a limitation of the data available. The workhorse of labor economics, the CPS, produces counts of persons in various insurance status categories that Short says are "essentially uninterpretable." The SIPP follows people for at most four years. The Panel Study of Income Dynamics has begun to ask regularly about health insurance, and it may eventually become the best source of insight into the time dimension of health insurance status. MEPS asks about respondents' health insurance coverage on a monthly basis, but this rich data set is largely unused by anyone outside health economics. The Health and Retirement Survey and the National Longitudinal Study of Youth offer promise for insight into longer-term dynamics in certain age groups.

While refinements can be made on the way the uninsured are counted and described, one can say with relative confidence that there is little new ground to be broken in this area. However, researchers and policy-makers alike need to be educated about the limitations of these commonly used cross-sectional estimates and about the need to look beyond them in assessing the scope of the problem and the appropriate policy response.

Reasons for Being Uninsured

In chapter 2, Linda Blumberg and Len Nichols describe what we know about *why* the uninsured go without health insurance. They synthesize the research on whether lack of coverage is a market failure and look at the supply and demand sides of employer-sponsored insurance.

Three main reasons have been found for lack of coverage: 1) people are healthy and choose not to have insurance because they are unwilling to pay the price for insurance; 2) people want insurance but cannot get it because of insurance underwriting practices or labor market rigidities; and 3) people want an insurance product that is available but cannot afford the coverage. Each category suggests a different set of policy prescriptions. Thus the path from research to policy requires a detailed understanding of the importance of each reason. Blumberg and Nichols separate unsubstantiated claims about causes from hypothesized causes that were based on theory and proven empirically. Beyond documenting the fact that barriers to coverage do exist, the chapter explores the reasons why some individuals have low demand for coverage and what barriers they face.

For most Americans, health insurance is a benefit provided by their employer, a practice that introduces additional players and complexity to the traditional model of supply and demand. Employers decide when, to whom, and at what out-of-pocket price to offer health insurance as a benefit. Employees, in turn, decide on job offers based not only on their skill set and wages, but also on the offer of health insurance for themselves and their families. Some of the components of these relationships are understood, and others are not. Generally, we know that employers offer health insurance to recruit and retain employees, but many of the finer details about employer offers of health insurance are not fully understood.

Blumberg and Nichols find evidence that employers' offers of insurance are influenced by worker preferences for health insurance, prevailing norms for attracting different types of workers, and the price of insurance faced by the firm. Premium price, tax incentives, and characteristics of firms and workers are significant factors in explaining the probability that an employer will offer health insurance. New, part-time, and temporary workers are less likely to be eligible for insurance, but it is not yet clear why employers make some workers rather than others eligible or what types of employers have differential eligibility policies. How do worker preferences affect employer decisions about offers? How and to what extent do preferences vary across workers? How are varied preferences taken into account in decisions about offers, eligibility rules, and the sharing of premium costs? Research has not yet satisfactorily answered these important questions.

Economic theory assumes that regardless of what percentage of the premium an employee pays out of pocket, he or she ultimately pays the remaining cost in the form of a wage-benefit trade-off. This hypothesized trade-off is not well documented empirically. Blumberg and Nichols present some evidence that employees do not pay 100 percent of insurance costs from their wages, based on how employers have responded to different policies and incentives. Some evidence indicates that the trade-off is greater when the definition of job benefits is broadened to include other things besides health insurance.

Employees do respond to the amount of the out-of-pocket premium, research shows. In fact, premium contributions have a greater effect on the rate at which employees take up the offer of insurance than total premium price does. Lower-income workers are more responsive to price than higher-income workers, and take-up rates increase with salary and earnings. Out-of-pocket premiums are even more important in determining take-up rates than the health status of the worker and family members.

Many questions remain unanswered. For example, how do workers who decline the offer of insurance differ from workers not offered insurance? What proportion of the uninsured is in transition between jobs and will soon secure coverage, as opposed to those who are continuously employed yet uninsured? What is the appropriate assumption regarding the percentage of insurance costs actually paid by workers? How does this vary by type of firm and worker, and by what mechanism are wages traded for employer premium payments? How do individuals weigh the pros and cons of private versus public coverage? Research is needed to shed light on the best way to ask and answer these questions.

Labor Supply and Job Mobility

Jonathan Gruber and Bridget Madrian focus on the interaction between health insurance and labor markets in chapter 3. Building on some of their previous work (Gruber 2000; Currie and Madrian 1999), they have developed a conceptual model outlining the hypothesized effects of worker demand for health insurance coverage on decisions regarding labor force participation (entry, exit, full-time vs. part-time work, firm), worker mobility, productivity, and wages. As they note, considerable research has looked at labor supply issues, but the majority of it merely points out the correlation between labor force participation and coverage and does not establish a causal link.

The authors' careful analysis of the literature yielded a number of findings. First, health insurance matters in people's decisions to retire or to change jobs. Second, while job lock—lack of job mobility because of fear of losing coverage—has been shown to exist, very little research has been done to determine the size of that effect or its implications for either the overall well-being of workers or the efficiency of the labor market. Third, research suggests that health insurance is not a major determinant in the decisions of low-income mothers to seek a job or leave welfare, but the authors note that more study of this topic needs to be done. There is still a lively debate about whether Medicaid expansions reduce welfare participation and increase labor supply, and there is room for significant contributions in this area.

Married couples' joint decisions with respect to health insurance coverage are also examined in this chapter. Spouses (usually identified as wives in the literature) may make their labor force decisions largely on the availability of health insurance to them and their families. Although flawed—most models are based on the assumption that the husband's health insurance coverage is exogenous, which may be increasingly unrealistic—the research indicates that health insurance is important to the labor supply decisions of "secondary" workers.

The effect of health insurance on labor markets has become an abundant field of research, and more is in the offing. New areas might take on phenomena that are puzzling to economists or not well understood. One puzzle to consider is the low rate at which part-time jobs come with health insurance offers. The standard economic account of firm behavior suggests that offers of health insurance should be independent of hours worked, and yet they are not. Another is our lack of insight into how decisionmaking among married couples affects health insurance outcomes. For example, retirement is often a joint decision. Given the higher expected health costs of the near-elderly, deciding to retire prior to becoming eligible for Medicare is likely to be influenced by health insurance options.

Impact of Health Insurance

In chapter 4, Helen Levy and David Meltzer focus on the health consequences of being uninsured. It is widely assumed that lack of coverage has deleterious effects on health status. This assumption is based on two important causative relationships: first, that being insured is critically important to receiving appropriate and timely medical care, and second, that receiving appropriate and timely medical care has a significant effect on health status.

Brown, Bindman, and Lurie (1998) reviewed much of the literature on this topic published between 1966 and 1996. They point out some of the weaknesses in the methodologies used and conclude that no causative links between lack of insurance and poor health have been supported. Levy and Meltzer build on this work. They develop a conceptual framework of the links, why one may expect different relationships among insurance coverage, health care utilization, and health status outcomes for different population groups (e.g., low income, racial and ethnic minorities) and for different diseases or treatment categories (e.g., chronic conditions, acute conditions). They also discuss what evidence would be needed to assert causation versus correlation. Very little research documents an effect of health insurance on health using the highest standard of proof, and what does exist points to small gains for people with specific ailments.

While a great many studies show a correlation between health insurance and improvements in health outcomes, Levy and Meltzer conclude that very few are controlled studies that permit a rigorous analysis of the specific contribution of health insurance on health outcomes. For a full understanding of how health insurance affects health utilization patterns and overall health, one needs an understanding of the incremental contribution of health insurance as opposed to the many other factors that affect health. Even most quasi-experimental studies have limited value because of questions regarding endogeneity. Only randomized controlled trials can provide indisputable evidence about the effect of health insurance on health status. The RAND Health Insurance Experiment was such a trial, but it was not designed to assess the impact of health insurance; rather, it was designed to test the relative impact of different types of coverage arrangements. Still, it provides some evidence that health insurance leads to limited improvements in health outcomes: namely, reduced blood pressure among low-income persons with hypertension, and improved vision.

Some readers will be frustrated by Levy and Meltzer's findings and argue that they set too high a bar for what qualifies as concrete evidence. Others will maintain that researchers and social scientists must be honest about the quality of the evidence at hand. Given problems of endogeneity and multicollinearity, as well as the lack of a controlled experiment, Levy and Meltzer conclude that we cannot definitively answer the following questions: What specific contribution does health insurance make on health status, and how does this vary across subpopulations? Does the effect differ depending on length of time with coverage? Or the frequency of spells without coverage? How do the gains and losses associated with coverage options differ across various subgroups? How cost-effective is expanded health insurance compared with other means of improving health status?

Health Insurance and Vulnerable Populations

No discussion of the dynamics of health insurance in the United States would be complete without a consideration of the special issues facing individuals who, for a variety of reasons, have a greater need for coverage and greater difficulty accessing and maintaining coverage through mainstream insurance markets. The type and degree of their vulnerability are difficult to define because they arise from varied and often interrelated factors. The way in which these factors interact and influence the availability of and demand for health insurance is also complex and difficult to specify. Some types of vulnerability, such as low socioeconomic status, are likely to influence the availability of coverage. Vulnerabilities related to language and culture, immigration status, and mental or cognitive capacity may influence the supply and demand for coverage, as well as the extent to which available coverage options are accessed and sustained.

It is important to understand whether and how traditional health insurance markets in the United States address the needs and constraints of vulnerable persons. Doing so requires knowledge about the characteristics of vulnerability and vulnerable groups, as well as an understanding of how those characteristics operate and interact within economic frameworks. For example, many economic studies include race as a dummy variable in regressions, but few go beyond this to understand the pathways by which racial minorities arrive at lower rates of insurance coverage.

In chapter 5, Harold Pollack and Karl Kronebusch provide an initial framework for thinking about vulnerability and summarize the literature on health insurance coverage of selected vulnerable populations. The authors bring together health services research and economics research on the health insurance status of vulnerable populations and provide a clear idea of how and why vulnerability affects a person's health insurance coverage. Four key components of vulnerability are set forth: barriers to accessing health insurance, poverty or economic disadvantage, discrimination, and impaired ability to make decisions. The authors then identify six populations that have one or more of these components: people with low incomes, children, racial or ethnic minorities and immigrants, people with chronic disease, the near-elderly, and individuals with psychiatric or substance abuse disorders. The authors' framework helps unravel the complexity of vulnerability and gives the reader a clearer sense of where research efforts have been targeted to date.

The authors summarize evidence from a literature review and statistical analysis of the health insurance coverage of these groups. The chapter evinces the complexity of issues affecting vulnerable populations and the need for further economic inquiry into their health insurance. While a wealth of literature discusses barriers to care for vulnerable populations, little of it focuses on the causes and consequences of lack of health insurance coverage.

Structural Models

Finally, chapter 6 synthesizes the structural models developed for and the methodological issues arising from studies of the uninsured. While the other syntheses focus on a specific aspect of the causes or consequences of the lack of insurance coverage, this synthesis focuses on how research in those areas fits together. It recognizes that almost all of the important observed phenomena discussed here are part of a grand system of interactions among employers, employees, and other consumers and decisionmakers acting to achieve their own particular objectives. How can one body of research inform the others, both substantively and methodologically? What do we learn about the relevant markets and impact of policy when we put all the pieces together?

Michael Chernew and Richard Hirth explore the connections among markets and identify aspects of the interconnections that seem to need further study. They discuss four key theoretical and methodological issues yet to be resolved that limit the ability to prescribe effective policies or predict the effect of market and policy changes: 1) the appropriate price of insurance; 2) the endogeneity of workers sorting into firms and firm decisions regarding benefit packages; 3) the frequency of transitions into and out of insurance coverage and the length of spells without coverage; and 4) the impact of labor market competition on firm behavior.

Chernew and Hirth also raise fundamental questions about the areas in which economic analysis is both most problematic and least plausible to noneconomists. For example, a fundamental proposition in economics is that consumers respond to prices. It is not clear, however, what consumers perceive to be the price of health insurance. One tradition considers the true price of insurance to be the amount above the expected cost of health care services, which is the load paid to health insurers for bearing risk, paying claims, and so on. Consumers may see the price of insurance very differently. There is substantial debate among economists about the best way to measure the price of health insurance—whether it is the load or some other measure. Without a good measure of price, economists' models cannot accurately predict behavior.

Economic reasoning about who pays for health insurance often seems implausible to noneconomists. The theory of compensating differentials suggests to economists that workers, not their employers, pay for health insurance. Even if economists generally agree with the theory, the picture of how workers pay is less clear. It surely is not the case that each individual sees his or her wage offset by his or her expected medical costs. In fact, Chernew and Hirth find evidence that employees appear not to act as if health insurance offsets wages at the individual level.

The uncertainty about how workers bear costs leads to questions about how workers sort themselves into firms that offer or do not offer health insurance. Economists make assumptions about sorting that have strong implications. If sorting is perfect, workers who place a lot of value on health insurance work for firms that offer health insurance, and those who value health insurance less work for employers that do not offer health insurance. Perfect sorting makes economic analysis easier, so it is often used in economic models; but perfect sorting suggests that we should observe things that we do not. For example, there should be some firms where workers have low demand for health insurance. These firms would rationally cater to the low demand by offering a bare-bones, high-deductible health insurance plan. Yet no such health insurance plan has been observed. Many factors make perfect sorting unlikely. To name a few, the number of firms is far from infinite. Firms are unlikely to demand homogeneous labor. Fixed costs limit the number of plans that firms offer. Efforts to discern the degree of sorting have been hampered by the possibility that sorting is based on unobservable as well as observable characteristics. Is the often-used assumption that worker characteristics are exogenous to the firm a valid one? This is one of the questions left unanswered by the structural modeling literature.

While academic economists are criticized for relying too heavily in their models on a restrictive set of possibly unrealistic assumptions, models are important because they serve as guideposts. Regression analyses developed with no theoretical underpinning can generate misleading and, in some cases, harmful conclusions about relationships. For example, specifying the endogeneity of certain worker and firm characteristics would yield important information about the degree of sorting in the market. With very strong sorting, employers are primarily a "pass through" whose decisions have little impact on the prevalence and distribution of coverage in the population. With imperfect sorting, employers become active and important players, and policies aimed at influencing employer decisions to offer health insurance are likely to be more effective.

Conclusion

Together, these chapters depict our understanding of the uninsured. They demonstrate that much of what passes for wisdom about the uninsured in policy circles is not founded on strong theoretical or empirical work, and they bring to light the tension between academics and policymakers. Social scientists will always search for better answers, whereas policymakers want the best available answers. Social scientists can wait; policymakers cannot.

This tension is not new. When Richard Doll and Bradford Hill studied the association of smoking with lung cancer and heart disease in 1950, their observational work was criticized by R.A. Fisher. Fisher argued that Doll and Hill's findings did not prove causation, and even undertook an analysis of smoking among twins to examine the possibility that a genetic factor predisposes people both to smoke and to develop lung cancer. Policymaking proceeded without waiting for evidence that would meet Fisher's standard of proof.

Since randomized controlled trials will continue to be rare in health services research, this tension between the right answer and the current answer is bound to continue. Social scientists will search for the causal linkages among health, health insurance, and the labor market, and as they do so, policymakers will draw on whatever is the best current evidence from social scientists.

The overarching message of this book is that research is badly needed to understand the links among health insurance, access to care, health outcomes, the labor market, and job choices. The uninsured are a heterogeneous group of individuals who are uninsured for differing lengths of time and for a great variety of reasons. The lack of insurance may have different effects across groups and may have different ramifications for short spells versus long spells. Understanding these differences will reveal the degree to which lack of insurance is a problem in this country and what solutions are needed.

REFERENCES

Brown, Margaret E., Andrew B. Bindman, and Nicole Lurie. 1998. "Monitoring the Consequences of Uninsurance: A Review of the Methodologies." *Medical Care Research and Review* 55(2):177–210.

Chollet, Deborah J. 2000. "A Survey of Surveys: What Does It Take to Obtain Accurate Estimates of the Uninsured?" *State Coverage Initiatives* 1(5–8). Washington, DC: The Alpha Center.

Currie, Janet M., and Brigitte C. Madrian. 1999. "Health, Health Insurance, and the Labor Market." In *Handbook of Labor Economics,* vol. 3, edited by Orley Ashenfelter and David Card (3309–3416). Amsterdam: Elsevier Science.

Gruber, Jonathan. 2000. "Health Insurance and the Labor Market." In *Handbook of Health Economics,* vol. 1, edited by Anthony J. Culyer and Joseph P. Newhouse (645–706). Amsterdam: Elsevier Science.

Swartz, Katherine, and Timothy D. McBride. 1990. "Spells without Health Insurance: Distributions of Durations and Their Link to Point-in-Time Estimates of the Uninsured." *Inquiry* 27(Fall): 281–88.

1

Counting and Characterizing the Uninsured

Pamela Farley Short

Researchers have been estimating the number and characteristics of Americans without health insurance for 50 years (Andersen and Anderson 1999). In 1953, the Health Information Foundation, which later became the Center for Health Administration Studies at the University of Chicago, collaborated with the National Opinion Research Center on the first nationally representative household survey of health care use, expenditures, and insurance. Over the next two decades, the centers conducted three more national surveys on these topics.

In 1964, the National Center for Health Statistics (NCHS) published the first nationwide estimates of health insurance (Hoffman 1964) from the National Health Interview Survey (NHIS). Ten years later, the center began planning a panel household survey with short recall periods that would capture reliable reports of health care expenditures and utilization from household respondents over a calendar year (Andersen and Anderson 1999). The plan resulted in the National Medical Care Expenditure Survey in 1977, a joint effort of NCHS and its sister agency in the U.S. Department of Health, Education and Welfare, the National Center for Health Services Research (NCHSR). With its six interviews during the calendar year, the survey allowed analysts to estimate for the first time changes in individuals' insurance. The study revealed that nearly as many people were uninsured for part of 1977 as for the entire year and that more than two-fifths of Medicaid recipients moved on or off Medicaid in a year (Walden, Wilensky, and Kasper 1985).

After fielding health insurance questions irregularly until 1989, the NCHS now produces annual estimates of the uninsured from NHIS data. The National Center for Health Services Research, now known as the Agency for Healthcare Research and Quality (AHRQ), continues to collect longitudinal health insurance data, fielding a new two-year Medical Expenditure Panel Survey (MEPS) every year since 1996.

At least six additional ongoing national surveys produce information about the number and characteristics of Americans who lack health insurance. In addition to the NHIS and MEPS, four surveys collect data about the uninsured of all ages:

- The Current Population Survey (CPS) is conducted monthly by the Census Bureau and has asked about health insurance every March since 1980 (except 1981). Because of its long time series, timeliness, and large sample (enabling analysts to make state-level estimates), the CPS is the most frequently cited source of statistics regarding the uninsured.
- The Survey of Income and Program Participation (SIPP) is a multi-year panel survey that has been fielded somewhat irregularly by the Census Bureau since 1983. Data are now available from a four-year survey that began in 1996.
- The Community Tracking Study (CTS), begun in 1996–1997, collects data every two years, primarily by telephone, from nationally representative households concentrated in 60 communities across the country. The CTS is conducted by the Center for Studying Health System Change, with funding from the Robert Wood Johnson Foundation.
- The National Survey of America's Families (NSAF) also collects data on a two-year cycle, primarily by telephone. Fielded in 1997 and 1999, the survey is part of the Urban Institute's *Assessing the New Federalism* project and is supported by funding from a number of foundations. The household sample is representative of the national population under age 65 and is drawn from 13 states.

Two other surveys are limited to adults:

- The Behavioral Risk Factor Surveillance Survey (BRFSS) interviews more than 150,000 adults each year by telephone. The survey is

conducted by the health departments of all the states and territo-
ries, with the support and guidance of the Behavioral Surveillance
Branch of the Centers for Disease Control and Prevention.
- The Health and Retirement Survey (HRS) is a panel survey that follows the aging of cohorts of Americans, starting at age 51. The survey began in 1992 with a cohort born between 1931 and 1941.
Respondents are interviewed every two years. HRS is conducted by
the Institute for Social Research at the University of Michigan, with
funding primarily from the National Institute on Aging.

Detailed, up-to-date descriptions of all of these surveys, except for
the HRS, are available from Fronstin (2000a) and Lewis, Ellwood, and
Czajka (1998).[1] Both reports compare and contrast methodologies and
estimates of the uninsured across surveys. As shown in table 1.1, adapted
from Fronstin, such comparisons reveal considerable variation in the
estimated number of Americans without health insurance—even for the
same year.

While earlier reports have focused on quantifying methodological
differences and reconciling their effects on estimates from various surveys, this chapter attempts to provide an understanding of the conceptual and methodological issues involved in counting, characterizing, and
studying the uninsured. In particular, it explains how most of the important issues can be traced back to two basic observations about the uninsured. The first is that the uninsured are by definition a residual group.
They are the people who fall between the cracks left by public and private insurance programs (figure 1.1). As a result, one cannot produce or
make sense of statistics about the *uninsured* without first producing or
making sense of statistics about the *insured*.

The second observation is that the insurance status of individuals
changes noticeably over time. With relatively large numbers of Americans flowing in and out of Medicaid and employer insurance over short
periods of time, people also move in and out of being uninsured at a
fairly rapid rate. Therefore, time is a very important consideration in
counting and characterizing the uninsured.

The far-reaching implications of these two apparently simple observations are discussed in the next two sections. Each section begins with
conceptual issues related to one of the observations and then turns to
the methodological and empirical implications of the observation. The
following section assesses the relative strengths and weaknesses of different health insurance surveys. The last section offers suggestions

Table 1.1. *Estimates of the Uninsured under Age 65 from Various Surveys*

Year	Uninsured	Sample size	Time frame of uninsured estimate	Location identifiers	Limitations
			Current Population Survey		
2001[a]	41 million	About 50% larger than earlier years	Uninsured throughout calendar year	All states	Some states have small sample sizes
1999	42 million, 39 million (revised)	131,000	Uninsured throughout calendar year	All states	Some states have small sample sizes
1998	44 million	116,000	Uninsured throughout calendar year	All states	Some states have small sample sizes
1995	40 million	118,000	Uninsured throughout calendar year	All states	Some states have small sample sizes
			Survey of Income and Program Participation		
1999[b]	37.5 million	116,000	Average monthly number of uninsured	41 states & DC	Many states have small sample sizes
1996[b]	40 million	116,000	Average monthly number of uninsured	41 states & DC	Many states have small sample sizes
1994	19 million	47,000	Uninsured throughout calendar year	45 states & DC	Many states have small sample sizes
10/1994–9/1995	35 million	47,000	Average monthly number of uninsured	45 states & DC	Many states have small sample sizes

Medical Expenditure Panel Survey					
2001	46 million	35,000	First 3–6 months of year	None	
1999	43 million	22,000	First 3–6 months of year	None	
1998	42 million	13,000	First 3–6 months of year	None	
1996	45 million	24,000	First 3–6 months of year	None	
1996	32 million	24,000	Uninsured throughout calendar year	None	
National Health Interview Survey					
1/2001–3/2001	39 million		Uninsured at time of interview	All states	Many states have small sample sizes
1999	38.5 million	97,059	Uninsured at time of interview	All states	Many states have small sample sizes
1997	41 million	103,000	Uninsured at time of interview	All states	Many states have small sample sizes
Community Tracking Study					
7/1998–7/1999	36 million	60,000	Uninsured at time of interview	60 communities	
7/1996–7/1997	35 million	60,000	Uninsured at time of interview	60 communities	
National Survey of America's Families					
1997	36 million	110,000	Uninsured at time of interview	13 states	
1999	36 million	110,000	Uninsured at time of interview	13 states	

Source: Adapted and updated from Paul Fronstin (2000a, 1).

a. A verification question that reduced the estimated number of uninsured was introduced in 2000.

b. Author's tabulations of longitudinal public use files.

Figure 1.1. *Measuring and Describing the Hole Left by Public and Private Insurance*

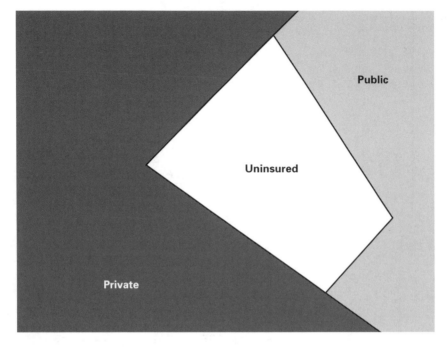

regarding future directions for both data collection and analyses aimed at counting and characterizing the uninsured.

The Uninsured Are a Residual Population

Conceptual Issues

Because the uninsured are people who do not have health insurance, the first step in defining "uninsured" is to define "health insurance." Most surveys do this implicitly, by listing different sources or types of coverage, asking respondents about each of them, and counting respondents without any of the listed types of coverage as uninsured. In order to achieve a reasonable degree of reliability across respondents, surveys rarely begin by asking people if they are uninsured. Thus, health insurance is defined as one of the items on the list.

For example, the list presented in the Current Population Survey defines health insurance as:

- A health plan provided through a current or former employer or union (as policyholder or dependent)
- A plan purchased directly from an insurance company (as policyholder or dependent)
- A health plan of someone who does not live in the household
- Medicare, the federal health insurance for persons 65 years old and over or persons with disabilities
- Medicaid, the federal assistance program that pays for health care, or the respondent's state government assistance program
- TRICARE, CHAMPUS, CHAMPVA, VA, or military health care
- A state health insurance program for low-income uninsured individuals or any other type of plan

In the past, people covered only by the Indian Health Service were counted as insured and included with Medicaid recipients in published statistics from CPS. Since 1998, however, they are counted as uninsured (Fronstin 2000a).

CPS interviewers are trained to exclude from the definition of health insurance any specialty plans that cover only dental, vision, or prescription expenses. In its questions, MEPS specifically limits the definition of health insurance to plans that cover hospital or physician services (thereby excluding specialty plans). Furthermore, MEPS does not consider extra cash plans, which are sometimes linked to specific diseases, or the services provided directly by the Veterans Administration to selected veterans to be health insurance.

No recent survey collects enough detailed information about health plans to quantify the effect of different definitions of health insurance on national estimates of the uninsured, but it is not likely that definitional differences have much empirical effect. Short and Vistnes (1992) found that 1 to 2 percent of the elderly who reported having private insurance in 1987 had only extra-cash or disease-specific coverage. Fronstin (2000a) estimates that the CPS change involving Indian Health Service recipients affected about 300,000 people and increased the estimated percentage of the population without health insurance from 18.1 to 18.3 percent in 1997.

Methodological Implications

Because the uninsured are always the residual group of survey respondents who do not answer positively to questions about coverage, forgetfulness and underreporting are likely to inflate survey estimates of the uninsured. All of the coverage that respondents forget or do not recognize from the wording used in a survey shows up in higher counts of the uninsured. There are no national benchmarks for cross-checking survey estimates of the total count of people with private insurance, but administrative records of Medicare and Medicaid can be used to evaluate the accuracy of survey-based counts of enrollment in these public programs.

Administrative records also have limitations in terms of reliability and validity. Nevertheless, comparisons of survey data to Medicaid data strongly suggest that Medicaid enrollment is often underreported, implying that surveys overestimate the number of uninsured.[2] In the past, many data collection organizations edited survey responses to correct for Medicaid underreporting, particularly by attributing Medicaid to welfare and Supplemental Security Income recipients, who automatically qualified for Medicaid before federal welfare reforms were instituted in 1996. Now, because Medicaid eligibility is no longer linked to the receipt of welfare and has been expanded to many low-income individuals (especially children) who are not eligible for welfare, it is more difficult to identify likely Medicaid recipients from the responses to other survey questions. Because of the emphasis on health expenditures in MEPS, analysts using that survey can cross-check and reconcile health insurance status with the sources of any third-party payments that are reported. The Urban Institute customarily adjusts CPS data, using the institute's microsimulation model, to match administrative Medicaid enrollment by age and disability status (Lewis, Ellwood, and Czajka 1998).

To guard against underreporting, the majority of surveys (including CPS, NHIS, CTS, and NSAF) ask respondents who have answered negatively to the list of questions about coverage types and sources to confirm that they are indeed uninsured. In addition, several surveys (including SIPP, MEPS, and CTS) ask a catchall question that allows respondents to report insurance that they did not associate with any of the types or sources mentioned by the interviewer. The use of a verification question reduces the number of uninsured by 20 percent in the National Survey of America's Families, a telephone survey without a catchall question, compared with 6 percent in the Community Tracking Study, a telephone survey with a catchall question (Rajan, Zuckerman, and Brennan 2000). Reportedly, the verification question in the NHIS has little effect in the context of the longer, more intensive, in-person interviews conducted for that survey (Rajan, Zuckerman, and Brennan 2000). Nelson and Mills (2001) report that the addition of a verification question to the CPS, incorporated for the first time in official estimates in 2000, reduced estimates of the uninsured by about 8 percent.

The fact that being uninsured is determined residually has other important methodological implications. Because private insurance typically covers all members of the policyholder's immediate family, it is very important to adopt a household or family perspective in studying the uninsured.[3] For example, it is more meaningful to relate a person's insurance or lack of insurance to the presence or absence of a worker in the family than to whether or not the person (who may be the child or the nonworking spouse of a working adult) is employed.

To identify the set of people whose health insurance status "goes together," analysts have invented and widely adopted a new, insurance-related concept of the family—the health insurance unit. The Census Bureau's official definition of family includes all of the people related by blood or marriage who are living at the same address; this definition is used in aggregating and adjusting family income in official poverty estimates. The concept of a health insurance unit is limited to the people who would typically be covered by a family health insurance policy. The CTS specifically samples and collects data for health insurance units instead of households or families. That approach collects data for fewer people, while preserving a picture of important coverage connections within families.

In defining health insurance units, adults are grouped with their spouses and their dependent children; that is, children who are either high-school age and younger or college age and full-time students. A 15-year-old boy and his mother constitute one family and one health insurance unit. A 50-year-old man who lives with his elderly mother are one family but two different health insurance units. Unlike the teenager and his mother, the 50-year-old and his mother are unlikely to have insurance from the same source, and few programs or proposals for covering the uninsured would combine the income of the two adults in determining either's eligibility for government assistance.

When income is aggregated over health insurance units instead of families, significantly more of the uninsured are categorized as poor

(Long and Marquis 1996). The distinction is particularly important for young adults, the age group with the highest percentage of uninsured persons (Short 2000). Using health insurance units to define poverty assigns young adults who live with their parents and are not in school to a different health insurance unit than their parents; thus the parents' income is not considered in measuring the economic well-being of the young adults.

Another important consideration in collecting and analyzing data about the uninsured is each person's eligibility for public or private insurance. Because Medicare's nearly universal coverage of the population age 65 and older means that virtually no one in that age group is uninsured, most statistics concerning the uninsured are limited to the population under 65. Now that Medicaid changes and the State Children's Health Insurance Program (SCHIP) have greatly expanded the coverage of children, compared with adults, it is equally important to distinguish between adults and children in studying the uninsured.

Employers and labor unions are the source of health insurance coverage for 80 percent of insured Americans under age 65 (Fronstin 2000b). Consequently, the most useful surveys for studying the uninsured ask lots of questions about employment status and job characteristics, in addition to health insurance. The most useful surveys also gather employment data for all adults in a family or health insurance unit because of the data's potential importance in explaining the coverage (or lack of coverage) of other family members.

Given the number of public programs and legislative proposals that target eligibility for insurance by income, survey questions that are well designed to measure income are also important for health insurance analyses.

Still another key piece of information is whether any family members were eligible for health insurance through an employer or union, regardless of whether or not they actually enrolled. According to CTS estimates (Cunningham, Schaefer, and Hogan 1999), all but 14 percent of people with access to insurance through their own or a family member's employment chose to enroll. Of that 14 percent, 9 percent had other coverage, leaving only 5 percent uninsured.[4] However, the uninsured who turned down insurance from a family member's employer accounted for about 20 percent of the total number of uninsured.

There are no comparable survey questions that can reliably establish eligibility for Medicaid or SCHIP. However, if a survey collects all of the necessary data elements and does not suppress the respondent's state of residence because of confidentiality concerns, analysts can simulate Medicaid/SCHIP eligibility according to the rules in the respondent's state. This line of research has established that Medicaid eligibility is a good but hardly perfect predictor of enrollment. Indeed, the discovery that a significant number of Medicaid-eligible children were uninsured in the mid-1990s (Selden, Banthin, and Cohen 1998; Dubay and Kenney 1996; Summer, Parrott, and Mann 1997) touched off a concerted effort in Medicaid and SCHIP to increase participation rates among eligible children by greatly expanding outreach efforts and simplifying application procedures.

Finally, the residual nature of the uninsured complicates analyses designed to identify individual characteristics and other factors that contribute to the probability of being uninsured. It is hard to make much sense of the effect of these variables by estimating binomial multivariate models where "insured" and "uninsured" are the two outcomes. Consider, for example, the relationship between income and the probability of being uninsured in a binomial model. This relationship is quite complicated, because low income is associated with Medicaid/SCHIP enrollment and high income is associated with enrollment in employment-related insurance. As a consequence, both high and low incomes are associated with lower probabilities of being uninsured.

Multinomial models (for example, with "private insurance," "Medicaid/SCHIP," and "uninsured" as outcomes) are likely to be more revealing and robust.[5] With such models, analysts can specify separate, structural determinants of the probabilities of public and private insurance in the population under age 65—and then calculate the probability of being uninsured as the residual that it is. Age, income, and other eligibility criteria that often vary by state are the primary determinants of enrollment in Medicaid and SCHIP. The employment status and job characteristics of adult family members are the primary determinants of private enrollment.

Related Empirical Findings

While surveys often disagree on the number of people who are uninsured, they all show that the risk of being uninsured is highest in the population subgroups that one would predict on the basis of eligibility (or lack of eligibility) for coverage from employers, Medicare, and

Medicaid/SCHIP. For example, because the rate of employer insurance increases dramatically with earnings and income, while Medicaid and SCHIP cover fewer than half of the nonelderly poor, the uninsured rate decreases dramatically with increasing income (figure 1.2).

The likelihood of being uninsured is also closely related to employment. Full-time workers and their families are much less likely to be uninsured than other people under age 65. Among working adults, those who work part-time or for small companies, who are self-employed, or who have jobs outside of manufacturing and the public sector are more likely to be uninsured.

The uninsured rate also varies noticeably by age. With the expansion of coverage to low-income children through Medicaid and SCHIP, children under 18 are now less likely to be uninsured than adults. Young adults in their late teens to mid-twenties are the age group with the highest percentage of uninsurance. Young adults do not qualify as dependents under their parents' plans if they leave school, and they are likely

Figure 1.2. *Percent Distribution of Insurance Status, by Family Income*

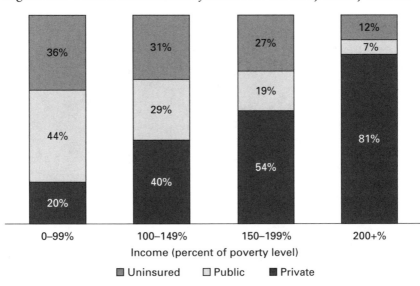

Source: Fronstin (2000b).

to have entry-level or short-term jobs that do not offer insurance benefits if they work.

The uninsured rate also varies by sociodemographic characteristics correlated with income and family employment, such as race and ethnicity or marital status. Racial and ethnic minorities, as well as noncitizens, are more likely to be uninsured. Single individuals or people in families headed by single adults are more likely to be uninsured than people in families headed by married couples.

There are noticeable geographic differences in the uninsured rate, which is generally higher in the South than elsewhere. A recent analysis using the CTS (Cunningham and Ginsberg 2001) suggests that about a third of the difference in uninsured rates across communities is due to differences in racial/ethnic composition and socioeconomic status; about a quarter is due to differences in employment characteristics; and about an eighth is due to differences in state Medicaid eligibility.

Two kinds of statistics are frequently used in characterizing the uninsured by population subgroup. The uninsured rate within a subgroup (i.e., the percentage of the subgroup that is uninsured) measures the risk or likelihood of being uninsured for people in that subgroup. The preceding discussion focused on variation in uninsured rates across subgroups, indicating that some groups are at much higher or lower risk of being uninsured. In contrast, the percent distribution of the uninsured across subgroups (i.e., the percentage of the uninsured who are in each subgroup) describes the composition of the uninsured population and its concentration in certain subgroups.

The composition of the uninsured population depends not only on the uninsured rate in each subgroup, but also on the absolute size of each subgroup. A low uninsured rate in a very large subgroup can account for a surprisingly large share of the overall uninsured population. For example, although the uninsured rate is relatively low for workers and their families, more than four out of five of the uninsured are in families with a working adult (Fronstin 2000b; Monheit and Vistnes 1997).

By the same token, about half of the uninsured under age 65 are in families with incomes *below* 200 percent of the federal poverty level (Fronstin 2000b), where the uninsured rate is relatively high. With nearly three-quarters of the entire population under age 65 in families with incomes *above* 200 percent of the poverty level, the higher income group accounts for the other half of the uninsured.

Insurance Status Changes over Time

Conceptual Issues

What is the best way to count and characterize the uninsured when people experience changes in insurance status over time, as illustrated in figure 1.3? The simplest approach is to focus on the uninsured at a particular point in time, such as the start of the calendar year (represented by the dotted line in figure 1.3). However, such cross-sectional estimates understate the number of people who are uninsured over time. For example, an estimate at the start of the first full calendar year in figure 1.3 will count A, B, and D as uninsured but will miss C and E, who are uninsured later in the year. As illustrated by the figure, longitudinal estimates that capture all of the uninsured spells for a sample of people over time should always produce higher counts of the uninsured than cross-sectional estimates. Furthermore, counting the uninsured over longer time periods (for example, two years instead of one year) should always produce a higher count of the uninsured, as illustrated by the addition of F to the count for one year.

Cross-sectional estimates of the uninsured are useful for projecting the average caseload that would be served by a new program to cover the uninsured. They are also useful for projecting program costs. By count-

Figure 1.3. *Changes in Insurance Status over Time*

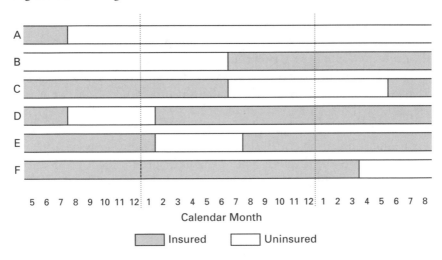

5 6 7 8 9 10 11 12 1 2 3 4 5 6 7 8 9 10 11 12 1 2 3 4 5 6 7 8
Calendar Month

Insured   Uninsured

Source: Adapted from Short and Klerman (1998).

ing the number of uninsured persons who would be covered by a new program on a given day, the cross-sectional approach yields an estimate of covered person-days for a one-day accounting period (and corresponds to a program's caseload). If there are no important seasonal considerations, multiplying the one-day estimate by 365 produces a reasonable estimate of the total number of covered person-days in a year (usually the accounting period of interest). Dividing by 365 then converts total person-days to person-years. Counting each uninsured person in the one-day cross section as an uninsured person-year is mathematically equivalent to these two operations, so that is how the calculation is actually performed in practice. Total annual program costs can then be approximated by applying an estimate of average costs per person-year (for example, the annual premium for covering each uninsured person in the cross section) to the total number of uninsured person-years.[6,7]

With longitudinal data that track a person's insurance status over days or months for a year or more, analysts can count the number of uninsured person-days or person-months over a year and then convert to person-years. Consequently, such data are also useful for projecting program costs or the average caseload that a new program will serve. Estimates from longitudinal surveys that do not break down insured and uninsured days (or months) for people who were uninsured for part of the year are not useful for these purposes. For example, the number or percentage of people who were *ever* uninsured in a year overstates the number of uninsured person-years. The number or percentage of people who were *always* uninsured in a year misses the part-year uninsured and understates the number of uninsured person-years.

The major advantage of longitudinal data, compared with cross-sectional data, is in assessing the welfare implications of being uninsured. First, recalling figure 1.3, the risk of being uninsured is considerably greater than cross-sectional statistics would imply. Second, being uninsured for a long time is likely to have a much bigger effect on a person's health and finances than being uninsured for a short time. After all, the likelihood of getting through a short uninsured spell without a health crisis is much greater than the likelihood of getting through a long spell. Also, the health effects of forgoing appropriate care because of its cost are likely to compound and accumulate over time. By definition, cross-sectional data do not distinguish between the short-term and long-term uninsured.

Although cross-sectional data do not allow analysts to distinguish the long-term uninsured from the short-term uninsured, it is possible to demonstrate mathematically that the long-term uninsured are represented more heavily in cross-sectional data than in longitudinal data. This difference between the two measurement approaches is attributable to length-based sampling, a feature of cross-sectional data that has been recognized in collecting statistics about other dynamic phenomena, such as unemployment or poverty. The heavier representation of long spells in the cross section can be seen intuitively in figure 1.3, where A's long spell is a third of the uninsured spells captured in the cross section (A, B, C) but only a fifth of the uninsured spells for the year (A, B, C, D, E). Because the short-term uninsured generally come from higher in the income distribution than the long-term uninsured (Monheit and Schur 1988; Swartz and McBride 1990; Short and Klerman 1998), cross-sectional estimates can be expected to show that more of the uninsured are poor or come from groups with lower socioeconomic status than longitudinal estimates.

As the preceding discussion illustrates, important conceptual questions regarding the best way to count and characterize the uninsured for a particular analytic purpose are raised by health insurance dynamics (Swartz 1994). Acknowledging the importance of health insurance dynamics also means introducing new concepts into one's thinking about health insurance. Important concepts in a dynamic framework include health insurance spells (time periods with a specific type of insurance, including none at all), the duration of insurance spells, and transitions from one type of insurance to another.

Methodological Implications

Health insurance dynamics affect both the collection of health insurance data and the comparability (or lack of comparability) of estimates from different surveys. First, because insurance status changes over time, surveys that ask about insurance status over different lengths of time will produce different estimates of the uninsured. For example, when NHIS or CTS asks if a respondent currently has any of a list of different types of coverage, that is not equivalent to asking in the CPS if he or she had any of the same types of coverage in the last year. Negative responses to the first set of questions imply that the person was uninsured for at least a day; negative responses to the second set of questions imply that the person was uninsured for at least a year. More people fall into the first category than the second. Therefore, surveys that ask about current coverage, as NHIS and CTS do, should count more people as uninsured than surveys with longer reference periods, such as CPS (the last calendar year), SIPP (the last four months), or MEPS (since the beginning of the calendar year or the last interview).

Extending the reference period back in time makes it more difficult for people who have experienced a recent change in insurance status to answer the questions about their health insurance correctly. Because it is undoubtedly easier for such people to answer correctly about their coverage now rather than about their coverage in the past, most surveys (NHIS, CTS, NSAF, BRFSS, and HRS) ask about health insurance in this cross-sectional fashion. When asked about the past, respondents have a tendency to forget coverage that they no longer have.

In order to reduce the errors associated with imperfect recall, while capturing monthly insurance status over relatively long periods of time, SIPP and MEPS are designed as longitudinal surveys that interview respondents every few months. Despite the relatively short reference period in SIPP, most of the changes in coverage that are reported occur in the months corresponding to the interviews. This pattern (the so-called seam problem) suggests that respondents tend to focus on their current insurance status when they are being interviewed, even when asked to think only a few months into the past.

Although CPS is the most frequently cited source of data regarding the uninsured, it poses the most difficult recall task for respondents. Respondents are asked in March if they had any of the listed types of coverage in the preceding calendar year. Consequently, respondents must remember back 14 months and then ignore the 2 months immediately preceding the interview. The resulting retrospective estimates of the number of people who were uninsured throughout a calendar year are much larger than comparable estimates from longitudinal surveys like SIPP and MEPS, which interview people several times during a year. Even with the introduction of a verification question that lowered the estimate for 1999 from 42 million to 39 million (Nelson and Mills 2001), the CPS annual estimate remains high in relation to annual estimates from MEPS and SIPP.

Methodological issues involving time also arise when measuring correlations and associations of other variables with health insurance status. For example, analysts using such surveys as NHIS and CTS should be cautious about relating cross-sectional information on insurance status from those surveys to annual measures of health services use (Long and Marquis 1994). The effects of being uninsured are disguised under those circumstances because some of the people who were uninsured in the cross section were not necessarily uninsured when they used health services. Moreover, some people who were uninsured for part of the year (and may have used fewer services during that time) were classified in the cross section as insured.

Finally, because insurance status changes over time, it is not really enough to know someone's current status—one must also know how long the person was insured or uninsured before the time of the survey. Otherwise, one can neither estimate the duration of insurance spells nor distinguish between short and long uninsured spells in terms of their welfare implications. Nor can one model eligibility rules that are based on recent insurance history, such as the portability rules in the Health Insurance Portability and Accountability Act or state rules that discourage people from dropping private insurance and applying for Medicaid. All of the surveys, except for CPS, currently ask something about coverage (or lack of coverage) prior to the start of the survey, but these questions seem to get surprisingly little attention from analysts.[8]

Without retrospective information, cross-sectional surveys do not enable analysts to distinguish between such situations as A and B in figure 1.3. Even in a longitudinal survey that covers the entire time window depicted in figure 1.3, the length of B's uninsured spell cannot be determined unless retrospective questions are asked at the start of the survey.

In technical terms, insurance spells are both left- and right-censored at the start and end of any survey, as illustrated in figure 1.3. Special techniques, such as life tables or survival models, which focus on the conditional probability of ending a spell in period $t + 1$ (after the spell has lasted t amount of time), can be used to accommodate right censoring.[9] However, those techniques require unbiased information about the prior duration of spells, without left censoring.

Related Empirical Findings

Going as far back as the 1977 National Medical Care Expenditure Survey, longitudinal surveys consistently show that turnover in the uninsured population is empirically important. As table 1.2 illustrates with longitudinal monthly data from the 1996 MEPS panel, the core of people who were uninsured throughout the two years of the survey made up a little more than one-quarter of the people who were ever uninsured

Table 1.2. Number and Characteristics of the Uninsured under Age 65 during Different Time Frames (United States, 1996–1997)

	Uninsured throughout 1996–1997			Uninsured throughout 1996			Average monthly uninsured 1996			Ever uninsured in 1996			Ever uninsured in 1996–1997		
	Millions	Rate[a] (%)	Relative risk[b]	Millions	Rate[c] (%)	Relative risk	Millions	Rate[d] (%)	Relative risk	Millions	Rate[c] (%)	Relative risk	Millions	Rate[a] (%)	Relative risk
Total	23.5	9.9	—	31.6	13.5	—	45.0	19.4	—	64.0	27.3	—	80.2	33.7	—
Age															
Under 18	4.5	6.2	1.00	7.0	9.8	1.00	10.9	15.7	1.00	17.4	24.4	1.00	22.1	30.7	1.00
18–24	3.5	13.4	2.16	5.6	22.3	2.28	8.3	33.0	2.10	11.6	45.8	1.88	13.6	52.4	1.71
25–54	13.6	11.5	1.85	16.8	14.3	1.46	22.9	19.6	1.25	31.2	26.7	1.09	39.3	33.3	1.08
55–64	2.0	9.1	1.47	2.2	10.7	1.09	2.9	13.9	0.89	3.8	18.3	0.75	5.2	23.4	0.76
Race/ethnicity															
White	12.4	7.5	1.00	16.9	10.3	1.00	24.9	15.2	1.00	36.5	22.2	1.00	46.9	28.3	1.00
African American	3.5	11.1	1.48	5.2	16.8	1.63	7.6	24.8	1.63	11.1	36.0	1.62	13.3	42.0	1.48
Hispanic	6.5	22.0	2.93	7.8	27.5	2.67	10.2	36.6	2.41	13.3	46.8	2.11	15.8	53.3	1.88
Other	1.1	10.1	1.35	1.7	15.9	1.54	2.4	22.9	1.51	3.1	29.2	1.32	4.2	37.1	1.31

(continued)

Table 1.2. *Continued*

Income (% of poverty level)	Uninsured throughout 1996–1997			Uninsured throughout 1996			Average monthly uninsured 1996			Ever uninsured in 1996			Ever uninsured in 1996–1997		
	Millions	Rate[a] (%)	Relative risk[b]	Millions	Rate[c] (%)	Relative risk	Millions	Rate[d] (%)	Relative risk	Millions	Rate[c] (%)	Relative risk	Millions	Rate[a] (%)	Relative risk
<100	5.5	16.5	3.67	8.0	23.4	4.42	11.1	33.2	4.00	15.4	45.1	3.44	17.2	51.5	2.72
100–125	1.8	18.4	4.09	2.6	25.5	4.81	4.1	40.4	4.87	5.5	53.9	4.11	6.1	61.3	3.24
126–199	6.1	18.8	4.18	8.0	24.2	4.57	10.7	32.7	3.94	14.5	43.8	3.34	16.3	50.6	2.68
200–399	6.4	8.0	1.78	8.8	11.4	2.15	12.5	16.4	1.98	18.1	23.6	1.80	24.8	31.3	1.66
400+	3.8	4.5	1.00	4.3	5.3	1.00	6.7	8.3	1.00	10.5	13.1	1.00	15.8	18.9	1.00

Source: Author's tabulations of the 1996 MEPS panel.

a. Denominator is all persons in the civilian noninstitutionalized population in 1996 or 1997 who were under age 65 in 1997.

b. Relative risk is the ratio of uninsured rates.

c. Denominator is the civilian noninstitutionalized population under age 65 in 1996.

d. Denominator is total person-years in the civilian noninstitutionalized population under age 65 in 1996.

during the two years (24 million out of 80 million). Of the 45 million who were uninsured each month in 1996, 32 million were uninsured throughout the year. As demonstrated by the difference between the 32 million who were uninsured throughout 1996 and the 64 million who were ever uninsured in 1996, the number of people who began or ended an uninsured spell during the year was about the same as the number who remained uninsured.

The relatively high turnover in the uninsured population is attributable to a large number of fairly short spells: half of uninsured spells end within five or six months (Swartz, Marcotte, and McBride 1993b; Bennefield 1996b). However, the long-term uninsured are important because of their numbers and their significance for public policy (Swartz 1994). Because people with long uninsured spells accumulate in the uninsured population while people with short spells replace each other, nearly three-quarters of the people in an uninsured cross section have been uninsured for six months or more (Short and Klerman 1998). More than 40 percent have been uninsured for 18 months or more. Such a cross section approximates the caseload of a universal program that would insure all of the uninsured.

Studies that have examined the factors associated with the likelihood of ending an uninsured spell and transitioning into coverage (Swartz and McBride 1990; Swartz, Marcotte, and McBride 1993a; Short and Friedman 1998; Bennefield 1996b) suggest that people with higher socioeconomic status have shorter uninsured spells. Also, although young adults are more often uninsured than older adults, they have shorter uninsured spells (Swartz et al. 1993a; Short and Friedman 1998; Bennefield 1996b). Nonworkers, Hispanics, and high school dropouts have longer uninsured spells (Bennefield 1996b; Short and Friedman 1998). There is also strong evidence that the likelihood of regaining coverage declines as people remain uninsured for longer and longer periods of time (Swartz et al. 1993a; Short and Friedman 1998).

Estimates of the total number of uninsured, ordered from left to right in table 1.2, increase over different time frames because they give increasing weight to the short-term uninsured. For example, the leftmost column counts only those people who were uninsured for 24 months and ignores anyone else who was ever uninsured. The rightmost column gives the same weight to people who were uninsured for as little as 1 month as to those uninsured for 24 months. There each person is counted once, regardless of the time uninsured. The center column weights each person according to the length of time that he or she was uninsured in 1996.

Because different time frames assign greater weight to the short-term uninsured, and relatively more of the short-term uninsured come from higher socioeconomic strata than the long-term uninsured, time frames also affect estimates of the uninsured by subgroup. For example, by looking across table 1.2 at the relative risk for each population subgroup, one can see how that group's risk of being uninsured varies in comparison with the most advantaged group with the lowest risk when different time frames are used. As expected, the relative risk of being uninsured generally declines from left to right across the table for more disadvantaged subgroups, as the time frames give less weight to the long-term uninsured. There is a noticeable exception to this pattern: the relative risk of being uninsured for all of 1996 and 1997 is lower for low-income groups and African Americans than the relative risk of being uninsured for all of 1996. This exception is attributable to the underlying trends from 1996 to 1997 in the risk of being uninsured all year by subgroup (data not shown).

Comparative Strengths and Weaknesses of Surveys

The Census Bureau's dependability in releasing CPS data on a regular, timely basis over many years is one of the major reasons for the popularity of that survey. As shown in table 1.3, data files are released from CPS more quickly than from any other survey. In addition, although its health insurance questions have been redesigned on several occasions since 1980 (Swartz 1997; Fronstin 2000a), no other survey offers as long a time series for studying trends in health insurance. The sample size, which is large enough to make state-specific estimates, is another important advantage. The rich employment and economic data, collected for all adults in the household, have been useful in many analyses. As the source of official estimates of poverty in the United States, CPS also has good income measures.

Unfortunately, there is overwhelming evidence that many respondents answer the CPS insurance questions incorrectly. Because CPS estimates are more similar to the cross-sectional estimates from other surveys and because respondents apparently tend to report their current coverage

text continues on page 27

Table 1.3. *Current Features of Six National Surveys with Health Insurance Data*

Feature	Current Population Survey	National Health Interview Survey	Medical Expenditure Panel Survey	Survey of Income and Program Participation	Community Tracking Survey	National Survey of America's Families
Survey Characteristics						
Organization managing the survey	Census Bureau	National Center for Health Statistics	Agency for Healthcare Research and Quality	Census Bureau	Center for Studying Health System Change	The Urban Institute
Survey design	March supplement is a cross section[a]	Cross section	Panel, five interviews over 2 years	Panel, every 4 months over 3–4 years	Cross section	Cross section
Mode	In person and telephone	In person	In person and telephone	In person and telephone	Telephone, supplemented in person	Telephone, supplemented in person
Response rate	86% (2000)	88% (1999) 90% (1998)	75% round 1 (1998) 68% annual (1998)	64.5% (1996), all interviews	65%	65% (1997) 60% (1997)
Sample Design						
Universe	Civilian noninstitutionalized population	Civilian non-institutionalized population	Civilian non-institutionalized population	Civilian non-institutionalized population	Civilian non-institutionalized population, excluding Alaska and Hawaii	Civilian non-institutionalized population under age 65

(continued)

Table 1.3. Continued

Feature	Current Population Survey	National Health Interview Survey	Medical Expenditure Panel Survey	Survey of Income and Program Participation	Community Tracking Survey	National Survey of America's Families
Sample frame	Area probability	Area probability	NHIS	Area probability	Random-digit dialing (supplemented by area probability)	Random-digit dialing (supplemented by area probability)
Sample size	50,000 households 130,000+ people	Varies around 40,000 households 100,000+ people	7,000–13,000 households 15,000–35,000 people[b]	37,000 households	60,000 people	44,000 households 100,000 people
Oversampling	Hispanics	Blacks, Hispanics	Blacks, Hispanics, disabled, low income, high expense, elderly	Low income	For community-specific estimates	For state-specific estimates, low income
Individual data	All members of household	Health insurance, all members of household; some topics, one adult and one child	All members of household	All members of household	All adults members of family insurance unit, one child per unit	One child < 6 and 6–17, parents of sampled children, childless adults
Location-specific estimates	All states	27 states	No state estimates	Some states	60 communities	13 states
Health Insurance Questions						
Timeframe	Preceding calendar year	Time of interview, throughout year, ever in year	Since start of calendar year or last interview; monthly	Last 4 months; monthly	Time of interview	Time of interview

Respondent	Household informant	One person familiar with family's health coverage	Family informant	Self-reporting for adults (15+)	Family informant	One spouse reports for parents and children, self-reporting or proxy for other adults.
Logical imputation	Medicaid of adults is attributed to their children	Medicaid attributed to AFDC/SSI[c] recipients until 1996	Minimal	Similar to CPS	Minimal	Medicaid attributed to TANF recipients
Catchall question	Asked	Not asked	Asked	Asked	Asked	Not asked
Verify uninsured	Added in 2000	Added in 1997	Reasons why uninsured[d]	Reasons why uninsured[d]	Asked	Asked
Eligibility for employer insurance	Not asked in March supplement	Asked	Asked	Asked	Asked	Asked
Status before survey	Not asked	Asked	Asked	Asked	Asked	Asked
Other Data						
Health care use	Not asked	2-week and 12-month recall	4–5 month recall	Selected interviews 12-month recall	12-month recall	12-month recall
Employment data	Extensive	Limited for all adults.[e] Additional detail for one adult.	Extensive	Extensive	Extensive	Extensive

(continued)

Table 1.3. *Continued*

Feature	Current Population Survey	National Health Interview Survey	Medical Expenditure Panel Survey	Survey of Income and Program Participation	Community Tracking Survey	National Survey of America's Families
			Data Availability			
Health insurance time series	Annual since 1980	Annual since 1989, selected years 1960–1986	Annual since 1996, 1977, 1980, 1987	Panels cover most years since 1983	1996–97, 1998–99	1997, 1999
Publication of most current estimates (as of October 2002)	P-60 report with data for 2001, September 2002	"Early release" on NCHS website for first quarter 2002, September 2002	"Compendium of Tables" with round 1 estimates for 2001, July 2002	P-60 report with data for 1992–1993, May 1996	*Issue Brief 29*, 1998/1999 for children, April 2000	*Snapshots of America's Families II: 1999 Results*, October 2000
Most current microdata (as of October 2002)	2002 survey with 2001 data	2000	1999 annual file, 2001 round 1 file, longitudinal weight for 1997–1998	1996 core files, topical modules, longitudinal weight	1998–1999	1999

a. Each CPS panel is interviewed for four months and then interviewed in the same four calendar months a year later.

b. Panels alternate between larger and smaller sample sizes. Two panels can be combined for 1997 and all subsequent years.

c. Aid to Families with Dependent Children/Supplemental Security Income.

d. Lack of insurance is not explicitly verified, but the uninsured are asked for "reasons why uninsured."

e. Employment status, hours, earnings, insurance eligibility for all adults.

when asked about the past, many analysts ignore the question wording and treat the estimates from CPS as a one-month cross section (Swartz 1986). Analysts are happy to treat CPS counts as cross-sectional because such estimates are more useful in costing out reform proposals than the all-year estimates of the uninsured that CPS is designed to produce. However, if some respondents interpret and answer the questions correctly, then the CPS estimates are really an ill-defined amalgam of annual and cross-sectional insurance status (with a good measure of recall error thrown in).[10] Ironically, if the Census Bureau continues to improve the validity of the all-year estimates by adding the new confirmation question and experimenting with other changes, analysts will have to stop interpreting the data as a cross section that can be used for cost estimates.[11]

Two other government surveys, NHIS and SIPP, approach CPS in terms of sample size (table 1.3), but they ask questions with shorter recall periods that respondents can answer more accurately. The NHIS questions about current insurance status are undoubtedly the most straightforward and easiest for respondents who have had recent changes in insurance status to answer. Recent improvements—shifting the insurance questions to the core, where they are asked each year, and adding more economic and employment questions—have made NHIS more suitable for studying health insurance issues that have historically been investigated with CPS. The release of statistical tables has been speeded to the point where the most up-to-date estimates of the uninsured are now from NHIS. However, some important employment questions are not asked of all adults in the family; some questions about families cannot be addressed, given the sampling of adults and children within the family; public use files have not been released as quickly for NHIS as CPS; the sample is too small to make reliable estimates for all states; and the income questions are probably not as good as those in CPS.

The 1996 SIPP panel also approaches the sample size of CPS but is not quite large enough to make estimates for all states. The Census Bureau plans to maintain the larger panel size instituted in 1996 by fielding one large panel every three years instead of overlapping panels every year. With a fixed, four-month reference period, each wave of SIPP is a nationally representative cross-sectional survey that could be used to make quick estimates of health insurance status. Like CPS, SIPP has the advantage of collecting a wealth of economic and employment data. Furthermore, the shorter reference period for these economic data (four months in SIPP, compared with a year in CPS) is probably better for measuring or simulating the relationship between insurance status and economic variables (such as employment or eligibility for Medicaid) that also change over time.

Because they ask retrospectively about insurance over a four-month period, the SIPP questions are known to be flawed by errors in recall. However, the apparent tendency of respondents to report changes in insurance (and many other variables) in the interview month should not detract from the validity of SIPP as a cross-sectional snapshot, because most changes in insurance should still be captured from interview to interview.

Probably the biggest factor discouraging use of SIPP is the hit-or-miss fielding of the survey. Not only have there been several lapses when SIPP was not fielded at all, but the panels have varied noticeably in length and sample size. Despite the potential advantages of SIPP compared with CPS, analysts have been understandably reluctant to invest in learning how to use a complicated survey that has not been fielded on a consistent basis.

All three of these surveys (CPS, NHIS, and SIPP) are limited in the quality and amount of health care utilization data that analysts can connect to health insurance differences and changes. With its shorter recall periods over an extended period of time, MEPS is the survey that best captures the effects of insurance on access to and use of health services. Although the individual panels are relatively small in comparison with CPS, NHIS, or SIPP, extensive oversampling and the possibility of combining overlapping MEPS panels makes possible analyses of relatively small, vulnerable population subgroups.

Timeliness is inevitably an issue with MEPS, because of its design. The quick estimates that the AHRQ publishes from the round 1 interview with each panel are not as analytically useful as the monthly data that are released much later. The round 1 questions count people who are uninsured for varying lengths of time (three to six months, depending on the time of interview). There are also two potential problems with any reported lack of insurance from interviews conducted toward the end of the round 1 reference period. First, recall error is likely to be significant. Second, because six months is a fairly long time in relation to the turnover in the uninsured population, and correct answers to the questions imply that uninsured respondents lacked coverage for the entire five to six months, the round 1 estimates undercount uninsured person-years. Furthermore, because the MEPS income questions are not asked until the calendar year has ended, the round 1 estimates cannot be tabulated by income, an essential variable in most policy analyses.

NSAF and CTS are privately funded efforts that are not aimed primarily at producing regular national estimates of the uninsured. While both survey designs maintain the capability to make reliable national estimates, the NSAF sample is optimized for state-specific estimates, and CTS is optimized for community-specific estimates. The central questions in both studies have to do with comparing estimates across geographic units and across time. To limit the cost of conducting so many interviews in so many different locations, both surveys rely heavily on telephone (instead of personal) interviews, and their samples are primarily based on random-digit dialing instead of area probability sampling. The reliance on telephone interviewing might explain the slightly lower estimates of the uninsured from these two surveys compared with the rest.

The estimates for 1999 from the six different surveys (shown in table 1.1) center on about 40 million uninsured, with a difference of 7 million between the smallest and largest estimates. SIPP and NHIS virtually agree on a cross-sectional estimate of around 38 million for that year, while the cross-sectional estimates from CTS and NSAF are slightly lower (36 million). Estimates from MEPS of people uninsured throughout the first half of the calendar year (43 million in 1999) are typically at the high end of the range. The CPS estimate of uninsured throughout 1999 (42 million, revised downward to 39 million with the new verification question) is characteristically consistent with the cross-sectional estimates.

New Directions for Data Collection and Analysis

Despite their limitations in capturing important insurance dynamics, accurate cross-sectional estimates of the uninsured can be produced more quickly and cheaply than longitudinal estimates. Consequently, cross-sectional estimates and surveys will continue to be important in monitoring and analyzing trends in health insurance, especially when there are policy changes (such as SCHIP) to be evaluated quickly.

Although the CPS sample has been expanded to facilitate the evaluation of SCHIP on a state-by-state basis, and analysts often interpret CPS estimates as a cross section, it is risky to translate annual questions incorrectly answered by respondents into program caseloads and costs.

Furthermore, to the extent that respondents answer the CPS questions correctly, the focus of the questions on coverage held at any time during a year gives relatively little weight to transitions out of coverage, a potentially important phenomenon in programs that experience as much turnover as SCHIP and Medicaid. For these reasons, a concerted effort should be made to improve the usefulness and timeliness of truly cross-sectional surveys, such as NHIS and SIPP, for policy purposes.

Some of the most fruitful new analyses of cross-sectional data are likely to involve pooling multiple years of data from the same survey. Pooled cross sections will provide more variation for exploring the determinants of health insurance status. Moreover, they will be useful in evaluating the effects of policy changes and investigating trends. It is important for data collection organizations that conduct cross-sectional surveys to keep survey questions and procedures consistent over time, in order to facilitate pooled and trend analyses.

State policies in determining Medicaid and SCHIP enrollment are correlated with the probability of being uninsured. Consequently, analysts need access to state identifiers and need to use statistical techniques that recognize intrastate correlations in cross-sectional studies of insurance status and the uninsured.

Much important territory remains to be explored with longitudinal data. As argued above, one cannot accurately assess the personal and social consequences of being uninsured without taking into account the distribution and duration of uninsured spells across people over time. Also, analysis of longitudinal data may help distinguish causality from correlation. Analysts can observe the ordering of events, model changes in individual behavior, and study outcomes more effectively with longitudinal data.

Historically, the lack of regular and timely longitudinal data has been one of the biggest impediments to studying the causes and consequences of gaps in health insurance over time. That situation may now be improving. AHRQ is releasing data for the two-year MEPS panels in a timely fashion and is committed to keeping MEPS in the field continuously. Because the median length of an uninsured spell is about six months, longitudinal panels do not need to be longer than the two years covered by MEPS. All of the SIPP data for the 1996 panel, covering 12 core interviews (3 each year) and all topical modules, are available for downloading from the Census Bureau's website, as is a longitudinally edited and imputed file with a longitudinal weight to adjust for sample attrition. A 2001 panel went into the field in February 2001, and the

Bureau plans to field abutting (instead of overlapping) SIPP panels every three years.

Future research that takes a dynamic view of health insurance will focus on describing and modeling transitions from one insurance status to another. Instead of static analyses that count and characterize the uninsured in cross-sectional data, these dynamic analyses will count and characterize *changes* in coverage (such as the likelihood and predictors of leaving Medicaid or employer insurance and becoming uninsured). Ideally, these dynamic models will imply flows from one type of coverage to another that are consistent with the stocks of each type in cross-sectional estimates.

Research should also be able to produce a more definitive picture of the consequences of being uninsured by characterizing the uninsured in terms of the timing and duration of their lack of insurance. Using longitudinal data to distinguish between the long-term and short-term uninsured is an obvious next step. More generally, research that relates individual or family changes in insurance status to changes in use of health services, employment, and health status (both in a causal sense and in time) will improve our understanding of the social and personal costs of being uninsured.

NOTES

This work was performed under the sponsorship of the Regents of the University of Michigan and The Robert Wood Johnson Foundation. The author is grateful to Kathy Swartz, Alan Monheit, Anne Polivka, and Catherine McLaughlin for comments on earlier drafts. Peter Cunningham (Center for Studying Health Systems Change), Diane Makuc (National Center for Health Statistics), Chuck Nelson (Bureau of the Census), Steve Zuckerman and Jennifer Haley (The Urban Institute), and Jeff Rhoades (Agency for Healthcare Research and Quality) were helpful in providing information about and from the surveys conducted by their organizations. Also, Paul Fronstin kindly provided additional, unpublished details regarding his estimates from the Current Population Survey.

1. Health insurance estimates from HRS, together with information about survey design, are available from Short, Shea, and Powell (2001); Sloan and Conover (1998); and Johnson and Crystal (1997).

2. The undercount of Medicaid in CPS has been discussed widely (Fronstin 2000a; Chollet 2000). Lewis, Ellwood, and Czajka (1998) report that there is also evidence of this problem in other surveys.

3. When Medicaid was automatically linked to welfare payments for a family, family eligibility for Medicaid was another reason for studying the insured and uninsured within families.

4. Similarly, estimates from MEPS for 1996 indicate that only 5 percent of workers age 16 to 64 who were offered insurance were uninsured (Monheit and Vistnes 1997).

5. There are a few examples of such multinomial models in the literature, including Rhine and Ng (1998), Johnson and Crystal (1997), and Short and Friedman (1998).

6. These calculations are only the starting point in costing proposed programs. Cost estimates incorporate additional adjustments to account for less than full participation in public insurance programs among the uninsured, for example, and for incentives to substitute enrollment in a new program for existing coverage among the insured. Adjustments to cross-sectional estimates may also be necessary to account for the frequency and timing of eligibility determinations. If a new program grants coverage for a specified time period, such as six months, its coverage will extend beyond the currently observed ending of some uninsured spells and will cover currently insured person-years (Kathy Swartz, personal communication).

7. Cross-sectional surveys do not collect information about the health insurance status of each sampled person on exactly the same day. Rather, they typically ask about the status of each sampled person on the day of the interview (or "now," in the wording of the survey questions). Although everyone in the sample is not literally interviewed on the same day, the survey still characterizes the status of each person on one day. Because one day is the same as another, in the absence of seasonal differences, the logic described in the text still applies.

8. For example, MEPS asks each person who was uninsured at the start of the calendar year when he or she was most recently covered by health insurance and the source of that insurance. NHIS asks how long it has been since each uninsured person last had health care coverage; the survey also asks each insured person if there were ever a time in the past 12 months when he or she did not have any health insurance and, if so, for how many months.

9. For example, see Swartz, Marcotte, and McBride (1993a), Bennefield (1996b), and Short and Friedman (1998).

10. When the Census Bureau experimented with questions about current insurance status in the March 1995 CPS, there was a discrepancy of about 10 percentage points between the cross-sectional estimates and those based on questions about the preceding year (Bennefield 1996a).

11. Even if the absolute numbers from CPS do not have a lot of meaning because of ambiguities about the timing of the coverage reported, it is possible that the survey still reliably measures relative differences across the population or over time. That is to say, the estimates can still be reliable, even if they are not valid. However, because the reporting errors in CPS are associated with changes in insurance status, the survey is unlikely to be reliable in comparing subgroups or time periods when the mix of short-term and long-term uninsured differs or changes over time.

REFERENCES

Andersen, Ronald, and Odin W. Anderson. 1999. "National Medical Expenditure Surveys: Genesis and Rationale." In *Informing American Health Care Policy: The*

Dynamics of Medical Expenditure and Insurance Surveys, 1977–1996, edited by Alan C. Monheit, Renate Wilson, and Ross H. Arnett III. San Francisco: Jossey-Bass.

Bennefield, Robert L. 1996a. *A Comparative Analysis of Health Insurance Coverage Estimates: Data from CPS and SIPP.* Joint Statistical Meetings. Chicago: Bureau of the Census.

———. 1996b. "Dynamics of Economic Well-Being: Health Insurance 1992 to 1993: Who Loses Coverage and for How Long?" *Current Population Reports* P70-54 (May): 1–5.

Chollet, Deborah J. 2000. "A Survey of Surveys: What Does It Take to Obtain Accurate Estimates of the Uninsured?" *State Coverage Initiatives* 1(5–8). Washington, DC: The Alpha Center.

Cunningham, Peter J., and Paul B. Ginsburg. 2001. "What Accounts for Differences in Uninsurance Rates across Communities?" *Inquiry* 38(1): 6–21.

Cunningham, Peter J., Elizabeth Schaefer, and Christopher Hogan. 1999. "Who Declines Employer-Sponsored Health Insurance and Is Uninsured?" *Issue Brief Findings from Health System Change* (22).

Dubay, Lisa C., and Genevieve M. Kenney. 1996. "The Effects of Medicaid Expansions on Insurance Coverage of Children." *The Future of Children* 6(1): 152–161.

Fronstin, Paul. 2000a. "Counting the Uninsured: A Comparison of National Surveys." *Employee Benefit Research Institute Issue Brief* 225. Washington, DC: Employee Benefit Research Institute.

———. 2000b. "Sources of Health Insurance and Characteristics of the Uninsured: Analysis of the March 2000 Current Population Survey." *Employee Benefit Research Institute Issue Brief* 228. Washington, DC: Employee Benefit Research Institute.

Hoffman, Carolanne H. 1964. "Health Insurance Coverage: United States, July 1962–June 1963." Series 10, Number 11. Rockville, MD: National Center for Health Statistics.

Johnson, Richard W., and Stephen Crystal. 1997. "Health Insurance Coverage at Midlife: Characteristics, Costs, and Dynamics." *Health Care Financing Review* 18(3): 123–48.

Lewis, Kimball, Marilyn R. Ellwood, and John L. Czajka. 1998. "Counting the Uninsured: A Review of the Literature." Washington, DC: The Urban Institute. *Assessing the New Federalism* Occasional Paper No. 8.

Long, Stephen H., and M. Susan Marquis. 1994. *Universal Health Insurance and the Uninsured: Effect on Use and Cost.* Report for Congress, 94-689EPW. Washington, DC: Office of Technology Assessment and Congressional Research Service.

———. 1996. "Some Pitfalls in Making Cost Estimates of State Health Insurance Coverage Expansions." *Inquiry* 33(1): 85–95.

Monheit, Alan C., and Claudia L. Schur. 1988. "The Dynamics of Health Insurance Loss: A Tale of Two Cohorts." *Inquiry* 25(3): 315–27.

Monheit, Alan C., and Jessica Primoff Vistnes. 1997. "Health Insurance Status of Workers and Their Families: 1996." *Medical Expenditure Panel Survey Research Findings No. 2.* (Agency for Health Care Policy and Research Publication No. 97-0065.) Washington, DC: U.S. Department of Health and Human Services.

Nelson, Charles T., and Robert J. Mills. 2001. "The March CPS Health Insurance Verification Questions and Its Effect on Estimates of the Uninsured." Paper presented at the annual meeting of the American Statistical Association in Atlanta, August.

Rajan, Shruti, Stephen Zuckerman, and Niall Brennan. 2000. "Confirming Insurance Coverage in a Telephone Survey: Evidence from the National Survey of America's Families." *Inquiry* 37(3): 317–27.

Rhine, Sherrie L. W., and Ying Chu Ng. 1998. "The Effect of Employment Status on Private Health Insurance Coverage: 1977 and 1987." *Health Economics* 7(1): 63–79.

Rhoades, Jeffrey A., and May C. Chu. 2000. "Health Insurance Status of the Civilian Noninstitutionalized Population: 1999." MEPS Research Findings No. 14, AHRQ Pub. No. 01-0011. Rockville, MD: Agency for Healthcare Research and Quality.

Selden, Thomas M., Jessica S. Banthin, and Joel W. Cohen. 1998. "Medicaid's Problem Children: Eligible but Not Enrolled." *Health Affairs* 17(3): 192–200.

Short, Pamela Farley. 2000. "Hitting a Moving Target: Income Related Health Insurance Subsidies for the Uninsured." *Journal of Policy Analysis and Management* 19(3): 383–405.

Short, Pamela Farley, and Vicki A. Freedman. 1998. "Single Women and the Dynamics of Medicaid." *HSR: Health Services Research* 33(5): 1309–36.

Short, Pamela Farley, and Jacob Klerman. 1998. *Targeting Long- and Short-Term Gaps in Health Insurance.* Report 259. New York: The Commonwealth Fund.

Short, Pamela Farley, and Jessica Primoff Vistnes. 1992. "Multiple Sources of Medicare Supplementary Insurance." *Inquiry* 29(1): 33–43.

Short, Pamela Farley, Dennis G. Shea, and M. Paige Powell. 2001. *Health Insurance on the Way to Medicare: Is Special Government Assistance Warranted?* Report 457. New York: The Commonwealth Fund.

Sloan, Frank A., and Christopher J. Conover. 1998. "Life Transitions and Health Insurance Coverage of the Near Elderly." *Medical Care* 36(2): 110–25.

Summer, Laura, Sharon Parrott, and Cindy Mann. 1997. *Millions of Uninsured and Underinsured Children Are Eligible for Medicaid.* Washington DC: Center of Budget and Policy Priorities.

Swartz, Katherine. 1986. "Interpreting the Estimates from Four National Surveys of the Number of People without Health Insurance." *Journal of Economic and Social Measurement* 14(3): 233–42.

———. 1994. "Dynamics of People without Health Insurance: Don't Let the Numbers Fool You." *Journal of the American Medical Association* 271(1): 64–66.

———. 1997. "Changes in the 1995 Current Population Survey and Estimates of Health Insurance Coverage." *Inquiry* 34(1): 70–79.

Swartz, Katherine, and Timothy D. McBride. 1990. "Spells without Health Insurance: Distributions of Durations and Their Link to Point-in-Time Estimates of the Uninsured." *Inquiry* 27(Fall): 281–88.

Swartz, Katherine, John Marcotte, and Timothy D. McBride. 1993a. "Personal Characteristics and Spells without Health Insurance." *Inquiry* 30(1): 64–76.

———. 1993b. "Spells without Health Insurance: The Distribution of Durations When Left-Censored Spells Are Included." *Inquiry* 30(1): 77–83.

Walden, Daniel C., Gail R. Wilensky, and Judith Kasper. 1985. "Changes in Health Insurance Status: Full-Year and Part-Year Coverage." NHCES Data Preview 21; DHHS Pub. No. PHS 85-3377. Rockville MD: National Center for Health Services Research and Health Care Technology Assessment.

2

Why Are So Many Americans Uninsured?

Linda J. Blumberg and Len M. Nichols

Numerous data sets count and describe the socioeconomic characteristics of the uninsured population in the United States. While precise estimates differ, by all accounts the number of uninsured persons is large (around 40 million in the best of economic times) and prone to grow, both in absolute terms along with the population and as a percentage of the population when the economy weakens.

There is some dispute about whether the widespread lack of insurance is a market failure that justifies policy intervention. There is less controversy about the substantial body of research showing that the uninsured have reduced access to care (Cunningham and Kemper 1998). Many researchers have also concluded that the uninsured often have inferior medical outcomes when an injury or illness occurs.[1] (The complex issue of causation between health insurance and health outcomes is addressed in chapter 4.) Regardless of final judgments about causation between health insurance and health outcomes or status, few dispute that many individuals cannot afford necessary health care on their own; therefore, at least since the mid-1980s (when the last large Medicaid expansions were enacted), policymakers have debated not whether but how best to enable more Americans to pay for needed health care services. This question inevitably leads to discussions of how best to expand access to health insurance coverage.

This chapter describes some of what economic research can and cannot yet offer policymakers who are concerned about reducing the number of uninsured persons. It focuses on a deceptively simple question: what do we know about why so many Americans under age 65 are uninsured? The answers are as varied as the subpopulations within this country's multifaceted health care delivery and financing "system." Therefore, identifying the causes requires one to review the institutional realities of the many sources of coverage, as well as the economic research literature.

This chapter first explores the reasons why demand for health insurance varies so much across individuals—why some with high demand are able to find arrangements with the lowest effective prices while others face barriers they cannot overcome without assistance. It then develops a theoretical and conceptual framework that can help explain why some individuals remain uninsured. The next sections review employer-based health insurance options and the supply-and-demand issues associated with them, public insurance options available to the nonelderly and the reasons why enrollment in them is less than 100 percent, and the private nongroup market, with its particular risk segmentation issues. The last section summarizes remaining research questions and data needs.

The Theory of Demand for Health Insurance

Unlike other industrialized nations, the United States does not compel any individual to have comprehensive health insurance. While many people have more than one option for obtaining coverage, each option is associated with a choice and an opportunity cost of taking it. For some people, the opportunity costs can be substantial. For others, insurance markets erect barriers that make some options inaccessible. This section explores those costs and barriers, but it is important to recognize that individual tolerance of risk is a key factor in the way people identify and choose among options.

Theoretical Framework for Private Demand for Health Insurance

The standard economic theory of behavior under uncertainty is well known: risk-averse individuals will pay to avoid severe financial consequences of the unfortunate state of the world. That willingness leads to the existence of contingent contracts, or insurance markets. In the health insurance context, the unfortunate state of the world can be described as illness or the fear of illness serious enough to require an individual or family to pay the full cost of necessary and efficacious medical care solely out of current income or wealth. Standard theory holds that risk-averse individuals who are offered actuarially fair prices will insure themselves fully; however, with unavoidable loading costs in the real world (discussed later), individuals prefer incomplete insurance. The optimal degree of coverage in the face of loading costs increases with the individual's aversion to risk.

In addition to avoiding financial risk, individuals may have an access motive for purchasing coverage (Nyman 1999). Nyman has developed a theoretical framework and rough empirical approximation of the value of being able to purchase medical care that would otherwise be unaffordable. For example, an individual needs a liver transplant to stay alive, at an approximate cost of $300,000, but his or her net worth is only $50,000. The individual cannot purchase the liver transplant out of net worth, so the financial protection issue is beside the point. At the same time, there is a positive value to the additional years of life that would result from having the procedure. This person can afford actuarially fair health insurance coverage for the possibility of needing a liver transplant (calculated as the cost times the probability of needing the procedure). The net gain from such insurance coverage is akin to the expected value of the care minus the cost of the care with insurance. Nyman's rough empirical estimates suggest that such an access benefit aggregated across the population may swamp the aggregated benefit of financial protection. The access motive may also include ensuring access to high quality providers and the full panoply of procedures rather than the anonymous safety net providers and the procedures that limited public subsidies might buy for the seriously ill uninsured.

Thus, it is useful to think about an individual's demand for health insurance as having two classes of arguments: those that reflect the individual's desire to protect his or her financial status and those that reflect his or her desire to ensure access to high-quality providers and expensive medical services. More formally:

$$V(B_i) = V(\textit{Financial Protection, Ensure Access}),$$

where *Financial Protection* $= FP(W, Y, RA)$, *Ensure Access* $= EA(EX(C,q,PC),$ $RA)$, and $RA = RA(\sigma_{EX}, ED, FS, G)$. $V(B_i)$ is the utility or satisfaction one derives from having a particular package of insurance benefits (B_i). With regard to financial protection, utility is a function of both wealth (W), as posited by standard theory, and current income (Y), since immediate consumption may be constrained by current income flows. As noted above, the potential financial loss from catastrophic illness is increasing in income, although after a very high threshold of wealth or income is reached, demand for insurance may decline again.

With regard to ensuring access to expensive services, as suggested by Nyman, expected expenditures (EX) are key, and they depend upon the quantity (C) and quality (q) of medical care that may be necessary (and efficacious), as well as the expected price of each unit of that medical care (PC). Implicit within the calculation of C is the health status (perceived as well as actual) of everyone in the family. Each insurance option may have a different PC and q, and each person will evaluate the relative value of each benefits package in this light. Take, for example, a person who is eligible for both public coverage and employer-sponsored insurance, and assume that the benefits packages are identical. In such a case, the PC and q values of the two options will play the central role in determining the relative values of $V(B_i)$. Similar comparisons of q and PC would take place in households where both spouses are offered employer-sponsored insurance.

Aversion to both financial and service quality risk (RA) is a function of the variance of expected expenditures (σ_{EX}), education (ED), family status (FS), and gender (G). When it comes to risk aversion and demand for health insurance, the expected value of necessary medical care is not more important than the potential demand or need for medical care—that is, the upper bound of potentially required medical care affects demand. Risk aversion is also a function of education (ED), because more educated people know the consequences, both financial and clinical, of not having insurance, they know that appropriate health care is likely to be efficacious, and they also may have more confidence that they can obtain efficacious care within an insurance and delivery system. Family status (FS) is included as a determinant of risk aversion, since parents and married partners may be more likely to seek coverage for family members whom they care about or for whom they feel responsible. Family status includes whether a spouse or other family member, if present, has access to alternative sources of insurance. Finally, gender (G) is included since men and women have different expected health use profiles and thus may need different degrees of financial protection and have different probabilities of needing access to high-quality providers.

Let the price of health insurance (to the individual) be P^*. Health insurance demand for a particular package of benefits is then:

$$HI^d = 0, \text{if } V(B_i) < P^* \text{ for all available } B_i, \text{ and}$$

$$HI^d > 0, \text{if } V(B_i) \geq P^* \text{ for at least one available } B_i.$$

It is a truism that people will be uninsured if the subjective value to them of the insurance benefit package they can buy is less than the price they have to pay. Moreover, those who value health insurance the most are likely to buy the most of it, depending on the price. This concept of $V(B_i)$ is similar to the notion of reservation price or willingness to pay for health insurance (Pauly and Herring 1999), and $V(B_i) - P^*$ is similar to consumer surplus, or the difference between what a consumer is willing to pay and what he or she actually pays.

An interesting feature of health insurance markets is that some persons who value health insurance the most are also the most likely to make choices—such as seeking jobs from employers that offer health insurance—that lead them to find the *lowest* prices of health insurance. Thus purchasers of insurance are likely to obtain substantial consumer surplus. Other people do not have the qualifications to obtain a job that offers health insurance, even if they value it highly. Still others with high demand—say, those who expect to be very sick—are unable to work. Often, these people qualify for public programs, end up facing very high prices in the private nongroup insurance market, or can find no one willing to sell them insurance at an actuarially fair price and are therefore uninsured (Pollitz, Sorian, and Thomas 2001). For these reasons, it is difficult to maintain that the prices paid in health insurance markets reflect willingness to pay on the margin, since some people get a consumer surplus while others cannot find a price they are willing to pay.

It is important to make clear that some eligible people do not enroll in insurance plans even though the monetary cost is zero, a situation that would not seem possible from this characterization of health insurance demand. Thus P^* represents more than just monetary cost; it includes time cost and any disutility from an enrollment process that is perceived as burdensome or embarrassing (which may be the case with Medicaid, since it is still associated with cash assistance). The ways in which $P*$ exceeds zero for various public insurance programs with zero nominal fees is discussed later.

Socially Optimal Levels of Health Insurance

The benefits of most health care services are seemingly private, as opposed to the public benefits of immunizations against communicable diseases. However, there is some evidence that many Americans derive some positive feelings from other people's consumption of health care services—after all, public funds are spent providing services to specific populations, and large tax expenditures are devoted to subsidizing employer-sponsored health insurance. Medicare, SCHIP, and Medicaid insure the elderly, children, and the severely disabled and low-income pregnant women, respectively. In addition, since hospitals are generally required to stabilize patients that need emergency services before discharging them, society has exhibited a desire to make sure people do not die immediately if provider capacity and ability permit, regardless of ability to pay.

Such expenditures can be interpreted as an externality, or social willingness to pay for catastrophic care to be available to all. They are financed through an implicit tax on hospitals in the form of service provision requirements. The cost of the requirements is borne by paying (insured) patients, through higher prices for their care; by providers, who earn less than they otherwise might; and by taxpayers, through direct financing of the health care safety net. General altruism also exists and is manifested in private charitable contributions to hospitals and some primary care clinics on behalf of those who are unable to pay. Still, it is reasonable to infer that a majority of voting Americans find 40 million uninsured people—and the patchwork of providers and services they have access to—an acceptable social outcome.

Although limited steps have been taken in the last two decades to expand access to insurance, the large uninsured population may create significant, and potentially measurable, inefficiencies. For example, receiving care in inappropriate settings is inefficient: primary care delivered in an emergency room is more expensive than similar care delivered in a doctor's office. Also, some low-wage uninsured workers might be more productive or miss fewer days of work if they and their family members had health insurance, but employers cannot reduce the workers' wages enough to pay for coverage due to minimum wage constraints. Greater efficiency might arise from expanding coverage if health insurance affects health outcomes and worker productivity in general. In addition, delays in receiving care due to lack of coverage may lead to more expensive treatments for conditions than would otherwise have been necessary; premature births are an example. Another potential inefficiency of uninsurance arises when healthy people systematically underestimate the probability that they will become seriously ill, leading to an underconsumption of insurance.

On balance, then, while it is ultimately an empirical question, there is a reasonable probability that subsidized coverage expansions could improve the efficiency of the overall resources allocated to health care. In other words, changing the present health insurance price structure to exploit differences in price responsiveness or elasticity of demand by different groups could increase coverage and enhance welfare as well.

To put the motivation for analyzing why people are uninsured into an efficiency framework, consider the current subsidy of employer-based insurance. Employers' premium payments are exempt from employee income and payroll taxes. This $100 billion per year subsidy effectively reduces the price of health insurance to persons insured through employers, and the subsidy's value increases with the individual's marginal tax rate. Ending the current tax subsidy would be like raising the price of insurance for the currently insured. If this were done, the savings to the government could be used to finance a larger per-person subsidy for individuals with low willingness to pay, presumably because they are constrained by their low income.[2]

It is impossible to determine the optimal level of coverage, because the social demand for insurance cannot be identified precisely. But it is at least possible, and plausible, that net social welfare could be enhanced by increasing the subsidy of insurance purchases by low-income populations and reducing the subsidy to high-income purchasers of health insurance since the former exhibit greater price responsiveness. The greater the disparity between the elasticities of demand of low-income and high-income groups, the greater the coverage expansion and welfare enhancement of a given redistribution of the current subsidy. This is why it is crucial for policy analysts to estimate correctly the elasticity of demand for different subgroups of the population.

Determining the Price of Health Insurance

Even without considering time and disutility costs, the price of health insurance is one of the most complex phenomena in all of economics. On the one hand, the price of $1 of insurance has long been interpreted as the administrative load (Pauly 1997). Load is the percentage markup on expected medical costs that insurers must have to cover the costs of selling and administering an insurance contract in a world of heterogeneous health risks, provider quality, and provider cost. Thus, any premium for a particular risk class, k, is

$$P = E[C^*q^*PC](1 + L),$$

where L is the load and $E[\ ]$ is the expectations operator, C is the number of units of medical care, q is the quality of medical care, and PC is the price per unit of medical care.[3] Competition among insurers keeps loads as low as possible, but they range from 5 percent to 40 percent, depending on the market (Congressional Research Service 1988).

Load is the appropriate concept of the price of insurance, as well as the right price of insurance to use operationally, *if* the individual expects to incur expenses of $E[C^*q^*PC]$ in the absence of insurance—that is, if the actuarial value of the insurance contract equals what the individual expects to spend. In this case, the person is paying for the convenience of having the insurance company pay bills they would have expected to pay themselves in the absence of insurance, as well as the promise to protect the individual financially if health care needs turn out to be much greater than expected. But all insurance contracts, even in the nongroup market, pool people with quite different health risks and expectations. These contracts typically charge all policyholders in the same pool, or subpopulation, the same price, which reflects the average expected C^*q^*PC for all members.

In real life, most of the group's members would have expected expenditures below the mean, while a few individuals would have expected expenditures well above the mean. Most individuals in any insurance pool expect to spend, and in fact do spend, less than the actuarial value of the policy in any given year, but they buy the policy because they are averse to risk of financial ruin and to being denied access to efficacious services and providers (Monheit, Nichols, and Selden 1996). They might buy a more parsimonious policy if they could find it, but transactions costs and economies of scale limit the degree to which insurance contracts can be tailored to individual expectations and health risks (Newhouse 1996). Thus, most people are paying a price that is well above the load, while some are paying less. The optimal amount of insurance is not likely to be available to every person—if, indeed, it is available to any person.

So how should the price of insurance be conceived? First, it must be noted that because of transactions costs, administrative economies of scale, and the high cost of hospitalization and attendant ambulatory visits, no one writes $1 insurance contracts. In fact, partially due to state mandatory benefit laws, minimum actuarial value health insurance contracts are quite large and lumpy in most markets. (Typical prices today are over $3,000 for singles and close to $8,000 for families [Kaiser Family Foundation 2002].) This means that the opportunity cost of buying health insurance at all—as opposed to the cost of one more dollar of coverage on the margin—can be quite high. Thus, the opportunity cost of purchasing insurance (that is, the market value of goods that the individual must forgo in order to buy insurance) is an appropriate way to conceive of the price of health insurance. The opportunity cost is equal to the premium or fraction of the premium the individual must actually pay, directly or indirectly.

But the net price of insurance to any particular consumer is even more complex. It is to some extent an outgrowth of the consumer's choices, even though external conditions may set many of the constraints under which the consumer makes those choices. The decision tree in figure 2.1 illustrates how individual decisions affect the price of health insurance with which the consumer is faced. The choices available to individuals are shown in ovals, constraints beyond the individual's control are in rectangles, and the pricing category faced as a result of these are in bold rectangles. The pricing categories can be ranked for an individual in a particular risk class, k, as follows:

$$P_k^{public} \; < \; P_k^{ESI/large} \; < \; P_k^{ESI/small} \; < \; P_k^{NG/se} \; < \; P_k^{NG/nse} \; < \; P_k^{unins},$$

where *public* refers to publicly sponsored coverage, *ESI/large* is employer-sponsored insurance available through a large firm, *ESI/small* is employer-sponsored insurance available through a small firm, *NG/se* is nongroup insurance purchased by a self-employed individual, *NG/nse* is nongroup insurance purchased by a non-self-employed individual, and

Figure 2.1. *Health Insurance Consumer Decision Tree*

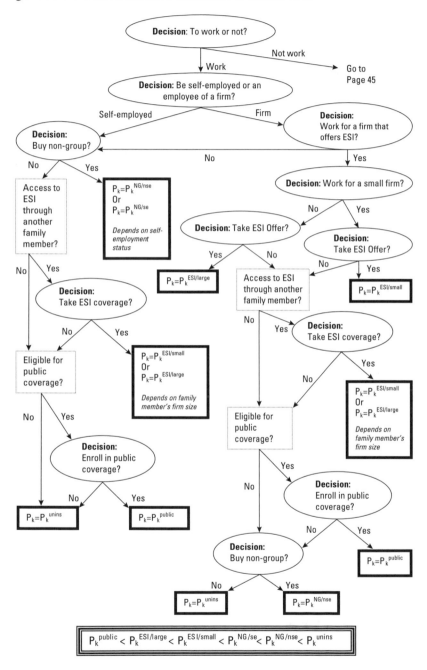

Figure 2.1. *Continued*

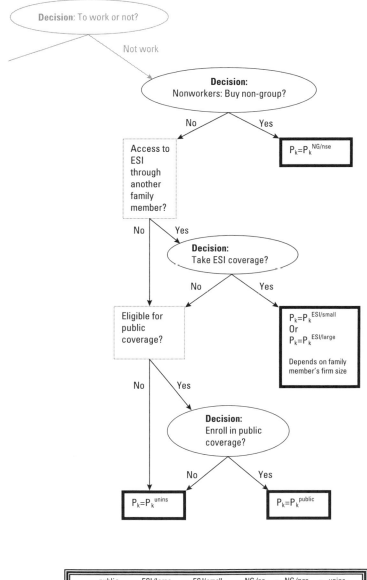

unins is the out-of-pocket cost per unit of care incurred by those without any insurance coverage at all.

The first key decision is whether or not to work. Such a decision separates those who have no potential for direct access to insurance in the group market from those who do have an opportunity to pursue group coverage directly. (Nonworkers may have access to group insurance indirectly, through a working family member.) If the individual decides to work, the second key decision is whether to be self-employed or work for a firm. This is another decision that can eliminate direct access to group coverage. For the person who decides to work for a firm, the third key decision is whether or not to choose a firm that offers health insurance. Those who choose a nonoffering firm also find themselves without direct access to group insurance. The fourth decision for a worker who chooses to work for an offering firm is whether or not to work for a small or a large firm. Because insurance is relatively less expensive in large firms than in small ones (for reasons discussed below), this decision also has significant implications for the relative price of health insurance a worker faces.[4]

Once the worker is employed by an offering firm, he or she must decide whether or not to accept the offer. Accepting the offer determines the price of coverage faced to be the lowest premium for a given set of benefits in the private sector. Declining the offer leaves the worker with the options of accessing coverage through a family member (if available), enrolling in public coverage (if eligible), or going uninsured.

Some low-income workers (typically those with incomes below 200 percent of the federal poverty level) find that they or some of their family members are eligible for Medicaid or another public program, such as the State Children's Health Insurance Program (SCHIP), which is administered by states and financed largely by the federal government. In this case, adults have to decide if they want to enroll themselves, their spouses, or their children in the public program. (Analysts have differing views of where in the decision sequence such choices regarding public coverage are made; this particular ordering is presented for illustrative purposes only.)

Those who choose to be self-employed, to not work for firms that offer health insurance, or to not work at all face more limited options for coverage. They may purchase nongroup coverage. Self-employed workers receive a price advantage relative to other purchasers in this market. Since 1986, unincorporated self-employed persons have been given a federal tax deduction on premiums. As a result of this tax break, the self-employed are more than twice as likely to purchase non-group insurance as other persons who are candidates for this insurance (Blumberg and Nichols 2000). The disparity will increase after 2003, when the self-employed deduction is increased to 100 percent. If persons without employer offers of insurance do not buy nongroup coverage, they can gain access to employer-sponsored insurance through another family member (if available), enroll in public coverage (if eligible), or be uninsured.

Each of these choices, or the fact of eligibility for Medicaid, will alter the net price of insurance to any given consumer. With the key choices identified, one can clarify how they affect prices at the end of each branch of the decision tree.

Group insurance: Group insurance, generally employer-sponsored insurance, provides a number of price advantages for consumers. First, premiums paid by an employer on the worker's behalf are exempt from federal income and payroll tax.[5] There is some dispute about how much of this employer premium payment is extracted from wages, and from whose wages, an issue discussed in some detail later. The basic point is this: if t represents an individual's marginal income tax rate plus his or her payroll tax rate, the degree of the tax subsidy is the product of the employer's share, s, and t, or st. If an employer pays 100 percent of the premium, the subsidy rate is equal to t. Thus it is clear that workers with higher incomes, and higher t, receive greater tax subsidies through their employers than workers with lower incomes, even with the exact same employer payment percentages.

The second price advantage of group insurance results from administrative economies of scale. These economies stem from the largely fixed costs of administering enrollment and from plan and provider screening activities, which can be spread over more employees in larger firms. Similar economies of selling and administering enable group insurers to offer health benefits packages with lower loads to larger groups. Finally, the variance of expected health care costs decreases with increasing group size, resulting in a kind of risk-pooling economy of scale that accrues only to groups, and to greater degrees in larger groups.

Each of the three price advantages of group insurance is large, since the average income plus payroll tax rate is about 30 percent, administrative loads can be 25 to 30 percent lower for group insurance products (Congressional Research Service 1988), and the risk premiums required for very small groups or individuals often exceed 15 percent (Cutler 1994). Moreover, the price advantages for large firms can be substantially greater than those for small firms (with fewer than 50 employees) or for individuals trying to buy in the nongroup market. Observed price differentials across markets—individual, small group, large group—are actually less than implied by these differences because purchasers in the small group and nongroup markets typically buy less generous packages than large firms do. Controlling for benefits package generosity is a serious empirical problem, but it is essential if one is to use premiums as the price of health insurance.

Another empirical problem concerns worker age. Firms with high percentages of older workers are likely to have high demand for health insurance, and they are also likely to incur higher health care costs and thus be more expensive to insure. One cannot know in advance whether the willingness to pay for insurance will increase more sharply than the expected costs of insuring older workers. The higher price for older workers may also be a function of their lower elasticity of demand for health insurance, since they expect to need more medical care.

For workers who receive an offer from their employer, the net price of insurance is

$$P* = P_k^{ESI} = (1-s)P_j^g + s(1-t)P_j^g\gamma.$$

This is the most complicated price, and the one applicable to most U.S. workers, since over 70 percent are offered health insurance by their own employer. Recall that s is the employer's share of the premium. P_j^g is the nominal total premium in the group market (the expected average medical costs of members of group j times $(1+L_j^g)$, where L_j^g is the load for the jth group), t is the worker's income plus payroll tax rate, and γ is the fraction of employer payments on the worker's behalf that the worker believes are actually extracted from his or her would-be wages. Thus $[(1-s)P^g]$ is the worker's out-of-pocket payment for health insurance, and $[s(1-t)P^g\gamma]$ is the wages lost to employer premium payments.[6] The various arguments and implications of $\gamma \le 1$ are discussed at some length in a later section. The price of insurance obtained through small employers, $P_k^{ESI/small}$, is estimated to be greater than that of insurance obtained through large employers, $P_k^{ESI/large}$, due to the administrative, risk pooling, and bargaining power advantages of large groups.

Nongroup insurance: Except for the self-employed, participants in the nongroup market are not subsidized by any government. Furthermore, in most states, insurers are allowed to adjust premiums—or their willingness to sell insurance altogether—to individual health status and other personal characteristics of those seeking nongroup coverage. Thus, the elements of an individual's demand affect price. At present, no one knows whether the increasing insurance prices associated with greater health risk (imagine a premium table arrayed by age group) rise as steeply as the willingness to pay associated with the same risk, but both influences increase the premiums that older and sicker Americans will face. The empirical difficulties of teasing out actual demand elasticities, given this complexity, are discussed later.

For those who are not self-employed and who end up as candidates in the nongroup market—that is, those who do not work or who work for a firm that does not offer or does not make them eligible for insurance—the price of nongroup insurance is:

$$P* = P_k^{NG/nse},$$

where k is the risk pool, or population subgroup believed to be similar by insurers. These pools are typically organized by age, gender, health status, geography, and family size. Note that $P_k^{NG/nse}$ is the expected average medical costs of members of subpopulation k times $(1+L^{ng})$, where L^{ng} is the load for the nongroup market.

For the unincorporated self-employed,

$$P* = P_k^{NG/se} = (1 - t)P_k^{NG/nse}$$

The normal nongroup premium is effectively reduced by the self-employed worker's income plus payroll tax rate, t, since current law makes self-employed premiums fully deductible starting in 2003.

Public insurance: Medicaid, and in most cases SCHIP, charge zero or low prices to those who are eligible for coverage (though a nonzero price may not seem low to a low-income family) and an infinite price to those who are not. Often this means that children, or a woman while she is pregnant, may be enrolled in a public program at no cost,[7] while other adults, and sometimes older children,[8] must buy any insurance they want for themselves in the nongroup market. Perhaps surprisingly, but indicating that deeper forces are at work in health insurance demand, millions of people who are eligible for "free" public insurance do not enroll. Of course, some workers decline zero out-of-pocket premium plans offered by employers, so it is not just people eligible for Medicaid who refrain from taking up "free" insurance (Chernew, Frick, and McLaughlin 1997). One reason low-income workers decline ostensibly free employer-sponsored insurance is because deductibles and copays are perceived as onerous, compared with the genuinely free care they may be able to obtain in clinics or outpatient departments of public hospitals. This rationale could also be at work in the lower-than-expected enrollment in some Medicaid and SCHIP programs that have copayments (Dubay, Kenney, and Haley, forthcoming). Possible reasons behind the decision to decline public insurance are discussed later.

For those eligible for Medicaid, SCHIP, or some other public program,

$$P^* = P^{public} = \varepsilon > 0.$$

Some SCHIP programs have nominal premiums, and those do deter enrollment, but most uninsured people who are eligible for Medicaid or SCHIP face zero out-of-pocket prices. Still, P^{public} is not zero, for time and hassle or stigma factors in the application process are not trivial and are clearly burdensome enough to affect enrollment. At the same time, some people are not aware that they are eligible for public programs, and thus for them, ε reflects search or transactions costs that are effectively infinite (Kenney, Haley, and Blumberg 2002).

Uninsurance: While many uninsured individuals pay for all or a significant portion of their care out-of-pocket, the availability of free health care for some uninsured persons lowers the price per unit of their medical care to nearly zero, thus lowering the demand for health insurance, everything else remaining equal. As Nyman (1999) noted, however, there is no guarantee of free, high-quality medical care. In fact, empirical evidence indicates that the uninsured tend to receive fewer services and less favorable medical outcomes than persons with insurance coverage.

EMPIRICAL ESTIMATION PROBLEMS THAT ARISE FROM THE THEORETICAL DISCUSSION

To summarize, net prices of health insurance are affected by, if not completely determined by, individual choices. This fact poses obvious econometric problems. Interestingly, many individuals with the highest demand for health insurance seem to undertake to obtain access to the lowest possible prices for health insurance by working for firms that offer insurance. Thus, the quantity they demand is maximized vis-à-vis persons who have a lower aversion to risk or a lower demand and who may end up facing higher net insurance prices.

To simplify, $HI^d = f(X,Z,P*)$, where X and Z are both vectors of variables that affect worker risk aversion and demand for health insurance and Z includes variables that affect demand but not price (e.g., education and wealth). But $P* = P*(X,ID)$, where ID represents identifying variables that affect insurers' offers, Ps, but not HI^d. Note that X variables—for example, age, health risk, family status, and so on—influence both HI^d and $P*$.

Two empirical solutions seem possible. One would be to estimate HI^d and $P*$ as a system; if appropriate Z and ID variables or instruments can be found, this is satisfactory. Alternatively, and this is the approach typically followed in the literature on an individual's demand for health insurance, one can use a $P*$ measure that is believed to be somewhat exogenous to the individual's specific circumstances, or X vector, and estimate HI^d directly. The potential bias and inefficiency in the estimated marginal effects of the X variables, as well as in highly policy-relevant price coefficients and calculated elasticities, are a function of how appropriate the assumptions regarding exogenous factors turn out to be. Furthermore, in all empirical work on health insurance demand, there is considerable controversy over the best way to impute premiums to workers who did not take, and firms that did not offer, employer-sponsored insurance. Only rarely does one observe prices nonpurchasers actually face. These issues are examined in the discussion of the literature, later.

Employer-Sponsored Insurance

Employer-sponsored insurance is the most common form of health coverage for Americans under age 65. Sixty-seven percent of the nonelderly had such insurance, through their own employer or a family member's, at some point in 1999, as did 73 percent of those who worked during the year (U.S. Census Bureau 2000b). However, 17 percent of workers (24.2 million) had no coverage of any kind during 1999, and 13 percent of workers' children (8.7 million) were uninsured. Why have some workers and their dependents obtained employment-based insurance, whereas others have not? That question is answered in this section.

Institutional Options for Coverage

An employer interested in sponsoring a health insurance plan for workers and their dependents has a number of options. The first is fully insured products for single employers. This option represents the purchase of an employment-based group health insurance policy from a licensed, risk-bearing carrier. There are many different types of licenses in each state, typically including Blue Cross Blue Shield (many of which remain not-for-profit), commercial, and health maintenance organizations (HMOs). Within these types, various products are made available, including indemnity plans, HMOs, preferred provider organizations, and point-of-service options for HMO products.

Fully insured plans determine their premiums based upon the sum of expected medical costs, or claims; margin, or reserve for higher-than-anticipated costs; expected expenses (i.e., administration); and profit or contribution to surplus funds. Expected claims are determined on the basis of the past experience of the insurer's group insurance business (particularly for employers of a similar type), the past experience of the employee group itself, and data from intercompany studies (Health Insurance Association of America 1994). This means that employers with an above average claims experience in the past (those with sicker enrollees) and employers of a type that tend to have above average costs (e.g., cab drivers, bartenders, hairdressers, loggers, etc.) will face higher premiums. The reliance of insurers on the claims experience of similar employers when setting premiums effectively means that the insurers pool the risk of like employers, even in the absence of regulatory constraints.

Because claims costs are uncertain, insurers also include a protective financial margin in the premium rate. This margin will vary with the size of the employer, since average claims of large groups are considerably more consistent over time than average claims of small groups. Administrative expenses are generally calculated as a share of premiums; the share decreases as the size of the group increases, reflecting real economies of scale.

The second option facing employers is to insure themselves. This option reflects the reality that firms can establish reserves and manage their own cash flow in such a way as to insure or indemnify their workers against most health-related expenses. Federal law—namely, the Employee Retirement Income Security Act of 1974 (ERISA)—exempts employers from state insurance regulations as long as they are providing self-funded health insurance to their workers, but such employers are not exempt from the federal Health Insurance Portability and Accountability Act of 1996. Most employers that self-insure their workers purchase stop-loss insurance from commercial carriers to protect themselves against very large losses. Stop-loss insurance policies have very large deductibles and are not regulated, unlike typical commercial health insurance products. Except for the stop-loss component, self-insuring employers effectively separate, or segment, the cost of insuring their employees from the risk of workers in other firms, a practice that is difficult to achieve when purchasing fully insured products from commercial plans, Blues, or HMOs. The efficiency with which this arrangement minimizes variance increases with firm size. Consequently, the probability of self-insuring is much higher for large firms than for small ones (Acs et al. 1996; Marquis and Long 1999).

The third option is for multiple employers to enter into insurance arrangements together. These options include Multiple Employer Welfare Arrangements (MEWAs), multi-employer plans (Taft-Hartley plans), business coalitions, and health insurance purchasing cooperatives. A MEWA is an insurance arrangement that offers benefits to the workers of more than one employer. These were defined in the 1983 amendments to ERISA.[9] A MEWA represents an agreement among employers alone—it is not collectively bargained by workers' representatives and multiple employers, as are Taft-Hartley plans. Legally, MEWAs can offer either self-insured plans or fully insured products. Regulation of MEWAs varies from state to state, with some states treating them the same way as the rest of the fully insured market, and others treating them more liberally than single-employer self-insured plans. MEWAs that are not fully insured are also subject to state insurance regulations, as long as those regulations are not inconsistent with ERISA. MEWAs tend to be vehicles for small employers to separate themselves from the broader employer-based risk pool without having to take on as much risk as they would have to under single self-insurance.

Taft-Hartley plans are defined and regulated by the 1947 Taft-Hartley Act, not by ERISA or the states. These plans are the result of collective bargaining agreements among multiple employers and their workers. The plans are particularly appropriate for employees of different firms in the same industry at different times throughout the year (e.g., longshoremen, construction workers). The boards of these plans typically comprise representatives of labor and management.

Purchasing cooperatives have been developed in a number of states and are generally designed to allow small employers to take advantage of economies of scale in purchasing, thereby reducing prices and often increasing health plan choices for workers.[10] While some large employers participate in pooled purchasing arrangements, small employers are much more likely to do so (Long and Marquis 1999). Some cooperatives began with seed money and management provided by the state. Purchasing cooperatives tend to be open to broad spectrums of employers (perhaps restricted only by size) and are oriented more toward increasing purchasing power than segmenting risk. Business coalitions and other purchasing groups vary in terms of their openness to employers with varying risk, their boards' acceptance of conflict-of-interest rules, and whether they offer a choice of health plans.

Although these three groupings of insurance options and the multitude of plans that fall within them potentially provide many coverage options to employers and their workers, significant numbers of workers and dependents remain uninsured. Why? The next sections summarize what is known, and what research questions remain, by examining why some employers offer insurance to their workers while others do not; why some offering employers deny eligibility to some workers; and why some eligible workers decline to enroll, remaining uninsured.

Why Do Some Employers Offer Insurance and Others Do Not?

Offering health insurance to workers can be an economically efficient decision. According to 2001 data from the MEPS-IC, 58 percent of private sector establishments offer health insurance to at least some of their workers. Offer rates vary dramatically by characteristics of the employer and its workers; for example, 99 percent of establishments with 1,000 or more workers offer insurance, compared with 39 percent of establishments with fewer than 10 workers. The same data indicate that 89 percent of workers are employed by establishments that offer coverage to at least some of their workers. Since about 80 percent of workers who are offered coverage take it up, each firm's offer decision is the key to widespread coverage or its absence. In addition, one forecast suggests that offer rates will be more important than take-up rates in explaining declines in employer-sponsored insurance in the near future (Acs and Blumberg 2001).

Before discussing the reasons why employers may offer health insurance, it is useful to review a theoretical framework of employers' offer decisions (Nichols et al. 2001). Assuming that employers care about health insurance only because workers do, the firm's demand represents an aggregation of individual workers' demands. Each worker's demand for health insurance (HI^{dw}) is a function of the net (relative) price of health insurance to the worker ($P*$) and the value he or she places on health insurance $V(B)$. In symbolic format,

$$HI^{dw} = f(V(B), P*),$$

where $P* = (1-s)P_j^g + s(1-t)P_j^g \gamma$. Note that even for the same benefits and cost-sharing structure, P_j^g will be different, depending on whether the employer chooses commercial insurance, self-insurance, or a multiple employer arrangement. In each case, P_j^g is a weighted average of the group's own recent medical costs and the recent cost experience of similar groups with which the group's risk is pooled. The net price to the worker is equal to the premium price multiplied by the share of the premium that would be required as an out-of-pocket payment by the worker (s is the employer share of the group premium), plus the net reduction in wages the worker must accept in order to prompt the employer to sponsor coverage. If wage incidence (γ) is 100 percent, then the employer has extracted all health insurance costs from the worker's wages.

The probability of a firm's offering health insurance to its workers is expressed as:

$$\Phi(Offer) = \Phi(f(HI^{dw}), COMPETITION, FP).$$

Here, $f(HI^{dw})$ is used to represent the distribution of the firm's many workers' demand for health insurance. Unfortunately, economists have yet to develop a satisfactory theory of how a firm actually aggregates the heterogeneous preferences of its workers. In pioneering work over 30 years ago, Goldstein and Pauly (1967) discussed this issue and developed two alternative mechanisms—the median voter/worker model and the average worker model. Neither option has been proven empirically, and alternative theories are possible. For example, the preferences of higher wage workers may receive disproportionate weight. Some empirical evidence supports this hypothesis, although further research is clearly needed (Gruber and Lettau 2000).

COMPETITION is the extent to which hiring workers of sufficient quality requires a firm to offer health insurance, given the other labor market options in the same geographic area or industry. It summarizes what one's labor market competitors are offering. Moreover, *COMPE-TITION* is likely to be a function of the wages of the workers employed by the firm, in that the nature of competition for low-wage workers is likely to be quite different from that for high-wage workers.

FP is the price the firm faces for health insurance. If wage incidence is 100 percent ($\gamma = 1$), as traditional economic theory holds, this price should be zero. The fact that firms act as if *FP* were not zero makes some analysts think that $\gamma < 1$ for many firms and workers. If $\gamma < 1$, then the premium the firm faces is the relevant price, as well as any administrative costs that the firm must bear and that are not financed out of wage reductions. Once the premium is on the firm's radar screen, then premium variance or fear of premium variance over time is also relevant.

Below are three reasons why some employers offer health insurance and others do not.

REASON 1: EMPLOYERS' OFFER DECISIONS REFLECT WORKER PREFERENCES
Workers with high demand for health insurance, those for whom $V(B) >> P*$, will prefer to work for firms that offer health insurance and offer it at the lowest $P*$, all else being equal. Thus, firms with high percentages or critical masses of high-income workers, older workers, married workers, educated workers, workers in areas with high health care costs, or workers with few acceptable alternatives are more likely to offer health insurance. Such workers are the most likely to be willing to pay for some or all of their employers' costs of health insurance in the form of reduced wages. Conversely, firms that employ a preponderance of low-wage, young, healthy workers are less likely to offer health insurance, since these workers are less likely to be willing to trade wages for health insurance coverage they do not value very highly. Firms that employ mostly minimum wage workers cannot lower wages to offset their health insurance costs and thus are extremely unlikely to offer coverage.

Workers with a spouse whose employer offers coverage or with family members who are eligible for public coverage may have weak demand for health insurance from their own employer. Employers with a large percentage of such secondary workers may not need to offer health insurance to attract the workforce they require. Sixty percent of nonoffering small employers interviewed for the 2002 Kaiser Family Foundation and Health Research and Educational Trust (Kaiser/HRET) Survey, of Employer-Sponsored Health Benefits reported that their employees' being covered elsewhere was very or somewhat important in their decision not to offer health insurance (Kaiser Family Foundation 2002). Some analysts have hypothesized that the expansions in Medicaid eligibility that took place in the late 1980s and early 1990s could have led employers to drop health insurance for their workers, but the only empirical study of this question found no evidence of such crowd-out behavior (Shore-Sheppard, Buchmueller, and Jensen 2000). The researchers did find some evidence that family coverage declined with increases in the share of workers eligible for Medicaid.

McLaughlin and Zellers (1992) found that almost half of nonoffering small employers surveyed in the 1990 Small Business Benefits Survey had no interest in offering health insurance because of a lack of demand on the part of their workers.

Using data from the May 1988 Current Population Study (CPS), Long and Marquis (1993) found that the characteristics of workers in nonoffering firms were more like those of workers who declined coverage offers than those who accepted them. This suggests that low demand by workers plays an important role in firms' coverage decisions. Yet only about 4 percent of workers in offering firms report that they declined coverage because they did not need insurance (Thorpe and Florence 1999). Given that most people who decline offers, and even those who are not offered insurance, obtain coverage through spouses, the most relevant comparisons are of workers who decline and are uninsured and workers who are not offered and uninsured.

Approximately 8 percent of the uninsured workers in nonoffering firms reported being in fair or poor health, compared with only 4 percent of those taking up offers of insurance (Blumberg and Nichols 2001a). Approximately 6 percent of those who decline an offer and are uninsured report being in bad health. These results indicate that at least some health characteristics of nonoffered workers would lead to higher demand for coverage. The problem of low demand may be a manifestation of low willingness to trade wages for health insurance. One of the main complexities in understanding employers' decisionmaking process is how they consider the heterogeneous demands of a diverse workforce. Not only do analysts have little insight into how such demands are taken into account, they have very little information about the actual extent of the heterogeneity of labor within different types of firms. Beyond including workforce summary statistics in estimation equations (percent over age 45, percent earning low wages, etc.), not much is known about how to model worker-firm interactions on this trade-off.

REASON 2: LABOR MARKET COMPETITION

Some employers do not offer health insurance coverage because the competition for workers does not require them to. This reason reflects underlying worker demand, but it may also be an independent factor, as offer and coverage rates vary considerably across the country. Survey results indicate that in 2002, 58 percent of small employers that did not offer health insurance said they could obtain good employees without it (Kaiser Family Foundation 2002).[11]

Industries and occupations with low offer rates are disproportionately made up of small firms (Nichols et al. 1997). Workers wanting jobs in a particular industry in a particular area may discover that small firms or low-wage firms dominate local employment opportunities, and those small firms tend not to offer coverage. Thus, even larger employers in these industries and locations do not have to offer health insurance to attract sufficiently good labor to run their business.

The industry with the lowest offer rate is agriculture (31 percent of agricultural establishments offered health insurance in 2001, according to the MEPS-IC[12]). Eighty-six percent of agricultural establishments have fewer than 10 workers, and 93 percent have fewer than 25 workers.[13] Construction also has a low offer rate (49 percent offered in 2001). Seventy-six percent of construction establishments have fewer than 10 employees and 90 percent have fewer than 25 workers.

Within such industries, offer rates vary considerably by occupation. While measured by worker rather than by firm, this finding is a further indication that firms' markets for particular types of labor may be very different. For example, white collar workers in agriculture and construction had high offer rates (virtually 100 percent for agriculture and 86 percent for construction), while offer rates for blue collar workers in those industries were only 32 percent and 49 percent, respectively (Nichols et al. 1997). This suggests that different labor markets and firms with different skill mixes will have different likelihoods of offering health insurance.

REASON 3: PRICE TO THE EMPLOYER

Conclusions about wage incidence are key to determining which price, if any, is relevant to the employer. There is some evidence that γ approaches 1 for workers in childbearing years (Pauly 1997; Gruber 1994), which implies that the price to the employer is zero, since all premium costs are extracted from wages. But there is also considerable evidence that workers behave as if $\gamma < 1$, at least on average (Levy and Feldman 2001;

Chernew et al. 1997; Blumberg, Nichols, and Banthin 2001), and at least one theory of how $\gamma < 1$ might be an equilibrium for a particular class of workers and firms has been advanced and some supporting evidence has been found (Garret and Nichols 1999).

A major reason for offering health insurance is to compete for workers, though having insured workers could be inherently valuable to employers if productivity is higher or work-loss days are fewer. Because the market for health insurance is complicated, multidimensional, heterogeneous, and at times fiercely competitive, employers may not be equally efficient at obtaining health insurance for their workers. Yet to compete for mobile workers, they must offer competitive total compensation packages.

An inefficient insurance-seeking employer—or a small firm with inherent disadvantages in spreading administrative costs—may find it impossible to recruit workers if it has to extract more from wages than more efficient insurance-seeking firms do. Thus, as long as there are heterogeneous insurance-searching skills or constraints, $\gamma < 1$ for many employers and workers. This is possible in equilibrium if inefficient firms earn some kind of economic rent in their product market that they then apply to the incomplete wage offsets. Most markets do have differentiated products; thus, given the host of other, more powerful factors affecting profitability that change over time (inflation, energy costs, etc.), some firms that offer health insurance may continue to make up the difference with product differentiation rents indefinitely, or at least until they drop coverage or go out of business altogether in a downturn.

Given the substantial administrative and risk-pooling advantages of large firms, γ might be quite a bit lower than 1 for small firms competing for the same types of workers as large firms. Garrett and Nichols (1999) have found evidence to support this hypothesis. Indeed, if γ is low enough for a given firm, it may not offer health insurance at all, for then the compensation package gets too expensive: the firm simply does not earn enough rent to finance $\gamma = 0$. Since small firms are inherently at a disadvantage in searching for efficient health insurance packages, they are less likely to offer health insurance, all else being equal. Similar logic predicts that γ and offer rates are low in large low-wage firms, since workers in those firms will naturally be resistant to having their wages reduced for any reason.

A neoclassical purist might counter that all inefficient insurance-seeking firms will simply offer higher cash wages and no insurance. But given the tax advantage to workers and the lower loads in group insurance products, efficiently purchased health insurance through the firm is much more valuable than the equivalent cash wages would be, *because workers cannot purchase insurance on their own in the nongroup market for the same amount.* This wedge, roughly $P_k^{ng} - [(1-s)P_j^g + s(1-t)P_j^g\gamma]$, acts as a constraint on firms that compete for workers who are able to obtain health insurance from competing employers. Recall that L^{ng} equals approximately $1.3*L^g$, so P_k^{ng} equals $1.3*P_j^g$, and since $st\gamma < 1$, the wedge between equivalent cash wages and price in the nongroup market can be quite large.

Firms that are inefficient at seeking insurance may have to offer it anyway, if they want to attract the kind of workers who command offers of health insurance on the open market. Monheit and Vistnes (2000) report that 79 percent of workers who value health insurance highly work for a firm that offers it, and 71 percent of workers who do not think they need health insurance at all work for firms that offer it. While these facts suggest that some worker sorting occurs among jobs with different compensation packages, they also suggest that job sorting among those who prefer wages to health insurance is highly imperfect. Though the notion has not yet been formally tested, it appears that most U.S. workers are in labor markets that attach health insurance to every relevant job, some are in labor markets that attach health insurance to no job, and a relatively small number of workers switch between jobs with and without health insurance attached. If labor markets are segmented this way, this could be one reason why it has been so difficult to trace the contours of wage–health insurance trade-offs empirically.

EVIDENCE ON WAGES AND THE INCIDENCE OF HEALTH INSURANCE COSTS
Workers employed by firms that offer health insurance have higher wages, on average, than workers whose firms do not offer it (Nichols et al. 1997). This fact, based on observed and unobserved productivity differences, makes it difficult to find trade-offs between wages and benefits.

One early study of public school districts found that an additional dollar of health benefits was associated with a $0.83 reduction in teachers' salaries (Eberts and Stone 1985). Another study found that when wage-nonwage trade-offs were estimated using pensions, health insurance, and life insurance, greater substitutability was found than when benefits were defined just as health insurance plus life insurance (Woodbury 1983). In other words, the broader the definition of benefits, the greater the wage-benefit trade-off. This finding implies that studies which do not take other potential benefit trade-offs into account may suffer from omitted variable bias.

The costs to employers of workers' compensation insurance have also been used to quantify wage incidence. One study found that 56 to 85 percent of such costs were shifted back to workers through reduced wages, depending upon the industry (Gruber and Krueger 1991). In other research, state and federal mandates for coverage of maternity benefits were used to measure wage effects (Gruber 1994). This study of all states found that 59 to 90 percent of the cost of the mandates fell upon the wages of the workers expected to benefit from the maternity services. The estimate for full-time workers was 75 percent.

However much wages are reduced to pay for health insurance, the precise mechanism is unclear. Are workers' wages adjusted individually or on average? Are they adjusted within each firm according to whether health insurance is taken or across firms in compensating differentials? How long do such adjustments take, and how does labor turnover play into the dynamics of these adjustments?

One study concluded that older workers pay for their higher health care costs in reduced wages (Sheiner 1999), but the study's design raises some concerns. First, the author did not control for a number of employment characteristics that are correlated with age and that have important effects on wages—such as firm size, industry, occupation, and length of time on the job. These omissions could bias the estimated coefficient of age. In addition, average employer health care costs for each age- and gender-specific category of workers were used to compare wage effects with appropriate health care costs. However, there is no universally accepted gradient measuring the relative differences in cost between individuals of different ages; in fact, premium-age gradients vary considerably across insurers and states. Since area averages instead of actual observed premiums were used in the study, any inferences about age incidence drawn from this study alone seem premature.

Observed wage-age gradients do not support the notion that costs are shifted to workers in this age-specific way. If they were, one would see steeper gradients in firms that do not offer health insurance, because the age-wage profile would not be attenuated by the effects of age on health care costs. In a simple test, the log of wage was estimated as a function of dummy variables for age categories.[14] The sample included full-time working men from the February 1997 Contingent Worker Supplement to the CPS. The equation was estimated separately for workers in firms that offered health insurance and those that did not. The statistical relationship between wage and age for workers in firms that did not offer insurance was considerably weaker than it was for those in firms that did. Wages increased monotonically by age in the offering firms, although the increment in wages did shrink at higher ages. In the non-offering firms, wages began to decline after age 49, precisely when high health care costs should have been bringing down wages in offering firms, if age-related incidence were indeed 100 percent. This model suggests that older workers in offering firms are paid more, relative to their younger coworkers, than older workers in nonoffering firms. This result strongly contradicts an age-incidence conclusion.

In another study, researchers found evidence that employers vary worker contributions to health insurance in a way that encourages employees to obtain coverage from a spouse's employer (Dranove, Spier, and Baker 2000). But if employers are able to pass the full cost of insurance on to their workers, and particularly if they are able to pass those costs along in direct relation to the costs imposed by the worker on the group, the employer should be indifferent about where the worker obtains coverage. Employers tend to resist with some passion mandates to provide health insurance, whereas if incidence were 100 percent, they should be indifferent. One can infer from such behavior that employers do not expect to be able to pass all of their employer payments on to workers.

Workers' perceptions of whether they themselves effectively pay for employer-sponsored health insurance—and if so, how much—have profound implications for whether they want their employer to offer it and, given an offer, the likelihood that they will take it up. There is at least anecdotal evidence that workers and employers do not believe in wage incidence of employer premium payments (Pauly 1997). These perceptions may be just as important for determining behavior as the currently unknown incidence dynamics. It is interesting to note that only 1 percent of eligible workers who decline insurance offers report that they did so because they preferred higher wages in lieu of coverage (Thorpe and Florence 1999).

Thus, the traditional assumption of $\gamma = 1$ does not hold everywhere, and it is wrong by varying degrees for different types of firms and workers. Because of this heterogeneity, analysis based upon the assumption that $\gamma = 1$ risks misleading policymakers quite seriously, at least in the short run. The measurement implication of this conclusion is that total premium, adjusted for benefit package generosity, is the right price to use in analyzing employers' decisions to offer or not offer insurance. In addition, γ could equal 1 for all benefits combined, but most data sets do not permit this hypothesis to be tested.

LABOR TURNOVER AND PRICE TO THE EMPLOYER

Labor turnover has two components: voluntary, or worker-motivated, separations and involuntary, or employer-motivated, separations. In addition, involuntary turnover may be permanent, in the case of firing, or temporary, in the case of layoffs. Employers with high rates of turnover have higher administrative costs of enrolling and disenrolling workers from health insurance than employers with more stable workforces. To the extent that these administrative costs cannot be recouped from workers, they are a kind of higher price and certainly represent disincentives to provide health insurance. The medical underwriting costs built into the price of insurance for small employers are also time-consuming and expensive. High turnover tends to lead to higher employer costs for recruitment and training and to lower worker productivity than is found in similar firms with lower turnover. Consequently, compensation may be lower, and not offering health insurance may be one outgrowth of that. Data from the 2002 Kaiser/HRET Survey reveal that 24 percent of nonoffering small firms report high turnover as a very important or somewhat important reason for not offering health insurance (Kaiser Family Foundation 2002).

From the worker's perspective, an expectation of short job tenure tends to decrease the demand for health insurance. Insurance is, by nature, more valuable as a long-term contract (the probability that a person in good health will be sick sometime during the year is much greater than the probability that the person will be sick in the next month). In addition, a person who expects to leave a job in the near term might also expect to be without significant income for some period, which tends to increase the subjective value of wages relative to benefits (Anderson and Meyer 1994).

The preponderance of evidence is that worker turnover is higher among small firms and among those that do not offer insurance. In addition, turnover seems to be concentrated in a subset of individuals (Anderson and Meyer 1994; Haber 1993; Groothuis 1994). However, no one knows at present the proportion of high-turnover workers in the uninsured population in a given year, nor what their actual demand for health insurance might be. The importance of this group relative to the total problem of uninsurance is also likely to fluctuate over the course of the business cycle.

As for price, 84 percent of small firms not offering health insurance report that high premiums were very important (68 percent) or somewhat important (16 percent) in their decision not to offer, according to the Kaiser/HRET employer survey. This finding could reflect a response to the demand for coverage by workers, since higher prices probably require greater wage offsets, or it might indicate that employers do not believe that health insurance costs can be sufficiently recouped through reductions in worker wages. According to the 1993 Robert Wood Johnson Employer Survey of 10 states, 40 percent of nonoffering employers had recently investigated the possibility of providing insurance coverage, but they did not find premiums low enough to entice them to do so (Cantor, Long, and Marquis 1995).

Three-quarters of employers cite possible premium increases over time as an important reason why they do not offer coverage (Morrisey, Jensen, and Morlock 1994). Apparently, employers were more worried about having to withdraw coverage than about not offering coverage at all. Withdrawing coverage would be an employer-motivated decision that would anger workers, rather than being a worker-driven response to future premium increases. Cutler (1994) found that premiums for small groups are subject to abrupt upward shocks following high-cost years and that the effects of these increases persist for a considerable time. Moreover, premiums varied more widely among small firms with higher turnover and less widely among small firms with larger percentages of high-wage workers.

Multivariate Analyses of the Probability of Offer

A number of studies have attempted to estimate the probability of an employer's offering health insurance. The difficulty in doing so is that price, obviously a key independent variable in this decision, can be observed only for firms that offer health insurance. Surveys rarely collect information on prices faced by those who do not offer insurance. Marquis and Long (2001) conducted an employer survey that did ask for quotes received by nonoffering firms, but less than 30 percent of respondents answered the question. While creative and quite interesting, their results cannot be considered representative.

As a consequence, researchers have tried to compensate for missing price data. One tack is to use tax rates as proxies for the premium price faced by the firm and its workers. Another is to impute premiums to firms that do not offer insurance. Yet another is to use employers' responses to questions about their willingness to offer coverage. Chernew and Hirth present the methodological disputes surrounding these approaches in chapter 6; this chapter summarizes recent studies and their findings.

Feldman and colleagues (1997) developed an approach to imputing premiums and used it to estimate the probability of small employers' offering insurance, using Minnesota data from the Robert Wood Johnson Foundation's 1993 Employer Survey. Their approach entailed treating the basic decision to offer insurance as a first-stage selection equation, estimating a selection-corrected premium equation for the purpose of deriving a premium imputation algorithm for all firms whether they actually offered or not, and then estimating a structural demand equation using the imputed premiums as a key explanatory variable.

This approach has yielded higher estimates of price elasticities than other studies have found. Feldman and colleagues used the selection correction term in the premium prediction or imputation equation, whereas Nichols and colleagues (2001) presented results both with and without the selection correction term.[15] The specifications and identification restrictions of the equations were also somewhat different. Feldman's estimated price elasticities were −3.9 for individual and −5.8 for family policies for small firms in Minnesota. This implies a 10 percent premium increase would lead to a 39 to 58 percent reduction in the probabilities of small firms offering health insurance. Nichols and colleagues estimated separate family price elasticities for each of four sizes of firms: fewer than 10 workers, 10 to 24 workers, 25 to 99 workers, and 100 or more workers. The data came from firms of all sizes. The price elasticities, in estimates derived from imputed premiums that were calculated without the selection correction term, declined with firm size; the largest group had a statistically insignificant response to price. The estimated elasticities for the three smaller groups were −1.2 (fewer than 10 workers), −0.5 (10 to 24 workers), and −0.4 (25 to 99 workers). Nichols and colleagues also found that the age and wage distributions of the workforce affected the probability of offer in predicted ways.

Hadley and Reschovsky (2002a) also used a variant of the Feldman and colleagues approach in their study of small firms, with a selection-corrected instrumental variable for price. They, too, found that the smallest firms had higher elasticities than larger ones (more than 10 but fewer than 100 employees), but all of their estimated elasticities were smaller (in absolute value) than −1.

Gruber and Lettau (2000) used Employment Cost Index and CPS data to estimate the probability of offer as a function of tax price for the median worker in the firm and other firm characteristics. They found an implied price elasticity of −.314. In addition, consistent with other work in the field, they found that the probability of offering insurance increases with firm size. Moreover, as higher wage jobs became an increasing share of jobs within a firm, the probability of offering insurance increased as well. Like the other studies, theirs found significant differences across industries.

Leibowitz and Chernew (1992) estimated the effect of the after-tax price of insurance on the decision of small firms to offer insurance. They also used premium quotes from small group insurers in different geographic areas. They found an estimated premium price elasticity of −0.8. Gentry and Peress (1994) analyzed data from the U.S. Bureau of Labor Statistics' Occupational Compensation Surveys for 1988 to 1992. They estimated the fraction of workers offered each of a number of benefits as a function of tax incentives and used regional data to capture how tax rules affect average benefits in a given region. They found that a 1 percentage point reduction in the marginal tax rate would decrease the share of employees offered health insurance by 1.8 percentage points.

Although they did not take a multivariate approach, Morrisey and colleagues (1994) calculated an implied price elasticity, using responses to an employer survey of small firms. A comprehensive health insurance plan was described by the survey team, and nonoffering employers were asked at what premium level they would be willing to offer the package to their workers. In 1993, 40 percent of respondents said that they would offer the policy if it could be purchased for $175 per worker per month. Lowering the premium by 15 percent increased the share to 53 percent. If the premium were lowered by 50 percent, 75 percent said they would offer the package. These responses imply a premium elasticity of −0.92. Whether responses to a hypothetical scenario such as this would be consistent with actual behavior is unknown, but the results are fairly consistent with other, empirical work.

Coburn and colleagues (1998) used the 1993 Robert Wood Johnson Foundation Survey to estimate the probability of offer with no price term. The analysis was designed to determine whether the lower rates of employer-sponsored coverage in rural areas relative to urban ones resulted from cultural or behavioral differences or simply from differences in characteristics of the employers. While 78 percent of rural employees are offered insurance, 88 percent of urban workers are. Coburn and colleagues found that the 10 percentage point gap would be reduced to 3 points if the distribution of firm size in rural areas were the same as it is in urban areas. If, in addition, the distribution of wages in rural areas were the same as in urban areas, the gap in offer rates would be reduced to just 2 percentage points.

In summary, multivariate studies have confirmed that premium price, tax incentives, and characteristics of the employer and workforce are significant in explaining the probability that an employer will offer health insurance. While the tax-based premium studies imply that at least some of the decision is driven by worker preferences, the continuing importance of employer characteristics, even after controlling for worker characteristics, indicates that employers may have independent reasons for choosing whether or not to offer health insurance. Clarification of these distinctions could be instrumental in designing effective public policies for expanding insurance coverage.

Why Are Only Some Workers Eligible for Insurance?

Employers who offer health insurance have a number of options for restricting access to that insurance for certain classes of workers. They can establish waiting periods, preventing new workers from receiving coverage until a specified period has passed, and they can permanently restrict coverage of certain types of workers (for example, part-time employees). All workers of a particular class must be treated the same, and their required contributions to health plans cannot vary within the group—that is, employers cannot make workers with particular health problems ineligible for insurance if similar workers are eligible. Nevertheless, employers can limit eligibility significantly if they so desire.[16]

Approximately 90 percent of workers in firms that offer health insurance are eligible for coverage (Garrett, Nichols, and Greenman 2001). Part-time workers and workers with short tenure (less than a year) are the least likely to be eligible. According to the 1997 Contingent Worker Supplement to the CPS, 3.7 million of 20.3 million uninsured workers (about 18 percent) were in offering firms but were not eligible for coverage (Thorpe and Florence 1999). An additional 6.4 million workers with insurance coverage from another source were also ineligible for coverage from their own employer. Of all these ineligible workers, 53 percent reported the reason as being that they do not work enough hours per week or weeks per year, about 8 percent said that contract or temporary workers are not allowed in the plan, 27 percent said they had not worked for the employer long enough to qualify, and 1 percent cited a preexisting medical condition. About 11 percent cited other reasons.

The reasons for lack of coverage cited most frequently by all uninsured workers were that they did not work enough hours to qualify (36 percent) and that they had not been with their firm long enough (48 percent). The former reason is indicative of a longer term uninsurance problem, while the latter implies that eligibility will come with more time on the job.

Those who are ineligible for insurance represent a minority of all uninsured workers, but this category appears to be growing in importance. Farber and Levy (2000) found that ineligibility was responsible for all of the decline in coverage of part-time workers (old and new) during their period of analysis.

Why do some employers choose to make some workers eligible for insurance and some workers not? No published literature on this question exists at present.[17] Perhaps employers use waiting periods in order to observe productivity or to screen out high-risk employees. If so, why do some employers use them while others do not? Little is known about the types of employers who do and do not use waiting periods to establish eligibility or how their use might vary by the characteristics and expected longevity of the workers.

While part-time workers may value health insurance less than wages because they are likely to have lower incomes, it is difficult to understand why their comparative valuation of health insurance would be declining over time. Some part-time workers have coverage through a spouse (another reason coverage may be less valuable to them), but Farber and Levy also found declines in spousal coverage of part-time workers. Do employers think they cannot recoup the costs of providing coverage to part-time workers to the same extent as they can from full-time workers? If they cannot, why not? Is it possible that the part-time labor market has reached a "tipping point" where employers accept denial of eligibility as a cultural or at least a competitive norm? With the share of part-time workers growing as a percentage of the labor market, eligibility may become a more prominent reason for uninsurance in the future.

Why Do Only Some Employees Take Up Offers of Insurance?

The participation rate of eligible workers offered health insurance is very high—85 percent in 1997 (Farber and Levy 2000). Yet participation is clearly not universal, and it has declined somewhat in recent years among full-time workers, particularly those who are less educated.[18] Of workers declining insurance, approximately 36 percent are uninsured, and the remainder obtain coverage elsewhere (Cunningham, Schaefer, and Hogan 1999). If workers were able to sort themselves perfectly into jobs with compensation packages that were consistent with their relative preferences for wages and benefits, the take-up rate for health insurance would be 100 percent.

As the out-of-pocket price of health insurance grows relative to wages, more workers will opt not to take up coverage. In addition, as more employers seek to create better matches between compensation and worker preferences by offering cafeteria plans, take-up of insurance should decrease (Thurston 1999). In the absence of cafeteria plans, workers who decline health insurance coverage receive no other benefits in its place; consequently, they are likely to enroll even if their demand for insurance is low. Under a cafeteria plan, those without strong demand for insurance are more likely to opt for another benefit that is more consistent with their preferences. Finally, expansions of public insurance increase the relative price of private insurance for more workers, leading to possible switching from private to public coverage. Estimates of the importance of this effect, first studied by Cutler and Gruber (1996), vary considerably (Blumberg, Dubay, and Norton 2000; Dubay and Kenney 1996; Dubay and Kenney 1997; Yazici and Kaestner 2000).

Jobs vary on many more dimensions than health insurance offers (McLaughlin 1999), and some types of workers may find it difficult to find a job that does *not* offer insurance. Some workers may not want to pay the out-of-pocket health insurance premium, preferring instead to obtain coverage through a spouse and perhaps negotiate higher wages with their own employer.

Two published studies have estimated multivariate models of eligible workers' take-up of their employers' offers of insurance (Blumberg et al. 2001; Chernew et al. 1997). Chernew and colleagues (1997) used data from the Small Business Benefit Survey, which was conducted in 1992 and 1993 in seven metropolitan areas and covered employers and workers in businesses with 2 to 25 employees. The person most knowledgeable about the firm's benefits was asked for information on the firm and specific workers in the firm. The analysis was confined to single workers.

Blumberg and colleagues (2001) used a linked file of the MEPS-IC and HH components (national surveys of employers and households), which allowed them to match actual employer premium data to a sample of workers offered insurance. It estimated separate models for singles (workers with no spouse or children) and for workers with a family (workers who were married or had dependent children, or both).

Both studies found that worker take-up was not significantly related to total premium price (employer contribution plus worker contribution), but it was significantly and negatively related to the worker's contribution. This finding is consistent with the hypothesis that workers do not perceive themselves as paying for the full cost of health insurance. Using the worker's out-of-pocket premium, the Chernew study estimated elasticities of $-.033$ to $-.095$, while the Blumberg study estimated elasticities of $-.0025$ for single workers and $-.04$ for workers with families. The Blumberg study also found that low-income workers (those with incomes of less than twice the poverty level) were more responsive to price than higher-income workers. In addition, salaried workers were more likely to take up coverage, and earnings were positively related to take-up, Chernew and colleagues found. The Blumberg study found that take-up was positively related to the log of family income, to the worker's being in fair or poor health, and to having one of a list of serious medical conditions.

Blumberg and colleagues also tested to see whether workers appear to sort into jobs with or without insurance offers as a function of their preferences for health insurance. They found evidence of this type of job sorting, but it did not seem to have an appreciable effect on the estimated take-up response to out-of-pocket premiums.

In another study, Blumberg and Nichols (2001b) used the National Health Interview Survey (NHIS) to estimate the probability of take-up. This analysis supported the inference that out-of-pocket premium price is more important in the take-up decision than health status of the worker and his or her family members. Lower-income workers again appeared to be more responsive to price than higher-income workers. Interestingly, low-income persons were more likely to enroll in a health plan if they had a family member in fair or poor health, but their own health status did not affect their purchase behavior significantly.

Workers' out-of-pocket premiums (even for the lowest cost plan offered) tended to be higher in firms with more low-wage workers, according to an analysis of data from the 1997 Robert Wood Johnson Foundation Employer Health Insurance Survey (Cunningham et al. 1999). When the typical wage in the firm was below $7 per hour, the average monthly employee premium amount for the lowest-cost plan was $27 for single and $130 for family, compared with only $17 and $84 in firms where the typical wage was over $15 per hour. The average take-up rates increased with income, at 78 percent for the lowest-wage firms and 89 percent for the highest-wage firms.

In a study on coverage, not take-up per se, researchers found that including psychological characteristics such as decisiveness and internal versus external locus of control in their model significantly increased the accuracy of their estimates, compared to estimates based on demographic characteristics alone (Dolinsky and Caputo 1997). Such psychological attributes may be relevant to the decision to take up offered coverage, as well as the decision to take a job with or without available health insurance.

Evidence indicates that some low-income workers decline employers' offers of health insurance even when their out-of-pocket costs are zero (i.e., the employer does not require a worker contribution). Researchers have suggested that such decisions are made because the coinsurance and deductibles required by an ostensibly free policy are more onerous than the charity care or uncompensated care low-income workers might receive through hospitals and other providers in the event of a serious illness or injury. In work related to that hypothesis, Rask and Rask (2000) found that public hospitals and uncompensated care reimbursement funds lower private insurance coverage.

Why Do People Work for Firms That Do Not Offer Insurance?

There are many reasons why workers might prefer to work for an employer that does not offer health insurance. These include preferences for wages relative to benefits, expectations of short job tenure, the cost of premiums relative to expected medical costs, or the availability of coverage from another source. Monheit and Vistnes (2000), using data from the 1987 National Medical Expenditure Survey (NMES), found that respondents stating "I'm healthy enough and really don't need insurance" or "health insurance is not worth the cost," or both, are significantly more likely to have a job that does not offer insurance. However,

72 percent of those stating they do not need health insurance and 69 percent of those who believe health insurance is not worth the cost work for employers that offer health insurance. There are clear mismatches in preferences for health insurance and job choice.

Another explanation is that firms that offer health insurance may attempt to screen out workers who have potentially high health costs. Buchmueller's analysis of 1984 Survey of Income and Program Participation (SIPP) data (1995) finds support for the hypothesis that there is a negative relationship between poor health and access to employer-sponsored insurance and that the relationship is stronger for men than for women. This means that employers may be effective screeners of worker health status, making it difficult for some workers with health problems or disabilities to obtain a job with insurance. The study was based on data obtained before the Americans with Disabilities Act was implemented, however. (The act prohibits hiring practices that discriminate against disabled workers.) In addition, the data were not derived from explicit questions regarding whether insurance was offered—Buchmueller assumed equivalence between an offer of insurance and coverage. As shown earlier, offer and take-up rates have diverged over time, so this assumption is probably less appropriate today than it was in 1984.

Furthermore, it is labor productivity, based on education, experience, and other aspects of human capital, that makes a worker valuable and able to command job offers from firms that offer insurance. Most people make decisions involving the acquisition of education and skills early in their adult life, long before they seriously consider health insurance or health plan choice in an employment setting. This is another way of saying that the specifics of health insurance may be less important to some workers than other job attributes, such as the nature of the work, the possibility that the job will move them forward in their career, and working conditions. Such considerations could also compensate a worker for selecting a job with a suboptimal health benefits package, whether because the plan is not generous enough, the worker's contribution is too high, or the price to the worker is just too high, all else being equal.

In summary, workers have no sure way of finding employment that offers health insurance options which are completely consistent with their individual preferences. While there are sure to be workers who do not value health insurance and who are able to sort themselves into firms that do not offer it, there are also workers who would prefer not to have coverage but who are in firms that do offer it, and workers who want coverage but cannot find a job that offers it. How efficient it is to search for the right job-insurance match, given the unavoidable real world costs of such a search, is unknown. However, considering the percentage of workers who appear to be mismatched, efficiency could probably be enhanced by an intervention that lowered search costs for workers in general. Low-wage jobs that offer insurance may have long, hidden queues of job-seekers because people looking for low-wage jobs cannot afford to search long while unemployed.

Many low-wage workers cannot afford employer-sponsored health insurance even though they want it. The higher take-home pay, even for workers who perceive the premium price as simply their out-of-pocket portion, may be worth far more to someone who earns 150 percent of the poverty level than to someone who earns 400 percent.

Public Insurance

Eligibility for public health insurance programs, whether federal or state, is generally limited to specific subgroups of the low-income population. In addition, eligibility guidelines for each subgroup vary by state. The largest public insurance programs for the low-income nonelderly population are Medicaid and SCHIP, both financed jointly by the federal government and the states.[19] Several states use their own funds to subsidize health insurance programs for certain low-income groups that are excluded from Medicaid and SCHIP.

Medicaid is available to families that would have qualified for coverage as recipients of cash assistance prior to welfare reform. In 1996, eligibility on the basis of income ranged from 15 percent of the federal poverty level for a family of three in Alabama, to 61 percent in New York (Liska et al. 1997). Many states also have programs for the medically needy, which extend Medicaid eligibility to some persons who have high medical expenses relative to income. These eligibility cutoffs vary by state as well, and in 1996 they ranged from 23 percent of the federal poverty level in Tennessee to 86 percent of poverty in California. Medicaid eligibility for persons receiving cash assistance through the Supplemental Security Income program is more uniform across the country, with the bulk of states setting it at 75 percent of the poverty level for children and adults with qualifying disabilities.

Federal law requires that Medicaid cover all children born after September 30, 1983, in families with incomes below the federal poverty level. Using Medicaid waivers or the 1902(r)(2) rules, some states expanded coverage to children born before that date or to children in families with higher incomes. Medicaid also covers pregnant women and children under the age of 6 up to at least 133 percent of the poverty level. SCHIP gives states the option of covering uninsured children in families with incomes up to 200 percent of the poverty level. States that had expanded Medicaid coverage beyond 150 percent of poverty prior to SCHIP can increase the maximum income by an additional 50 percentage points.[20]

State participation in Medicaid and SCHIP is voluntary, although every state now has both a Medicaid and a SCHIP program in place. The costs of Medicaid are shared between the states and the federal government according to a formula that takes into account each state's per capita personal income. The federal matching rates for SCHIP are 30 percent higher than each state's matching rate for the Medicaid program.

Under Medicaid, some states provide only the mandatory minimum benefits for children (e.g., Alabama, Alaska, Louisiana, Nevada, Wyoming), whereas others have gone much further (Bruen and Ullman 1998). Minnesota, for example, used an 1115 waiver to subsidize coverage of children up to 275 percent of the poverty level (some premiums are charged for those with family incomes between 133 and 275 percent of the poverty level). On average, only about 54 percent of low-income children (those in families with incomes below 150 percent of the poverty level) are Medicaid beneficiaries. SCHIP initiatives vary considerably as well. Eligibility ranges from a low of 140 percent of the federal poverty level in North Dakota to a high of 350 percent in New Jersey (Ullman, Hill, and Almeida 1999).

Many low-income persons fall into the so-called insurance gap—that is, they are not eligible for public insurance, yet they do not have access to or resources sufficient to purchase private insurance. The number of persons in this gap varies by state and surely contributes to the overall number of uninsured persons in the United States.

Participation in public insurance programs by those who are eligible is significantly below 100 percent. While participation among persons receiving cash assistance has historically been quite high (90 percent for children) (Dubay and Kenney 1996), the more recent expansions, which extended eligibility beyond the cash assistance population, have engendered much lower participation rates. An estimated 31 to 41 percent of children who are eligible for Medicaid and who do not have other sources of coverage are not enrolled in the program and are therefore uninsured (Dubay and Kenny 1996; Selden, Banthin, and Cohen 1998). Evidence indicates that these children are more likely to report having unmet medical, dental, and other health care needs than children enrolled in the program (Davidoff et al. 2000). Moreover, eligible but uninsured children are more likely to have delayed care in the last year because of cost (11 percent vs. 3 percent), and their families are more likely to have spent more than $500 out-of-pocket on health care (29 percent vs. 13 percent).

Why do individuals who can enroll in public insurance for little or no cost choose to stay uninsured or to have their children be uninsured? Hypotheses abound: the social stigma of being in a public program is a deterrent; many people do not know they are eligible; people know they can enroll in the event of medical need; and administrative requirements pose barriers to enrollment. No empirical study has yet determined the relative importance of these factors.

Researchers have attempted to predict the probability of participation in Medicaid. A recent study using data from the 1994 and 1995 NHIS found that enrollment of eligible children in Medicaid was positively related to the number of community and migrant health centers per 100,000 low-income persons in the child's county (Davidoff and Garrett 2001). This finding contradicts the safety net price of care argument advanced earlier and may reflect providers signing people up so they can be reimbursed. Welcoming safety net providers lower the application hurdles for eligible persons with fairly low latent demand for health insurance. The study also found that participation declined as the child grew older. Eligible children who are black were more likely to participate than those who are white, and children with limitations on their activity were more likely to enroll than those without. Participation declines with the age of the older parent. It is also negatively related to the parents being immigrants and to the income of the family unit. As the number of children in the family increases, so does participation. Enrollment is more likely for children with a parent in fair or poor health and for children who are eligible for Medicaid through the cash assistance program.

Although SCHIP is still in its infancy and no formal evaluations have been completed yet, concerns about take-up rates within the program have arisen. Byck (2000) used a very rough proxy to identify children in the 1993 and 1994 NHIS who were uninsured and who would have been eligible for SCHIP had it been implemented in those years.[21] She compared this group with children enrolled in Medicaid and with children with private health insurance. She draws on the differences between the groups and on experience with the Medicaid program to identify causes for concern in SCHIP take-up rates. Medicaid take-up has been low among higher-income families and higher-educated working families. Children eligible for SCHIP tend to come from such families, implying that achieving high participation will be more difficult for SCHIP than for Medicaid generally. Because the stigma hypothesis is credible, some states have implemented SCHIP using a different name than Medicaid. Still, residual stigma associated with a public program may reduce participation rates. Stigma effects may be greater among families with higher incomes, who have less experience with public programs. Educating parents about the eligibility of their children is also more of a challenge for SCHIP because the parents do not tend to have contact with welfare offices and other locations where outreach for low-income programs traditionally occurs. And even modest cost-sharing requirements may deter the working poor from enrolling.

An additional concern about SCHIP is low retention of children in the program. A study of eight SCHIP programs by researchers at the Urban Institute found that less than 50 percent of eligible children were reenrolling (Hill and Lutzky 2003). While specific causes are difficult to identify because of substantial limitations in state data, areas of greatest potential concern are parents' failure to respond to renewal notices and their failure to pay premiums.

Reform of the welfare system in 1996 had a negative effect on Medicaid participation. Kronebusch (2001) used data from multiple years of the CPS to estimate participation rates of children before and after the implementation of welfare reform. Enrollment grew between 1989 and 1995, largely because of the poverty-related eligibility expansions implemented during that period. Depending upon income, enrollment peaked in 1995 or 1996. Since then, it has fallen dramatically, even for children in the poorest families—that is, those with no income. In 1995, the enrollment participation rate for children with no income was 81 percent, but by 1998 that rate had fallen to 68 percent. For children at 50 percent of the poverty level, participation rates fell from 61 percent in 1995 to 53 percent in 1998. The study also found that state declines in Medicaid participation were strongly associated with declines in state welfare enrollment.

In another study, Garrett and Holahan (2000) used the 1997 National Survey of America's Families to examine the health insurance status of women leaving welfare between January 1995 and mid-1997. While much of this study period predates welfare reform, the analysis should hold for the post-reform period as well. In fact, welfare rolls were declining rapidly just before reform because of the strong economy and changes in Medicaid under state waivers.

In many cases, families leaving welfare can retain Medicaid coverage. If they leave because of increased income, Transitional Medicaid Assistance will cover them for six months, with another six months available if income does not exceed 185 percent of the federal poverty level. As noted previously, alternative means of coverage are available for children, pregnant women, and persons with high medical expenses, depending upon income and state of residence.

Of the women who had left welfare within six months of the survey, 56 percent still had Medicaid coverage, 12 percent had some form of private coverage (with some overlap between the two groups), and 34 percent were uninsured. Of those who had left a year or more before the survey, 49 percent were uninsured. Children fared better, with 19 percent of those who had left recently and 29 percent of those who had left earlier being uninsured. Clearly, large gaps in coverage exist, even during periods when former recipients are guaranteed eligibility for Medicaid.

Madden and colleagues (1995) examined participation in Washington State's Basic Health Plan (BHP), a subsidized insurance program for the low-income population. All persons with family incomes of less than 200 percent of the federal poverty level who live in the service area of participating plans and who are not eligible for Medicare may participate. Insurance coverage is provided through managed care plans contracting with the state. At the time of the study, no enrollment caps were in place, but since then, enrollment has been limited because of state budget constraints. The study included four counties and used enrollment data from BHP, as well as a telephone survey of applicants and eligible families that were not enrolled. The premiums charged enrollees vary with family income, the minimum being $7 per month and the average $34 in 1989. Copayments at the time of service were $5 per office visit and $25 for nonemergency care received in a hospital emergency room.

The results indicated that families with part-time workers only were more likely to enroll than those with no workers, and families with a full-time employed worker were least likely to enroll. Families with children age 5 or younger were more likely to enroll, as were single-mother families and those with higher recent out-of-pocket health care costs. Health status had no significant effect on enrollment. The price of coverage had a significant negative effect on enrollment, with a $10 increase in the monthly family premium reducing the odds of enrolling by 13 percent. Having family members with insurance from another source reduced enrollment. Larger families were more likely to enroll, as were those with no usual source of care. More highly educated eligible persons were more likely to join, as were families with older adults.

The great sensitivity of low-income eligible persons to price found in that study was reinforced by a Washington Hospital Association survey of persons who applied for BHP but did not join. More than 70 percent said they did not enroll because the premiums were too expensive (Washington State Health Care Authority 1994). This evidence poses a powerful dilemma for those hoping to reduce the number of uninsured: people who need subsidies have very little willingness to pay for health insurance. While administrative complexity and the stigma traditionally associated with low-income programs such as Medicaid have been largely overcome by new programs designed to be less stigmatizing, more like enrolling in private health insurance plans, and less complex from the standpoint of determining eligibility, even modest premiums charged to enrollees may deter enrollment. At the same time, policy-makers view premiums as a means of addressing state budget constraints and discouraging privately insured persons from switching to subsidized public coverage. Consequently, the question of how much to require public enrollees to pay will continue to interact with the question of how many uninsured persons society can tolerate under a voluntary system.

Outside of limited evaluations such as that of Washington's BHP, relatively little research has been done on the probability that different types of eligible persons (single adults, families, children) at different income levels will enroll in public programs. Nor is much known about the character of low- and moderate-income workers' demand for public insurance relative to private insurance. At what premium price will workers choose to enroll in an employer-offered plan instead of a public plan for which they are eligible in order to avoid the public sector's jungle of administrative complexities and obtain greater perceived quality of care? Knowledge of such trade-offs would be very useful in designing public insurance programs that would increase participation rates within budget constraints.

Beyond program design components such as premiums, administrative processes, outreach, and logistical access to providers, which surely have substantial implications for expanding coverage, more subtle factors are at play. Behavior, attitudes, and training of those responsible for enrolling eligible persons in public insurance may reflect a state's concerns about expanding programs for which it is at least partially financially responsible. Such factors may exert a powerful influence on eligible persons' desire to follow through with the enrollment process, and they are difficult, if not impossible, to measure or influence through policy.

The Nongroup Market

Almost 25 million Americans have some kind of private insurance purchased in the nongroup market (U.S. Census Bureau 2000a). These people and the insurance they buy are very diverse, including older people who buy supplements to the rather parsimonious Medicare benefit package, as well as some nonelderly people who buy dental and other specific policies to supplement their employer-provided insurance. The number of nonelderly people whose primary insurance is purchased in the nongroup market is much lower, less than 10 million, and has been declining slowly in recent years (Pauly and Nichols 2002; Pauly and Percy 2000). Four percent of the poor and 7 percent of those with incomes above 200 percent of the poverty level buy nongroup insurance. Rural Americans are slightly more likely than urban Americans to buy such insurance (Chollet 2000). Those who buy nongroup insurance are healthier than the uninsured, on average (Pauly and Percy 2000).

Institutional Realities of the Nongroup Market

Relatively little health economics scholarship has focused on the nongroup market, perhaps because of its size relative to the group market.[22] Chollet and Kirk (1998) have reported that the nongroup market varies considerably in size across the country, from 15 percent of the nonelderly population in North Dakota to less than 5 percent in Massachusetts. This variation is probably related to the availability of employer-sponsored insurance as well as to the generosity of public insurance and the insurance regulatory environment. Less than 2 percent of workers who have access to group insurance turn it down and then buy nongroup insurance; the vast majority of workers who have access to both reveal a clear preference for group insurance (Blumberg and Nichols 2000).

This is the market for which classic adverse selection is the most serious problem: all else being equal, those most inclined to seek nongroup coverage are those with higher health risks. Thus insurers have to worry that their applicant pool is not a random draw from the population at large. This problem is at the core of the well-known model developed by Rothschild and Stiglitz (1976), which predicts that a purely voluntary nongroup market will break down until only the very sickest individuals would pay the high but actuarially fair premiums required. Relatively few of the sickest individuals could afford to do so, however. Pauly and Herring (1999), based on their analysis of 1987 NMES data, argue that these concerns are overstated in real markets, since transactions costs force some pooling, even in the nongroup market (an interpretation that is consistent with Newhouse [1996]). Pauly and Herring concluded that the nongroup market pools risk about as well as the small group market, though nongroup insurance remains more expensive (by as much as 15 to 20 percent) because of unavoidably higher administrative loads.

A study of the enrollment experience of New Jersey's Individual Health Coverage Program (Swartz and Garnick 1999) concluded that adverse selection did not take place, even though medical underwriting was prohibited. It did note that premiums were relatively high and showed that good health status and income are highly correlated. The inference is that price acted, at least in this case, as an effective risk-screening device, since individuals at highest risk of health problems could generally not afford to pay high prices. Recent experience in this market, however, suggests that a more classic adverse selection death spiral[23] has occurred in the years since this study was written (Monheit et al. 2002).

There is no doubt that insurers in the nongroup market take greater pains to protect themselves from the risks of adverse selection than group insurers do: they exclude preexisting medical conditions from coverage, attach riders that exclude specific conditions or procedures from coverage for the life of the policy, engage in medical underwriting (the process whereby insurers assess an applicant's relative health risk and then charge higher premiums to those whose risk is deemed to be higher than normal [nonstandard]), refuse to cover specific conditions or body parts, or refuse to sell an applicant insurance altogether (Hall 2000; Pollitz et al. 2001; U.S. General Accounting Office 1996). The success of these techniques helps explain why nongroup purchasers are healthier than the uninsured, on average, even though fewer healthy people should have such strong demand for health insurance. These risk-avoidance techniques have prompted repeated calls for legislative reform—they are seen as unfair to the unfortunate sick and as violating some philosophical views of what insurance is supposed to be about (Stone 1993).

Many people with chronic conditions are able to find nongroup policies they are willing to buy, even though they probably face higher-than-average premiums and exclusion of their preexisting condition from coverage (Pauly and Nichols 2002). Persons in fair or poor health are less likely to buy nongroup insurance than those reporting good or better health, so judgments about the net effects of medical underwriting on the nongroup market depend in part upon what measure of health status one uses.

Some states and now the federal government have tried market reforms—that is, restrictions on the behaviors and techniques insurers would like to use to protect themselves against adverse selection and to segment risks into homogeneous pools (Blue Cross Blue Shield Association 1999; Marsteller et al. 1998; Nichols and Blumberg 1998; Swartz and Garnick 2000). Predictably, however, market reforms produce trade-offs rather than unambiguously increased access, and all empirical evidence to date suggests that nongroup market reforms have reduced, not increased, insurance coverage. Simply put, this is because the market reforms put forth—guaranteed issue (selling to all comers), guaranteed renewal, limits on exclusions of preexisting conditions, restrictions on variations in premium prices, and mandated benefits—all force a degree of risk pooling that would not obtain if the market were left alone.

Because of the highly skewed distribution of actual and expected health expenditures—10 percent of any insured population typically accounts for 70 percent of all spending by that group (Berk and Monheit 1992)—forced pooling raises premiums for more people than it lowers premiums for (Nichols 2000). Thus reform leads to a drop in coverage, despite the best of intentions, while undoubtedly improving access for the sickest individuals, who would often otherwise be underwritten out of the market altogether (Pollitz et al. 2001; U.S. General Accounting Office 1996). Partly because of this outcome, most states permit nongroup insurers to adjust premium rates or refuse to sell altogether based on an individual's or family member's health risk. This raises important measurement issues, which are discussed later. Only 13 states currently have guaranteed issue regulations in place in their nongroup insurance markets, and only 8 have guaranteed issue for all products (Laudicina, Yerby, and Pardo 1998). Nineteen states have some type of rating regulations in the nongroup market, but some of these states still allow rate adjustments for health status.

Candidates for Nongroup Purchase

Basically, candidates for insurance in today's nongroup market are individuals who have no less expensive alternative source of insurance, whether employer-sponsored or public. There are three classic types of potential candidates: the self-employed, workers whose employers do not offer health insurance or who are not eligible for what is offered, and nonworkers who are not eligible for Medicaid or similar public insurance. The demand for nongroup insurance in the first two groups is discussed below.

The self-employed. If a business is incorporated, 100 percent of an employer-paid premium is deductible as a business expense and excluded from income tax. Beginning in 1986, self-employed owner-operators of unincorporated businesses and partnerships were allowed to deduct 25 percent of the cost of their premium from their federally taxable income. This still left the unincorporated self-employed person at a disadvantage relative to the incorporated self-employed and to wage earners of incorporated employers that offer health insurance. Furthermore, the new deduction is allowed only if the self-employed owner-operator also provides coverage for any employees he or she may have; it is not allowed if the owner-operator has access to employer-sponsored insurance through a spouse or through another job.

In 1987, 25 percent of the self-employed were uninsured (compared with 15 percent of wage earners), 25 percent of the self-employed sponsored a small group plan for themselves and their employees, 28 percent had coverage through their spouse's employment, and 22 percent purchased nongroup coverage (compared with 4 percent of wage earners) (Monheit and Harvey 1993). This section focuses on the self-employed who are not eligible for coverage through a spouse's employer and who do not have employees, for they are the candidates for the nongroup market.

Monheit and Harvey show that the unincorporated self-employed are less likely to have group insurance than the incorporated self-employed, but they also report that 30 percent of the self-employed with incomes below 125 percent of the poverty level bought nongroup insurance in 1987, a much higher percentage than in any other group of low-income individuals (Chollet 2000; Pauly and Percy 2000). Thus, the 25 percent deduction is important in inducing even low-income self-employed persons to buy health insurance. Interestingly, poor health status had no effect on the probability of any self-employed person's obtaining employment-related health insurance, but the authors were not able to include a price variable, so this model should not be interpreted as definitive.

Gruber and Poterba (1994) used the introduction of the health insurance deduction in 1986 as a natural experiment in price reduction, from which they deduced an elasticity of demand for the self-employed of −1.8, which is 3 to 5 times larger than the elasticity of demand usually estimated for others in the nongroup market. They used data from the CPS to compare coverage of the self-employed and the employed (in order to control for changes in the economy that might have affected health insurance coverage) and to compare the self-employed before and after the tax reform. Their innovation was to identify the change in tax price as the relevant price change to model. The question that remains is, how applicable is this elasticity to non-tax-price changes for persons who are not self-employed? The findings may not be generalizable to other populations or policy interventions.

Workers who are not offered insurance by their employers. The most frequently cited estimates of demand for health insurance by this group were derived by Marquis and Long (1995). To complement the worker characteristics in both CPS and SIPP data, they used premiums taken from a price list provided by a prominent nongroup insurance company. The price list included the premiums charged for a standard product by zip code. The premiums also varied by age, sex, and type of coverage (self only, employee and spouse, employee and dependents, family). Marquis and Long aggregated the premiums at the metropolitan statistical area and combined metropolitan statistical area levels, using weighted averages of the county population. Thus, they used premium prices—reflecting opportunity cost, not administrative load—that were not actually observed by individuals but that were presumed to be representative of the prices faced by workers with different family structures and in different locales. Swartz (1988) used a similar approach for nongroup purchasers and the uninsured, with price data obtained from a nongroup insurer with a much larger market share (Blue Cross Blue Shield plans, nationwide).

This approach addresses two key problems often encountered in estimating health insurance demand. First, when worker characteristics that affect demand are used by the insurer to adjust premiums, the price variable in a nongroup demand equation may be jointly determined with the dependent variable. If the premium from the standard price list is correlated with, but not identical to, the premium offered to the individual, this premium proxy is more exogenous to the individual and better for statistical purposes than the premium actually faced. Second, the insurer's price list provides a relevant and presumably unbiased way to impute premiums to those who did not buy insurance.

In general, insurers offer applicants a contract with two dimensions, premium (or price) and benefits (which include covered services and providers as well as cost-sharing obligations). In the nongroup market, where adverse selection is more likely and feared, some insurers classify individuals according to risk class much more precisely than they do individuals in the group market; this leads them to both increase premiums and decrease benefits to individuals with certain health conditions. This insurer behavior makes it difficult to estimate price elasticities in this market because it is hard to know what prices individuals in any survey actually did or would face.

These considerations lead to the following general model of empirical choices in the study of demand in the nongroup market:

$$Y = a_0 + a_1 P + a_2 X + a_3 Z + a_4 B + e_y. \tag{1}$$

$$P = b_0 + b_1 B + b_2 C + b_3 X + e_p. \tag{2}$$

$$B = c_0 + c_1 P + c_2 X + e_B. \tag{3}$$

where Y is the probability of buying insurance, P is the premium, B is benefits, X is a set of personal or family characteristics that affect both demand and supply offers (e.g., age and health status), Z is a set of personal or family characteristics that affect demand but not supply offers (e.g., education and income), and C is the cost of delivering a set of benefits to a standard risk person in a particular location, which can vary by local practice patterns as well as by local medical prices. The e_i are error terms. The terms a_0, b_0, and c_0 are constants, and the remaining a, b, and c terms are vectors of regression coefficients for the applicable independent variables.

The empirical approaches of Marquis and Long and of Swartz estimated (1) directly, essentially using a standard price vector adjusted for geography (C in place of P). Dismissing benefit variance for the moment, this approach would yield unbiased estimates of a_1 (and price elasticities) as long as b_3 is actually zero. But b_3 is very likely to be positive for older and sicker individuals in the sample.

An advance might be to estimate (1) and (2) as a system. Hadley and Reschovsky (2002b) have taken the first step by estimating (2) directly. This equation can then be used to generate predicted prices for a second-stage structural estimation of (1).

But benefit package offers do vary with X. Because coverage exclusion riders are so common in this market, c_2 is unlikely to be zero. This fact will render a systems estimation of (1) and (2) alone unsatisfactory. Thus an empirical approach that minimized the risk of omitted variable bias would require knowledge of the exact benefit package offered to each person so that (1) and (2) could be specified completely or (3) could be estimated directly and then substituted into (1) and (2) as a predicted variable.

Since benefit packages vary relatively little in the group market, at least among covered services, these problems are much less severe for studies of group demand. In the nongroup case, however, one must conclude that fully satisfactory approaches to specifying the distribution of the benefit packages offered have not been found.

Marquis and Long and Swartz, whose elasticity estimates are similar, have probably devised the best price measures currently in use in demand equations. However, in any real policy analysis situation, fairly broad ranges of their elasticity estimates should probably be used, since there is still legitimate concern about the bias of even their price coefficients.

Concluding Remarks on a Research Agenda

This chapter has explained what analysts do and do not know about why some Americans are uninsured. The concluding section lays out a research agenda organized around two types of gaps in the knowledge needed to make intelligent policy choices regarding expansion of coverage: conceptual gaps and empirical complexities.

Conceptual Gaps

Is the absence of health insurance coverage a market failure or not? Answering this question is a prerequisite for policy analysis, so it is surprising that so few economists have addressed this issue directly. Clearly, the existence of small group and individual market reforms, as well as the Health Insurance Portability and Accountability Act, suggests that in at least some quarters, the absence of coverage is considered a market failure. Part of the difficulty in answering this question comes from an inability to measure the social value of coverage as an externality, but part also comes from the inability to determine when constraints—such as high nongroup loading factors—prevent purchases that would have occurred at lower, feasible prices because the lower prices could not be observed. Why are these prices not observed? Is there an informational intervention that could improve efficiency in this market? These are questions with which to begin this line of inquiry.

How do worker preferences affect firms' decisions? Perhaps the most basic problem is lack of information about how heterogeneous worker preferences are taken into account by different kinds of firms before their decisions about offer, eligibility, and employer share are made. This makes it difficult to assess the efficiency of, for example, current eligibility patterns and to predict how employers might respond to fundamental changes such as replacing the current tax preference for employer premium payments with individual tax credits. Apparently, little creative thinking has gone into testing hypotheses about worker-firm interactions that seem fairly basic to understanding the health insurance choices a majority of Americans face each year. These issues span pension and other benefit decisions as well, so perhaps a unified conceptual approach would be best.

What IS the appropriate wage incidence assumption? The extent of wage incidence by type of firm and worker is not well understood, nor is the mechanism by which wages are traded for employer premium payments. Even the most recent research in this area demonstrates the difficulty of producing robust estimates of how wages adjust to compensate for different levels of employer payments.[24] Some economists are comfortable asserting that in the long run, wages must adjust to compensate. Others worry that in the short term, incomplete wage adjustments could jeopardize the success of an individual tax credit proposal that subsidized purchases of coverage only in the nongroup market. If economists could assure policymakers that workers' wages would be raised, then employers discontinuing sponsorship of insurance for their workers would not be a major concern. Current evidence does not seem to warrant such assurances, however.

What are the major implications of imperfect sorting of workers into jobs with different compensation packages? If workers cannot find the jobs they really want—with health insurance and somewhat lower wages attached—then perhaps market failure in access to private health insurance is greater than previously thought and non-employment-based mechanisms for buying insurance should be investigated more thoroughly. Imperfect sorting also makes aggregating heterogeneous worker preferences more complicated. Assessing the links between job choice and health insurance options and choices is an important area for future empirical work.

What are the intangible elements of some potential enrollees' preferences for private versus public insurance? Why do some people turn down ostensibly free insurance, both public and private? Despite tenable hypotheses and some limited evidence, analysts really do not understand the extent to which low-income individuals weigh the pros and cons of public versus private coverage. Policymakers need to know which kinds of people prefer each, why, and how much are they willing to pay for their preference, given a choice.

Empirical Complexities

Prices are inherently endogenous. This is especially true in the nongroup market, but it is also true in the group market, particularly when job choice—with different health insurance packages attached—is considered part of the equation. Analysts must develop techniques for measuring the presence of specific health conditions that insurers consider if structural demand estimation is to proceed. Only structural estimation can adequately inform policymakers trying to gauge likely responses to new subsidies or other price changes.

Benefit packages are heterogeneous, and differences among them, especially in the nongroup market, are difficult, if not impossible, to measure. Such measures are extremely important if inferences about estimated demand relations are to be drawn. Given the preponderance of exclusions in the nongroup market, as well as network and coverage differences in the group market, structural equations that do not control for benefits are based on the heroic assumption that all benefit packages are identical. Variation in benefits is a potential source of omitted variable bias in demand analyses. The consequences of falsely assuming that all benefit packages are the same should be explored in all empirical work from now on.

To what extent do uninsured person-years comprise workers in transition or turnover? Researchers need to find out the extent to which being uninsured results from labor market transitions, which end and from which most workers settle into jobs with offers attached, and to what extent it stems from the presence of a permanent low-wage labor force. Until the relative importance of these two sources is determined, it is premature to recommend any specific type of subsidy as an effective remedy for uninsurance.

NOTES

1. See also Institute of Medicine (2002) and Hadley (2002).

2. Some portion of those who are covered under the current system, but who would lose coverage due to the elimination of the current tax subsidy, might not receive enough of the redirected subsidy to induce them to continue purchasing coverage. If this were indeed the case, a first best scenario still would not obtain, although the new state of affairs would probably be an improvement, in terms of social welfare, over the current system.

3. The assumption is that quality, q, works like an index, such that higher q is equivalent to higher C and can be priced per $C*q$ unit at PC.

4. Some might suggest that the size of the firm is a decision made prior to the decision regarding whether to offer health insurance, and that may be true. The precise order of these decisions is irrelevant to the discussion presented here, however.

5. Many states exempt this in-kind income from state taxes as well, since they use federal definitions of adjusted gross income as the starting point for state income tax liability calculations.

6. Employers may also set up an arrangement through which employees pay their out-of-pocket share with pretax dollars, but only about 25 percent of workers are in these plans, mostly because employers do not offer them.

7. It is useful to remember that low-income pregnant women are guaranteed eligibility only for pregnancy-related services, not the comprehensive health care typically associated with Medicaid. Their limited Medicaid eligibility expires one month after giving birth.

8. SCHIP has subsidized states that wish to equalize eligibility thresholds for children of all ages. Medicaid mandates alone made infants, toddlers, preadolescents, and adolescents eligible at different income levels across the states.

9. Institute of Medicine (1993).

10. See the Institute for Health Policy Solutions website www.ihps.org, and its directory of consumer choice health purchasing groups.

11. Twenty-one percent of nonoffering firms with 3 to 199 workers reported this as a very important reason, and 37 percent reported it as a somewhat important reason for not offering health insurance.

12. http://www.meps.ahrq.gov/MEPSDATA/ic/2001/Tables_I/TIA2.pdf.

13. http://www.meps.ahrq.gov/MEPSDATA/ic/2001/Tables_I/TIA1a.pdf.

14. Linda Blumberg, Urban Institute internal memorandum, July 1999.

15. Including the selection correction term in the imputation algorithm has been shown to bias the elasticity estimates upward (Marquis and Louis 2002).

16. Farber and Levy (2000) summarize recent changes in nondiscrimination law. Basically, firms may not use health status, but they may use class of employee (e.g., full-time) to determine eligibility for health insurance.

17. Royalty (2000) examines the extent to which the probability that a worker is offered *and* is eligible for health insurance is affected by his or her tax rate. She does not, however, distinguish between workers who are and are not eligible for offers made by their employers.

18. See also Cooper and Schone (1997).

19. Almost all persons age 65 and over are eligible for and enrolled in the Medicare program, which is financed federally. Certain disabled persons and persons with end-stage kidney disease are also eligible for Medicare. Consequently, this chapter focuses on programs applicable to the nonelderly population, among whom an uninsurance problem persists.

20. Medicaid also finances long-term care and assistance with out-of-pocket Medicare payments for the low-income elderly. Those aspects of Medicaid are not discussed here.

21. There is clearly error in Byck's measurement of children who would be eligible. She does not use state-by-state Medicaid rules to determine which children are actually eligible or which children who are eligible for Medicaid are not eligible for SCHIP. In addition, income is measured in categories in the National Health Interview Survey, which does not permit precise measurement of income or comparison with eligibility rules. In addition, SCHIP eligibility varies by state, and Byck assumes that all children between 133 percent and 200 percent of the poverty level who are uninsured are eligible for SCHIP. Not only does this exclude state variations, but it also excludes older lower-income children who are not eligible for Medicaid but are eligible for SCHIP. Nonetheless, her analysis provides a rough approximation that is useful.

22. See Pauly and Nichols (2002) for an overview of what is known, unknown, and still in dispute about the way this market works.

23. This is a dynamic in which low-risk individuals exit an insurance risk pool as more high-risk individuals enter. As premiums increase further, more and more of the healthier individuals exit, until premiums increase to such an extent that the risk pool is no longer sustainable.

24. See Levy and Feldman (2001) and Jensen and Morrisey (2001).

REFERENCES

Acs, Gregory P., and Linda J. Blumberg. 2001. "How a Changing Workforce Affects Employer-Sponsored Health Insurance." *Health Affairs* 20(1): 178–83.

Acs, Gregory P., Stephen H. Long, M. Susan Marquis, and Pamela F. Short. 1996. "Self-Insured Employer Health Plans: Prevalence, Profile, Provisions, and Premiums." *Health Affairs* 15(2): 266–78.

Anderson, Patricia M., and Bruce D. Meyer. 1994. "The Extent and Consequences of Job Turnover." *Brookings Papers on Economic Activity.* Washington, DC: Brookings Institution.

Berk, Marc L., and Alan C. Monheit. 1992. "The Concentration of Health Expenditures: An Update." *Health Affairs* 11(4): 145–49.

Blue Cross Blue Shield Association. 1999. *State Legislative Health Care and Insurance Issues.* Washington, DC: Blue Cross Blue Shield Association.

Blumberg, Linda J., and Len M. Nichols. 2000. "Decisions to Buy Private Health Insurance: Employers, Employees, the Self-Employed, and Non-working Adults in The Urban Institute's Health Insurance Reform Simulation Model (HIRSM)." Washington, DC: U.S. Department of Labor, Pension and Welfare Benefits Administration.

———. 2001a. "The Health Status of Workers Who Decline Employer-Sponsored Insurance." *Health Affairs* 20(6).

———. 2001b. "Price Versus Health Status: What Matters More in Workers' Decisions to Purchase Employer-Sponsored Health Insurance." Washington, DC: U.S. Department of Health and Human Services, Office of the Assistant Secretary for Planning and Evaluation.

Blumberg Linda J., Lisa C. Dubay, and Stephen A. Norton. 2000. "Did the Medicaid Expansions for Children Displace Private Insurance? An Analysis Using the SIPP." *Journal of Health Economics* 19(1): 33–60.

Blumberg, Linda J., Len M. Nichols, and Jessica Banthin. 2001. "Worker Decisions to Purchase Health Insurance." *International Journal of Health Care Finance and Economics* 1(3/4).

Bruen, Brian K., and Frank C. Ullman. 1998. "Children's Health Insurance Programs: Where States Are, Where They Are Headed." Washington, DC: The Urban Institute. *Assessing the New Federalism* Issue Brief No. A-20.

Buchmueller, Thomas C. 1995. "Health Risk and Access to Employer-Provided Health Insurance." *Inquiry* 32(1): 75–86.

Byck, Gayle R. 2000. "A Comparison of the Socioeconomic and Health Status Characteristics of Uninsured, State Children's Health Insurance Program-Eligible Children in the United States with Those of Other Groups of Insured Children: Implications for Policy." *Pediatrics* 106(1): 14–21.

Cantor, Joel C., Stephen H. Long, and M. Susan Marquis. 1995. "Private Employment-Based Health Insurance in 10 States." *Health Affairs* 14(2): 197–211.

Chernew, Michael E., Kevin Frick, and Catherine G. McLaughlin. 1997. "The Demand for Health Insurance Coverage by Low-Income Workers: Can Reduced Premiums Achieve Full Coverage?" *Health Services Research* 32(4).

Chollet, Deborah J. 2000. "Consumers, Insurers, and Market Behavior." *Journal of Health Politics, Policy and Law* 25(1): 27–44.

Chollet, Deborah J., and Adele M. Kirk. 1998. "Understanding Individual Health Insurance Markets." Menlo Park, CA: Henry J. Kaiser Foundation.

Coburn, Andrew, Elizabeth H. Kilbreth, Stephen H. Long, and M. Susan Marquis. 1998. "Urban-Rural Differences in Employer-Based Health Insurance Coverage of Workers." *Medical Care Research and Review* 55(4): 484–96.

Congressional Research Service. 1988. *Costs and Effects of Extending Health Insurance Coverage.* Washington, DC: U.S. Government Printing Office.

Cooper, Philip F., and Barbara S. Schone. 1997. "More Offers, Fewer Takers for Employment-Based Health Insurance: 1987 and 1996." *Health Affairs* 16(6): 142–49.

Cunningham, Peter J. and Peter Kemper. 1998. "Ability to Obtain Medical Care for the Uninsured." *Journal of the American Medical Association* 280(10): 921–27.

Cunningham, Peter J., Elizabeth Schaefer, and Christopher Hogan. 1999. "Who Declines Employer-Sponsored Health Insurance and Is Uninsured?" Issue Brief No. 22. Washington, DC: Center for Studying Health System Change.

Cutler, David M. 1994. "Market Failure in Small Group Health Insurance." Working Paper No. 4879. Cambridge, MA: National Bureau of Economic Research, Inc.

Cutler, David M., and Jonathan Gruber. 1996. "Does Public Insurance Crowd-Out Private Insurance?" *Quarterly Journal of Economics* 111(2): 391–430.

Davidoff, Amy J., and Bowen Garrett. 2001. "Determinants of Public and Private Insurance Enrollment among Medicaid-Eligible Children." *Medical Care* 39(6): 523–35.

Davidoff, Amy J., Bowen Garrett, Diane M. Makuc, and Matthew Schirmer. 2000. "Children Eligible for Medicaid but Not Enrolled: How Great a Policy Concern?" Washington, DC: The Urban Institute. *Assessing the New Federalism* Issue Brief A-41.

Dolinsky, Arthur L. and Richard K. Caputo. 1997. "Psychological and Demographic Characteristics as Determinants of Women's Health Insurance Coverage." *The Journal of Consumer Affairs* 31(2).

Dranove David, Kathryn E. Spier, and Laurence Baker. 2000. "'Competition' among Employers Offering Health Insurance." *Journal of Health Economics* 19(1): 121–40.

Dubay, Lisa C., and Genevieve M. Kenney. 1996. "Revisiting the Issues: The Effects of Medicaid Expansions on Insurance Coverage of Children." *The Future of Children* 6(1): 152–61.

———. 1997. "Did the Medicaid Expansions for Pregnant Women Crowd-Out Private Insurance?" *Health Affairs* 16(1).

Dubay, Lisa C., Genevieve M. Kenney, and Jennifer M. Haley. Forthcoming. "Medicaid and SCHIP Programs for Children: What Do We Know about Participation?" Washington, DC: The Urban Institute. *Assessing the New Federalism* Policy Brief.

Eberts, Randall W. and Joe A. Stone. 1985. "Wages, Fringe Benefits, and Working Conditions: An Analysis of Compensating Differentials." *Southern Economic Journal* 52(1): 274–80.

Farber, Henry, and Helen Levy. 2000. "Recent Trends in Employer-Sponsored Health Insurance Coverage: Are Bad Jobs Getting Worse?" *Journal of Health Economics* 19(1): 93–119.

Feldman, Roger, Bryan Dowd, Scott Leitz, and Lynne A. Blewett. 1997. "The Effect of Premiums on the Small Firm's Decision to Offer Health Insurance." *Journal of Human Resources* 32(4).

Garrett, Bowen, and John Holahan. 2000. "Health Insurance Coverage after Welfare." *Health Affairs* 19(1): 175–84.

Garrett, Bowen, and Len M. Nichols. 1999. "Do Workers in Small Firms Pay for Health Insurance with Reduced Wages?" Paper presented to American Economic Association Meetings, Atlanta, Georgia.

Garret, Bowen, Len M. Nichols, and Emily K. Greenman. 2001. "Workers without Health Insurance: Who Are They and How Can Policy Reach Them?" Report to the Kellogg Foundation. Washington, DC: The Urban Institute.

Gentry, William M. and Eric Peress. 1994. "Taxes and Fringe Benefits Offered by Employers." NBER Working Paper No. 4764. Cambridge, MA: National Bureau of Economic Research.

Goldstein, Gerald S., and Mark V. Pauly. 1967. "Group Health Insurance as a Local Public Good." In *The Role of Health Insurance in the Health Services Sector*, edited by Richard N. Rossett. New York: National Bureau of Economic Research.

Groothuis, Peter A. 1994. "Turnover: The Implication of Establishment Size and Unionization." *Quarterly Journal of Business and Economics* 55(Spring): 433–64.

Gruber, Jonathan. 1994. "The Incidence of Mandated Maternity Benefits." *The American Economic Review* 84(3): 622–41.

Gruber, Jonathan, and Alan B. Krueger. 1991. "The Incidence of Mandated Employer-Provided Insurance: Lessons from Workers' Compensation Insurance." In *Tax Policy and the Economy*, vol. 5, edited by David Bradford. Cambridge, MA: MIT Press.

Gruber, Jonathan, and Michael Lettau. 2000. "How Elastic Is the Firm's Demand for Health Insurance?" NBER Working Paper No. 8021. Cambridge MA: National Bureau of Economic Research.

Gruber, Jonathan, and James Poterba. 1994. "Tax Incentives and the Decision to Purchase Health Insurance: Evidence from the Self-Employed." *Quarterly Journal of Economics* 109(3): 701–33.

Haber, Sheldon E. 1993. "Aspects of Labor Market Turnover and the Impact of Fringe Benefits in Small and Large Firms." Small Business Administration Report, SBA-3052-OA-88. Washington, DC: U.S. Small Business Administration.

Hadley, Jack. 2002. "Sicker and Poorer: The Consequences of Being Uninsured." Menlo Park, CA: Henry J. Kaiser Family Foundation.

Hadley, Jack and James D. Reschovsky. 2002a. "Small Firms' Demand for Health Insurance: The Decision to Offer." *Inquiry* 39(2): 118–37.

———. 2002b. "Tax Credits and the Affordability of Individual Health Insurance." *Issue Brief #53*. Washington, DC: Center for Studying Health System Change.

Hall, Mark A. 2000. "An Evaluation of New York's Reform Law." *Journal of Health Politics, Policy and Law* 25(1): 71–99.

Health Insurance Association of America. 1994. *Group Life and Health Insurance, Part A*, 5th ed. Washington, DC: Health Insurance Association of America.

Hill, Ian, and Amy W. Lutzky. 2003. *Is There a Hole in the Bucket? Understanding SCHIP Retention*. Washington, DC: The Urban Institute. *Assessing the New Federalism* Occasional Paper No. 67.

Institute of Medicine. 1993. *Employment and Health Benefits*. Washington, DC: National Academy Press.

———. 2002. *Care Without Coverage: Too Little, Too Late*. Washington, DC: National Academy Press.

Jensen, Gail A., and Michael A. Morrisey. 2001. "Endogenous Fringe Benefits, Compensating Wage Differentials and Old Workers." *International Journal of Health Care Finance and Economics* 1(3/4): 203–26.

Kaiser Family Foundation, Health Research and Educational Trust. 2002. *Employer Health Benefits: 2002 Annual Survey.* Menlo Park, CA: Henry J. Kaiser Family Foundation.

Kenny, Genevieve M., Jennifer M. Haley, and Stephen Blumberg. 2002. *Awareness and Perceptions of Medicaid and SCHIP among Low-Income Families with Uninsured Children: Findings from Early 2001.* Washington, DC: U.S. Department of Health and Human Services.

Kronebusch, Karl. 2001. "Medicaid for Children: Federal Mandates, Welfare Reform, and Policy Backsliding." *Health Affairs* 20(1): 97–111.

Laudicina, Susan S., Jaqueline Y. Yerby, and Kathy Pardo. 1998. *State Legislative Health Care and Insurance Issues: 1998 Survey of Plans.* Washington, DC: Blue Cross Blue Shield Association.

Leibowitz, Arleen A., and Michael E. Chernew. 1992. "The Firm's Demand for Health Insurance." In *Health Benefits and the Workforce.* Washington DC: U.S. Department of Labor, Pension and Benefits Administration.

Levy, Helen, and Roger Feldman. 2001. "Does the Incidence of Group Health Insurance Fall on Individual Workers?" Paper presented at *Why Do Employers Do What They Do?* conference sponsored by the U.S. Department of Labor.

Liska, David, Brian K. Bruen, Alina Salganicoff, Peter Long, and Bethany Kessler. 1997. "Medicaid Expenditures and Beneficiaries: National and State Profiles and Trends, 1990–1995." Menlo Park, CA: Henry J. Kaiser Family Foundation.

Long, Stephen H., and M. Susan Marquis. 1993. "Gaps in Employer Coverage: Lack of Supply or Lack of Demand?" *Health Affairs* 12(Supplement): 282–93.

———. 1999. "Pooled Purchasing: Who Are the Players?" *Health Affairs* 18(4): 105–11.

Madden, Carolyn W., Allen Cheadle, Paul Diehr, Diane P. Martin, Donald L. Patrick, and Susan M. Skillman. 1995. "Voluntary Public Health Insurance for Low-Income Families: The Decision to Enroll." *Journal of Health Politics, Policy and Law* 20(4).

Marquis, M. Susan and Stephen H. Long. 1995. "Worker Demand for Health Insurance in the Non-Group Market." *Journal of Health Economics* 14(1): 47–63.

———. 1999. "Recent Trends in Self-Insured Employer Health Plans." *Health Affairs* 18(3): 161–66.

———. 2001. "To Offer or Not to Offer: The Role of Price in Employers' Health Insurance Decisions." *Health Services Research* 36(5): 935–58.

Marquis, M. Susan and Thomas A. Louis. 2002. "On Using Sample Selection Methods in Estimating the Price Elasticity of Firms' Demand for Insurance." *Journal of Health Economics* 21(1):137–45.

Marsteller, Jill A., Len M. Nichols, Adam Badawi, Bethany Kessler, Shruti Rajan, and Stephen Zuckerman. 1998. "Variations in the Uninsured: State and County Analyses." Washington, DC: The Urban Institute. http://www.urban.org/health/variatfr.html.

McLaughlin, Catherine G. 1999. "Health Care Consumers: Choices and Constraints." *Medical Care Research and Review* 56(Supplement 1): 24–59.

McLaughlin, Catherine G., and Wendy K. Zellers. 1992. "The Shortcomings of Voluntarism in the Small-Group Insurance Market." *Health Affairs* 11(2): 28–40.

Monheit, Alan C., and P. Holly Harvey. 1993. "Sources of Health Insurance for the Self-Employed: Does Differential Taxation Make a Difference?" *Inquiry* 30(3): 293–305.

Monheit, Alan C., and Jessica Primoff Vistnes. 2000. "Health Insurance Availability at the Workplace: How Important are Worker Preferences?" *Journal of Human Resources* 34(4): 771–85.

Monheit, Alan C., Len M. Nichols, and Thomas M. Selden. 1996. "Winners and Losers in the Employment-Related Health Insurance Market: How Are Net Health Benefits Distributed?" *Inquiry* 32(4).

Monheit, Alan C. et al., 2002. "Regulating the Individual Market in New Jersey: Evidence of a Classic Death Spiral?" University of Medicine and Dentistry of New Jersey Working Paper.

Morrisey, Michael A., Gail A. Jensen, and Robert J. Morlock. 1994. "Small Employers and the Health Insurance Market." *Health Affairs* 13(5): 149–61.

Newhouse, Joseph P. 1996. "Reimbursing Health Plans and Health Providers: Efficiency in Production versus Selection." *Journal of Economic Literature* 34(3): 1236–63.

Nichols, Len M. 2000. "State Regulation: What Have We Learned So Far?" *Journal of Health Politics, Policy and Law* 25(1): 175–96.

Nichols, Len M., and Linda J. Blumberg. 1998. "A Different Kind of 'New Federalism'? The Health Insurance Portability and Accountability Act of 1996." *Health Affairs* 17(3): 25–42.

Nichols, Len M., Linda J. Blumberg, Gregory P. Acs, Cori E. Uccello, and Jill A. Marsteller. 1997. *Small Employers: Their Diversity and Health Insurance.* Washington, DC: The Urban Institute.

Nichols, Len M., Linda J. Blumberg, Phillip Cooper, and Jessica Primoff Vistnes. 2001. "Employer Demand for Health Insurance: Evidence from the Medical Expenditure Panel Survey." Paper presented at the 2001 American Economic Association Meetings.

Nyman, John A. 1999. "The Value of Health Insurance: The Access Motive." *Journal of Health Economics* 18(2): 141–52.

Pauly, Mark V. 1997. *Health Benefits at Work: An Economic and Political Analysis of Employment-Based Health Insurance.* Ann Arbor: University of Michigan Press.

Pauly, Mark V., and Bradley Herring. 1999. *Pooling Health Insurance Risks.* Washington, DC: American Enterprise Institute Press.

———. 2002. *Cutting Taxes for Insuring: Options and Effects of Tax Credits for Health Insurance.* Washington, DC: American Enterprise Institute Press.

Pauly Mark V., and Len M. Nichols. 2002. "The Non-Group Insurance Market: Short on Facts, Long on Opinion and Policy Disputes." *Health Affairs Web Exclusive, October 23, 2002.* Arlington, VA: National Association of Health Underwriters.

Pauly, Mark V., and Allison M. Percy. 2000. "Cost and Performance: A Comparison of the Individual and Group Health Insurance Markets." *Journal of Health Politics, Policy and Law* 25(1): 9–26

Pollitz, Karen, Richard Sorian, and Kathy Thomas. 2001. "How Accessible Is Individual Health Insurance for Consumers in Less-Than-Perfect Health?" Menlo Park, CA: Henry J. Kaiser Family Foundation.

Rask, Kevin N., and Kimberly J. Rask. 2000. "Public Insurance Substituting for Private Insurance: New Evidence Regarding Public Hospitals, Uncompensated Care Funds, and Medicaid." *Journal of Health Economics* 19: 1–31.

Rothschild, Michael, and Joseph E. Stiglitz. 1976. "Equilibrium in Competitive Insurance Markets: An Essay on the Economics of Imperfect Information." *Quarterly Journal of Economics* 90(4): 629–50.

Royalty, Anne B. 2000. "Tax Preferences for Fringe Benefits and Workers' Eligibility for Employer Health Insurance." *Journal of Public Economics* 75(2): 209–27.

Selden, Thomas M., Jessica S. Banthin, and Joel W. Cohen. 1998. "Medicaid's Problem Children: Eligible but Not Enrolled." *Health Affairs* 17(3): 192–200.

Sheiner, Louise. 1999. "Health Care Costs, Wages, and Aging." Finance and Economics Discussion Series No. 1999-19. Washington, DC: Board of Governors of the Federal Reserve System.

Shore-Sheppard L., Thomas C. Buchmueller, and Gail A. Jensen. 2000. "Medicaid and Crowding Out of Private Insurance: A Re-Examination Using Firm Level Data." *Journal of Health Economics* 19(1): 61–91.

Stone, Deborah. 1993. "The Struggle for the Soul of Health Insurance." *Journal of Health Politics, Policy and Law* 18(2): 287–318.

Swartz, Katherine. 1988. "The Demand for 'Self-Pay' Health Insurance: An Empirical Investigation." Urban Institute Working Paper 3308-04. Washington, DC: The Urban Institute.

Swartz, Katherine, and Deborah W. Garnick. 1999. "Can Adverse Selection Be Avoided in a Market for Individual Health Insurance." *Medical Care Research and Review* 56(3): 373–88.

———. 2000. "Lessons From New Jersey." *Journal of Health Politics, Policy and Law* 25(1): 45–70.

Thorpe, Kenneth E., and Curtis S. Florence. 1999. "Why Are Workers Uninsured? Employer-Sponsored Health Insurance in 1997." *Health Affairs* 18(2): 213–18.

Thurston, Norman K. 1999. "On the Decline of Employment-Based Health Insurance in the U.S." *Applied Economics Letters* 6(10): 683–86.

Ullman, Frank C., Ian Hill and Ruth A. Almeida, 1999. "CHIP: A Look at Emerging State Programs." Washington, DC: The Urban Institute. *Assessing the New Federalism* Issue Brief No. A-35.

U.S. Census Bureau. 2000a. "Health Insurance Coverage, 1999." Current Population Reports, P60-211. Washington, DC: U.S. Department of Commerce.

———. 2000b. Current Population Survey, table HI01. Washington, DC: U.S. Department of Commerce. http://ferret.bls.census.gov/macro/032000/hlthins/01_001.htm (accessed June 6, 2001; site now discontinued).

U.S. General Accounting Office (GAO). 1996. *Private Health Insurance: Millions Relying on Individual Market Face Cost and Coverage Trade-Offs.* HEHS-97-8. Washington, DC: U.S. General Accounting Office.

Washington State Health Care Authority. 1994. *BHP Highlights* vol. 1. Olympia: Washington State Health Care Authority.

Woodbury, Stephen A. 1983. "Substitution between Wage and Nonwage Benefits." *American Economic Review* 73(1): 166–82.

Yazici, Esel Y., and Robert J. Kaestner. 2000. "Medicaid Expansions and the Crowding Out of Private Health Insurance among Children." *Inquiry* 37(1): 23–32.

3

Health Insurance, Labor Supply, and Job Mobility

A Critical Review of the Literature

Jonathan Gruber and Brigitte C. Madrian

A distinctive feature of the health insurance market in the United States is that group insurance is available almost exclusively through the workplace: over 90 percent of privately insured persons obtain their coverage through their own employment or the employment of a family member (Employee Benefit Research Institute 2000). This distinction can affect the functioning of the U.S. labor market along many dimensions. For example, the high cost of health insurance, currently almost 7 percent of compensation (McDonnell and Fronstin 1999), has been shown to affect the determination of wages, employment, and hours.[1] It can also affect the labor supply and job mobility. Given the high and variable costs of health care for many workers, health insurance can be a key factor in the decision to work, retire, leave welfare, or switch jobs.

The potential impacts of health insurance on workers' decisions have prompted many researchers to study this topic over the past decade. While there was virtually no research in this area before 1990, over 50 scholarly articles have been written in the 10 years since. These studies are wide-ranging in both substance and empirical approach, yet they have enough important features in common that a thorough review of their findings reveals fairly clearly what the past decade of work has taught us about health insurance, labor supply, and job mobility. This chapter presents such a review.

Two primary conclusions emerge. First, these studies have gone far toward quantifying the importance of health insurance for labor supply and job choice decisions. There is some disagreement among studies, but the evidence shows fairly consistently that health insurance matters quite a bit for decisions such as whether to retire or to change jobs.

Second, the studies have essentially failed to advance our knowledge about the implications of their results. For example, we know that people with health insurance who particularly value that insurance are less likely to leave their jobs than people who value it less, but we do not know whether this finding substantially reduces either economic growth or personal welfare. Given the importance of labor mobility in the U.S. economy, it seems likely that the welfare costs of such labor market distortions may be large, yet essentially no attempts have been made to quantify them. Similar limitations exist in the literature on health insurance and labor supply.

This chapter provides a framework for thinking about recent research. It begins with a general model of health insurance and mobility that documents why job lock, or reluctance to change jobs for fear of losing health insurance, may arise. The model can be applied easily to health insurance and labor supply decisions as well. The chapter then provides a critical review of the exciting, large, and almost exclusively empirical literature that has arisen on these topics over the past decade. Finally, it presents a heuristic discussion of how one might think about the implications of these findings for welfare. The chapter does not provide direct evidence of implications for welfare or even a rigorous framework for computing welfare costs. Instead, it lays out the issues that must be tackled by those who will take on this important task.

A Model of Employer-Provided Health Insurance and Labor Mobility

A simple model of employer-provided health insurance and labor mobility shows that job lock may be an important concern. While the model focuses on mobility, it is easily extended to consider labor supply effects as well, as discussed below.[2] The very notion that health insurance is responsible for imperfections in the functioning of the U.S. labor market is somewhat curious. After all, health insurance is a voluntarily provided form of employee compensation. There is little discussion of the distortions to the labor market from cash wages, so why is health insurance different?

To see the difficulties introduced by health insurance, it is useful to begin with a very stylized "pure compensating differentials" model (Rosen 1986). In this model, health insurance exerts no distorting effect on the labor market. By then relaxing the very rigid assumptions required by such a model, one can illustrate the source of distortions to mobility.

Thus, health insurance coverage in this model consists of a binary, homogeneous good; individuals are either covered or not, and those who are covered have the exact same insurance plan. Insurance is perfectly experience-rated at the worker level. That is, firms essentially purchase insurance on a worker-by-worker basis and are charged a separate premium for each worker. Jobs that offer health insurance feature a negative compensating wage differential—that is, they pay workers less to compensate for the price of insurance to the employer. Moreover, each individual job (worker-job match) can have its own compensation structure; firms can offer insurance to some workers and not others and can pay lower wages to workers whose insurance costs more.

Assume that individuals have preferences about wages and health insurance:

$$U_{ij} = U(W_{ij}, H_{ij}), \tag{1}$$

where U represents the utility, or preferences, W_{ij} is the wage of worker i at firm j, and H_{ij} is a binary indicator of insurance coverage of worker i at firm j ($H_{ij} = 1$ or 0). The wage for each worker-job match (before the compensating wage differential) is equal to the worker's marginal productivity at that job.

Given these preferences, individuals will desire health insurance coverage if there is a compensating wage differential ΔW_{ij} such that:

$$U(W_{ij} - \Delta W_{ij}, 1) - U(W_{ij}, 0) = V_{ij} \geq 0, \tag{2}$$

where V_{ij} is the worker's valuation of insurance.

Suppose there is a continuum of jobs in the economy and that the labor market is perfectly competitive. Firms face identical worker-specific insurance price schedules; a given worker i incurs a cost of insurance $C_{ij} = C_i$

wherever he or she works. In this world, firms will provide insurance to their workers if:

$$\Delta W_{ij} \geq C_i. \tag{3}$$

As a result of perfect competition, firms will bid the compensating differential down to C_i. Thus, all workers covered by insurance will earn exactly:

$$W_{ij} - \Delta W_{ij} = W_{ij} - C_i, \tag{4}$$

regardless of what job they hold.

In this simplified model, the introduction of health insurance leads to lower wages for workers who value that insurance at its cost or more. If individuals wish to change jobs, they can ask their new employer to provide them with insurance and lower their wage by C_i. Workers for whom $V_{ij} > 0$ will benefit, or earn economic rents, from the fact that the value they place on insurance is greater than its cost. Firms cannot extract those rents from the workers—if they tried, the workers would be hired away by other employers who charged them the appropriate compensating differential. Most important, there is no inefficiency from health insurance: since workers will pay the same compensating differential wherever they work, they will choose the job with the highest wages. Thus workers will find the best job match, regardless of how much they value insurance.

This highly stylized model is useful for illustrating the conditions necessary to generate no effects of insurance on mobility, but reality departs from it in at least two important ways. First, employers are constrained in their ability to offer insurance to some workers and not others. The Internal Revenue Code gives favorable tax treatment to employer expenditures on health insurance only if most workers are offered an equivalent benefits package. Moreover, the costs of administering such a complicated benefits system would absorb much of the economic rent that workers would earn from its existence. The problem of worker preferences in this context is daunting. It is difficult to see how firms could set appropriate worker-specific compensating differentials; the implication is that there would be specific economic rents for workers attached to particular jobs.

Second, the underlying costs of providing health insurance differ dramatically among employers. The cost of insurance is much higher for small firms, for example, because they do not benefit from economies of scale—that is, they must pay the same fixed administrative costs when purchasing insurance as larger firms. Larger workplaces have larger risk pools, allowing insurers to spread the risk of claims across a larger number of people and thereby allowing individual employees to purchase insurance without the adverse selection premium that insurers demand in the individual health insurance marketplace. Smaller groups face the risk that insurance purchase is driven by the needs of one or two (unobservably) very ill employees, whose costs cannot possibly be covered by the premium payments of healthier workers. As the Congressional Research Service (1988) reported, the load, or markup insurers charge to cover their administrative and other expected costs on insurance purchases by the very smallest firms (with fewer than 5 employees) is more than 40 percent higher than that on very large groups (more than 10,000 employees); the load on individual insurance is even higher. Moreover, Cutler (1994) finds more dispersion of per-worker health insurance premiums among small firms than among larger ones, which is consistent with greater adverse selection problems in the small group market.

Even after accounting for observable factors such as firm size and benefits package, huge variations in insurance premiums exist across otherwise identical firms (Cutler 1994). This variation arises both from unobserved differences in the relationship between firm characteristics and insurance supply prices and from heterogeneity in the workforce health status, indicating that workers may be unable to obtain health insurance on comparable terms across jobs.

As a result of these two features, workers and firms will be matched in labor market equilibrium: workers who most desire health insurance coverage will work at firms offering insurance, and firms that can provide insurance most cheaply will offer it. In the case of a perfectly competitive labor market, there would be a marketwide compensating differential ΔW. Workers would only work at firms offering insurance if their valuation of insurance were at least as great as this compensating differential, or $V_{ij} > \Delta W$. Firms would only offer insurance if the per worker cost of insurance to the firm, C_j, were less than the compensating differential, $C_j < \Delta W$. This is the compensating differentials equilibrium described by Rosen (1986). As highlighted in his discussion, all of the workers whose valuation of insurance V_{ij} is greater than ΔW will be earning economic rents from working at a job with health insurance; similarly, all firms whose costs of insurance C_j are below ΔW will earn economic rents.

Adding these complications introduces the possibility of job lock. Suppose that an individual now holds job 0 but would be more productive on job 1 ($W_{i1} > W_{i0}$). The cost of insurance to firm 1 is much higher, however ($C_1 > C_0$). The high cost might arise from a high load or from the fact that the firm has a relatively unhealthy workforce and must therefore pay higher, experience-rated insurance premiums. As a result, firm 1 does not offer health insurance. Even though insurance would attract worker i, the cost is too great to provide for the rest of the workforce. And most important, the insurance cannot be provided just for worker i. As a result, if:

$$U(W_{i0} - \Delta W, 1) - U(W_{i1}, 0) > 0, \tag{5}$$

then the worker will not switch jobs, even though he would be more productive on the new job. This is the welfare loss from job lock: switches that would improve productivity are not made.

In theory, firm 0 could extract the surplus from this worker, knowing that he will not move to firm 1, but full extraction of these rents would mean that the employee was not ultimately locked into his job at firm 0. The key question is the extent to which firms can discriminate in wages on the basis of the value of insurance.

A great deal of research has been done on this question. It finds clear evidence that the costs of insurance are shifted to workers' wages, at least in the medium to long run. Gruber (1994) and Sheiner (1999) find cost shifting to broad demographic groups within the workplace, with relatively high-cost groups (such as older workers or women of child-bearing age) receiving lower wages as a result. To date, however, no evidence of worker-specific shifting has been found. In practice, full capture of economic rent on a worker-by-worker basis seems unlikely, because of preference revelation and administrative difficulties. As long as pay discrimination by valuation of insurance does not take place on a person-by-person basis, there will be job lock.

Job lock can arise from any employee benefit for which there is differential valuation across workers, differential costs of provision across employers, and an inability to set worker-specific compensation packages (examples include workplace safety or the location of the firm). In practice, however, job lock is likely to be stronger for health insurance relative to other benefits, since both the variation in valuation across workers and the variation in costs of provision across firms are much higher than for other workplace amenities.

In theory, the problem arises only for workers considering switches from firms offering insurance to those not offering insurance. But job lock may arise even among firms offering insurance, because health insurance coverage is not a homogenous good. For example, a new policy that excludes preexisting medical conditions may expose the worker to large medical costs if he or she switches plans. Other plans include probationary periods for new enrollees and, in extreme cases, medical underwriting and the exclusion of costly new employees from insurance coverage. Workers who change plans may lose credit toward deductibles and out-of-pocket payment limits under their old plans. In addition, health insurance is a continuum of policy features. The worker's current job may offer a wider range of insurance options than other jobs that offer insurance, making job switching unattractive, particularly if the worker is constrained through a managed care plan from using preferred medical providers. Finally, insurance purchased in the individual market is very expensive, less comprehensive, and potentially not even available to very unhealthy applicants, raising the costs of an off-the-job search. All of these factors mitigate against leaving a job that currently has insurance, even if the next job offers insurance as well.

Employer-Provided Health Insurance and Labor Supply

The discussion thus far has centered on job mobility, but the same model can be applied to labor supply decisions. In that case, the choice for the worker is not between one job and another, but between employment and nonemployment. Consider an older worker thinking about whether to retire. Even if the value of leisure is greater than the marginal product of labor, a less healthy older worker may be unwilling to retire from a job that offers health insurance if health insurance is not available or is prohibitively expensive outside of employment. This is a form of lock.

Retirement is not the only labor supply decision that might be affected by health insurance. The decision to leave public assistance programs that have health insurance benefits attached to them and enter the labor market is another. Most people who leave welfare programs move to jobs where health insurance is not available. As a result, the decision to move from welfare to work is akin to the decision to move from a job with insurance to one without. Therefore, welfare lock may be an important consequence of the desire to maintain health insurance coverage.

The decision of secondary workers to be employed is another important labor supply decision that can be affected by health insurance. In many cases, secondary earners in a family may be the source of health insurance coverage for the family, particularly if the primary earner is self-employed or in a very small firm. As these secondary earners think about leaving a job, perhaps to attend to family matters, they face the same decision as someone switching from a job with health insurance to one without it—once again a form of lock.

The next three sections review what empirical studies have discovered about the impact of health insurance on labor supply in the three types of situations described above. The chapter then addresses the question of whether health insurance affects job mobility and concludes with a discussion of how these findings might affect welfare considerations.

Health Insurance and Retirement

Anecdotal evidence indicates that health insurance is an important determinant of retirement. In a Gallup poll, 63 percent of working Americans reported that they "would delay retirement until becoming eligible for Medicare [age 65] if their employers were not going to provide health coverage," despite the fact that 50 percent said "they would prefer to retire early—by age 62" (Employee Benefit Research Institute 1990). Despite these persuasive arguments, and despite the existence of an enormous body of research on the effects of health status on retirement decisions,[3] it is only in the past decade that researchers have focused on the effect of the availability of health insurance on the retirement decision.

As highlighted above, the existence of economic rents attached to jobs with health insurance implies that workers will be reluctant to move from such jobs to nonemployment. One might expect this effect to be strongest for older workers, who are likely to benefit most from within-workplace pooling of insurance purchase[4] because their exposure to medical costs is generally greater and more variable.

A variety of indicators of health status, by age, are shown in table 3.1.[5] It is clear from the table that health deteriorates and that utilization of and spending on medical care increase after age 55. Compared with persons age 35 to 44, for example, those age 55 to 64 are twice as likely to report being in fair health and four times as likely to report themselves as being in poor health; four times as likely to have had a stroke or have cancer, seven times as likely to have had a heart attack, and five times as

Table 3.1. *Health Risks by Age*

Measure of risk	Age				
	25–34	*35–44*	*45–54*	*55–64*	*65+*
Self-reported health					
Fair	9.5%	11.9%	15.6%	24.9%	36.1%
Poor	1.1%	1.5%	4.1%	6.4%	11.4%
Incidence of specific diseases					
Stroke	0.4%	0.8%	1.6%	3.6%	7.4%
Cancer	1.6%	2.4%	4.7%	9.7%	13.3%
Heart attack	0.3%	1.1%	3.8%	7.7%	13.3%
High blood pressure	10.1%	18.2%	29.1%	41.9%	49.8%
Emphysema	0.4%	1.0%	2.6%	5.2%	8.0%
Diabetes	1.7%	3.0%	5.7%	9.8%	14.7%
Heart disease	0.8%	2.2%	6.1%	11.9%	22.2%
Health care utilization					
Admitted to hospital?	9.2%	6.8%	8.7%	11.0%	20.1%
Nights in hospital	5.5	6.8	9.3	11.8	13.8
Prescribed medicines?	52.9%	55.6%	61.1%	71.1%	81.9%
Number of medicines	5.2	6.6	11.5	14.7	18.5
Visit to doctor?	64.1%	67.1%	71.1%	77.9%	85.8%
Number of visits	4.6	4.6	5.5	6.0	7.4
Medical expenditures					
Mean	$1176	$1135	$1395	$2144	$2877
Standard deviation	$4025	$3537	$4001	$6532	$7070

Source: Gruber and Madrian (1996), tables 1–4.

likely to have heart disease; twice as likely to be admitted to a hospital (with twice as many nights in the hospital, if admitted); and 40 percent more likely to be taking a prescribed medicine (with twice as many medicines, if receiving a prescription). As a result, the medical spending of 55- to 64-year-olds is almost twice as great, and twice as variable, as that of 35- to 44-year-olds.

Older workers with declining health face an interesting dilemma. On the one hand, their health status makes retirement more attractive. On the other hand, being in poor health raises the value of employer-provided health insurance and increases the cost of leaving the labor force. As noted earlier, if the loss of health insurance is costly, the desire to maintain coverage will favor continued employment over retirement.

Not all individuals lose their health insurance upon retirement. Some employers continue to provide early retirees with equivalent or nearly equivalent coverage to that offered active workers at a similar cost.[6] In such situations, health insurance will not be a factor in determining when to retire. Rather, the decision will rest solely upon individual preferences and the financial incentives associated with pensions, Social Security, and other personal assets.

At age 65, everyone becomes eligible for Medicare. For persons whose employer-provided health insurance does not extend into retirement, Medicare replaces their coverage, thereby lowering the cost of retirement.[7] Such individuals have an incentive to postpone retirement until age 65. Medicare should have little impact on the retirement decisions of persons who will continue to have employer-provided health insurance in retirement.

What empirical evidence is there that health insurance affects retirement decisions? Table 3.A1 (at the end of this chapter) surveys the 16 studies on this topic. Despite their varied estimation techniques and data sets, almost every one has found an economically and statistically significant impact of health insurance on retirement decisions (see table 3.2). The few notable exceptions are discussed in more detail below.

Research on how health insurance affects retirement has proceeded along parallel lines, with one taking a structural approach to modeling retirement behavior (i.e., a utility-based model) and the other looking at reduced-form relationships (i.e., direct relationships between health insurance and retirement). In both cases, the earliest studies focused on estimating the effect of health insurance coverage for retirees, while subsequent studies considered other types of health insurance as well.

Several studies have estimated reduced-form models. They suggest that the availability of health insurance increases the likelihood of retirement in a given year by 30 to 80 percent (Blau and Gilleskie 2001b; Gruber and Madrian 1995; Karoly and Rogowski 1994) and reduces the age at retirement by 6 to 24 months (Blau and Gilleskie 2001b; Madrian 1994a).[8] In a similar vein, Johnson, Davidoff, and Perese (1999) calculated the net present value of the health insurance costs an individual would have to bear if he or she retired at a given age and found that the higher the costs are, the less likely the individual is to retire.

Table 3.2. *Summary Statistics of Studies on Health Insurance and Labor Market Outcomes*

| | Employment decisions | | | | | | Job choice (table 3.A4) | |
| | Older adults (table 3.A1) | | Single mothers (table 3.A2) | | Men/married women (table 3.A3) | | | |
	Number	Percent	Number	Percent	Number	Percent	Number	Percent
Number of studies	16	100	16	100	7	100	18	100
Published in refereed journal	7	44	9	56	4	57	9	50
Published elsewhere	3	19	1	6	1	14	1	6
Working paper/dissertation	6	38	6	38	2	29	8	44
Data sets used[a]								
CPS	3	19	9	56	3	43	1	6
SIPP	3	19	3	19	1	14	7	39
PSID	0	0	0	0	0	0	3	17
U.S. Census	1	6	0	0	0	0	0	0
RHS	2	13	0	0	0	0	0	0
HRS	7	44	0	0	0	0	0	0
NMCUES or NMES	1	6	2	13	1	14	3	17
NLSY	0	0	1	6	0	0	3	17
Other	1	6	3	19	2	29	4	22

Sample								
Men only	11	69	0	0	1	14	6	33
Women only	0	0	16	100	5	71	0	0
Men and women	5	31	0	0	1	14	12	66
Estimation technique								
Reduced form	10	63	15	94	7	100	17	94
Structural	6	38	1	6	0	0	3	17
Characterization of results[b]								
Positive and significant	12	75	8	50	7	100	6	33
Insignificant	1	6	3	19	0	0	6	33
Negative and significant	0	0	0	0	0	0	0	0
Mixed	2	13	5	31	0	0	5	28
Unable to evaluate	1	6	0	0	0	0	1	6

Note: Please see appendix tables 3.A1–3.A4 for individual study results.

a. Use of multiple data sets in a study results in totals that exceed the number of studies and percentages that add to more than 100%.

b. The results of a study are categorized as positive (negative) if they suggest that health insurance motivates employment outcomes in the way predicted (opposite of that predicted) by the theoretical framework in this chapter.

All of the reduced-form studies that examined the impact of retiree health insurance on retirement (Headen, Clark, and Ghent 1997; Hurd and McGarry 1996; Karoly and Rogowski 1994; Madrian 1994; Rogowski and Karoly 2000) suffer from the potential effects of endogeneity, or workers' preferences, whether between the availability of retiree health insurance and the pension incentives associated with retirement, or between the availability of retiree health insurance and individual preferences for leisure. Many companies have pension plans that encourage retirement before age 65; those same companies are more likely to offer retiree health insurance benefits. Thus, the pension-related incentives for early retirement are correlated with the health insurance incentives. Yet none of the reduced-form studies accounts for the pension-related incentives satisfactorily. If those incentives are positively correlated with the availability of health insurance, the estimates of the effect of retiree health insurance on retirement are probably too large.[9] Similarly, the selection of jobs that offer retiree health insurance by individuals with strong preferences for leisure will lead to an upward bias in estimates of the effect of retiree health insurance on retirement.[10]

Two approaches have been taken to the problem of endogeneity. The first is to find variations in the availability of retiree health insurance that are exogenous to workers' preferences for retirement. Gruber and Madrian (1995, 1996) studied the impact of state and federal continuation of coverage laws (e.g., COBRA), which allow individuals to maintain their health insurance from a previous employer for up to 18 months.[11] The coverage comes at some cost to the former employee, both directly, in terms of premium costs, and indirectly, as COBRA premiums do not receive the same favorable tax treatment as employer-provided health insurance expenditures. COBRA recipients do benefit from other price-reducing aspects of employer-provided health insurance: notably, the continuous coverage, which may be important to families that could be denied coverage because of a preexisting medical condition. The value of identifying the effects of COBRA-like coverage on retirement is twofold: such coverage is completely independent of omitted personal characteristics that may be correlated with both retiree health insurance and incentives to retire, and it is completely independent of omitted job characteristics (such as pension plan provisions) that may be correlated with both employer-provided and retiree health insurance. Thus, establishing the effects of continuation of coverage provides a relatively clear source of variation for identifying the effect of health insurance on retirement.

Gruber and Madrian (1995) found that continuation of coverage increases the rate of retirement by 30 percent. While this is at the lower end of the estimated magnitudes, it is nevertheless a very large effect, given that COBRA provides only 18 months of coverage, for which individuals must pay the full average group cost. Thus, these findings use a relatively exogenous source of variation to confirm that retirement is very sensitive to the availability of health insurance.

Berger and colleagues (2000) examined the impact of COBRA on the joint employment and retirement decisions of husbands and wives. They used variation in firm size to identify the impact: firms with fewer than 25 employees are exempt from the federal law requiring continuation of coverage. The researchers found little impact of COBRA on retirement using this approach, but the approach is not a particularly compelling one. First, firm size is likely to be correlated with other factors that influence retirement, such as availability and generosity of pension coverage, and the effects of these omitted variables on retirement behavior is uncertain. Second, the group studied is relatively small, so the statistical precision of the resulting estimates are likely to be low no matter what the true effect is.

The second approach to dealing with the potential effects of workers' preferences is to develop a stronger structural model of retirement decisions. Gustman and Steinmeier (1994) were the first to adopt this approach. They used data from the Retirement History Survey (RHS) to estimate a structural model that incorporates both pension-related and insurance-related incentives to retire. They estimated that retiree health insurance reduces age at retirement by a mere 1.3 months and decreases the labor supply at age 62 by only 1 percentage point. However, they also found that retiree health insurance increases the rate of retirement at age 62 by 6 percentage points (47 percent). These seemingly disparate results arise because the model relies on the assumption that eligibility for retiree health insurance coincides with eligibility for early retirement pension benefits.[12] The assumptions imply that, as with pensions, individuals who are not yet eligible to receive their retiree health insurance benefits will delay retirement until they are eligible and that once eligible, they will retire at a greater rate. A model making different assumptions about eligibility for retiree health insurance could yield very different estimates. Nonetheless, Gustman and Steinmeier found that retiree health insurance has a strong influence on the *timing* of retirement, even if its estimated effects on overall labor supply are not large.

A very sophisticated structural dynamic programming model of retirement was designed by Rust and Phelan using RHS data (1997). The model is computationally demanding, but it may provide a sturdier framework for the dynamics of the retirement decision. Even after accounting for the Social Security incentives associated with retirement, Rust and Phelan found sizable effects of health insurance on retirement. For example, the availability of retiree health insurance decreased the probability of working full-time by 10 percentage points (12 percent) at ages 58 and 59, by 20 percentage points (29 percent) at ages 60 and 61, and by 16 percentage points (25 percent) at ages 62 and 63. The major obstacle to generalizing from the results of this study is that the study was restricted to men without a pension, a somewhat nonrepresentative sample. While it is difficult to compare these estimates with those in most of the reduced-form studies, results from both types of studies suggest a rather large effect of health insurance on retirement.

Two working papers using structural models and recent Health and Retirement Study (HRS) data found smaller effects of retiree health insurance on retirement behavior. The first, by Blau and Gilleskie (2001a), used the first two waves of the HRS to estimate a joint model of retirement for husbands and wives. They found little impact of health insurance on individual or joint retirement behavior when the effect was forced to operate solely through the budget constraint in the model. When they allowed preferences to be affected directly by health insurance availability, they found that availability does lead to earlier retirement, although they hesitated to place an economic interpretation on the results. The authors did not speculate about what might drive the discrepancy: Is the availability of retiree health insurance a proxy for some other factor, perhaps a preference for early retirement? Do individuals value health insurance coverage too highly? Or does the model miss some important costs associated with being uninsured?

While the results suggest that health insurance may not be as important a factor in retirement decisions as previous research has suggested, one must bear in mind some important caveats in interpreting them. First, the sample used in the estimation had a much lower rate of health insurance coverage than a representative sample of HRS respondents. To the extent that the sample is skewed toward people whose actions are less likely to be responsive to the availability of health insurance, the model may understate the effects of health insurance on retirement. Second, at age 51 to 63, the sample is young for a study in which retirement decisions are actually observed only over the next two years. The extent to which Medicare eligibility motivates retirement is not actually observed in the data, even though the value of Medicare is modeled.

The second working paper also suggested that health insurance has little impact on retirement behavior (French and Jones 2001). The authors posited that wealthy people should be less sensitive to the availability of health insurance in their retirement decisions because they can afford to self-insure. However, they found little difference in the rate of retirement between wealthy individuals with health insurance and less wealthy individuals with health insurance, perhaps because the study did not account adequately for other differences that affect both assets and retirement. For example, professionals such as doctors and lawyers have many assets, jobs that are likely to allow gradual transitions from full-time work to retirement, and jobs that are less likely to be affected by the declines in health that accompany aging. Thus, wealthy individuals are less likely to retire early than people with fewer assets, even if their valuation of retiree health insurance is the same. Overall, this approach to identifying the effect of health insurance on retirement does not seem well-grounded.

Identifying the effect of Medicare eligibility on retirement is complicated by the fact that Medicare eligibility coincides with Social Security's normal retirement age. Rust and Phelan (1997) identified the effect of Medicare from the expected distribution of medical care expenditures and a risk aversion parameter included in the dynamic program. They found that men with employer-provided health insurance that did not extend into retirement were indeed less likely to leave the labor force before age 65 than men whose health insurance continued. Somewhat paradoxically, they found that even after age 65, men with employer-provided health insurance but without such insurance in retirement were less likely to retire in a given year. They suggest that this situation may stem from the fact that Medicare coverage is much less generous than the coverage provided by employers.

Employer-provided health insurance typically covers dependents, whereas Medicare does not. The lack of dependent coverage gives workers with employer-provided health insurance who are themselves eligible for Medicare an incentive to continue working until their spouses reach age 65 and are eligible as well.[13] Madrian and Beaulieu (1998) show that at all ages, the retirement rate among 55- to 69-year-old married men increases substantially when their wives reach age 65, suggesting yet another link between health insurance and retirement. The results remain suggestive, because the 1980 and 1990 Census data used in their analysis contain no information on either pensions or health insurance.

In contrast, Lumsdaine, Stock, and Wise (1994) found that Medicare has little effect on retirement decisions. They incorporated the value of Medicare into a structural retirement model that used the personnel records from a large U.S. firm. The firm provided health insurance to its retirees, so there was little additional value associated with Medicare. In this context, the lack of an effect is not surprising, and one would certainly be hesitant to generalize from these conclusions.

Although the preponderance of the evidence shows that health insurance does have an effect on retirement decisions, the magnitude of the effect has yet to be determined. This lack stems in large part from limitations in the data.[14] The next step should be to account more fully for the age-specific retirement incentives associated with Social Security and pensions—using current data. For several years now, researchers have been pinning their hopes on the HRS because it contains the information needed to provide the "ultimate answer" to the question of how health insurance affects retirement. While several studies have used data from the HRS, only one has used data beyond wave II.[15] Incorporating the later waves is clearly critical, because none of the respondents had reached age 65 in wave II. Any hopes that the HRS will provide the ultimate answer must be tempered somewhat by sample size. After restricting their sample to eligible couples with valid data from both the Social Security and Health Insurance and Pension Provider Supplement (HIPPS) supplements, Blau and Gilleskie (2001a) were left with a sample of fewer than 700 couples. This is a rather small sample and is likely to result in imprecise estimates for many variables. Adding in single individuals or individuals who were not eligible on the basis of age would increase the sample size, but it might not be appropriate in some contexts.

Beyond estimating the combined effects of Social Security, pensions, health insurance, and health on retirement, several other research refinements are warranted. Recent research recognizes that for many people, retirement is not the "absorbing state" that simplified theories portray. That is, a nontrivial fraction of workers move from full-time employment to part-time employment and then to complete retirement.[16] Many other older workers make several transitions in and out of the labor force before making the final switch to retirement. Moreover, a sizable fraction of workers would prefer a gradual transition from work to retirement

(Hurd and McGarry 1996). But health insurance may limit the ability of workers to "retire" as they wish. Because coverage is usually attached to full-time rather than part-time jobs, most workers will have to relinquish health insurance if their transition to retirement involves part-time work. Rust and Phelan (1997) found that men with employer-provided retiree or other non-employment-based health insurance were much less likely to be working full-time than men whose employers provide health insurance but not retiree health insurance—and they were much more likely to be working part-time.

Like most research on retirement, that on health insurance and retirement has focused almost exclusively on men,[17] largely because so few older women are in the labor force and because a sizable fraction of those who do work receive coverage under their husbands' plans. As more older women work, and as an increasing number of older women become the head of household or the primary insurer of their families, the question of whether health insurance affects women differently than men will warrant further investigation.

Health Insurance and Low-Income Single Mothers

Health insurance may also affect the decisions of low-income single women and other potential recipients of public assistance regarding whether or not to work. Table 3.A2 describes the 16 studies surveyed here, and the results are summarized in table 3.2. A key feature of both Temporary Assistance for Needy Families (TANF, formerly Aid to Families with Dependent Children, or AFDC) and the Supplemental Security Income (SSI) programs is that, in addition to providing cash and other benefits, they qualify recipients for Medicaid. Because the groups who qualify for these programs—low-income families headed by single women and low-income disabled and elderly persons—tend to qualify for low-wage, low-skilled jobs without health insurance, the coupling of Medicaid with public assistance encourages individuals to sign up for and remain enrolled in public assistance programs. The budget set for these individuals is shown by budget constraint MABC in figure 3.1. The nonlinearity in the budget set generated by the loss of Medicaid (segment AB) creates an incentive to reduce labor supply from H to H'.

Because Medicaid receipt has historically gone hand in hand with receipt of public assistance, the Medicaid effect on labor supply has been difficult to distinguish from the welfare effect.[18] Four strategies for doing

Figure 3.1. *The Impact of Medicaid Loss on the Budget Set and the Choice of Hours Worked*

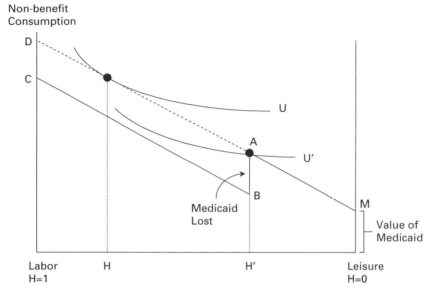

so have been pursued. The first exploits variation in the demand for health insurance coverage generated by differences in expected medical expenditures. Ellwood and Adams (1990) followed this approach, using Medicaid administrative claims data, as did Moffitt and Wolfe (1992), using SIPP data. Both found that the probability of leaving public assistance decreases substantially as the imputed value of Medicaid rises. Moffitt and Wolfe also showed that the value of maintaining Medicaid coverage has a significant negative impact on single mothers' decision to work.

Although these results support the notion that individual labor supply decisions are made in such a way as to maintain health insurance coverage, the strategy for identifying the effect is faulty. The primary determinant of differences in the valuation of Medicaid benefits—namely, differences in health status—is likely to have a strong independent effect on both labor supply and welfare participation.[19] Both studies recognize this criticism and attempt to address it by examining the health status of the family head separately from that of the children. Ellwood and Adams (1990) found little difference between the two groups in the effect of health status on expected increases in expenditures. In contrast, Moffitt and Wolfe (1992) found that expected increases generated by the health status of children led to labor supply effects that are one-third as large as those generated by the health status of the family head. Wolfe and Hill (1995) showed that having a disabled child led to a reduction in maternal labor supply, so even this approach to disentangling the effect of expected medical expenditures from the effect of health is problematic.

A second approach has been to use variation in the generosity of state Medicaid programs to identify the value of Medicaid to potential welfare recipients. Generosity is typically specified as some measure of per capita Medicaid spending, such as spending per recipient or average spending for a family of a given size. This general approach has been pursued by Blank (1989), Winkler (1991), and Montgomery and Navin (2000). Blank found no effect of Medicaid expenditures on either AFDC participation or labor supply. The other two studies found small effects on labor supply, although the effects in Montgomery and Navin disappeared once they controlled for fixed state differences.

Using average state Medicaid expenditures as a proxy for the value of Medicaid to potential recipients is problematic for two reasons. First, variation in average expenditures is likely to reflect not only variation in the generosity of the insurance, but also variation in the underlying health of those covered and in the utilization patterns of patients and practice patterns of physicians. This type of measurement error will result in attenuation bias, which makes it less likely that an effect of Medicaid on the labor market will be found, if such an effect exists. Second, variation in state Medicaid expenditures that is driven by the underlying health of the Medicaid population is likely to be spuriously correlated with decisions to work. Because health is a significant determinant of labor supply, states with relatively healthy populations are likely to have both high employment rates and low average Medicaid expenditures. This spurious correlation between employment rate and average Medicaid expenditures will also create a bias against finding a relationship between the value of Medicaid and the decision to work.

More recent studies have attempted to exploit the fact that a series of legislative initiatives in the late 1980s severed the link between Medicaid and welfare participation for various groups of mothers and children. These initiatives allowed women to maintain their Medicaid coverage for a specified period of time after leaving welfare and extended Medicaid coverage to many groups of low-income children indefinitely (in figure 3.1, these initiatives change the budget constraint from MABC to

MD). Currie and Gruber (1996a, b) estimated that as a result of these expansions, almost one-third of children and one-half of pregnant women are eligible for Medicaid coverage.

Yelowitz (1995) was the first to use the Medicaid expansions as a way to identify the effect of Medicaid coverage on AFDC and labor supply. He found evidence that the expansions in Medicaid availability led to a small but statistically significant increase in the number of single mothers who work. Meyer and Rosenbaum (2000b) contested the findings, claiming that the effects resulted from a miscalculation of the income limits for AFDC eligibility, which forced both AFDC and Medicaid income limits to have the same effect. When Meyer and Rosenbaum corrected the calculation to allow for different coefficients of the AFDC and Medicaid income limits, they found that the effects on labor supply noted by Yelowitz were driven entirely by AFDC and not by the Medicaid expansions.[20] In an unpublished note, Yelowitz (1998c) claimed that his findings remained relatively robust. Regardless of whether the effects exist or not, even the largest estimates suggest they are small.

Yazici (1997) also found little effect of the Medicaid expansions on labor supply, although her sample from the National Longitudinal Study of Youth (NLSY) is so small that it is unlikely she could have obtained statistically significant effects unless they were particularly large. In another study based on longitudinal data, Ham and Shore-Sheppard (2000) found that the Medicaid expansions shortened both nonemployment and welfare spells of single mothers, with stronger effects for the long-term nonemployed and long-term welfare recipients. Those effects largely disappeared when the authors controlled for the survey year, although year effects removed a substantial fraction of the variation in Medicaid expansions that can be used to identify the effects of Medicaid.

Decker (1993) pursued a related strategy, examining the effect of the introduction of Medicaid in the late 1960s and early 1970s on individual participation in AFDC and labor supply. Because the Medicaid program was phased in over a period of several years, this strategy provides a credible means of identifying the effect of Medicaid on welfare participation and labor supply. Using both state-level data on AFDC caseloads and individual data on AFDC participation from the Current Population Survey (CPS), Decker found a sizable and statistically significant 21 percent increase in the likelihood of individuals' participating in AFDC after Medicaid was introduced. The effects of Medicaid on labor supply were insignificant, however, suggesting that participation increased primarily because the decision not to work increased the number of people eligible.

A final strategy for identifying the effects of Medicaid on labor supply has been to exploit differences in the availability or generosity of employer-provided health insurance that welfare recipients might obtain if they were employed. This approach was pursued by Perreira (1999), using administrative data on Medicaid enrollment in California, and by Meyer and Rosenbaum (2000b), using CPS data. Perreira found that a 2.5 percentage point (5 percent) increase in the availability of employer-provided health insurance nationwide decreased the median length of time on Medicaid by 3 to 11 months (10 to 37 percent). Meyer and Rosenbaum (2000b) obtained somewhat contradictory results. They found that higher worker contribution rates to employer-provided health insurance led to a decrease in the employment of single mothers, consistent with the notion that as employer-provided health insurance becomes more expensive, Medicaid becomes more valuable. Yet they also found that an increase in the value of employer-provided health insurance decreased the employment of single mothers. The authors posit a demand-side argument for the latter effect—that is, when employers are more likely to offer health insurance, they take steps to reduce employment.

In practice, using variation in the availability of employer-provided health insurance to identify the effect of health insurance on the labor supply of single mothers is a tricky proposition at best. Health insurance coverage rates vary significantly by geographic area, income, and hours worked. Given this heterogeneity, any measure of health insurance availability or health insurance value for single mothers is likely to be quite arbitrary. Consequently, any variation in these measures is likely to be dominated by measurement error, and the results are quite likely to be subject to significant attenuation bias.

In a series of other studies, Yelowitz examined the effect of Medicaid on receipt of public assistance through programs other than TANF or AFDC. Although the studies did not examine effects on labor supply directly, they all found that coupling Medicaid with other types of public assistance programs increases enrollment in those programs.[21]

Overall, the research literature suggests that the availability of health insurance, particularly Medicaid, has little or no effect on the decisions of low-income single mothers to work. This finding is somewhat surprising, given the potential importance of health insurance for these women and their children. On the other hand, some evidence suggests that the decision to participate in welfare programs, conditional on decisions regarding whether to work, is fairly responsive to the availability of health insurance.

Clearly, the last word on this topic has not been written. The continuing controversy over whether Medicaid expansions reduced the number of single women on welfare and increased the number working indicates the need for more research on these effects. And the significant new expansions of children's eligibility for public insurance through the State Children's Health Insurance Program (SCHIP), along with changes in state welfare programs resulting from welfare reform, provide further variation that can be studied to assess the impact of public insurance on the welfare and work decisions of single mothers.

Health Insurance and the Labor Supply of Married Couples

Married women, and to a lesser extent married men, are another group whose decisions to work or not are likely to be affected by the availability of health insurance. Although policymakers and analysts have been interested mostly in the effect of health insurance on the employment decisions of older workers and welfare recipients, the potential impact in terms of aggregate effects on total hours worked may very well be greatest for workers between the ages of 20 and 64, particularly married women, who are typically estimated to have a great deal of flexibility in making employment decisions. Given the responsiveness of married women to wage changes, one might expect them to be sensitive to the availability of health insurance coverage as well.

Seven studies of the labor supply of nonelderly workers who are not single mothers are described in table 3.A3, with the results summarized in table 3.2. In most of them, the effect of health insurance on labor supply is identified by comparing the labor supply and hours worked of married women whose husbands have employer-provided health insurance with the labor supply and hours worked of married women whose husbands do not. This strategy rests on the assumption that a husband's employer-provided health insurance is exogenous to the wife's decision regarding work.[22] The assumption is clearly problematic if husbands and wives make joint labor supply and job choice decisions. Putting this caution aside, all four studies that looked at the labor supply of married women using U.S. data found strong evidence that employment and hours decisions of married women do in fact depend on whether or not health insurance is available through the husband's employment. Buchmueller and Valletta (1999) estimated that the availability of spousal health insurance reduces the labor supply of married women by 6 to 12 percent, Olson (1998) estimated a 7 to 8 percent reduction, Schone and Vistnes (2000) a 10 percentage point reduction, and Wellington and Cobb-Clark (2000) a substantial 20 percentage point reduction in the labor supply of married women.

Health insurance seems to affect not only the decision of whether or not to work, but also the choice of job for women who do work. Buchmueller and Valletta (1999) found that spousal health insurance reduced the probability of working in a full-time job with health insurance by 9 to 13 percentage points, increased the probability of working in a full-time job without health insurance by 4 to 8 percentage points, and increased the probability of working in a part-time job by about 3 percentage points. Schone and Vistnes (2000) found a 14 percentage point reduction in full-time work, a 2 percentage point increase in part-time work, and a 15 percentage point decrease in the likelihood of having a job with employer-provided health insurance. Wellington and Cobb-Clark (2000) found an 8 to 17 percent reduction in hours worked per year by married women. Finally, Olson estimated an average decline in weekly hours of 20 percent (5 hours per week) for married women whose husbands have health insurance.

A problem with all of these studies is that the husbands' employer-provided health insurance coverage could be determined by their wives' decisions to work. However, at least some evidence indicates that the results are driven by the availability of health insurance per se, not by its correlation with any underlying desire of wives to work. First, Buchmueller and Valletta (1999) found that the negative effect of husbands' health insurance on wives' labor supply was strongest in larger families, which is consistent with the notion that the value of health insurance is driving decisions. In addition, Olson (1998) showed that wives who work at least 40 hours per week have very similar distributions of hours, regardless of whether their husbands have health insurance. Finally, both Buchmueller and Valletta and Olson found that husbands' having health insurance substantially reduced the probability of their wives' working full-time but had only small effects on the probability of their wives' working part-time. Taken together, these findings suggest that the availability of husbands' health insurance exerts a negative effect on their wives' decisions to work, leading wives to work fewer hours or not at all.

One of the few studies that used non-U.S. data examined the effects of health insurance on the labor supply of wives in Taiwan (Chou and Staiger 2001). Before March 1995, when Taiwan implemented a national health insurance program, coverage was provided primarily through one of three government-sponsored health plans for workers in different sectors of the economy. Historically these plans covered only workers, not their dependents. Thus, the only way for most individuals to obtain health insurance was through their own employment—with one exception: coverage of spouses was extended to government workers in 1982, and subsequently to children and parents as well. By examining this variation in the availability of dependent health insurance coverage, Chou and Staiger were able to identify the effect of health insurance on employment. They found that employment of women married to government workers declined by about 3 percent after they were able to obtain coverage as dependents. A similar decline occurred in the employment rate of wives of private-sector workers following implementation of national coverage. The results are largely corroborated in an analogous study by Chou and Liu (2000).

Only two empirical studies have examined the effect of health insurance on the labor supply of nonelderly men. The first, by Wellington and Cobb-Clark (2000), examined the effect of spousal health insurance on the employment decisions of both husbands and wives. As noted earlier, they found that husbands' health insurance had large effects on wives' decisions to work. They also found that having a wife with health insurance reduced husbands' employment by 4 to 9 percentage points and reduced the number of hours worked per year by up to 4 percent.

The effect of continuation of coverage mandates such as COBRA on workers' transition from employment to nonemployment and on the subsequent duration of nonemployment were studied by Gruber and Madrian (1997). They found that mandated continuation of coverage increased the likelihood of experiencing a spell of nonemployment by about 15 percent. It also increased the amount of time without a job by about 15 percent.

Overall, empirical studies give strong and consistent support to the notion that health insurance affects individuals' decisions regarding employment. When health insurance not attached to one's own employment is readily available, individuals (particularly married women) are much less likely to be employed. This suggests that the link between health insurance and employment may be a significant factor in the employment decisions of individuals. To date, however, studies of health insurance's effect on labor supply are somewhat limited by a lack of convincing strategies for identifying the effects, unlike studies of health insurance and retirement, welfare, and job mobility.

Health Insurance and Job Mobility

The most thoroughly studied outcome in the area of health insurance and labor markets is job mobility—that is, a worker's choice of job and his or her decision to change jobs, also described as job turnover. The 18 studies of health insurance and job turnover surveyed here are described in table 3.A4, with the results summarized in table 3.2. Recognizing that health insurance provided by one's own employer is likely to be correlated with potentially unobserved job attributes that also affect turnover, only a few studies have looked directly at the impact of such health insurance on job mobility. The first (Mitchell 1982) makes no claim to identifying the effect of health insurance on job choice. Two others (Buchmueller and Valletta 1996; Gilleskie and Lutz forthcoming), used different controls to account for the positive correlation between health insurance and other job amenities that are likely to reduce turnover (the Buchmueller and Valletta study employed both this identification strategy and the one discussed below). The last one (Dey 2000) estimated a highly structural model of job choice.

Most of the other analyses of job turnover have compared the probability of job turnover among employees who value a current employer's health insurance policy and the probability of turnover among apparently equivalent employees who place less value on their current coverage. Various measures of the value of health insurance have been used, including:

- Health insurance from a source other than one's current employer, most often a spouse's employer or continuation of coverage such as COBRA (Anderson 1997; Berger, Black, and Scott 2001; Buchmueller and Valletta 1996; Cooper and Monheit 1993; Gilleskie and Lutz forthcoming; Gruber and Madrian 1994; Holtz-Eakin 1994; Holtz-Eakin, Penrod, and Rosen 1996; Kapur 1998; Madrian 1994b; Madrian and Lefgren 1998; Penrod 1994; Slade 1997; Spaulding 1997).
- Family size (Berger, Black, and Scott 2001; Kapur 1998; Madrian 1994)

- Health conditions (Anderson 1997; Berger, Black, and Scott 2001; Brunetti et al. 2000; Cooper and Monheit 1993; Holtz-Eakin, Penrod, and Rosen 1996; Kapur 1998; Madrian 1994b; Penrod 1994; Stroupe, Kinney, and Kniesner 2000)
- Health status (Anderson 1997; Berger, Black, and Scott 2001; Brunetti et al. 2000; Holtz-Eakin 1994; Penrod 1994; Slade 1997)

Evaluating the likely effect on job turnover of health insurance from a source other than one's own employer is most appealing if the alternative source is in fact exogenous. The problem is that it may well not be. By far the most prevalent source of alternative coverage is a spouse's employment-based health insurance; thus, to the extent that couples make joint decisions, the health insurance available through one spouse could affect the employment and job choice decisions of the other spouse. Madrian (1994b) first used the availability of spousal health insurance as a means of measuring differences in job mobility and thus identifying job lock. She found that having this alternative source of insurance increased job turnover by 25 percent. Others who followed the same strategy obtained qualitatively similar results (Buchmueller and Valletta 1996; Berger, Black, and Scott 2000). In their study of job turnover, Buchmueller and Valletta tried to account for the potential influence of spousal health insurance and found that it had little impact. This suggests that even though spousal health insurance may be jointly determined by husbands and wives, from the standpoint of job turnover it can perhaps be treated as exogenous. This conclusion is echoed by Buchmueller and Valletta (1999) and Olson (1998) in studies of spousal health insurance and the labor supply of married women discussed above.

Using a similar strategy, Holtz-Eakin (1994) failed to find a significant impact of spousal health insurance on job turnover. His results are difficult to evaluate, however, because of well-documented problems with the turnover variables in the data he used (the Panel Study on Income Dynamics, or PSID). Because the PSID does not track job changes very well, different definitions of job change can result in very different job turnover rates (which suggests the possibility of measurement error, regardless of what definition is chosen). With a continuous dependent variable, such measurement error will simply result in a loss of efficiency (bigger standard errors); in the context of a limited dependent variable model, however, it can lead to biased estimates. Hausman, Abrevaya, and Scott Morton (1998) showed how this occurs in a general context. Brown and Light (1992) showed that in the specific context of job choice in the PSID, the definition of the dependent variable is critical—and varying definitions can result in statistically significant, opposite results! Clearly, PSID data may not be appropriate for investigations of job turnover.[23]

Measurement error in the dependent variable is also likely to be quite important in the one study that used CPS data. Because the CPS does not ask questions about job change, Brunetti and colleagues (2000) used industry and occupation changes as a measure of job change. However, industry and occupation can change without a change of employer, and the significant variation in their measure of job change, depending on how this variable is defined (change in industry, change in occupation, or change in both) suggests that these variables are very likely to contain a substantial degree of measurement error.

Kapur (1998) criticized the approach used in Madrian (1994b) and in Buchmueller and Valletta (1996) not because of the potential endogeneity of spousal health insurance, but because the identification of job lock rested on differences in mobility between those who do and do not have health insurance. She claimed that substantial differences in the characteristics of individuals employed in jobs with and without health insurance invalidate such a comparison. It is true that workers with and without their own employer-provided coverage differ substantially (Kapur 1998, table 1), but in using spousal health insurance to identify job lock, Madrian (1994b) obtained extremely similar estimates.

Kapur (1998) suggested an alternative approach: restrict the sample to individuals with employer-provided health insurance and examine the differential effect of health conditions or health status on those with and without spousal health insurance. The notion here is that lack of an alternative source of health insurance should pose a greater impediment to mobility for workers with family health conditions. Similar strategies have been pursued by a number of other researchers, including Monheit and Cooper (1994), Penrod (1994), Holtz-Eakin (1994), Holtz-Eakin, Penrod, and Rosen (1996), Brunetti and colleagues (2000), Stroupe, Kinney, and Kniesner (2000), and Berger, Black, and Scott (2001). Although the details vary, the basic approach is one of the following:

- Include all individuals with and without employer-provided health insurance in the sample and identify job lock from an interaction between employer-provided health insurance and some measure of health conditions.

- Include only individuals with employer-provided health insurance in the sample and identify job lock from an interaction between the availability of health insurance through a spouse and some measure of health conditions.
- Include all individuals with and without employer-provided health insurance in the sample and identify job lock from a three-way interaction between one's own health insurance, the spouse's health insurance, and some measure of health conditions.

With the exception of Stroupe, Kinney, and Kniesner (2000), none of the studies in this genre found any statistically significant effect, positive or negative, of health insurance on job to job mobility. Although the approach suggested above has intuitive appeal, implementation presents several problems.

First, the prevalence of severe health problems or extensive utilization of medical care in the nonelderly working population is low, leading to less precise estimates. The problem is further compounded when the identification of job lock rests on the interaction between health status or medical care utilization and health insurance coverage. The prevalence of both health problems and spousal health insurance, or of health problems, own insurance, and spousal health insurance, is even lower. Thus, the likelihood of being able to estimate statistically significant effects of health insurance on job turnover is small. Stroupe, Kinney, and Kniesner (2000) overcame the low prevalence of severe or chronic illnesses by using data that vastly oversample people who themselves have or whose family members have chronic illnesses. Interestingly, this is the only study that found a statistically significant effect of health insurance on job turnover: the results suggested that health insurance reduces voluntary job turnover by about 40 percent.

Second, one would like to have a measure of *expected* medical care utilization or health needs. Such measures are generally calculated on the basis of past experience, but past experience may not be a very reliable predictor of future outcomes for the nonelderly working population. For example, in married couple families with a household head under the age of 45, a substantial fraction of physician visits and hospital admissions are pregnancy-related. For such families, last year's hospital admissions are unlikely to be predictive of next year's medical needs. Madrian (1994b) argues that pregnancy is one of the most prevalent health conditions among nonelderly workers that is likely to generate job lock (at least in the short term), yet pregnancy is unlikely to be predicted accurately by health or medical care utilization in the previous year (if anything, it is likely to be negatively related). Thus, the likelihood of extensive measurement error in many of these variables will lead to attenuation bias.

Third, to the extent that health problems impose costs on employers, both directly, in terms of increased medical costs, and indirectly, in terms of decreased productivity of workers dealing with their own or a family member's health problems, employers may actually be more likely to dismiss such workers. Such action would bias studies against finding any evidence of job lock.

Finally, these variables may depend somewhat on the nature of the health insurance coverage that individuals have. For example, a person who has only his or her own employer-provided health insurance and who plans on changing jobs may have a greater incentive to take care of certain medical problems before changing jobs than a person who has spousal health insurance as well. Such behavior will also bias studies against finding job lock.

None of the studies that used various measures of health conditions or medical care utilization to identify job lock addressed any of these issues. Until it can be shown that the criticisms leveled above are likely to generate only small biases in estimates and their standard errors, it seems unlikely that they can provide compelling evidence of job lock.

Gruber and Madrian (1994) used continuation of coverage mandates, a completely exogenous source of health insurance, to estimate job lock and found that continuation of coverage appears to increase turnover by about 10 percent. The finding suggests that having health insurance in fact lessens job turnover. However, since continuation of coverage is expensive, it is unlikely to alleviate the full extent of job lock. Gruber and Madrian's estimates could therefore be viewed as a lower bound.

Cooper and Monheit (1993) used a two-stage procedure, first estimating the likelihood that an individual will gain or lose health insurance coverage if he or she changes jobs, and then identifying job lock by including variables that measure the likelihood of gaining or losing coverage in a job turnover regression. They found that being likely to gain health insurance increased turnover by 28 to 52 percent, while being likely to lose health insurance reduced turnover by 23 to 39 percent. Anderson (1997) discovered a similar effect—namely, that individuals who would benefit most from obtaining health insurance coverage (because of pregnancy or disability) were more likely to change jobs. She labels this behavior "job push."

Slade (1997) took a completely different tack in his effort to identify job lock. He first documented a substantial negative correlation between health insurance coverage and the propensity of individuals for changing jobs. In light of this correlation, he noted, the dampening effect of employer-provided health insurance on job mobility should not be construed as evidence of job lock because it may largely reflect unobserved variation in the propensity for changing jobs. Much of the previous literature recognized this potential bias, and it is one reason behind the difference-in-difference strategy for identifying job lock first propounded by Madrian (1994b). Slade looked directly at the effect of health insurance availability on job mobility at the state level and at room charges in state hospitals. The notion behind the first measure is that if the likelihood of obtaining health insurance in another job is high, one's current employer-provided health insurance is less valuable. The latter measure is assumed to be a proxy for the former under the presumption that higher hospital room charges will decrease the availability of health insurance. He found little evidence that these health insurance variables affect worker turnover.

It is not clear that Slade's strategy will really enable one to identify the effect of health insurance on job mobility. The measure of health insurance availability he uses is the fraction of the nonelderly population in the state covered by private health insurance. If employers base their decisions about whether to offer health insurance on the turnover propensities of the workforce—because health insurance is more expensive to offer when turnover is high—then states in which mobility is high for non-insurance-related reasons will have a lower rate of health insurance coverage. The spurious correlation between mobility and statewide private health insurance coverage will bias studies against finding an effect of health insurance availability on job mobility, even if greater availability does indeed increase turnover. In any case, this measure would not pick up job lock generated by the exclusion of preexisting medical conditions from coverage by firms that do offer health insurance.

Looking at hospital room charges for evidence of job lock is also problematic. Higher room charges might decrease the overall availability of health insurance by raising prices, but firms might be able to recoup their increased costs by lowering wages. This would mitigate any decrease in mobility that one would expect to see from higher health care costs. Moreover, higher hospital room charges might affect mobility differently for those with and without health insurance. Health insurance becomes more valuable to those who have it when health care costs are high, so one would expect to see reduced mobility among insured workers. In contrast, obtaining health insurance becomes more important to those who do not have it when health care costs are high, so one would expect to see increased mobility among uninsured workers as they change jobs to obtain insurance. Slade (1997) did not separate the effects of hospital room charges on these two groups, so the resulting coefficient is likely to reflect two effects that work in opposite directions.

Two studies examined the effect of health insurance on a very specific type of job turnover, namely, the transition from employment to self-employment. While the self-employed receive some limited tax benefits for their health insurance purchases, they generally face high prices for health insurance in addition to the potential costs associated with relinquishing the health insurance provided by a current employer. Holtz-Eakin, Penrod, and Rosen (1996) found no effect of health insurance on the transition from employment to self-employment, but since most of the other variables they studied (income, race, education) had no effect either, the lack may speak more to the quality of the data than to the actual effect of health insurance. Madrian and Lefgren (1998) found some evidence that both continuation of coverage and spousal health insurance increased transitions to self-employment.

The results of both studies should be interpreted with caution. The issue of measurement error is likely to be of particular concern for transitions from employment to self-employment. Although the idea of self-employment is simple enough, the empirical identification of the self-employed is complicated because many individuals hold a wage-paying or salaried job in addition to being self-employed. In such cases, classifying someone as employed for wages or self-employed is necessarily arbitrary. Madrian and Lefgren (1998) showed that the various schemes for classifying workers as self-employed or not self-employed in the SIPP resulted in a 40 percent variation in the self-employment rate. Moreover, defining the transition from employment to self-employment resulted in transition rates that vary by as much as 100 percent.

Madrian and Lefgren claim that, for some very specific groups of individuals, the transition rate between employment and self-employment is as high as 70 percent, suggesting that there were serious flaws in the initial categorization of individuals as employed or self-employed. In addition, they suggest that the estimated effects of health insurance on self-employment can be sensitive to how this specific group of individuals is treated. If so, it seems clear that any definition of such a transition will probably be subject to significant measurement error, casting doubt on the ability to identify the true effect of health insurance on transitions from employment to self-employment. Measurement error is further compounded by the relatively low transition rates from employment to self-employment—precise estimates of an effect, if one exists, are difficult with so little data.

Overall, the research findings on health insurance and job turnover are more divided than those on health insurance and labor supply. About one-third of the studies analyzed in this chapter found that health insurance significantly affected the job choices made by workers (Anderson 1997; Cooper and Monheit 1993; Gruber and Madrian 1994; Madrian 1994b; Stroupe, Kinney, and Kniesner 2000); another one-third found no significant relationship between health insurance and job choice (Holtz-Eakin 1994; Holtz-Eakin, Penrod, and Rosen 1996; Kapur 1998; Mitchell 1982; Penrod 1994; Slade 1997; Spaulding 1997); and the remaining one-third found evidence that varied with the subgroup analyzed or effects that were not statistically significant at standard levels (Berger, Black, and Scott 2001; Brunetti et al. 2000; Buchmueller and Valletta 1996; Gilleskie and Lutz, forthcoming; Madrian and Lefgren 1998). Yet despite differences in data and in strategies for identifying job lock, a fair number of the studies that found a significant effect estimated that employer-provided health insurance reduces job mobility by 25 to 50 percent (Buchmueller and Valletta 1996; Cooper and Monheit 1993; Madrian 1994; Stroupe, Kinney, and Kniesner 2000).

In general, using the availability of spousal coverage to identify the effect of health insurance on job turnover results in positive and significant estimates of job lock (Holtz-Eakin [1994] was the notable exception, but the data concerns discussed above may explain his results). In contrast, identifying job lock from an interaction between spousal health insurance and the worker's own health, family health, or expected medical expenditures (or a three-way interaction among these measures and the worker's own employer-provided health insurance) tends to result in statistically insignificant coefficients that are both positive and negative. Thus, conclusions regarding job lock seem to hinge on the strategy used to identify it.

Both strategies suffer from potential problems of endogeneity, but the health or expected expenditures approach has a host of additional difficulties that the alternative insurance approach does not. Perhaps the greatest limitation of the alternative insurance approach is that it is most often obtained through a spouse's employer, making it less useful for estimating job lock among single individuals or married individuals in single-earner families.[24] It is possible, however, to set reasonable bounds on the extent of job lock even for such individuals. Continuation of coverage is available to all employees, whether single or married, but it is costly, and estimates of job lock based on the availability of continued coverage are best viewed as a lower bound. For married, dual-earner couples, a rich array of job controls, particularly tenure and the availability of other benefits, greatly reduces the bias in job turnover results stemming from the availability of employer-provided health insurance (Buchmueller and Valleta 1996).[25] Buchmueller and Valleta suggest that for single individuals, the effect of health insurance on job turnover *when these other job controls are included* may represent a reasonable upper bound on the true effect of job lock. Interestingly, when including such job controls, they found that the magnitude of job lock among single women and men in single-earner households is very similar to that estimated for men in dual-earner households using the interaction between spousal and own health insurance to identify job lock.

In conclusion, using variation in continuation of coverage mandates to identify job lock yields a conservative lower bound estimate of 10 percent (Gruber and Madrian 1994), while using spousal insurance to identify job lock provides a reasonable upper bound estimate of 25 to 35 percent (Madrian 1994b; Buchmueller and Valletta, 1996). Clearly, the widely divergent results of the many studies of health insurance and job turnover need to be reconciled. A study that systematically compared the results obtained using different data sets, strategies for identifying job lock, and research methodologies would be particularly valuable.

The Missing Piece: Implications for Welfare

The foregoing review of research literature documents the exciting approaches and important conclusions that have emerged from a decade of high-quality empirical work on health insurance and the labor market. Given the wide variety of empirical approaches in these studies, they provide a fairly firm basis for concluding that health insurance affects workers' decisions regarding retirement, whether to work, and whether to change jobs. This is no small contribution.

But this literature has largely failed to document, or even discuss, the implications of these results for the overall efficiency of the U.S. job market. Developing a model of the implications of job lock for the country is beyond the scope of this chapter, but the chapter does lay out the promises and pitfalls of four different approaches to measuring the implications of job lock stemming from health insurance. The discussion is written with reference to job mobility, but the points and conclusions carry over to any other model of health insurance and labor supply: the key question is the consequences of a barrier to mobility from one position to another where individuals are better off.

Approach A: Structural Modeling

The first approach is to devise a structural model of the job mobility decision, beginning with maximizing well-being across job alternatives. The advantage of this approach is that it allows analysts to evaluate utility in different states and to measure the utility lost through reduced job mobility.

Dey (2000) created a structural model of job turnover to estimate the consequences of job lock on welfare. While he suggests that job lock does exist (and estimates a highly variable 2 to 16 percent reduction in mobility caused by employer-provided health insurance), he found very small effects on welfare. It is difficult to evaluate his results or to generalize from them—first, because it is not clear where the identification of job lock comes from, and second, because the sample consisted of unemployed persons. Assuming that individuals who value employer-provided health insurance highly take steps to avoid becoming unemployed, then this sample will be composed largely of people whose decisions about whether to work are not likely to be affected by the availability of health insurance. Therefore, changing the nature of the availability of health insurance for this sample will have small consequences for welfare. Changing the availability of health insurance for individuals who value health insurance more highly could presumably have much greater effects.

While deriving results from this model is straightforward in theory, doing so in a credible fashion is likely to prove daunting in practice. This is because the data are unlikely to be varied enough to pin down all of the base parameters required to evaluate the model. One would need, at a minimum, estimates of time discount rates, parameters of risk aversion, direct utility from consumption of medical care relative to cash, and the disutility of labor. As a result, any estimates derived from this approach are likely to be heavily dependent on assumptions about the particular specification of the empirical model.

Moreover, this approach, as well as most of the others reviewed below, misses a potentially key component of the welfare gain from reducing job lock: spillover. In increasing returns models, such as Kremer's (1993), there can be important social benefits (complementarities) from having skilled workers produce together. In such a world, the gains to society from improved matches of workers to jobs can significantly exceed any gains that would emerge from a structural model focused on the worker alone.

Approach B: Computing Productivity Loss

A second approach is to use data on the value of mobility to infer the cost of restrictions on mobility. Monheit and Cooper (1994) used their estimate of the health-insurance-induced reduction in job mobility to calculate roughly the effects on welfare. They derived the number of individuals affected by job lock and multiplied it by the average wage increase that accrues to individuals who change jobs. This yielded a productivity loss equal to about one-third of 1 percent of the gross domestic product (GDP).

This approach has its own difficulties. First, the information on average wage increase is quite crude. Accurately estimating the increase is difficult because individuals whose wages are likely to increase if they change jobs are more likely to change jobs, whereas individuals who already have high-productivity, high-wage jobs are likely to stay put, fearing their wages would be lower elsewhere. Studies of job mobility and wage changes (including Monheit and Cooper 1994) have also focused almost exclusively on the short-term changes in wages that accompany job mobility, ignoring any effects that could potentially compound or dissipate increases over time.

Another key difficulty of this approach is that wages may be a poor proxy for the marginal productivity of workers in long-term employment relationships. The nature of the bias is not obvious. On the one hand, if workers have invested a lot of firm-specific human capital in their jobs, their wages may be lower than their marginal productivity at their current firm but above their marginal productivity at another job. On the other hand, if workplace norms or some other factors result in apparently inefficient long-term contracts for workers, then workers' wages may be above their marginal productivity at the current firm. Moreover, the important issue of impacts beyond the workers themselves arises: if there are positive complementarities in production, then a worker's own wage would once again understate his or her marginal productivity. Finally, while potentially useful for thinking about job mobility, this approach does not speak to the value of leisure and therefore is not helpful in thinking about the welfare implications of labor supply decisions that are distorted by health insurance.

Approach C: Limiting the Cost of Mobility

Another approach is to infer an upper bound on the costs of job lock. As long as an individual can buy insurance at some price, the costs of the forgone job change cannot be infinitely large; at some point, individuals would simply buy insurance coverage on their own and change jobs. In principle, the cost of the alternative form of insurance can be used to limit the costs of job lock.[26] This approach is appealing because it is market based and incorporates the full utility costs of job lock, while putting a dollar limit on those costs.

In practice, the approach has important limitations. The first is positing the cost of the alternative insurance option. For the first 18 months, this cost can be set at the cost of COBRA for workers in medium and large firms. Thus, for example, the approach can clearly be used to assess the loss from retirement lock among persons over the age of 63½. But for other groups, the cost of alternative health insurance rises after 18 months to the cost of purchasing a policy on the nongroup market. These costs are not well defined, for two reasons. First, nongroup policies are typically much less generous than policies provided in the group market. Second, nongroup premiums are much more variable: if an individual becomes ill, his or her premium could rise exponentially. States with high-risk pools or some other insurance backstop can limit premium increases, but even this limit is subject to the political risk that the subsidy of high-risk pools will end.

Liquidity constraints pose another problem. Take the case of a worker considering an alternative position that will result in higher productivity but that provides only delayed compensation (such as stock options). In this case, neither the firm nor the worker may have much cash up front. Even if there is a reasonably priced alternative insurance, the firm and the employee may jointly be unable to front the funds to purchase that insurance.

Nonetheless, this approach lends itself to some fairly straightforward limit calculations. For the first 18 months, assuming full shifting of insurance costs to wages, insurance has the same gross cost on the current job as on any new job, thanks to COBRA. Of course, since employer insurance payments are tax deductible and individual insurance payments are not, there is a net cost of moving from the current group onto COBRA coverage (the worker's tax rate times insurance costs). After the first 18 months, nongroup coverage must be priced, but for almost all nonelderly workers, such coverage should be available for no more than 50 percent higher than the current cost of group coverage.

The bounding approach suggests very modest costs of job lock. For example, suppose that current nongroup coverage for a family costs $6,000 per year, of which the employee is already paying $2,000. Suppose that a worker has a tax rate on wages of 35 percent (a 15 percent federal rate, 15 percent payroll tax rate, and 5 percent state rate). If the worker leaves a current job for another job at which he or she must purchase insurance, the net cost to the worker is the $1,400 in lost tax subsidy of the health insurance for 18 months and, at most, $4,400 per year thereafter (the loss of the tax subsidy plus the differential cost of the nongroup policy).

Today, roughly 50 million married workers are covered by health insurance on the job.[27] Suppose that each year, job lock accounts for a reduction in job mobility of 25 percent, or 4 percentage points, resulting in 2 million (50 million × 0.04) workers affected by job lock.[28] The maximum cost of job lock, in steady state, is therefore between $3 and $9 billion per year. These costs are between 0.03 percent and 0.09 percent of GDP, a fairly small cost relative to the $100 billion-plus price tag for any comprehensive reform to eliminate the problem of the uninsured in America.

Admittedly, this is a very crude calculation. First and foremost, it is, in theory, only an upper bound. Such an approach may be more useful for ruling out very large welfare losses than for putting an actual cost estimate on job lock. On the other hand, much of the welfare loss from job lock may be due to very-high-cost workers for whom nongroup insurance coverage is not available or for whom such coverage is more expensive than assumed above. If so, welfare losses due to job lock would be dramatically underestimated. Moreover, the lack of long-term health insurance contracts in the nongroup market, and the resulting variability in premiums over time, may mean that such coverage is not an attractive option, even if the immediate costs are modest relative to the higher wages that can be obtained on a new job. Finally, this approach continues to miss any spillover effects of improved productivity, implying that even this "upper bound" may be understated.

Approach D: Examining the Impacts of Loosening Job Lock

The fourth potential approach is to examine the impact on labor market outcomes of interventions that reduce job lock. Suppose an exogenous change suddenly removed the possibility of job lock for a worker or class of workers. If job lock has an important impact on productivity, one should see productivity rise when this change occurs. Moreover, this approach is the only one that holds out the possibility of including spillover.

An analysis in this spirit was carried out by Gruber and Madrian (1997). A clear example of an intervention that reduces job lock is the continuation of coverage mandate. Gruber and Madrian modeled workers' earnings upon reemployment as a function of whether continued coverage was available and examined whether such coverage improved subsequent job matches. They found that one year of available continued coverage *doubled* the reemployment earnings of those who took up that coverage.

This is an enormous estimate that needs to be confirmed.[29] In particular, these effects seem very large relative to the bounds established above. In the data used by Gruber and Madrian, typical reemployment earnings were roughly $15,000 per year. The implication is that offering insurance at the average group cost, even for only 18 months, gave unemployed workers more time to search for jobs, resulting in earnings that increased by $15,000. Extrapolating a gain of this magnitude to the 2 million job-locked married workers in the United States would cause earnings to rise by $30 billion. But this is an upper bound, because individuals who take continuation coverage are likely to be those who have the least access to an attractive nongroup product. In addition, $30 billion is not an enormous figure relative to the size of the economy.

Even this large estimate does not account for any spillover effects. As noted above, this approach holds out some hope of measuring spillover because it allows analysts to examine aggregate impacts of changes that reduce job lock. However, such an examination would require a substantial loosening of job lock for the aggregate impact to be detectable.

This approach may also be useful for looking at effects of job lock on labor supply, as Gruber and Madrian (1995) did in the case of retirement. They found that a year of continued coverage raised the retirement rate by 30 percent and then noted that the effect could be implicitly "dollarized" by comparing it with estimates of the impact of pension wealth on retirement. Doing so, they found that a year of continuation of coverage for an older worker has the same impact on retirement as $13,600 in pension wealth. They used data on the expected distribution of medical expenses to note that this large dollar value is not inconsistent with a relatively low aversion to risk, relative to most empirical estimates of this parameter, given the highly variable medical costs facing an older person who retires without insurance.

Conclusion

The past decade has witnessed the development of a large and exciting body of research on health insurance, labor supply, and job mobility. Of the more than 50 studies reviewed here, only one was written before 1990. As with any large body of research, few unanimous conclusions emerge. Yet relative to other areas of research, some fairly clear conclusions can be drawn from these studies:

- *Health insurance is quite important for retirement decisions.* The finding on which there is probably the greatest consensus is that health insurance is a key determinant of the decision to retire. This is not surprising, given the potentially high, variable medical costs of persons near the age of Medicare eligibility. The studies suggest that the availability of retiree health insurance raises the odds of retirement by 30 to 80 percent. This conclusion emerges consistently from very different approaches using very different data sets.
- *Health insurance is not very important to low-income mothers' decisions about whether or not to work.* While there is some debate over whether health insurance availability has a statistically significant impact on the labor supply of low-income mothers, the consensus is that such effects, if they exist, are not large.

- *Health insurance appears to be important for married women's decisions regarding whether or not to work.* The much smaller literature on health insurance and the labor supply of married women is remarkably consistent in its conclusion that health insurance is important. Confidence in this conclusion should be tempered by the fact the studies are relatively similar, and all suffer from the fact that the strategy used to identify the effect (an assumption that the husband's health insurance is exogenous) is contestable.
- *Alternative health insurance coverage is important for job mobility, implying that significant job lock exists.* There is truly a schism in the literature on job lock. With rare exceptions, studies that use alternative sources of coverage (mostly spousal insurance) as a proxy for the value of health insurance find sizable and significant estimates of job lock. Studies that use health spending as a proxy for the value of health insurance find little evidence of job lock. The former approach has much more to recommend it, given the endogeneity and faulty measurement of expected medical spending. Overall, there is strong evidence that job lock occurs.
- *Much work remains to be done on the implications of health insurance for welfare.* Empirical work has run way ahead of theory in this area, and nowhere is that more evident than in the lack of research on, or even lack of attention to, the overall implications of mobility for the economy. Four approaches to measuring the implications for welfare of job lock stemming from health insurance are presented in this chapter, but much more work needs to be done on each of them. To the extent that these approaches are useful, they suggest that the economic costs of job lock may be modest.

While the studies reviewed in this chapter have revealed a great deal about the effect of health insurance on labor supply and job mobility, they have revealed relatively little about the implications of these results. Clearly, this is where research needs to head in the next decade.

NOTES

Prepared for the Research Agenda Setting Conference held at the University of Michigan, July 8–10, 2001. We thank Catherine McLaughlin, Hilary Hoynes, Tom Buchmueller, and conference participants for helpful comments. Financial support from the Robert Wood Johnson Foundation is gratefully acknowledged.

1. See Gruber (2000) and Currie and Madrian (1999) for literature reviews.

2. This section draws heavily on the model developed in Gruber (2000).

3. See, for example, Diamond and Hausman (1984); Bazzoli (1985); Bound (1989); and Stern (1989). See also the recent review in Currie and Madrian (1999).

4. Unless employers are able to shift the higher insurance costs to older workers' wages. Sheiner (1999) suggests that this is indeed what happens. Even so, older workers may value employer-provided insurance particularly highly, for two reasons. First, the variance of medical expenditures grows with age, increasing the value of having insurance. Second, the differential cost of individual and group policies also grows with age, so that even if older workers are essentially paying for their health insurance through lower wages, they would rather have group coverage than face the individual insurance market.

5. This table summarizes tables 1–4 in Gruber and Madrian (1996). The medical expenditure statistics in the column labeled "65+" are restricted to persons age 65 to 74, corresponding to table 4 in Gruber and Madrian.

6. Presumably, retirees have already paid for the full cost of their health insurance through lower wages during their employment years. To date, the magnitude of this particular wage-health insurance trade-off has not been empirically estimated.

7. In fact, Medicare is much less generous than the typical employer-provided health insurance policy. As a result, the majority of Medicare recipients have some type of supplemental (Medigap) insurance, either through their former employers or purchased in the private market. The private market for this type of insurance is extensively regulated and is not in general plagued with the adverse selection problems typical of the private market for basic nongroup coverage.

8. Blau and Gilleskie (2001b) also find that the effects of employer-provided health insurance for both active and retired employees increase with age.

9. Because of the correlation between early retirement incentives and the availability of health insurance, the estimated effects of pensions on retirement in the extensive pension literature are also likely to be overstated.

10. Madrian (1994a) suggests that the extent of the bias generated by selection issues is probably mitigated by the fact that a substantial fraction of younger employees have no idea whether their employers offer retiree health insurance. Thus, the availability of retiree health insurance does not appear to be a factor in the employment decisions of many individuals when they accept a job, although it may become a factor in their retirement decisions later.

11. Continuation of coverage laws require employers to allow employees and their dependents to continue purchasing health insurance through the employers' health plan for a specified period of time after coverage would otherwise have ended (health insurance might end because of job change, a reduction in hours, or, in the case of a dependent, divorce). Minnesota was the first state to pass a continuation of coverage law, in 1974. Several states passed similar laws over the next decade. The federal government mandated this coverage at the national level in 1986 with a law now commonly referred

to as COBRA. See Gruber and Madrian (1995, 1996) for more detail on continuation of coverage laws.

12. Employee benefit data from the Bureau of Labor Statistics suggest that eligibility for retiree health insurance is contingent on pension eligibility for only 25 percent of those working in firms that provide retiree health insurance.

13. Wives are, on average, three years younger than their husbands (Madrian and Beaulieu, 1998).

14. Data limitations include lack of information on pension plan availability (Gruber and Madrian 1995, 1996; Karoly and Rogowski 1994; Madrian 1994a) or specific pension plan incentives (Blau and Gilleskie 2001a; French and Jones 2001; Rogowski and Karoly 2000); the lack or poor quality of measures of employer-provided or retiree health insurance (Gustman and Steinmeier 1994; Karoly and Rogowski 1994; Madrian 1994a; Rust and Phelan 1997); the restrictiveness of the sample (Lumsdaine, Stock, and Wise 1994; Rust and Phelan 1997); and the age of the data (Gustman and Steinmeier 1994; Rust and Phelan 1997).

15. French and Jones (2001) use data from waves I through IV.

16. See Ruhm (1990) and Peracchi and Welch (1994) for a more complete discussion of bridge jobs to retirement.

17. Lumsdaine, Stock, and Wise (1994); Headen, Clark, and Ghent (1997); Hurd and McGarry (1996); Blau and Gilleskie (2001a); Johnson, Davidoff, and Perese (1999); and Berger et al. (2000) are the notable exceptions.

18. This also suggests that estimates of the effect of AFDC on labor supply that do not recognize the colinearity of AFDC and Medicaid may overstate the effects of AFDC.

19. See Currie and Madrian (1999) for a survey of the extensive literature on health and labor supply.

20. See Meyer and Rosenbaum (2001) and Meyer and Rosenbaum (2000a) for additional evidence suggesting that the Medicaid expansions had little impact on the labor supply increases of single mothers over the past 15 years.

21. See Yelowitz (2000) for evidence on elderly SSI recipients; Yelowitz (1998a and 1998b) for evidence on disabled SSI recipients; and Yelowitz (1996) for evidence on receipt of food stamps.

22. Schone and Vistnes (2000) attempt to address the potential endogeneity of spousal health insurance coverage by instrumenting for its availability with characteristics of the husband's job (e.g., firm size, industry, and occupation). To the extent that husbands seek out jobs with health insurance, however, the job characteristics that make employers more likely to offer health insurance are simply the mechanism through which the health insurance endogeneity operates.

23. Holtz-Eakin (1994); Holtz-Eakin, Penrod, and Rosen (1996); and Spaulding (1997) all use PSID data to examine the impact of health insurance on job mobility.

24. From a policy perspective, these individuals should be of the greatest interest precisely because they do not have access to health insurance from multiple sources.

25. In particular, they find that controlling for tenure and pension availability substantially reduces the magnitude of the negative main effect of health insurance on job mobility and that the magnitude of this main effect becomes similar to the magnitude of the interaction effect of having health insurance through both one's own and a spouse's employer on increasing turnover.

26. We are grateful to Sherry Glied for suggesting this point to us.

27. Authors' tabulations from March 2000 CPS.

28. Madrian (1994b) reports that 16 percent of her sample changed jobs over an approximately 12-month period. A 25 percent reduction in mobility using this as a baseline implies a 4 percentage point decrease in turnover.

29. Gruber and Madrian (1997) do try to test this estimate internally, by showing, for example, that there is no effect on the earnings of those who do not separate.

REFERENCES

Anderson, Patricia M. 1997. "The Effect of Employer-Provided Health Insurance on Job Mobility: Job-Lock or Job-Push?" Unpublished paper, Dartmouth University.

Bazzoli, Gloria J. 1985. "The Early Retirement Decision: New Empirical Evidence on the Influence of Health." *Journal of Human Resources* 20(2): 214–34.

Bound, John. 1989. "The Health and Earnings of Rejected Disability Applicants." *American Economic Review* 79(3): 482–503.

Berger, Mark C. et al. 2000. "Spouse Health Insurance and the Retirement Decision." Unpublished paper, University of Kentucky.

Berger, Mark C., Dan A. Black, and Frank A. Scott. 2001. "Is There Job-Lock?" Unpublished paper, University of Kentucky.

Blank, Rebecca M. 1989. "The Effect of Medical Need and Medicaid on AFDC Participation." *Journal of Human Resources* 24(1): 54–87.

Blau, David M., and Donna B. Gilleskie. 2001a. "Health Insurance and Retirement of Married Couples." Unpublished paper, University of North Carolina.

———. 2001b. "Retiree Health Insurance and Labor Force Behavior of Older Men in the 1990s." *Review of Economics and Statistics* 83(1): 64–80.

Brown, James N., and Audrey Light. 1992. "Interpreting Panel Data on Job Tenure." *Journal of Labor Economics* 10(3): 219–57.

Brunetti, Michael A., Kamran Nayeri, Carlos E. Dobkin, and Henry E. Brady. 2000. "Health Status, Health Insurance, and Worker Mobility: A Study of Job Lock in California." Working Paper, UC DATA/Survey Research Center, University of California Berkeley.

Buchmueller, Thomas C., and Robert G. Valletta. 1996. "The Effects of Employer-Provided Health Insurance on Worker Mobility." *Industrial and Labor Relations Review* 49(3): 439–55.

———. 1999. "The Effect of Health Insurance on Married Female Labor Supply." *Journal of Human Resources* 34(1): 42–70.

Chou, Ying-Jeng, and Douglas Staiger. 2001. "Health Insurance and Female Labor Supply in Taiwan." *Journal of Health Economics* 20(2): 187–211.

Chou, Shin-Yi, and Jin-Tan Liu. 2000. "National Health Insurance and Female Labor Supply: Evidence from Taiwan." Unpublished paper, New Jersey Institute of Technology.

Congressional Research Service. 1988. *Costs and Effects of Extending Health Insurance Coverage.* Washington, DC: U.S. Government Printing Office.

Cooper, Philip F., and Alan C. Monheit. 1993. "Does Employment-Related Health Insurance Inhibit Job Mobility?" *Inquiry* 30(4): 400–416.

Currie, Janet M., and Jonathan Gruber. 1996a. "Saving Babies: The Efficacy and Cost of Recent Changes in the Medicaid Eligibility of Pregnant Women." *Journal of Political Economy* 104(6): 1263–96.

———. 1996b. "Health Insurance Eligibility, Utilization of Medicare Care, and Child Health." *Quarterly Journal of Economics* 111(2): 431–66.

Currie, Janet M., and Brigitte C. Madrian. 1999. "Health, Health Insurance, and the Labor Market." In *Handbook of Labor Economics,* vol. 3, edited by Orley Ashenfelter and David Card (3309–3416). Amsterdam: Elsevier Science.

Cutler, David M. 1994. "Market Failure in Small Group Health Insurance." NBER Working Paper No. 4879. Cambridge, MA: National Bureau of Economic Research.

Decker, Sandra L. 1993. "The Effect of Medicaid on Access to Health Care and Welfare Participation." PhD diss., Harvard University.

Dey, Matthew S. 2000. "Welfare and Mobility Effects of Employer-Provided Health Insurance." Unpublished paper, University of Chicago.

Diamond, Peter A., and Jerry A. Hausman. 1984. "The Retirement and Unemployment Behavior of Older Men." In *Retirement and Economic Behavior,* edited by Henry Aaron and Gary Burtless (97–134). Washington, DC: Brookings Institution.

Ellwood, David, and Kathleen Adams. 1990. "Medicaid Mysteries: Transitional Benefits, Medicaid Coverage, and Welfare Exits." *Health Care Financing Review, 1990 Annual Supplement,* 119–131. Washington, DC: U.S. Department of Health and Human Services.

Employee Benefit Research Institute. 1990. *Employee Benefit Notes, November 1990.* Washington, DC: Employee Benefit Research Institute.

———. 2000. *Sources of Health Insurance and Characteristics of the Uninsured.* Washington, DC: Employee Benefit Research Institute.

French, Eric, and John Bailey Jones. 2001. "The Effects of Health Insurance and Self-Insurance on Retirement Behavior." Unpublished paper, Federal Reserve Bank of Chicago.

Fronstin, Paul. 1996. *Sources of Health Insurance and Characteristics of the Uninsured.* EBRI Issue Brief No. 179. Washington, DC: Employee Benefit Research Institute.

Gilleskie, Donna B., and Brian Lutz. Forthcoming. "The Impact of Employer-Provided Health Insurance on Dynamic Employment Transitions." *Journal of Human Resources.*

Gruber, Jonathan. 1994. "The Incidence of Mandated Maternity Benefits." *American Economics Review* 84(3): 622–41.

———. 2000. "Health Insurance and the Labor Market." In *Handbook of Health Economics* vol. 1, edited by Anthony J. Culyer and Joseph P. Newhouse (645–706). Amsterdam: Elsevier Science.

Gruber, Jonathan, and Brigitte C. Madrian. 1994. "Health Insurance and Job Mobility: The Effects of Public Policy on Job-Lock." *Industrial and Labor Relations Review* 48(1): 86–102.

———. 1995. "Health Insurance Availability and the Retirement Decision." *American Economic Review* 85(4): 938–48.

———. 1996. "Health Insurance and Early Retirement: Evidence from the Availability of Continuation Coverage." In *Advances in the Economics of Aging,* edited by David A. Wise (115–143). Chicago: University of Chicago Press.

————. 1997. "Employment Separation and Health Insurance Coverage." *Journal of Public Economics* 66(3): 349–82.

Gustman, Alan L., and Thomas L. Steinmeier. 1994. "Employer-Provided Health Insurance and Retirement Behavior." *Industrial and Labor Relations Review* 48(1): 124–140.

Ham, Jon, and Lara Shore-Sheppard. 2000. "The Impact of Public Health Insurance on Labor Market Transitions." Unpublished paper, Ohio State University.

Hausman, Jerry A., Jason Abrevaya, and Fiona M. Scott-Morton. 1998. "Misclassification of the Dependent Variable in a Discrete-Response Setting." *Journal of Econometrics* 87(2): 239–69.

Headen, Jr., Alvin E., Robert L. Clark, and Linda Shumaker Ghent. 1997. "Effects of Retiree Health Insurance and Pension Coverage on the Retirement Timing of Older Workers: Sensitivity of Estimates." Unpublished paper, North Carolina State University.

Holtz-Eakin, Douglas. 1994. "Health Insurance Provision and Labor Market Efficiency in the United States and Germany." In *Social Protection Versus Economic Flexibility: Is There a Tradeoff?* edited by Rebecca M. Blank (157–187). Chicago: University of Chicago Press.

Holtz-Eakin, Douglas, John R. Penrod, and Harvey S. Rosen. 1996. "Health Insurance and the Supply of Entrepreneurs." *Journal of Public Economics* 62(1–2): 209–235.

Hurd, Michael, and Kathleen McGarry. 1996. "Prospective Retirement: Effects of Job Characteristics, Pensions, and Health Insurance." Unpublished paper, University of California at Los Angeles.

Johnson, Richard W., Amy J. Davidoff, and Kevin Perese. 1999. "Health Insurance Costs and Early Retirement Decisions." Unpublished paper, The Urban Institute, Washington DC.

Kapur, Kanika. 1998. "The Impact of Health on Job Mobility: A Measure of Job Lock." *Industrial and Labor Relations Review* 51(2): 282–97.

Karoly, Lynn A., and Jeannette A. Rogowski. 1994. "The Effect of Access to Post-Retirement Health Insurance on the Decision to Retire Early." *Industrial and Labor Relations Review* 48(1): 103–123.

Kremer, Michael. 1993. "The O-Ring Theory of Economic Development." *Quarterly Journal of Economics* 108(3): 551–76.

Lumsdaine, Robin L., James H. Stock, and David A. Wise. 1994. "Pension Plan Provisions and Retirement: Men and Women, Medicare, and Models." In *Studies in the Economics of Aging,* edited by David A. Wise (183–220). Chicago: University of Chicago Press.

Madrian, Brigitte C. 1994a. "The Effect of Health Insurance on Retirement." *Brookings Papers on Economic Activity* 1994(1): 181–232.

————. 1994b. "Employment-Based Health Insurance and Job Mobility: Is There Evidence of Job Lock?" *Quarterly Journal of Economics* 109(1): 27–54.

Madrian, Brigitte C., and Nancy D. Beaulieu. 1998. "Does Medicare Eligibility Affect Retirement?" In *Inquiries in the Economics of Aging,* edited by David A. Wise (109–131). Chicago: University of Chicago Press.

Madrian, Brigitte C., and Lars John Lefgren. 1998. "The Effect of Health Insurance on Transitions to Self Employment." Unpublished paper, University of Chicago.

McDonnell, Ken, and Paul Fronstin. 1999. *EBRI Health Databook.* Washington, DC: Employee Benefit Research Institute.

Meyer, Bruce D., and Dan T. Rosenbaum. 2001. "Welfare, The Earned Income Tax Credit, and the Labor Supply of Single Mothers." *Quarterly Journal of Economics* 116(3): 1063–1114.

———. 2000a. "Making Single Mothers Work: Recent Tax and Welfare Policy and Its Effect." *National Tax Journal* 53(4): 1027–61.

———. 2000b. "Medicaid, Private Health Insurance, and the Labor Supply of Single Mothers." Unpublished paper, Northwestern University.

Mitchell, Olivia S. 1982. "Fringe Benefits and Labor Mobility." *Journal of Human Resources* 17(2): 286–98.

Moffitt, Robert, and Barbara L. Wolfe. 1992. "The Effect of the Medicaid Program on Welfare Participation and Labor Supply." *Review of Economics and Statistics* 74(4): 615–26.

Monheit, Alan C., and Philip F. Cooper. 1994. "Health Insurance and Job Mobility: Theory and Evidence." *Industrial and Labor Relations Review* 48(1): 68–85.

Monheit, Alan C., Mark M. Hagan, Mark L. Berk, and Pamela J. Farley. 1985. "The Employed Uninsured and the Role of Public Policy." *Inquiry* 22(4): 348–64.

Montgomery, Edward, and John C. Navin. 2000. "Cross-State Variation in Medicaid Program and Female Labor Supply." *Economic Inquiry* 38(3): 402–18.

Olson, Craig A. 1998. "A Comparison of Parametric and Semiparametric Estimates of the Effect of Spousal Health Insurance Coverage on Weekly Hours Worked by Wives." *Journal of Applied Econometrics* 13(5): 543–65.

Penrod, John R. 1994. "Empirical Essays in the Economics of Labor and Health." PhD diss., Princeton University.

Peracchi, France, and Finis Welch. 1994. "Trends in Labor Force Transitions of Older Men and Women." *Journal of Labor Economics* 12(2): 210–42.

Perreira, Krista M. 1999. "Exits, Recidivism, and Caseload Growth: The Effect of Private Health Insurance Markets on the Demand for Medicaid." PhD diss., University of California Berkeley.

Rogowski, Jeannette A., and Lynn A. Karoly. 2000. "Health Insurance and Retirement Behavior: Evidence from the Health and Retirement Survey." *Journal of Health Economics* 19(4): 529–39.

Rosen, Sherwin. 1986. "The Theory of Equalizing Differences," in *Handbook of Labor Economics*, vol. 1, edited by Orley Ashenfelter and Richard Layard (641–92). Amsterdam: Elsevier Science.

Ruhm, Christopher J. 1990. "Bridge Jobs and Partial Retirement." *Journal of Labor Economics* 8(4): 482–501.

Rust, John, and Christopher Phelan. 1997. "How Social Security and Medicare Affect Retirement Behavior in a World of Incomplete Markets." *Econometrica* 65(4): 781–831.

Schone, Barbara Steinberg, and Jessica Primoff Vistnes. 2000. "The Relationship between Health Insurance and Labor Force Decisions: An Analysis of Married Women." Unpublished paper, Agency for Healthcare Research and Quality.

Sheiner, Louise. 1999. "Health Care Costs, Wages and Aging." Finance and Economics Discussion Series 99/19. Washington, DC: Board of Governors of the Federal Reserve System.

Slade, Eric P. 1997. "The Effect of the Propensity to Change Jobs on Estimates of 'Job-Lock.'" Unpublished paper, Johns Hopkins University.

Spaulding, James Wallace. 1997. "Fringe Benefits, Job Quality, and Labor Mobility: Pension and Health Insurance Effects on Job-Change Decisions." PhD diss., University of Wisconsin-Madison.

Stern, Steven. 1989. "Measuring the Effect of Disability on Labor Force Participation." *Journal of Human Resources* 24(3): 361–95.

Stroupe, Kevin T., Eleanor D. Kinney, and Thomas J. Kniesner. 2000. "Chronic Illness and Health Insurance-Related Job Lock." Center for Policy Research Working Paper No. 19. Syracuse, NY: Maxwell School of Citizenship and Public Affairs, Syracuse University.

Wellington, Allison J., and Deborah A. Cobb-Clark. 2000. "The Labor-Supply Effects of Universal Health Coverage: What Can We Learn from Individuals with Spousal Coverage?" In *Worker Well-Being: Research in Labor Economics,* vol. 19, edited by Simon W. Polachek. Amsterdam: Elsevier Science.

Winkler, Anne E. 1991. "The Incentive Effects of Medicaid on Women's Labor Supply." *Journal of Human Resources* 26(2): 308–37.

Wolfe, Barbara L., and Steven C. Hill. 1995. "The Effect of Health on the Work Effort of Single Mothers." *Journal of Human Resources* 30(1): 42–62.

Yazici, Esel Y. 1997. "Consequences of Medicaid Expansions on Three Outcomes: Demand for Private Insurance, Infant and Child Health, and Labor Supply." PhD diss., City University of New York.

Yelowitz, Aaron S. 1995. "The Medicaid Notch, Labor Supply and Welfare Participation: Evidence from Eligibility Expansions." *Quarterly Journal of Economics* 110(4): 909–40.

———. 1996. "Did Recent Medicaid Reforms Cause the Caseload Explosion in the Food Stamp Program?" UCLA Working Paper No. 756; IRP Discussion Paper 1109–96, University of California Los Angeles.

———. 1998a. "The Impact of Health Care Costs and Medicaid on SSI Participation." In *Growth in Disability Benefits: Explanation and Policy Implications,* edited by Kalman Rupp and David C. Stapleton. Kalamazoo, MI: W.E. Upjohn Institute for Employment Research.

———. 1998b. "Why Did the SSI-Disabled Program Grow So Much? Disentangling the Effect of Medicaid." *Journal of Health Economics* 17(3): 321–50.

———. 1998c. "Evaluating the Effects of Medicaid on Welfare and Work: Evidence from the Past Decade." Unpublished paper, University of California Los Angeles.

———. 2000. "Using the Medicare Buy-In Program to Estimate the Effect of Medicaid on the SSI Participation." *Economic Inquiry* 38(3): 419–41.

Table 3.A1. *Health Insurance and the Employment Decisions of Older Individuals*

Authors / data set / sample	*Labor force, health insurance, and health measures*	*Estimation technique*	*Results*
Madrian (1994a) NMES (1987) Men 55–84 not in the labor force SIPP (1984, 1985 and 1986 panels) Men 55–84 not in the labor force	LF: age of self-reported retirement (NMES), age last worked (SIPP) HI: retiree health insurance Hlth: none	1) truncated regression for age at retirement; 2) probit for retirement before age 65 (sample restricted to ages 70–84)	Retiree health insurance leads to retirement 14–18 mos. earlier in the NMES and 5–14 mos. earlier in the SIPP. Retiree health insurance increases the probability of retirement before age 65 by 15 percentage points in the NMES, and 6 to 7.5 percentage points in the SIPP.
Karoly and Rogowski (1994) SIPP (1984, 1986, 1988 panels) Men 55–62 employed during 1st wave	LF: permanent (6+ months) departure from the labor force HI: probability of retiree health insurance (imputed from firm size, industry, and region) Hlth: poor self-reported health status (0/1)	Probit for labor force departure	Retiree health insurance increases probability of retirement by 8 percentage points (47%); poor health increases probability of retirement by 15 percentage points (88%).

(continued)

Table 3.A1. *Continued*

Authors / data set / sample	*Labor force, health insurance, and health measures*	*Estimation technique*	*Results*
Gustman and Steinmeier (1994) RHS (1969–79) Men 58–63 in 1969 NMCES (1977)	LF: full-time work, full-time or partial retirement HI: value of health insurance provided by own employer and retiree health insurance (imputed from the NMCES) Hlth: none	Structural model of labor force participation (full-time work, full-time retirement, or partial retirement)	Retiree health insurance delays retirement until age of eligibility for retiree health insurance and accelerates it thereafter; overall retiree health insurance decreases retirement age by 3.9 months.
Lumsdaine, Stock, and Wise (1994) Proprietary data from a single large firm (1979–88) Men and women employed at the firm	LF: departure from the firm HI: value of health insurance provided by own employer, retiree health insurance (imputed as average firm cost), and Medicare (avg. per person Medicare expenditures) Hlth: none	Structural model of retirement (departure from the firm)	Value of Medicare has little effect on age at retirement.
Gruber and Madrian (1995) CPS March 1980–90 Men 55–64 worked in previous year SIPP 1984–87 panels Men 55–64 worked in 1st wave	LF: self-reported retirement (CPS), departure from the labor force (SIPP) HI: availability and months of continuation coverage Hlth: none	(1) probit for self-reported retirement (CPS); (2) hazard for labor force departure (SIPP)	1 year of continuation coverage increases the retirement hazard by 30 percent. There are no apparent differences by age, and the effects are similar in both the CPS and the SIPP.

Gruber and Madrian (1996) CPS MORG 1980–90 All men 55–64	LF: self-reported retirement, not in the labor force HI: availability and months of continuation coverage Hlth: none	Probit for self-reported retirement or being not in the labor force	1 year of continuation coverage increases the probability of self-reported retirement by 1.1 percentage points (5.4%) and the probability of being not in the labor force by 1.0 percentage points (2.8%).
Hurd and McGarry (1996) HRS (wave I) Men 51–61, women 46–61 Full-time, not self-employed	LF: self-reported probability of working full-time after age 62 and after age 65 HI: health insurance provided by own employer, retiree health insurance Hlth: self-reported health status, self-reported prospective mortality	Non-linear regression for probability of working full-time past age 62 or age 65	Health insurance provided by own employer increases probability of working past age 62 (but insignificant) and age 65 (5.3 percentage points). Retiree health insurance decreases probability of working past age 62 (5.3 percentage points); smaller impact on working past 65. Poor health or higher prospective mortality decreases probability of working past 62 or 65.

(continued)

Table 3.A1. *Continued*

Authors / data set / sample	*Labor force, health insurance, and health measures*	*Estimation technique*	*Results*
Rust and Phelan (1997) RHS (1969–79) Men 58–63 in 1969 without a pension	LF: employment status of full-time, part-time or not in the labor force HI: health insurance provided by own employer, private health insurance or retiree health insurance, Medicaid, not insured Hlth: self-reported health status	Structural dynamic programming model of labor supply	Private health insurance, retiree health insurance and Medicaid decrease full-time work by 10.0 percentage points (12%) at ages 58–59, 20.0 percentage points (29%) at ages 60–61, and 16.2 percentage points (25%) at ages 62–63. Poor health decreases full-time work by 4.4 percentage points (5.1%) at ages 60–61, 5.0 percentage points (6.3%) at ages 62–63.
Headen, Clark, and Ghent (1997) CPS August 1988 Men and women 55–64 either active workers or self-reported retirement	LF: categorical length of time retired (active worker, retired <2 yrs, 2–4 yrs, 5–9 yrs, 10+ yrs) HI: health insurance provided by own employer Hlth: covered by Medicare (proxy for disability status)	Ordered probit for length of time retired	Retiree health insurance increases the probability of being retired by 6 percentage points (30%), and the effect is stronger at younger ages. Medicare increases the probability of being retired by 48 percentage points (280%).

Madrian and Beaulieu (1998) U.S. Census (1980, 1990) Married men 55–69 who worked 1+ week in the previous calendar year	LF: not in the labor force HI: spouse is age-eligible for Medicare Hlth: none	Linear probability model for being not in labor force	The probability of retirement increases with the age of a man's spouse until the spouse becomes eligible for Medicare at age 65, after which it is constant.
Johnson, Davidoff, and Perese (1999) HRS (waves I and II) Men and women 51–61 and employed full-time in 1992	LF: transition out of full-time work HI: present discounted value until Medicare eligibility of premium differences between retiree health insurance and health insurance from own employer	Probit for transition out of full-time work between waves I and II	A 10% decrease in the health insurance cost of retirement increases the retirement hazard by 1.1–1.4% for men, and 1.4–1.9% for women. The reduction in the health insurance cost of retirement associated with retiree health insurance increases the retirement hazard by 25% for men and 28% for women.
Rogowski and Karoly (2000) HRS (waves I and II) Men 51–61 in 1992 employed full-time in 1992	LF: not in the labor force and self-reported retirement in wave II HI: health insurance provided by own employer; retiree health insurance, private health insurance Hlth: 2+ self-reported chronic conditions (0/1), body mass index, self-reported health status, activities of daily living impairments	Probit for retirement between waves I and II	Retiree health insurance increases the probability of retirement by 4.3 percentage points (62%). No significant interaction between retiree health insurance and health status. No significant impact of other types of health insurance.

(continued)

Table 3.A1. *Continued*

Authors / data set / sample	*Labor force, health insurance, and health measures*	*Estimation technique*	*Results*
Berger et al. (2000) HRS (waves I and II) Married couple families with both spouses under age 62 in 1992	LF: employment transition from wave I to II between the states: 1) neither spouse employed, 2) only husband employed, 3) only wife employed, 4) both spouses employed HI: health insurance provided by own employer, spouse has employer-provided health insurance, COBRA eligibility (approximated by firm size)	Multinomial logit for employment state transition probabilities between waves I and II	No significant effect of health insurance on transitions out of states (2) or (3) to any of the other states. If both spouses work in wave I, health insurance coverage by either spouse increases the probability of both spouses working in wave II by 5 percentage points, and decreases the probability that only the husband works in wave II by 3–5 percentage points. No significant effect of COBRA eligibility on any employment transitions.
Blau and Gilleskie (2001a) HRS (waves I and II) Men 51–61 in 1992	LF: employment transition from wave I to wave II (stay in same job, move to new job, exit labor force, or enter labor force)	Dynamic multinomial logit for employment transition between waves (model allows for unobserved heterogeneity and endogeneity of initial job characteristics)	Retiree health insurance decreases moves to a new job by 4.1–5.3 percentage points (50–65%); increases labor force departures by 2–6

Blau and Gilleskie (2001b)
HRS (waves I and II)
Married age-eligible couples with wife not older or 10+ years younger than husband and with valid data from Social Security earnings and Health Insurance and Pension Provider Survey supplements

LF: employment transition from wave I to wave II (stay in same job, move to new job, exit labor force, enter labor force, or remain not in the labor force)

HI: health insurance provided by own employer, spouse has employer-provided health insurance, own retiree health insurance, spouse has retiree health insurance

HI: health insurance provided by own employer, spouse has employer-provided health insurance, retiree health insurance

Hlth: Self-reported health status fair or poor (0/1)

Structural dynamic programming model of labor supply

percentage points (26–80%); and increases labor force entry by 1–3.3 percentage points (6–20%).
There is no differential impact on these transitions by health status. There is no effect of having a spouse with employer-provided health insurance on any employment transitions.
Continued health insurance availability after retirement results in a greater likelihood of retirement for both men and women, but the model substantially underpredicts the magnitudes actually observed in the data. No standard errors available to gauge significance of the results.

(continued)

Table 3.A1. *Continued*

Authors / data set / sample	*Labor force, health insurance, and health measures*	*Estimation technique*	*Results*
French and Jones (2001) HRS (waves I–IV) Men 51–69	LF: 1) labor force participation; 2) annual hours HI: Self-reported health costs for individuals with health insurance provided by their own employer, retiree health insurance, COBRA, private insurance, or no insurance at all	Structural dynamic programming model of labor supply	Little effect of health insurance on retirement.

Data set acronyms: CPS = Current Population Survey; CPS MORG = Current Population Survey Merged Outgoing Rotation Group; HRS = Health and Retirement Study; NMCES = National Medical Consumption and Expenditure Survey; NMES = National Medical Expenditure Survey; RHS = Retirement History Survey; SIPP = Survey of Income and Program Participation.

Table 3.A2. *Health Insurance and the Employment and Welfare Decisions of Single Mothers*

Authors / data set / sample	*Labor force, health insurance, and health measures*	*Estimation technique*	*Results*
Blank (1989) NMCUES (1980) Female heads of household with at least one child<21	LF: 1) hours per week; 2) AFDC participation HI: state-specific value of Medicaid for 1 adult + 3 child household Hlth: 1) Number of restricted activity days of head and of others in household, 2) activity limitation of head (0/1), 3) household avg. self-reported health status	Joint estimation of AFDC participation (probit), Medicaid participation (probit), and hours worked (Tobit)	Value of Medicaid has no impact on AFDC participation (effect on weekly hours and labor force participation not estimated). All health measures have negative impact on hours worked and positive impact on AFDC participation.
Ellwood and Adams (1990) Medicaid claims data for GA and CA (1980–86) Women receiving AFDC	LF: AFDC participation HI: expected medical expenses Hlth: none	AFDC exit as a function of future medical expenses predicted on the basis of medical usage in the previous six months	100% increase in expected medical costs lowers the AFDC exit probability by 6.5–11%.

(*continued*)

Table 3.A2. *Continued*

Authors / data set / sample	*Labor force, health insurance, and health measures*	*Estimation technique*	*Results*
Winkler (1991) CPS March (1986) Female heads of household 18–64 with at least one child <18	LF: 1) labor force participation; 2) annual hours; 3) AFDC participation HI: state-specific value of Medicaid for family of 3 Hlth: none	1) probit for labor force participation; 2) Heckman 2-step model for hours worked; 3) Tobit for hours worked; 4) probit for AFDC participation	A 10% increase in the value of Medicaid leads to a 1 percentage point decline in labor force participation but has no impact on annual hours or AFDC participation.
Moffitt and Wolfe (1992) SIPP (1984 panel, waves 3, 9) Female heads of household NMCUES (1980)	LF: 1) labor force participation; 2) AFDC participation HI: 1) family-specific value of expected medical expenditures if covered by Medicaid or private health insurance; 2) state-specific value of Medicaid Hlth: none	1) expected medical expenditures under Medicaid and private health insurance imputed from the NMCUES based on personal characteristics and self-reported health and disability status; 2) probit for labor force participation; 3) probit for AFDC participation	A $50/mo. increase in the value of Medicaid raises AFDC participation by 2.0 percentage points and decreases labor force participation by 5.5 percentage points. A $50/mo. increase in the value of private health insurance decreases AFDC participation by 5–7 percentage points and increases labor force participation by 12–16 percentage points. The state-specific value of Medicaid has no effect on AFDC or labor force participation.

Study	Variables	Method	Results
Decker (1993) State AFDC caseload data (1964–74) CPS (1966–72) Single female heads of household	LF (caseload data): state AFDC caseloads LF (CPS): 1) AFDC participation; 2) labor force participation HI: Medicaid availability Hlth: none	1) state AFDC caseloads; 2) individual AFDC participation	Caseload data: Medicaid introduction increased state AFDC caseloads by 21%. CPS: Medicaid introduction increased AFDC participation by 6.4 percentage points (21%); insignificant effect on labor force participation.
Yelowitz (1995) CPS March (1989–1992) Single women 18–55 with at least one child <15	LF: 1) labor force participation; 2) AFDC participation HI: extent to which Medicaid eligibility is independent of AFDC recipiency Hlth: none	1) probit for labor force participation; 2) probit for AFDC participation	Expansions in Medicaid eligibility increased labor force participation by 1 percentage point (1.4%) and decreased AFDC recipiency by 1.2 percentage points (3.5%).
Yelowitz (1996) SIPP (1987, 1988, 1990–1993 panels) Household heads 18–64	LF: food stamps receipt HI: child in household eligible for Medicaid (0/1) Hlth: none	Probit for food stamp participation	Making all households eligible for Medicaid would increase food stamp receipt by 0.6 percentage points (7.5%). Actual Medicaid expansions increased food stamp participation by 0.2 percentage points (about 10% of the growth in food stamp participation observed in the data).

(continued)

Table 3.A2. *Continued*

Authors / data set / sample	*Labor force, health insurance, and health measures*	*Estimation technique*	*Results*
Yazici (1997) NLSY (1989, 1992) Single women with at least one child <18 in 1989	LF: 1) labor force participation in last week; 2) labor force participation in last year; 3) AFDC participation in last month; 4) AFDC participation in last year; 5) hours worked in last week HI: difference between AFDC and Medicaid income thresholds Hlth: none	1) logit for labor force participation; 2) logit for AFDC participation; 3) ordinary least squares for labor force participation; 4) ordinary least squares for AFDC participation; 5) fixed effect logit for labor force participation; 6) fixed effect logit for AFDC participation; 7) difference-in-difference estimates for mean changes in labor force participation, AFDC participation, and hours worked for treatment vs. control groups in 1989 and 1992	No significant effect of expansions in Medicaid eligibility on labor force participation, AFDC participation, or hours worked except in the logit regression for labor force participation.

Yelowitz (1998a, b) CPS (1988–94) Individuals 18–64	LF: SSI participation HI: state Medicaid spending per disabled SSI recipient, and per blind SSI recipient Hlth: work limitation	1) linear probability model for SSI participation as a function of Medicaid spending for disabled SSI recipients; 2) two-stage least squares for SSI participation using Medicaid spending per blind SSI recipient to instrument for Medicaid spending per disabled recipient	The value of Medicaid increases SSI participation by 0.1 percentage points and explains 20% of the increase in SSI participation over the period studied.
Perreira (1999) California Work Pays Demonstration Project (1987–95) Individuals/families with children enrolled in Medicaid in 1987 or who enroll in 1988–95	LF: Medicaid participation HI: 1) fraction of county population covered by employer-provided health insurance; 2) fraction of county population earning <200% of poverty and covered by employer-provided health insurance Hlth: none	Hazard for months until Medicaid spell ends	A 2.5 percentage point (5%) increase in the availability of employer-provided health insurance decreases median Medicaid spell length by 3–11 months (10–37%).

(continued)

Table 3.A2. *Continued*

Authors / data set / sample	*Labor force, health insurance, and health measures*	*Estimation technique*	*Results*
Montgomery and Navin (2000) CPS March (1988–93) Single women 18–65 with at least one child <15	LF: 1) labor force participation; 2) hours per week HI: state Medicaid spending 1) per recipient, 2) per adult recipient, 3) per child recipient, 4) per scaled family Hlth: none	1) probit for labor force participation; 2) ordinary least squares for hours (with a Heckman correction for participation); 3) include state fixed effects; 4) include state random effects	A 10% increase in the value of Medicaid w/o fixed effects, random effects or instrumental variables leads to a 0.36 percentage point decrease in labor force participation (0.6%) and an increase in weekly hours of 0.04 to 0.10 hours (0.11 to 0.25%). With state random effects the effect on labor force participation is substantially reduced and there is no effect on hours. With state fixed effects, there is no effect on labor force participation or weekly hours.

Ham and Shore-Sheppard (2000) SIPP (1987–88 and 1990–93 panels) Single mothers 18–55	LF: 1) employed; 2) duration of employment spells; 3) duration of non-employment spells HI: 1) Medicaid income limit for youngest child; 2) fraction of children age-eligible for Medicaid Hlth: none	1) probit for employment; 2) hazard for duration of employment spells; 3) hazard for duration of non-employment spells	Medicaid expansions shorten non-employment and welfare spells, with stronger effects for the long-term non-employed and long-term welfare recipients. Little evidence that Medicaid affects the duration of employment or non-welfare spells.
Yelowitz (2000) CPS (1988–93) Individuals 66–75	LF: SSI participation HI: Qualified Medicare beneficiary eligibility and generosity Hlth: none	Ordinary least squares linear probability model for SSI participation	Expansions in the Qualified Medicare Beneficiary program led to a 1.7 percentage point (45%) reduction in SSI participation.
Meyer and Rosenbaum (2000a) CPS March (1968–1996) CPS MORG (1984–1996) Single women 19–44	LF (March): worked last year LF (MORG): worked last week HI: number of people covered by Medicaid if employed Hlth: none	Mean differences in the employment rates of single women in states with large expansions in Medicaid coverage relative to states with only small expansions in Medicaid coverage	Over the entire 1984–96 period, employment rates for single women increased more in states with large Medicaid expansions, but the timing of the employment increases does not correspond well with the timing of the Medicaid expansions.

(continued)

Table 3.A2. *Continued*

Authors / data set / sample	*Labor force, health insurance, and health measures*	*Estimation technique*	*Results*
Meyer and Rosenbaum (2000b) CPS March and MORG (1984–96) Single women 19–44	LF (March): worked last year LF (MORG): worked last week HI: 1) number of people covered by Medicaid if employed; 2) value of employer-provided health insurance if employed; 3) cost of employer-provided health insurance if employed; 4) extent of small-group health insurance reforms in a state; 5) availability and generosity of state medically needy programs; 6) extent to which Medicaid eligibility is independent of AFDC eligibility Hlth: none	1) mean differences in the employment rates of single women in states with large expansions in Medicaid coverage relative to states with only small expansions in Medicaid coverage; 2) structural model of labor force participation	1) Medicaid expansions and small-group health reforms had little effect on the employment of single mothers; 2) higher employee costs for employer-provided health insurance decrease employment of single mothers; 3) lower employer-provided health insurance coverage rates and medically needy programs slightly increase the employment of single mothers.

Meyer and Rosenbaum (2001) CPS March and MORG (1984–96) Single women 19–44	LF (March): 1) worked last year; 2) annual hours LF (MORG): 1) worked last week; 2) hours per week HI: family-specific expected value of Medicaid at different levels of income Hlth: none	1) structural model of labor force participation; 2) Tobit for hours worked; 3) ordinary least squares for hours worked conditional on labor force participation	Medicaid has no statistically significant effect on labor force participation or hours per week, and a small statistically significant effect on annual hours.

Data set acronyms: CPS = Current Population Survey; CPS MORG = Current Population Survey Merged Outgoing Rotation Group; NLSY = National Longitudinal Survey of Youth; NMCUES = National Medical Care Utilization and Expenditure Survey; SIPP = Survey of Income and Program Participation.

Table 3.A3. *Health Insurance and the Employment Decisions of Men and Married Women*

Authors / data set / sample	Labor force, health insurance, and health measures	Estimation technique	Results
Gruber and Madrian (1997) SIPP (1984–88 panels) Men 25–54 employed in 1st wave	LF: 1) transition from employment to not in the labor force; 2) weeks not in the labor force; 3) earnings HI: 1) health insurance provided by own employer; 2) continuation coverage Hlth: none	1) probit for transition from employment to not in the labor force; 2) ordinary least squares for weeks not in the labor force; 3) ordinary least squares for reemployment earnings	Continuation coverage increases the transition from employment to not in the labor force by 15%, increases time spent not in the labor force by 15%, and increases reemployment earnings by 22%.
Olson (1998) CPS March (1993) Married women <64 in single-family households	LF: 1) labor force participation; 2) hours per week (full-time vs. part-time) HI: health insurance provided by own employer, spouse has employer-provided health insurance Hlth: none	1) probit for labor force participation; 2) ordered probit for being not in the labor force, part-time and full-time work; 3) Tobit for labor force participation and hours per week; 4) semi-parametric analysis of hours per week and labor force participation	Ordered probit: having a spouse with health insurance reduces labor force participation by 10–11 percentage points, increases part-time work by 2 percentage points, and decreases full-time work by 13 percentage points. Tobit: having a spouse with health insurance reduces labor force participation by 7 percentage points and weekly hours by 5.3 hours. Semiparametric: having a spouse with health insurance reduces labor force participation by 7 percentage points and weekly hours by 4.5 hours.

Buchmueller and Valletta (1999) CPS April EBS (1993) Married women 25–54 not self-employed	LF: 1) labor force participation; 2) hours per week; 3) job offers health insurance HI: spouse has employer-provided health insurance, spouse is offered employer-provided health insurance, health insurance provided by own employer Hlth: none	1) probit for labor force participation; 2) Tobit for labor force participation and hours worked; 3) multi-nomial logit for being not in the labor force and hours worked in combination with whether or not job offers health insurance	Having a spouse with insurance reduces labor force participation by 6–12% (probit) and reduces weekly hours by 15–36% (Tobit). Multinomial logit: having a spouse with insurance reduces the probability of full-time work with own employer-provided health insurance by 8.5–12.8 percentage points, increases the probability of full-time work w/o own employer-provided health insurance by 4.4–7.8 percentage points, and increases the probability of part-time work by about 3 percentage points.

(*continued*)

Table 3.A3. *Continued*

Authors / data set / sample	*Labor force, health insurance, and health measures*	*Estimation technique*	*Results*
Schone and Vistnes (2000) NMES (1987) Married women 21–55 with employed husband 21–55	LF: 1) labor force participation; 2) hours per week (full-time vs. part-time) HI: health insurance provided by own employer, spouse has employer-provided health insurance Hlth: 1) chronic conditions indicators; 2) self-reported health status; 3) pregnancy	1) probit for whether husband is employed in a job offering health insurance; 2) simultaneous full information maximum likelihood estimation of an ordered probit for wives' labor supply (full-time, part-time, or not in the labor force) and a probit for having a job that offers health insurance. The predicted probability of whether husband has health insurance from (1) is used to instrument for whether husband has health insurance; 3) multinomial logit instead of ordered probit for wives' labor supply in model (2) above.	Having a spouse with health insurance reduces labor force participation by 10.3 percentage points, reduces full-time work by 13.8 percentage points, increases part-time work by 1.6 percentage points, and reduces work in a job with health insurance by 15.1 percentage points.

Wellington and Cobb-Clark (2000)
CPS March (1993)
Married couple households with both husband and wife 24–62 and not covered by CHAMPUS, Medicare, or Medicaid

LF: 1) labor force participation; 2) annual hours
HI: spouse has employer-provided health insurance
Hlth: none

1) bivariate probit for husbands' and wives' labor force participation; 2) ordinary least squares for hours (two-stage and three-stage least squares estimated with similar results and not reported)

Having a spouse with employer-provided health insurance reduces labor force participation by 19.5 percentage points (23%) for both white and black women; reduces labor force participation by 4.1 percentage points (4%) for white men and by 9.1 percentage points (10%) for black men. Having a spouse with employer-provided health insurance reduces annual hours by 17% for white women, 8% for black women, 4% for white men, and has no effect for black men.

(continued)

Table 3.A3. *Continued*

Authors / data set / sample	*Labor force, health insurance, and health measures*	*Estimation technique*	*Results*
Chou and Liu (2000) Taiwan Human Resource Utilization Survey (1990–1997) Married women 20–54 with husbands employed in the public or private sector	LF: 1) not in the labor force, part-time or full-time employment; 2) hours per week HI: availability of non-employment-based health insurance Hlth: none	1) Tobit for hours per week; 2) symmetrically trimmed least squares Tobit for hours per week; 3) multinomial logit for being not in the labor force, part-time work, and full-time work	For married women, the introduction of national health insurance in Taiwan significantly reduced labor force participation by 3% and working hours by 12–14%.
Chou and Staiger (2001) Taiwan Survey of Family Income and Expenditure (1979–85 and 1991–95) Married women	LF: labor force participation HI: availability of non-employment-based health insurance Hlth: none	Probit for labor force participation	The availability of non-employment-based health insurance reduces labor force participation by 2.5 to 6.0 percentage points; effects are larger for wives of less-educated husbands.

Data set acronyms: CPS = Current Population Survey; NMES = National Medical Expenditure Survey; SIPP = Survey of Income and Program Participation.

Table 3.A4. *Health Insurance and Job Choice*

Authors / *data set* / *sample*	*Labor force, health insurance, and health measures*	*Estimation technique*	*Results*
Mitchell (1982) QES (1973, 1977)	LF: voluntary job change, job departure HI: health insurance provided by own employer Hlth: none	Probit for job change and job departure	No significant effect of health insurance on job change or job departure
Cooper and Monheit (1993) NMES (1987) Wage earners 25–54 not covered by governmental health insurance	LF: voluntary job change HI: health insurance provided by own employer, spouse has employer-provided health insurance, private health insurance Hlth: recoding of self-reported chronic conditions to reflect whether they would lead to denial of health insurance coverage, exclusion of coverage for those conditions, or higher premiums	Four-step procedure: 1) estimate reduced form job change probit and calculate inverse Mill's ratio; 2) estimate change in wages and health insurance as a function of turnover (including Mill's ratio); 3) compute difference between actual and predicted wages and health insurance associated with job change; 4) include these variables in a probit for job change	The lack of portability of employer-provided health insurance reduces turnover by 25% for married women, 38% for married men, 29% for single men, and 30% for single women. Being likely to gain health insurance as a result of turnover increases turnover by 28–52%; being likely to lose health insurance as a result of turnover reduces turnover by 23–39%. The effect of health conditions on turnover varies in sign and significance with condition. (*continued*)

Table 3.A4. *Continued*

Authors / data set / sample	*Labor force, health insurance, and health measures*	*Estimation technique*	*Results*
Madrian (1994b) NMES (1987) Married men 20–55 employed but not self-employed at first interview	LF: voluntary job departure HI: health insurance provided by own employer, spouse has employer-provided health insurance, private health insurance Hlth: pregnancy	1) probit for job departure; 2) random effects probit for job departure	The lack of portability of employer-provided health insurance reduces turnover by 25–30% when identified from whether a spouse has employer-provided health insurance, by 32–54% when identified from family size, and by 30–71% when identified from pregnancy; these magnitudes correspond to expected medical expenses for each group.
Gruber and Madrian (1994) SIPP (1984–87 Panels) Men 20–54 not self-employed	LF: job departure HI: health insurance provided by own employer, availability and months of continuation coverage Hlth: none	Probit for job departure	One year of continuation coverage increases job turnover by 10%.

Holtz-Eakin (1994)
PSID (1984–87)
Men and women 25–54
  employed full-time in 1984
GSOEP (1985–87)
Not specified (presumably
  similar to PSID)

LF: 1-year and 3-year job
  change
HI (PSID): health insurance
  provided by own employer,
  spouse has employer-
  provided health insurance
HI (GSOEP): health insurance
  premium likely to increase
  with job change
Hlth (PSID): 1) self-reported
  health status in 1984, 2) self-
  reported health status in
  1986 (future health), 3)
  change in self-reported
  health status from 1982–84
  (worse health), 4) work
  limitation (0/1)

Probit for job change

PSID: No effect of employer-
  provided health insurance on
  job turnover. GSOEP: Some
  estimates are significant and
  suggest that health insurance
  does reduce turnover, but
  results are sensitive to the
  definition of whether the
  health insurance premium is
  likely to increase and are not
  consistent across various
  samples (married men, single
  men, single women); paper
  only presents probit
  coefficients (no marginal
  probabilities calculated).

Penrod (1994)
SIPP (1984) panels 3–9
Men 24–55 who are employed
  but not self-employed
NMCUES (1980)

LF: voluntary job departure
HI: health insurance provided
  by own employer, spouse has
  employer-provided health
  insurance
Hlth: 1) self-reported health
  status; 2) predicted
  medical care expenditures;
  3) pregnancy; 4) medical care
  utilization; 5) disability status

Probit for job departure

Little evidence supporting an
  effect of health insurance on
  job departure.

(continued)

Table 3.A4. *Continued*

Authors / data set / sample	Labor force, health insurance, and health measures	Estimation technique	Results
Buchmueller and Valletta (1996) SIPP (1984 panel) Individuals 25–54 employed but not self-employed in August 1984	LF: 1-year job change HI: health insurance provided by own employer, spouse has employer-provided health insurance Hlth: none	1) probit for job change; 2) jointly endogenous probit for job change in dual-earner couples (estimate reduced form job change probit for husbands and wives and generate fitted job change probabilities; then include fitted probability for spouse's job change in job turnover probit)	Own employer-provided health insurance reduces turnover by 35–59% for married men, 37–53% for married women, 18–33% for single men, and 35% for single women. Among those with own employer-provided health insurance, having a spouse with health insurance increases turnover by 26–31% for married men and 34–38% for married women. Endogenous probit estimates are of similar magnitude but slightly reduced significance. In general, estimated magnitudes are stable but statistical significance varies.

Holtz-Eakin, Penrod, and Rosen (1996) SIPP (1984, 1986, and 1987 panels waves 3–6; 1985 panel waves 5–8) Individuals 16–62 PSID (1984–86) Individuals 16–62 working 5+ hours/week	LF: one-year (SIPP) and two-year (PSID) transitions from employment to self-employment HI (SIPP and PSID): health insurance provided by own employer, spouse has employer-provided health insurance, months of continuation coverage Hlth (SIPP): 1) disabled child (0/1); 2) hospital nights and doctor visits in last 4 mos. and last 12 mos.; 3) predicted medical expenditures Hlth (PSID): self-reported health status	Logit for transition from employment to self-employment.	No significant impact of health insurance on job-to-self-employment transitions in either the SIPP or the PSID using a variety of measures for the value of maintaining one's own employer-provided health insurance.
Anderson (1997) NLSY (1979+) Non self-employment jobs held by men and women older than 20	LF: job duration, job departure HI: health insurance provided by own employer, other health insurance Hlth: 1) pregnancy; 2) work limitation	1) proportional hazard for job departure; 2) probit for job departure	Own employer-provided health insurance reduces job mobility for those for whom losing coverage would be costly; the lack of own employer-provided health insurance increases mobility for those who would benefit most by attaining it. *(continued)*

Table 3.A4. *Continued*

Authors / data set / sample	Labor force, health insurance, and health measures	Estimation technique	Results
Spaulding (1997) PSID (1984–1985) Men and women 25–54 working full-time in 1984 (1,000+ hours)	LF: voluntary job departure HI: health insurance provided by own employer, spouse has employer-provided health insurance Hlth: none	Probit for voluntary job departure	No significant impact of health insurance on job departures.
Slade (1997) NLSY (1979–1992) Continuously employed men and women who were interviewed at least eight times after reaching age 21	LF: job change HI: 1) health insurance provided by own employer; 2) state private health insurance coverage rate; 3) state hospital room charge rate Hlth: illness-related work absence	1) Probit for job change; 2) probit for health insurance coverage; 3) discrete factor probit model for job departure and health insurance coverage with correlated errors; 4) fixed effect probit for job change	Individuals who change jobs frequently are less likely to be employed in jobs with health insurance. Effect of health insurance availability and demand for health insurance on job changes is sensitive to empirical specification.
Kapur (1998) NMES (1987)	LF: voluntary job departure HI: health insurance provided by own employer, spouse has employer-provided health insurance	Probit for voluntary job departure	No significant or substantive impact of health insurance on job departure.

Married men 20–55 employed but not self-employed at first interview and not laid off during the sample year	Hlth: 1) number of chronic medical conditions in family; 2) cost-weighted medical conditions index; 3) health utilization index		
Madrian and Lefgren (1998) SIPP (1984–88 and 1990–93 panels) CPS (March 1983–1997) Men and women 20–64	LF (SIPP): 1-year and 2-year transitions from employment to self-employment LF (CPS): 1-year transition from employment to self-employment HI: 1) health insurance provided by own employer; 2) spouse has employer-provided health insurance; 3) months of continuation coverage Hlth: none	Linear probability model for transition from employment to self-employment	Having own employer-provided health insurance reduces the probability of a transition from employment to self-employment for men and women when identified from whether a spouse has employer-provided health insurance; for women when identified from family size; and for men when identified from continuation coverage.

(continued)

Table 3.A4. *Continued*

Authors / data set / sample	*Labor force, health insurance, and health measures*	*Estimation technique*	*Results*
Brunetti et al. (2000) CWHS (1998–99) Individuals working in both 1998 and 1999 CPS (March 1997 and 1998) Individuals working in both 1997 and 1998	LF (CWHS): job change LF (CPS): 1) change in industry; 2) change in occupation; 3) change in both industry and occupation HI: health insurance provided by own employer, other health insurance Hlth (CWHS): 1) health status index; 2) self-reported health status; 3) diagnoses of chronic or acute conditions; 4) activity limitations Hlth (CPS): 1) self-reported health status; 2) work limitation	Logit for job change on having health insurance provided by own employer, health measures and an interaction between the two (in the CWHS, the health measures include a health status index derived from regressing subjective health measures on objective measures of health)	Using the CWHS, no significant impact of own employer-provided health insurance on job departure. Using the CPS, no significant impact of own employer-provided health insurance on industry and/or occupation change when identified from self-reported health status. Significant negative impact of own employer-provided health insurance on industry and/or occupation change when identified from work-limiting disabilities.

Stroupe, Kinney, and Kniesner (2000) Robert Wood Johnson Barriers to Insurance Survey (1994) Respondents <65 and employed at some time during 1984–94	LF: job duration HI: health insurance provided by own employer Hlth: health conditions	Hazard model for job duration	For individuals confronting a chronic illness (their own or a child's), own employer-provided health insurance reduces the probability of a voluntary job departure by 41% for men and by 39% for women.
Dey (2000) SIPP (1990–1993 panels) High school educated men 22–55 either initially unemployed or who became unemployed during survey panel	LF: job duration, job change, unemployment HI: health insurance provided by own employer Hlth: none	Structural model of employment and job duration	Own employer-provided health insurance reduces job turnover by 2–8% for individuals with a high demand for health insurance, and by 10–16% for individuals with a low demand. Employer-provided health insurance also increases mobility for those with health insurance.

(continued)

Table 3.A4. *Continued*

Authors / data set / sample	*Labor force, health insurance, and health measures*	*Estimation technique*	*Results*
Berger, Black and Scott (2001) SIPP (1987, 1990 panels) Employed individuals 18+ at the beginning of each panel	LF: job duration HI: health insurance provided by own employer, spouse has employer-provided health insurance with family coverage Hlth: 1) work limitation; 2) functional limitations; 3) activities of daily living limitations; 4) health conditions; 5) self-reported health status; 6) inpatient hospital utilization	Hazard model for job duration	Own employer-provided health insurance increases job duration if identification is based on availability of health insurance from a spouse or family size. No significant effect of own employer-provided health insurance on job duration if identification is based on health conditions or health conditions interacted with availability of health insurance from a spouse.

| **Gilleskie and Lutz** (forthcoming)
NLSY (1989–1993)
Men not in school, the armed forces, or self-employed | LF: employment transitions (stay in same job, move to new job, or exit the labor force)
HI: employer offers health insurance, individual covered by own employer-provided health insurance, individual covered by other health insurance
Hlth: 1) disability; 2) health limitation; 3) body mass index | 1) multinomial logit for employment transitions; 2) dynamic multinomial logit for employment transitions allowing for unobserved heterogeneity and endogeneity of initial job and individual characteristics | Having own employer-provided health insurance has no significant or substantive impact on moving to a new job for married men; it reduces the likelihood of moving to a new job by 10–15% for single men. |

Data set acronyms: CPS = Current Population Survey; CWHS = California Work and Health Survey; GSOEP = German Socio-Economic Panel Survey; NLSY = National Longitudinal Survey of Youth; NMCUES = National Medical Care Utilization and Expenditure Survey; NMES = National Medical Expenditure Survey; PSID = Panel Study on Income Dynamics; QES = Quality of Employment Survey; SIPP = Survey of Income and Program Participation.

4

What Do We Really Know about Whether Health Insurance Affects Health?

Helen Levy and David Meltzer

Almost 18 percent of nonelderly Americans—approximately 43 million people—lacked health insurance during 1999 (AHRQ 2000). The uninsured are the focus of policy concern primarily because health insurance is believed to contribute to better health by improving access to medical care. Literally hundreds of studies have documented the fact that the uninsured have worse health outcomes than the insured, and these studies form an important part of the case for expanding health insurance coverage in the United States.

Very few of the studies establish a *causal* relationship between health insurance and health, however. Causation is difficult to establish because one almost never observes truly random variation in health insurance status. People who have health insurance and people who do not almost certainly differ in many ways besides their health insurance coverage. Moreover, the causal relationship between health insurance and health is likely to run in both directions: that is, at the same time that insurance affects health, health status determines insurance coverage. This makes it difficult to determine whether a correlation between health insurance and health status reflects the effect of health insurance on health, the effect of health on health insurance, or the effect of some other attribute, such as socioeconomic status, on both health insurance and health status.

This chapter reviews the evidence on the causal effect of insurance on health—what we really know about whether health insurance affects health. In doing so, it distinguishes between observational studies, which do not account for the problems identified above, and experimental or quasi-experimental studies, in which health insurance coverage varies randomly, minimizing those problems. As discussed in more detail below, it is generally not possible to make any causal inference about the effect of health insurance on health from observational studies. Therefore most of the chapter is devoted to reviewing the findings of experimental and quasi-experimental studies, which do provide evidence on the nature of the causal relationship.

Three other obstacles to answering the question posed in the title are worth mentioning, although this review does not focus on them. The first is that health insurance is a complex, multidimensional good. A generous indemnity policy with first-dollar coverage and a bare-bones catastrophic coverage policy are not likely to have the same effect on health.[1] A precise answer to the question "What is the impact of health insurance on health?" would require a much more complete specification of what is meant by health insurance, as well as a careful enumeration of other relevant factors, such as income. For example, is health insurance provided as a public benefit funded by a payroll tax? Or is the purchase of private health insurance simply mandated for all individuals? These are very different scenarios and their implications for health may be very different. Since this review of the literature focuses on experimental and quasi-experimental studies, one can draw causal inferences about the impact of health insurance on health from a limited range of situations, such as the expansion of Medicaid eligibility in the 1980s and early 1990s. One's ability to extrapolate from this expansion to the hypothetical effects of a different kind of insurance expansion, such as a Medicare buy-in for individuals age 55 to 64, is limited.

Second, health itself is a complex, multidimensional construct, and our ability to measure it is imperfect. In practice, the measures of health used in most studies may not be very powerful in that they may fail to detect significant changes in true, underlying health. Mortality rates, for example, are a blunt instrument for measuring health; studies that rely on these rates (as many do) may not capture health-related changes in quality of life that are quite important. The less powerful one's measures of health, the more cautious one must be in interpreting results that find no effect of health insurance on health.

Third, the most plausible pathway through which health insurance may exert a causal effect on health is improved access to medical care:

having health insurance increases the quality and quantity of medical care, which in turn improves health. Since the impact of health insurance on health depends on an intermediate factor, medical care, focusing on health insurance and health without considering medical care allows one to say, at most, *whether* there is any causal link between health insurance and health. If studies find no effect of health insurance on health, it may be because health insurance does not in fact affect access to medical care, or because medical care has no measurable effect on health, or both. Therefore analysis of the causal effect of health insurance on health is only a starting point that leaves many interesting questions, such as the causal effect of medical care on health, unanswered.

Any one of these three issues could be the subject of a lengthy discussion, and all are certainly relevant to the question at hand. This chapter focuses instead on the endogeneity of health insurance. By endogeneity, we mean the fact that health insurance is likely to be correlated with other factors that may also determine health that have been left out of the model, so that any observed relationship between health insurance and health may in fact not be causal but instead be due to the effect of these omitted factors on health. This is among the least carefully considered and potentially most important issues to be addressed in reviewing the evidence on whether health insurance affects health. A critical review of the literature suggests that when one considers only studies that convincingly address the endogeneity of health insurance, the bulk of the evidence points to a small, positive effect of insurance coverage on health outcomes among the populations most likely to be the targets of public coverage expansions: infants, the elderly, and the poor. There is also evidence to suggest that in some cases, expansions in health insurance may not result in measurable improvements in health.

The discussion proceeds as follows. First, a basic framework for thinking about the links between health, health insurance, medical care, and other relevant factors is presented. The framework highlights the endogeneity of health insurance. Second, studies are classified with respect to how they approach the problem created by the endogeneity of health insurance. Observational studies, which make up most of the literature on health insurance and health, either ignore the endogeneity of insurance status or address it by controlling for observable differences between people with and without coverage. Quasi-experimental studies, a much smaller group, rely on naturally occurring situations in which variation in health insurance coverage is plausibly exogenous: for example, changes in public policies that result in changes in insurance coverage. Only one truly randomized experimental study examines the effects of health insurance on health, the RAND Health Insurance Experiment.

The next three sections discuss each of the three classes of studies, and the last section summarizes the lessons drawn from the review.

Understanding the Relationship between Insurance and Health

Health depends not only on medical care but also on a host of other factors, such as stress, income, behavior, beliefs about the effectiveness of Western medicine, and genetic predisposition to disease. Factors such as income and beliefs about Western medicine also affect whether or not an individual has insurance coverage, which in turn affects access to medical care. The state of one's health affects consumption of medical care, since individuals in poor health are more likely to seek care. Figure 4.1 presents a

Figure 4.1. *Factors Affecting Health Insurance Coverage*

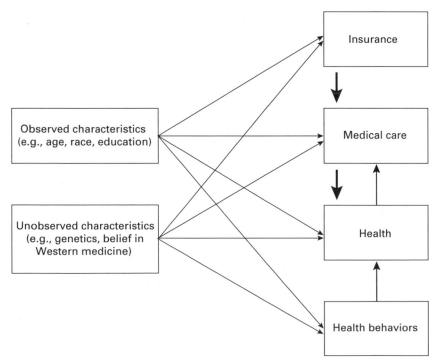

stylized diagram of the many relationships that exist between health, insurance, medical care, and other factors, which may or may not be observable.[2]

Identifying the *causal* impact of health insurance on health is complicated by the fact that health insurance is not usually assigned at random to individuals.[3] Instead, as figure 4.1 shows, coverage is directly affected both by health status and by the same underlying factors that determine health and the consumption of medical care. As a result, simple comparisons of outcomes for insured and uninsured individuals may reflect either a causal effect of health insurance or other differences.

Approaches to the Endogeneity of Health and Insurance Status

Most studies simply ignore the endogeneity of health insurance. Others attempt to deal with the problem using a variety of techniques. This chapter classifies studies of health and health insurance on the basis of whether and to what extent they address the question of endogeneity and discusses their findings.

Observational studies do little or nothing to acknowledge endogeneity. Most simply compare health outcomes for the insured with outcomes for the uninsured. Some use regression analyses to control for covariates such as income, age, gender, race, behavior (e.g., smoking), and other medical conditions. Such analyses, representing the vast majority of studies of the association between health insurance and health, are confounded by both observable and unobservable differences between people who do and do not have health insurance. As a result, such studies are not likely to provide much insight into the causal effect of health insurance on health. Moreover, the complexity of the underlying relationships makes it impossible to say whether the bias that results from the omitted variables is positive or negative.

Quasi-experimental studies, also called natural experiments, rely on a policy change or other exogenous event to introduce variation in coverage that is plausibly unrelated to health or the other underlying determinants of insurance coverage. These situations offer an opportunity to estimate the causal effect of insurance on health. Some natural experiments are quite small in scale and are perhaps best thought of as case studies. Other natural experiments are much broader in scale.

Randomized experiments are true experiments in which health insurance coverage is randomly assigned to some individuals and subsequent differences in health outcomes are compared across groups. Such studies correspond to randomized clinical trials in the field of medicine, the gold standard of biomedical evidence. Only the RAND health insurance experiment falls into this category.

Which studies provide credible evidence that can be used to make inferences about the *causal* impact of health insurance on health? As we have mentioned, and as explained in more detail below, only the quasi-experimental and experimental analyses offer any basis for making such inferences.[4] This does *not* mean that observational studies are uninteresting or without value. Quite the contrary: observational studies documenting differences in medical care use and health outcomes between insured and uninsured populations provide essential information to researchers and to policymakers. The studies illustrate disparities in health care utilization and health outcomes among identifiable groups, suggesting the need for better ways to understand and ultimately address the disparities. Since experimental and quasi-experimental studies are far less numerous than observational studies, and their results are often quite different, this chapter discounts the stated conclusions of a great deal of published work. The following discussions explain why experimental and quasi-experimental evidence are preferable in analyzing causal effects.

Observational Studies

Literally hundreds of studies have examined the association between health insurance and health, and several comprehensive reviews of those studies have been done (e.g., U.S. Congress 1992; Brown, Bindman, and Lurie 1998). The reviews typically focus on important methodological issues, such as how the samples of individuals were identified (at a site of care, in the community, and so on) and how health utilization or health outcomes were measured. While the utilization studies clearly suggest that use of health services increases among persons with health insurance, they also emphasize that the increases do not necessarily translate into improved health. As a result, the studies place less weight on results concerning effects on health care utilization than on results concerning effects on health.

The reviews cite many studies showing a direct association between health insurance and health status. Outcomes shown to be correlated with health insurance range from death to objective physiological measures of health (such as hypertension), to subjective measures (such as self-reported health status) (Brown et al. 1998). In reviewing these studies, Brown and colleagues noted, "because there were no randomized trials, none of the articles reviewed fulfills criteria for the highest quality evidence." This statement is not true, strictly speaking, for the RAND Health Insurance Experiment meets these criteria; however, it is mostly true. Hundreds of studies attempt to analyze the effect of insurance on health using nonexperimental data that do not take into account the nonrandom nature of insurance status.

Studies that do not use some random or quasi-random variation in insurance status cannot provide clear evidence of a causal connection between insurance status and health. This problem is easily illustrated by considering a simple comparison of health status among persons with and without insurance. Depending on the population studied, uninsured persons may be young, healthy people in entry-level jobs that lack health insurance or older persons not yet eligible for Medicare but with health conditions that prevent them from purchasing insurance. Thus, this simple comparison would not indicate whether any correlation found between health insurance and health status reflects an effect of health insurance on health, an effect of health on health insurance status, or the effects of some third variable (such as age) on both health and health insurance status.

The vast majority of observational studies suggest a positive correlation between health insurance status and health. This suggests either that there is a true positive effect of health insurance on health or that some other factors such as income or education are positively correlated with both health and health insurance. On the other hand, important factors such as underlying illness may produce a downward (negative) bias in the observed relationship between health insurance and health status. Consider the landmark study by Ayanian and colleagues (1993) documenting lower survival rates, conditional on stage of diagnosis, among uninsured women with breast cancer than among privately insured women with the disease. This finding would seem to suggest that health insurance improves outcomes. However, the study documented even lower survival rates for women covered by Medicaid. Is one to conclude from this that Medicaid is bad for health? Presumably not; other factors that were not included in the analysis may have influenced the outcome.

In the same way, one cannot rule out the possibility that omitted factors may explain the positive relationship observed between private health insurance and health outcomes, as the authors of the study explain.

Because there is good evidence from a variety of sources that observable aspects of socioeconomic status such as education, income, and social integration are associated both with improved health outcomes (Pincus et al. 1998; Ross and Mirowsky 2000) and with health insurance coverage, many authors have attempted to control for these factors using multivariate analysis. Unfortunately, this does not necessarily mitigate the problem. Controlling for socioeconomic factors might be useful if variation in insurance status were determined solely by observable variables. However, after controlling for observable differences, any variation in insurance status that remains will be more heavily driven by unobservable differences between insured and uninsured people. Moreover, there is no guarantee that the unobservable attributes will be any less closely correlated with health outcomes than the observable attributes. As a result, analyses that control for observable differences may not be any less biased than analyses that do not control for them.

Consider the relationship between health insurance status and health around age 65. Health status improves markedly at that age, when people become eligible for Medicare (Lichtenberg 2001). This finding seems to suggest that health insurance has a positive effect on health. Yet when one controls for the observable characteristic (age) that drives the variation and focuses on persons with or without health insurance just below age 65, the relationship between health insurance status and health becomes more complicated. Factors such as preexisting illness may compromise health and make it less likely that someone can obtain or afford health insurance, creating a correlation between health insurance and health that is due to the effect of health on health insurance, rather than the effect of health insurance on health. This illustrates the more general point that controlling for differences does not necessarily improve one's ability to estimate accurately the effects of health insurance on health.

Other largely unobservable factors that may complicate the relationship between health insurance status and health include one's underlying belief in the efficacy of health care or one's valuation of health and similar factors that could affect care-seeking behavior. Some of the very best observational studies have attempted to address such concerns by considering plausibly exogenous health shocks. For example, Doyle

(2001) has analyzed data on serious car crashes. Using data from police accident reports linked to hospital discharge records, he found that the uninsured are significantly more likely than either the publicly or privately insured to die after a car accident in which they were incapacitated at the scene of the accident. Although this study cleverly surmounts the problem of selection into initial treatment—since both insured and uninsured accident victims are all taken to the hospital and, being incapacitated, have no say in the matter—such studies can never ensure that unobservable differences may not remain and affect outcomes. In Doyle's study, it is possible that even though the observable attributes of the auto accidents are similar, they may differ in some unobservable ways. Even if the accidents were truly identical, a positive bias in the relationship between health insurance and health might be created if insured persons were more compliant patients or had better underlying health status. Alternatively, a negative bias might be created if insured persons had better access to home care; in this case, insured people who were hospitalized would be likely to have more severe injuries.

There may be certain observational studies in which positive or negative biases can be clearly determined or perhaps bounded in magnitude, but to date no observational study appears to have succeeded in doing so. That is why this analysis focuses instead on quasi-experimental and experimental studies.

Quasi-Experimental Studies

The quasi-experimental approach to solving the evaluation problem relies, as the name suggests, on a situation in the real world that approximates what might be achieved in a randomized experiment. Such opportunities arise when a "natural experiment" causes health insurance coverage to vary for some measurable reason or reasons not related to an individual's health status; when that variation is not correlated with other, unobserved determinants of health, such as income; and when individuals whose coverage was not affected can be used as a control group. The control group is needed to pick up any unrelated changes in health outcomes, such as those due to improvements in medical technology.

The following section covers natural experiments that provide credible evidence of the causal effect of insurance coverage on health (see also figure 4.2). It places greater emphasis on studies of insurance and health

Figure 4.2. *What Experimental and Quasi-Experimental Studies Found about How Health Insurance Affects Health*

Fihn and Wicher 1988: Cancellation of VA outpatient benefits associated with significant increases in blood pressure.

Lurie et al. 1984, 1986: Termination of Medi-Cal benefits associated with significant increases in blood pressure, especially among persons with lower incomes.

Haas 1993a, Haas 1993b: Expansions of Healthy Start in Massachusetts to women between 100 and 185 percent of federal poverty level associated with no effect on birth outcomes relative to privately or publicly insured women.

Currie and Gruber 1996a: Expansions of Medicaid among children associated with declines in child mortality.

Currie and Gruber 1996b: Significant decline in infant mortality associated with expansions of Medicaid to pregnant women; smaller decline in the incidence of low birth weight.

Currie and Gruber 1997: Expansions of Medicaid to low-income pregnant women had positive effect on those living close to neonatal intensive care units; procedure use (e.g., fetal monitors) increased among women with less education and decreased among women with more education; relative birth outcomes did not change.

Hanratty 1996: Enactment of Canadian National Health Insurance associated with improvements in infant mortality and smaller improvements in the incidence of low birth weight.

Lichtenberg 2001: Improvements in mortality rate of 65-year-olds associated with the passage of Medicare in 1965.

Meer and Rosen 2002: The self-employed were far less likely to be insured than wage earners, but appeared to suffer no adverse health outcomes as a result.

Brook et al 1983; Keeler et al. 1985; Newhouse et al. 1993: Persons randomized to health insurance policies that provided free care versus only catastrophic coverage experienced no change in health outcomes except for reductions in blood pressure for low-income persons with hypertension and small improvements in corrected vision.

Goldman et al. 2001: More generous state-level policies to increase access to effective HIV therapies reduced mortality among HIV-positive individuals.

---

than on studies of insurance and health care utilization, because increased utilization does not necessarily translate into improved health. Studies of utilization are sometimes useful to explain the absence of insurance effects on health. That is, if insurance affects health only indirectly, through its effects on medical care, and a study *does not* find effects on medical care, one should not expect to see any effects on health. In the studies examined below, this reasoning is not relevant because they generally *do* find effects on health. In such cases, findings on utilization are used, when possible, to clarify the mechanism by which health insurance affects health.

Small-Scale Natural Experiments (Case Studies)

MEDI-CAL CUTBACKS

In 1982, California terminated Medi-Cal benefits for all 270,000 medically indigent beneficiaries, defined as those with "economic or medical need but . . . not eligible for assistance from a federal program for the aged, blind or disabled for families with dependent children." Lurie and colleagues (1986) examined changes in health outcomes for 186 patients at a Los Angeles clinic whose Medi-Cal benefits were terminated and compared them with changes in outcomes for a control group of 109 patients at the same clinic who were continuously covered by Medi-Cal. Those who lost benefits experienced, on average, a statistically significant increase in diastolic blood pressure (9 mm Hg six months after benefit termination, 6 mm Hg one year after termination), while the comparison group experienced no significant change. Self-reported health status also declined significantly for those who had lost coverage but not for controls. The authors did not focus on the mechanism by which the loss of insurance might have contributed to these declines in health, but they did note a 45 percent drop in the use of outpatient services among those who lost benefits.

The results may have been biased by the fact that the authors, alarmed at the increases in blood pressure observed at the six-month follow-up, intervened to help some of the subjects regain insurance coverage. However, this action would have been expected to bias the results toward zero, and the authors found significant increases in blood pressure a year after benefits were terminated. Since the termination was motivated by financial pressures on the state, it is possible that the state simultaneously cut back on other welfare programs that may have affected the group who lost benefits (and who were not categorically eligible for any federal assistance programs) but did not affect the control group. Though this hypothesis is plausible, there is no specific evidence that such cutbacks occurred. It is also possible that whatever criteria led the individuals to be excluded from Medicaid are correlated with less favorable health outcomes over time. For example, people who were continuously insured may have had more stable living circumstances and perhaps had a greater interest in maintaining coverage and being compliant with medical advice; persons whose benefits were cut might not have continued to be enrolled, even without cuts. Overall, this case study offers evidence that losing health insurance coverage is associated with declines in health status.

CUTBACKS IN VETERANS' HEALTH BENEFITS
Because of a budget shortfall, regular outpatient services at the Seattle Veterans' Administration Medical Center (VAMC) were terminated in 1983 for veterans who had no "service-connected disability," had not been admitted to the VAMC during the previous year, and had not had a scheduled outpatient visit in the past three months (Fihn and Wicher 1988). Physicians could appeal the terminations on a case-by-case basis and, if they could demonstrate the "medical instability" of a given patient, his benefits would not be cancelled. As a result, 89 of the original 360 patients targeted for cancellation in fact retained their eligibility for outpatient services. These 89 patients were treated as a control group. Twenty patients who were initially retained were later discharged and excluded from the analysis. The remaining 251 had their benefits terminated.

The authors obtained follow-up data 16 months after termination on 69 percent ($N = 172$) of the veterans who were no longer eligible and 91 percent ($N = 82$) of the control group (6 percent of the ineligible group and 8 percent of the control group had died). In addition to asking questions about access to medical care and general health status, the authors measured the veterans' blood pressure. Both systolic and diastolic blood pressure appeared very similar among the two groups before the discharge decision (the authors do not report a test of the hypothesis that the before-discharge means differ across groups).

At the follow-up, the ineligible group showed statistically significant increases in both systolic (+11.2 mm Hg, $p<.001$) and diastolic (+5.6 mm Hg, $p<.001$) blood pressure. In contrast, the control group experienced insignificant changes in both systolic (+0.5 mm Hg) and diastolic (−2.5 mm Hg) blood pressure. In addition, a significantly higher fraction of the ineligible group reported that their health had become "much worse" (41 percent vs. 8 percent, $p<0.001$). The ineligible group was substantially less likely than the control group to identify a usual source of care (70 percent vs. 100 percent, $p<0.001$) or to be satisfied with their present medical care (41 percent vs. 100 percent, $p<0.001$). Finally, the ineligible vets were substantially more likely to report having reduced the number of prescribed medications they took, including antihypertensive medication (47 percent vs. 25 percent, p<0.002). Several of the effects were greater for persons with lower incomes.

The combination of worsened outcomes and declines in utilization that are especially prominent among low-income persons who lose coverage is certainly suggestive of a true effect of insurance on health, but there are also some clear problems with this study. In addition to the very small sample size, the groups were not truly randomized, because some patients remained eligible because of doctors' efforts on their behalf. One might expect this selection to result in the eligible group's being sicker than the ineligible group, since they were those for whom doctors demonstrated "medical instability." Moreover, the selection might result in a conservative estimate of the treatment effect, assuming sicker patients are more likely to experience declines in health status.

In fact, this seems not to have been the case: some medical conditions related to high blood pressure, such as coronary artery disease, were more prevalent among the ineligible group. The authors attribute this "to the fact that physicians in the busy cardiology clinic allowed almost all targeted patients to be discharged and rarely appealed the decision" (Fihn and Wicher 1988, 359). This statement raises the possibility that some patients may have played a role in advocating for maintenance of their benefits. It is not unlikely that patients who were more concerned about their health not only advocated for maintenance of their insurance but were also more compliant with the treatment regimen. If so, the relationship between continued coverage and health status could well reflect unobservable patient characteristics rather than the effects of health insurance. This feature of the study makes it very unclear how successful the "randomization" was at eliminating any correlation between treatment and unobservable determinants of health.

Another thing to note about the study is that the natural experiment on which it is based may be more appropriate for studying the impact of access to care on health than for studying the effect of insurance on health. Eligibility for VA outpatient services functioned as a form of insurance, but in practice the usual source of care for these men had shut down. Thus, they not only lost their insurance coverage, they also lost access to their usual set of health care providers, with whom at least some of them had presumably established meaningful relationships. The impact of such events on health is interesting in its own right, but it may be fundamentally different from the impact of a change in insurance on health.

HEALTHY START EXPANSIONS

The Massachusetts Healthy Start program was begun in December 1985 to provide health insurance coverage for pregnant women with incomes up to 185 percent of the federal poverty level (Haas et al. 1993a, b). Medicaid coverage in Massachusetts at that time extended to pregnant women with incomes at or below the poverty level. In 1987, according to the authors, 54 percent of women who gave birth and who had neither private insurance nor Medicaid were covered by Healthy Start. The data consist of hospital discharge records merged to vital statistics records for nearly all live in-hospital births in Massachusetts in fiscal year 1984 ($N = 57,257$) and fiscal year 1987 ($N = 64,346$).

The authors' research strategy was to compare changes in medical care utilization and maternal and infant health among a group of women with neither private insurance nor Medicaid with changes among women who had Medicaid benefits or private insurance.[5] Any change in outcomes for the women without Medicaid or private insurance, compared with the control groups, is attributed by the authors to the expansions of Healthy Start coverage that occurred between 1984 and 1987.

No statistically significant changes were found in the following outcomes for the group without private insurance or Medicaid, compared with the controls: the incidence of adverse birth outcomes (low birth weight or premature birth), the fraction of women receiving satisfactory prenatal care, the fraction of women initiating care before the third trimester, and adverse maternal health outcomes (pregnancy-related hypertension, placental abruption, and a hospital stay longer than the infant's). In fact, the only outcome showing a significant change between 1984 and 1987 in the group without Medicaid or private insurance versus the control groups was the cesarean section rate, which increased among women without insurance (from 17.2 percent to 22.4 percent) and among privately insured women (from 23.0 percent to 25.9 percent). However, as the authors noted, there was no change in either maternal or infant outcomes corresponding to this change in cesarean section rates.

The studies assumed that all of the women newly insured by Healthy Start had been uninsured before then, whereas some of them may have had private insurance. To the extent that some of them had been covered—one study of Medicaid recipients found that approximately one-third of newly eligible recipients had previously been covered by private insurance (Currie and Gruber 1996)—the measured effect on birth outcomes might be smaller than if the expansions had reached a group of truly previously uninsured women. This is not so much a problem with the design of the study as a feature of the expansions themselves. If the expansions did not result in net increases in insurance, then it would not be surprising that there was no improvement in health outcomes.

SUMMARY
Taken as a whole, these three case studies provide mixed evidence on the effect of insurance on health. The first two studies strongly suggest that cutting back on insurance coverage of a vulnerable, low-income population has the potential to increase blood pressure significantly. On the other hand, the Haas papers suggest that expanding coverage to pregnant women may not affect health outcomes for them or their infants, even though it may result in changes in medical care utilization.

Large-Scale Natural Experiments

Five large-scale natural experiments have been studied: the enactment of Medicare in 1965, expansions of Medicaid eligibility in the 1980s and 1990s, the implementation of National Health Insurance in Canada, the variation across states in the generosity of insurance coverage for HIV patients, and the much lower rates of health insurance coverage among self-employed workers than among wage-and-salary workers. Each of these studies is discussed in detail.

THE ENACTMENT OF MEDICARE
Drawing on data from U.S. Vital Statistics, the National Hospital Discharge Survey, the National Health Interview Survey, and the National Ambulatory Medical Care Survey, Lichtenberg (2001) examined the effects of Medicare on the health of older Americans by looking for evidence of abrupt discontinuities in health care utilization and outcomes at age 65, when people typically become eligible for Medicare. He found that utilization of ambulatory care and, to a smaller extent inpatient care, increased abruptly at age 65. Lichtenberg then examined whether sickness and death dropped off at age 65 relative to outcomes prior to that age. The results showed a 13 percent reduction in the number of days spent in bed and a 13 percent reduction in the probability of death after age 65, compared with what the results would have been in the

absence of Medicare. Finally, Lichtenberg looked at whether the increase in health care utilization and the improvements in outcomes around age 65 over time were associated with each other.

The study found that, depending on age and the death rate in the previous year, the elasticity of the death rate with respect to the number of physician visits was −0.095 in the short run and −0.497 in the long run. Thus, a sustained 10 percent increase in the number of physician visits would reduce the death rate by 5 percent. Further insight into this association may be provided by the fact that the number of physician visits in which at least one drug was prescribed also increased suddenly at age 65; therefore, knowing which drugs were prescribed could be particularly useful in understanding how additional physician visits resulted in improved health. Another interesting finding was that the increase in the consumption of hospital services at age 65 was preceded by a decline in hospital utilization at ages 63 and 64, suggesting that at least some of the increase resulted from postponement of hospitalization in the prior two years.

These findings suggest a powerful effect of Medicare on both health outcomes and utilization of services, but alternative interpretations are possible. One is that 65 is a common age for retirement, and retirement may result in more time available for health care and thus improved health. Lichtenberg pointed out that 62 percent of workers have already retired by age 64, but that fact does not rule out the possibility of a spike in retirement at age 65 that might result in a (negative) spike in mortality. The possibility could be tested definitively by determining whether the spike in utilization and decline in mortality at age 65 are present for people who remain employed. Lichtenberg did not perform this test, but he did examine whether there was a difference in the discontinuity of mortality rates at age 65 before and after 1965, the year in which Medicare began. He found no evidence of a discontinuity at age 65 before the establishment of Medicare in 1965, but strong evidence after 1965. This finding probably reflects a change caused by the implementation of Medicare, but it may also reflect a change in the spike in retirement at age 65, which may have intensified with the establishment of Medicare. A valuable area for future work would be tests to determine whether discontinuities in outcomes differ depending on whether people have health insurance before age 65. Lichtenberg's preliminary findings suggest that health insurance has a significant effect on the health of persons at retirement age.

THE MEDICAID EXPANSIONS

Federally mandated expansions of Medicaid eligibility provide another natural experiment in which insurance coverage varies in a way that is plausibly exogenous. Three studies estimate the health effects associated with expansions of Medicaid eligibility that occurred between 1979 and 1992.[6] Two of them (Currie and Gruber 1997, 1996b) focus on the impact of eligibility expansions on birth-related health outcomes among pregnant women and infants; the third (Currie and Gruber 1996a) analyzes the impact of eligibility expansions on children's health outcomes.

Although the expansions for pregnant women and for children occurred at slightly different times and different outcomes were examined, all three studies exploit the fact that some states expanded Medicaid eligibility more than others, and the states did so at different times. The basic idea is that by correlating the magnitude and timing of the eligibility expansions with the magnitude and timing of changes in health outcomes, it is possible to determine whether there is any causal effect of insurance on health.

More specifically, the authors construct a variable, which they refer to as simulated Medicaid eligibility, that is equal to the fraction of a nationally representative sample of individuals (either children or women age 15 to 44) who would have been eligible for Medicaid under a given state's rules in a given year. The variable measures the generosity of the state's Medicaid program and is independent of the economic conditions prevailing in the state and of any demographic fluctuations in the size of the population eligible for benefits. The authors measure whether health outcomes are associated with changes in this simulated eligibility.

The study of children's coverage (1996a) included the following outcomes: the probability of no doctor visit during the last year, the probability of any doctor visit in the past two weeks, the probability of a hospital stay during the last year, and the child mortality rate (deaths per 10,000 children). Of these outcomes, only the last one is a measure of child health; the others measure utilization of health services, or health input. Currie and Gruber found that utilization increased significantly as a result of the expansion of eligibility and that child mortality dropped significantly (by 1.277 deaths per 10,000 children, relative to a baseline of 3.087 deaths per 10,000 children). Therefore, they concluded that expanding children's health insurance reduced child mortality.

The two studies that focused on expansions of coverage for pregnant women and infants (1996b, 1997) took the same basic approach, but they used variation in the timing and magnitude of eligibility expansions for pregnant women to estimate the effect of expansions on health outcomes for infants (low birth weight, infant mortality) and the use of obstetric services (specifically, cesarean section). The first one found a small, weakly significant effect of the Medicaid expansions on the incidence of low birth weight and a larger, significant effect on infant mortality (1996b). The estimates suggested that the 30 percentage point increase in eligibility was associated with an 8.5 percent decline in the infant mortality rate.

The second study focused on the expansions for pregnant women in an effort to find the specific mechanisms through which the impact on infant mortality operated. The impact, it turns out, depended on how close the infant's mother lived to a high-tech hospital with a neonatal intensive care unit, with the impact being greater on infants close to such hospitals. Interestingly, the use of cesarean section, fetal monitors, induction of labor, and ultrasound technology increased among teens and high school dropouts as a result of the eligibility expansions but decreased among more highly educated women. Currie and Gruber attribute this to the fact that many of the more highly educated women may have shifted from private insurance coverage to Medicaid (Currie and Gruber 1997). There was no decline in infant health associated with reductions in the use of these procedures,[7] a finding that is consistent with the broader literature suggesting that the rate of delivery by cesarean section is too high (Menard 1999). However, the study does raise the question of whether the increased rate of cesarean section among teens and high-school dropouts should be considered a desirable outcome of the Medicaid expansions.

ENACTMENT OF NATIONAL HEALTH INSURANCE IN CANADA

Canada's national health insurance program was enacted in different provinces at different times between 1962 and 1972. As a result, "it should be possible to identify the impact of national health insurance from variations across provinces in the dates of its implementation" (Hanratty 1996, 277). Hanratty used county data on infant mortality and individual data on low birth weight, and she controlled for various demographic and economic characteristics (age, average income, and urban location in county data; marital status and parity in individual data). The results suggest that there was a statistically significant, 4 percent reduction in infant mortality as a result of national health insurance and a 1.3 percent reduction in low birth weight.

While the findings suggest an effect of health insurance on health outcomes, it is also possible that systematic differences between persons in the various provinces explain the observed differences in health outcomes. For example, the differential adoption of new technologies by physicians in the various provinces might have led both to a demand for universal coverage and to improved health outcomes. If this were the case, one would expect to see differential improvements across the provinces before universal coverage was established. Hanratty investigated the possibility by testing for improvements in health outcomes across provinces before the implementation of national coverage, but she did not find any evidence of such effects. It is theoretically possible that the use of beneficial technologies accelerated suddenly, generating a demand for national health insurance, but this scenario seems unlikely.

HEALTH INSURANCE AND MORTALITY OF PEOPLE WITH HIV
Medicaid eligibility for and generosity to HIV-positive persons varies across states. One study uses this variation to construct instrumental variables for insurance coverage in order to estimate the impact of insurance coverage on mortality (Goldman et al. 2001). Using data from the HIV Cost and Service Utilization Survey, Goldman and colleagues found that insurance lowered the probability of dying within six months by 71 percent following the survey's initial round of interviews in 1996–1997. They estimated the effect at 85 percent following the survey's second round of interviews, which were conducted after the introduction of Highly Active Antiretroviral Therapy (HAART). The authors hypothesized that the larger estimate in the later period is due to the increased benefit associated with insurance coverage after the introduction of HAART. The study provides strong evidence that health insurance can have a dramatic effect on mortality among HIV-positive persons.

HEALTH INSURANCE AND THE HEALTH OF SELF-EMPLOYED WORKERS
Health insurance premiums received as an employment benefit are entirely deductible from a worker's taxable income, whereas only a fraction of the cost of premiums (currently 60 percent) is deductible from a self-employed person's taxable income. This difference in tax treatment, in addition presumably to other differences in the small versus large group markets for insurance, results in much higher rates of insurance

coverage among wage earners (Meer and Rosen 2002). Almost 82 percent of wage and salary workers under age 63 had health insurance coverage in 1996, compared with 69 percent of the self-employed (Perry and Rosen 2001).

Meer and Rosen used self-employment status to investigate whether insurance coverage led to any detectable difference in health outcomes. In order for self-employment status to be a valid instrument, they had to demonstrate that it was not affected directly by health status. For example, if very healthy people who place a low value on health insurance precisely because they are healthy are more likely to become self-employed because they do not value the tax subsidy for wage-earners, then the variation in health insurance is endogenous and the instrument is not valid. Meer and Rosen documented that health status was not significantly related to the probability of a person's becoming self-employed. An earlier study by Perry and Rosen (2001) had documented that self-employment status, as well as transitions into and out of self-employment, do not seem to be driven by the health of either the self-employed individual or his or her children.

The evidence is consistent with Meer and Rosen's hypothesis that the difference in rates of health insurance coverage of the self-employed and wage earners forms the basis of a valid natural experiment and that it would be possible to draw causal inferences from the results. The authors used data from the 1996, 1997, and 1998 rounds of the Medical Expenditure Panel Survey ($N = 37,331$) to estimate the impact of health insurance on health, using self-employment as an instrument for insurance coverage. Their results suggest that insurance coverage results in a small, statistically insignificant reduction (−0.3 percentage points) in the probability that a respondent will report being in good, very good, or excellent health. This result stands in contrast to the significant positive effect of health insurance on health (an increase of 1.8 percentage points in the probability of good or better health) estimated using ordinary least squares. The authors concluded that the public policy concern over low rates of insurance coverage among the self-employed may be misplaced, or at least that the concern should not be motivated by fear of adverse health outcomes. The conclusion is consistent with their findings, but the standard error on their estimates is about 2.5 percentage points, leaving open the possibility that the true effect of insurance on health could still be positive and substantial.

SUMMARY

It is difficult to summarize the results of the quasi-experimental studies since they relied on very different situations and looked at very different populations: infants (both American and Canadian), children, the medically indigent, persons with HIV, veterans, and 65-year-olds. But with the exception of the Healthy Start (Haas et al. 1993a, b) and self-employment studies (Meer and Rosen 2002), they found evidence of significant improvements in health outcomes as result of expansions of insurance coverage and, conversely, declines in health as a result of reductions in insurance.

Randomized Experiments

The final category, randomized experiments, includes only the RAND Health Insurance Experiment. Although the study is now 20 years old, having run from 1974 through 1982, it continues to be important because it remains the only study of its type in the United States. The experiment covered 2,005 families containing a total of 3,958 people between the ages of 14 and 61 who were free of any disability that precluded work. The families were assigned at random to either a free care plan or one of several plans that required varying copayments.

No significant effects on a wide range of measures of health status were found for the average person, with quite narrow confidence intervals (Brook et al. 1983; Keeler et al. 1985; Newhouse et al. 1993).[8] However, health benefits were found for persons with poor vision and for persons with elevated blood pressure (table 4.1). Specifically, visual acuity increased by 0.2 Snellen lines for persons with poor vision, and diastolic blood pressure went down by 3 mm Hg for persons with hypertension. The reduction in blood pressure was converted into an estimated relative risk of dying, based on epidemiological estimates of the effects of risk factors such as hypertension on mortality. The result suggested that a person in the highest quartile would have an annual risk of dying of 2.11, relative to the average participant in the study, if he or she was in one of the cost-sharing plans, compared with a relative risk of only 1.90 if he or she was in a free care plan. This 10 percent reduction in mortality risk was significant at $p<0.05$ and was found to result primarily from reductions in hypertension. Further analysis suggested that the reduction in blood pressure among low-income persons with hypertension in the free care plan occurred because they were more likely to visit the doctor than those in the cost-sharing plans; as a result, those in the free care plan were more likely to have previously undetected hypertension diagnosed (Keeler et al. 1985).

Several caveats accompany the RAND experiment. One is that the analyses do not control for the presence of multiple comparisons (that is, the hypothesis tests for multiple health outcomes). Also, the results are now 20 years old, and it is possible that changes in medical technology may have altered the effects of insurance. Another caveat is that the minimum insurance policy was not no insurance, but a so-called catastrophic coverage policy; therefore, no conclusions can be drawn about the effect of having no insurance.

The results are particularly interesting because control of hypertension is regarded as a major cause of the reduction in mortality from cardiovascular disease, and reduced mortality from cardiovascular disease has been the main reason for the overall decline in adult mortality rates in the United States over the past several decades (Cutler and Kadiyala 1999). If one accepts Lichtenberg's conclusion that Medicare increased ambulatory care utilization and improved mortality, and Cutler's conclusion that the control of hypertension was a key reason for the decline in adult mortality over this period, it raises the interesting possibility that Medicare may have reduced mortality at least partially by improving the control of hypertension.

So What Do We Know about the Effects of Health Insurance on Health?

Observational studies of the effect of health insurance on health clearly suggest an association between the two but provide little evidence on whether the relationship is causal. Quasi-experimental and experimental studies, on the other hand, provide a basis for drawing causal inferences. The results of small quasi-experimental studies provide only mixed evidence that health insurance affects health, while larger quasi-experimental studies and the RAND Health Insurance Experiment provide consistent evidence that health insurance improves health. Only one large-scale quasi-experimental study (Meer and Rosen's study of self-employment) fails to show a relationship between health insurance and health, and this study may not have adequate power to rule out the possibility that health insurance improves health. Taken as a whole, these high-quality studies strongly suggest that policies to expand health insurance can also promote health.

Another lesson that can be drawn from these studies is that the size of the effect of health insurance on health depends very much on whose health is being considered. Vulnerable populations, such as infants and children on the fringes of Medicaid eligibility and low-income individuals in the RAND experiment, have the most to gain from additional resources, and they do appear to benefit from them. But the effects on higher-income adults and children seem to be smaller. Moreover, it is difficult to extrapolate from these studies to the potential health benefits of completely different policies, such as a Medicare buy-in for people age 55 to 64, for example, making it very hard to predict the benefits associated with innovative policies. It is also worth noting that most of the insurance expansions described in this chapter included coverage of ambulatory care and that many of the outcomes that improved in response to insurance coverage (such as blood pressure control and HIV mortality) are plausibly affected by ambulatory treatment. In other words, the studies do not indicate what the effect of catastrophic insurance coverage alone might be.

One is left with the conclusion that health insurance can improve health but with no evidence of exactly what interventions related to insurance will do so most effectively. The uncertainty is even greater when one also considers interventions that target health or access to medical care directly. It is clear that expanding insurance is not the only way to improve health. Public spending on health could support community health centers, screening programs for hypertension, or advertising campaigns to encourage good nutrition, to name just a few possibilities. Policies could also be aimed at factors that may fundamentally contribute to poor health, such as poverty and low levels of education. There is no evidence at this time that money aimed at improving health would be better spent on expanding insurance coverage than on any of these other possibilities.

NOTES

This work was supported by a grant from the Robert Wood Johnson Foundation. We are grateful to Dana Goldman, Emmett Keeler, Willard Manning, and participants in the Agenda Setting Meeting of the Coverage Research Initiative, Ann Arbor, Michigan, July 9–10, 2001, for helpful comments and suggestions.

1. For evidence that this is true, see the discussion of the RAND experiment below.

2. One other effect is worth mentioning: there should also be an arrow running from insurance to health behaviors, to represent the "moral hazard" associated with insurance coverage. Moral hazard refers to a change in risk behavior induced by the presence of insurance; in this context, for example, people with health insurance might be less likely than they would otherwise have been to take precautions, such as wearing seat belts, that would lessen their risk of medical expenses.

3. The same problem arises in evaluating workforce training programs. Many studies discuss the problem in that context; see Heckman, LaLonde, and Smith (1999) for a review.

4. LaLonde (1986) makes the argument for relying on experiments to evaluate the impact of workforce training programs. Heckman, LaLonde, and Smith (1999) summarize the current state of the debate over the use of different econometric estimators to solve the evaluation problem using nonexperimental data on workforce training programs.

5. Haas et al. use the term "the uninsured" to describe their treatment group, but this may be somewhat misleading. The group was presumably entirely uninsured in 1984, but by 1987, 54 percent of the group were Healthy Start recipients.

6. Two other studies have examined the Medicaid expansions. Lykens and Jargowsky (2002) used data from the 1988 and 1991 National Health Interview Surveys. They described two sets of results, one at the individual level and one using mean values of children's insurance eligibility and health outcomes at the primary sampling unit (PSU) level. The results of the individual-level analysis did not show a significant effect of eligibility on children's health, whereas the PSU-level analysis did; it is unclear whether this discrepancy results from an ecological fallacy or from the presence of "network effects", as the authors hypothesize. Lykens and Jargowsky did not report the results of a test of the network effects hypothesis (e.g., individual-level regressions including the mean value of insurance eligibility as an explanatory variable), so it is impossible based on their evidence to rule out the ecological fallacy. Kaestner, Joyce, and Racine (2001) compared the incidence of hospitalizations for ambulatory-care-sensitive (ACS) diagnoses (e.g., asthma) for children from low-income and higher income areas in 1988 and 1992. They found mixed evidence of reductions in ACS admissions of children in the groups most likely to have experienced gains in coverage; as the authors acknowledge, their research design biased the result toward zero. Another issue is that their measures of the incidence of ACS hospitalizations were calculated as the ratio of total ACS hospitalizations to (1) all children's hospitalizations or (2) contemporaneous births, which makes it difficult to interpret the outcome variable as a measure of children's health.

7. This result, as Currie and Gruber point out, is consistent with the interpretation that the availability of a fixed "lumpy" amount of public insurance coverage at a very low price induces women to drop private coverage that may have been more generous but was also far more expensive, resulting in a net *decrease* in the quantity of insurance these women have, with a corresponding reduction in the use of medical procedures. To the extent that this reduction in use might be considered a desirable outcome (Menard 1999), it is ironic that a benefit from the Medicaid expansion stems from an unintended *reduction* in coverage of persons previously covered by private insurance.

8. The study was not powered to be able to detect effects on mortality because the cost of such a large sample would have been prohibitive.

REFERENCES

Agency for Healthcare Research and Quality. See AHRQ.

AHRQ. 2000. *MEPS Research Findings #14.* AHRQ Pub. No. 01-0011. Washington, DC: U.S. Department of Health and Human Services.

Ayanian, John, Betsy Kohler, Toshi Abe, and Arnold Epstein. 1993. "The Relation between Health Insurance and Clinical Outcomes among Women with Breast Cancer." *New England Journal of Medicine* 329(5): 326–31.

Brook, Robert H., John E. Ware, Jr., William H. Rogers, Emmett B. Keeler, Allyson R. Davies, Cathy A. Donald, George A. Goldberg, Kathleen N. Lohr, Patricia C. Masthay, and Joseph P. Newhouse. 1983. "Does Free Care Improve Adults' Health? Results from a Randomized Controlled Trial." *New England Journal of Medicine* 309(23): 1426–34.

Brown, Margaret E., Andrew B. Bindman, and Nicole Lurie. 1998. "Monitoring the Consequences of Uninsurance: A Review of Methodologies." *Medical Care Research and Review* 55(2): 177–210.

Coate, Stephen. 1995. "Altruism, the Samaritan's Dilemma, and Government Transfer Policy." American Economic Review 85(1): 46–57.

Currie, Janet, and Jonathan Gruber. 1996a. "Health Insurance Eligibility, Utilization of Medical Care and Child Health." *Quarterly Journal of Economics* 111(2): 431–66.

———. 1996b. "Saving Babies: The Efficacy and Cost of Recent Changes in the Medicaid Eligibility of Pregnant Women." *Journal of Political Economy* 104(6): 1263–96.

———. 1997. "The Technology of Birth: Health Insurance, Medical Interventions, and Infant Health." National Bureau of Economic Research Working Paper No. 5985. Cambridge, MA: National Bureau of Economic Research.

Cutler, David, and Srikanth Kadiyala, 1999. *The Economics of Better Health: The Case of Cardiovascular Disease.* Cambridge, MA: Harvard University.

Doyle, Joseph J. 2001. "Does Health Insurance Affect Treatment Decisions and Patient Outcomes? Using Automobile Accidents as Unexpected Health Shocks." Unpublished manuscript, University of Chicago.

Fihn, Stephan D., and John B. Wicher. 1988. "Withdrawing Routine Outpatient Medical Services: Effects on Access and Health." *Journal of General Internal Medicine* 3: 356–362.

Goldman, Dana P., Jayanta Bhattacharya, Daniel F. McCaffrey, Naihua Duan, Arleen A. Leibowitz, Geoffrey F. Joyce, and Sally C. Morton. 2001. "The Effect of Insurance on Mortality in an HIV+ Population in Care." *Journal of the American Statistical Association* 96(455): 883–94.

Haas, Jennifer S., Steven Udvarhelyi, and Arnold M. Epstein. 1993a. "The Effect of Health Coverage for Uninsured Pregnant Women on Maternal Health and the Use of Cesarean Section." *Journal of the American Medical Association* 270(1): 61–64.

———. 1993b. "The Effect of Providing Health Coverage to Poor Uninsured Pregnant Women in Massachusetts." *Journal of the American Medical Association* 269(1): 87–91.

Hanratty, Maria. 1996. "Canadian National Health Insurance and Infant Health." *The American Economic Review* 86(1): 276–84.

Heckman, James J., Robert J. Lalonde, and Jeffrey A. Smith. 1999. "The Economics and Econometrics of Active Labor Market Programs." In *Handbook of Labor Eco-*

nomics, vol. 3, edited by Orley C. Ashenfelter and David Card. Amsterdam: Elsevier Science.

Kaestner, Robert, Theodore Joyce, and Andrew Racine. 2001. "Medicaid Eligibility and the Incidence of Ambulatory Care Sensitive Hospitalizations for Children." *Social Science and Medicine* 52(2): 305–13.

Keeler, Emmet B., Robert H. Brook, George A. Goldberg, Caren J. Kamberg, and Joseph P. Newhouse. 1985. "How Free Care Reduced Hypertension in the Health Insurance Experiment." *Journal of the American Medical Association* 254(14): 1926–31.

LaLonde, Robert J. 1986. "Evaluating the Econometric Evaluations of Training Programs with Experimental Data." *American Economic Review* 76(4): 604–20.

Lichtenberg, Frank. 2001. "The Effects of Medicare on Health Care Utilization and Outcomes." Paper prepared for presentation at the Frontiers in Health Policy Research Conference, National Bureau of Economic Research, June 7, 2001. Washington, DC.

Lurie, Nicole, N. B. Ward, Martin F. Shapiro, and Robert H. Brook. 1984. "Termination from Medi-Cal—Does It Affect Health?" *New England Journal of Medicine* 311(7): 480–4.

Lurie, Nicole, N. B. Ward, Martin F. Shapiro, C. Gallego, R. Vaghaiwalla, and Robert H. Brook. 1986. "Termination of Medi-Cal Benefits. A Follow-Up Study One Year Later." *New England Journal of Medicine* 314(19): 1266–8.

Lykens, Kristine A., and Paul A. Jargowsky. 2002. "Medicaid Matters: Children's Health and Medicaid Eligibility Expansions." *Journal of Policy Analysis and Management* 21(2): 219–38.

Meer, Jonathan, and Harvey Rosen. 2002. "Insurance, Health, and the Utilization of Medical Services." Unpublished manuscript.

Menard, M. Kathryn. 1999. "Cesarean Delivery Rates in the United States: The 1990s." *Obstetrics and Gynecology Clinics in North America* 26(2): 275–86.

Newhouse, Joseph P., and the Insurance Experiment Group. 1993. *Free for All? Lessons from the RAND Health Insurance Experiment.* Santa Monica, CA: RAND.

Perry, Craig William, and Harvey S. Rosen. 2001. "The Self-Employed Are Less Likely to Have Health Insurance than Wage Earners. So What?" National Bureau of Economic Research Working Paper No. 8316. Cambridge, MA: National Bureau of Economic Research.

Pincus, Theodore, Robert Esther, Darren A. DeWalt, and Leigh F. Callahan. 1998. "Social Conditions and Self-Management Are More Powerful Determinants of Health than Access to Care." *Annals of Internal Medicine* 129(5): 406–11.

Ross, Catherine E., and John Mirowsky. 2000. "Does Medical Insurance Contribute to Socioeconomic Differentials in Health?" *Milbank Quarterly* 78(2): 291–321.

U.S. Congress, Office of Technology Assessment. 1992. "Does Health Insurance Really Make a Difference?" OTA-BP-H-99. Washington, DC: U.S. Government Printing Office.

5

Health Insurance and Vulnerable Populations

Harold Pollack and Karl Kronebusch

This chapter considers the causes of lack of insurance coverage for vulnerable populations. It is a daunting task because there are as many kinds of vulnerability as there are bad things that happen to human bodies or to human life. Although the term *vulnerable population* conjures images of a discrete and insular minority, every person's vulnerability to illness, injury, and disease makes health insurance necessary and possible for the vast majority of the U.S. population.

A Medline search on "vulnerable populations" yielded 191 entries covering a broad range of groups, including children of immigrants, parents of immigrants, and undocumented or recently documented immigrants; recipients of Aid to Families with Dependent Children (AFDC) or Temporary Assistance for Needy Families (TANF) (Andrulis 2000); families ineligible for welfare; unattached adults ineligible for public assistance; men and women with psychiatric disorders, substance abuse disorders, or developmental disabilities; racial and ethnic minorities (Shirley 1995); prison inmates and current or former offenders (Hammett, Gaiter, and Crawford 1998); residents of rural areas (Goody 1993); residents of inner-city communities (Shah-Canning, Alpert, and Bauchner 1996); individuals with chronic illnesses; the disabled poor; children and the elderly; the near-elderly; foster children; and children with special health care needs. Foreign populations noted in the same Medline search include residents of

Cuba, Iraq, Guatemala, and other nations subject to U.S. economic sanctions.

The diversity of these populations calls into question whether vulnerability is a useful organizing principle of policy analysis. If so many groups are vulnerable for so many reasons, does this concept really provide insight into public policies regarding insurance coverage? The argument of this chapter is that there indeed are commonalities among these groups concerning health insurance and public programs. The construct of vulnerable populations, though admitting of many interpretations, highlights an important set of issues for the design and management of health insurance, as well as essential linkages between health insurance and social policy.

This chapter starts by defining the concept of vulnerability and by considering components of vulnerability that are relevant for health policy and health insurance: Who are the disparate groups identified as vulnerable by health policy analysts and public health researchers? What distinctive features of these groups are pertinent to health insurance coverage? How do programs created to address specific vulnerabilities constrain subsequent policy interventions?

Four dimensions of vulnerability are discussed—needs that hinder access to insurance, general economic disadvantage, discrimination, and impaired and proxy decisionmaking—along with the major public programs that provide insurance for vulnerable populations. Six specific groups provide the focus of the discussion: low-income individuals, children, members of racial or ethnic minorities (including immigrants), individuals facing the challenges of chronic disease, the near-elderly (persons age 55 to 64), and individuals with psychiatric and substance use disorders.

Next, the basic demographics of health insurance coverage are presented. Using the health insurance supplement of the 1996 National Health Interview Survey (NHIS), the chapter examines the prevalence of coverage across the most readily identifiable vulnerable groups and presents multivariate models to identify risk factors for lack of coverage. The discussion uses a common data set to highlight the patterns identified by previous researchers. It also provides a framework for considering the shortcomings of wholly descriptive models as guideposts for public policy.

The chapter then reviews the extensive research literature on why individuals in vulnerable populations lack insurance coverage. The analysis focuses on structural factors that underlie economic decision-making as well as the important issues raised by the government programs designed to address their insurance needs. Vulnerable groups often face significant economic disadvantages and have readily identifiable medical or social needs that limit their access to health insurance. Each group raises distinct concerns for public policy, health insurance, and the health care delivery system, and each presents important challenges to the traditional system of private, employer-based coverage.

The chapter concludes with a discussion of several important issues for research and policy, particularly the inadequacy of data regarding many vulnerable populations; the complex interactions between public programs, private insurance, and other funding streams that provide health care; and the difficulties of setting priorities for expanding insurance coverage.

What Is Vulnerability?

A definition of health-related vulnerability starts with the concept of need. Social consensus frays at the margin when one asks which medication or service is most efficacious or cost-effective for a particular diagnosis. Yet few dispute the basic argument that poverty or lack of insurance should not block access to widely accepted treatments that significantly extend life or relieve illness. Health care is a prominent "merit good"—in this case, a good that, based on social altruism, society desires to provide to all citizens at some minimum level (Tobin 1970). Health care is not the only merit good. Subsidies for housing, preschool education, and food are often justified in similar terms (Currie 1995). But there is a social consensus in favor of assuring access to some minimal quantity and quality of health care services that leads policymakers to pay special attention to the distribution of health status and health care services across the population (Schelling 1979).

Vulnerability and health insurance coverage are closely linked. Many people who are uninsured, or who have limited coverage, face obstacles in obtaining medical treatment and preventive services. Twenty-seven percent of families in which all family members are uninsured report that they had delayed or not received needed health care, compared with only 8 percent of families in which all members are insured. Differences in use of care are not simply a function of insurance status. They can also occur among individuals who have similar insurance coverage. Thus, a simple comparison of 1987 expenditures for Medicare beneficiaries shows average spending of $4,316 for whites compared with $4,049 for blacks; $4,523 for high school graduates compared with $4,959 for college graduates; and $3,648 for poor persons, compared with $4,661 for persons with high income.[1] A large health services research literature on vulnerable populations has scrutinized barriers to access and utilization faced even by people with insurance coverage. The focus here, however, is on how vulnerable populations face barriers to insurance coverage itself.

Obstacles to health insurance coverage can arise from many factors, but four are especially important for vulnerable populations:

- Medical and social needs that hinder access to traditional insurance markets,
- General economic disadvantage, including both low income and limited access to employer-based health insurance,
- Discrimination based on race, ethnicity, or language, and
- Impaired decisionmaking and proxy decisionmaking.

Vulnerability can operate in each of these domains to limit access to coverage and to care. Some vulnerabilities are associated with suboptimal consumer demand, as when barriers to information prevent people from seeking care that they would willingly purchase given full information. In other cases, people do not obtain insurance coverage because of transaction costs, such as when families are thwarted by administrative barriers when applying for public programs. On the supply side, individuals may not be offered care if they have a costly or complex condition, and they may not be able to obtain insurance coverage if their expected expenditures exceed the premiums that insurers can charge.

Medical and Social Needs

The last possibility highlights the most basic vulnerability that individuals experience: ill health, disease, or disability. Insurance starts with the presence of risk and seeks to spread the financial burdens of that risk. Vulnerability to disease and its attendant costs motivates consumers to buy insurance. Yet the nature of disease and medical treatment presents difficulties for pooling risk within an unregulated market. Under appropriate competitive conditions, insurance markets provide for efficient allocation of resources. They do not, however, provide a vehicle for addressing distributional concerns, which are often central policy goals. And in the presence of market failures, they fail even to achieve efficient resource allocation.

Adverse selection and moral hazard prevent many individuals from obtaining coverage for which they are willing to pay actuarially fair premiums. Health status and the existence of disease underlie consumer demand for both medical care and insurance coverage. Those who are most likely to need care are most likely to seek coverage; those who are less likely to need care may not purchase coverage. Adverse selection occurs when risk characteristics can be observed and used as the basis of market transactions. When such characteristics are known to the individual but cannot be acted on by insurers, consumer self-selection can prevent markets from providing actuarially fair coverage to all consumers who wish to purchase such policies. In an adverse selection spiral, the insurance market shrinks entirely to the high-risk group, resulting in high premiums that are actuarially fair for individuals with chronic illness but that are too high to attract other, healthier potential consumers. The result can be lack of coverage for low-risk individuals who would have been willing to purchase coverage at actuarially fair rates (Rothschild and Stiglitz 1976).

To guard against adverse selection, insurers may charge high premiums or deny coverage to individuals with high expected expenditures. In less extreme cases, insurers lessen their risk by imposing restrictions on coverage, such as waiting periods, exclusions of preexisting medical conditions, and cost-sharing requirements. These measures discourage consumers in poor health from obtaining coverage and result in lack of coverage for higher-risk consumers. Such market outcomes thwart a common redistributive goal of public policy—to shift resources from healthy individuals to those with severe or chronic illness.

Some market failures arise because markets are missing. As Richard Zeckhauser has noted, some of life's most important lotteries are run before one is born (Cutler and Zeckhauser 2000). An individual with spina bifida might be able to purchase an actuarially fair, albeit expensive insurance policy to provide care for the condition, but he or she cannot purchase insurance against the possibility of being born with the condition. The absence of a market for prior risk aggravates adverse selection in a voluntary insurance market. An uncoordinated market will not, therefore, protect chronically ill consumers from the burden of actuarially fair premiums. Thus, missing markets provide an important economic justification for social insurance.[2]

Economic Disadvantage

A second vulnerability arises from general economic disadvantage. Individuals with low income (including children in low-income families) are less likely or able to purchase insurance coverage and are less likely or able to purchase care directly. Moreover, the primary mechanism for obtaining health insurance for persons under age 65 is through an employer. Many low-income Americans, however, have a weak connection to stable jobs, and the jobs they do hold may not provide health benefits (Gruber 2000). When health benefits are offered, they may require premiums, especially for dependent coverage. Existing data suggest that consumer purchases of health insurance coverage are sensitive to income. Nyman (2002) reports higher sensitivities to income among persons who use more health care. The result is that many low-income workers do not purchase health insurance for themselves or other family members.

Economic disadvantage can also be caused by poor health. Poor health can hinder job performance, thereby limiting income as well as access to employment-linked health insurance. These issues are considered in chapter 2, and are therefore not considered here.

Discrimination

A third vulnerability arises from race, ethnicity, language, and citizenship status. The disadvantages associated with race and ethnicity are partly due to poverty and low income. Yet these categories are also distinct from economic need, raising issues of social discrimination, access to pertinent information, cultural norms, and cross-cultural difficulties that may impede access to medical services and health insurance.

Racial and ethnic discrimination poses barriers to using the health care delivery system effectively and to obtaining insurance coverage. Real and perceived discrimination concerning individuals and their health care providers has received increased research attention, especially regarding medical encounters of African-American patients. Hispanic citizens, noncitizens, and recent citizens are the largest single population of uninsured men, women, and children in the United States (Weinick,

Zuvekas, and Cohen 2000). Barriers associated with language skills and immigration status keep members of many ethnic groups from seeking public coverage for which they are eligible.

Impaired Decisionmaking

A fourth vulnerability concerns individuals' ability to act as effective agents on their own behalf. Although most people are effective judges of their own well-being, are competent decisionmakers, and can advocate for their own interests, some persons with cognitive or psychiatric disorders are not. Such individuals may not be sophisticated consumers and may be unaware that they are entitled to health insurance coverage. People with stigmatizing disorders and circumstances and those with social and economic disadvantages are also likely to be less effective agents within the health care delivery system. The social stigma attached to receipt of welfare and other means-tested programs may also deter them from applying for programs for which they are eligible.

Poor health status interacts with many of these concerns to create especially significant vulnerability for individuals with chronic illness. Chronic conditions limit access to insurance and may limit individuals' capacity to take actions on their own behalf. Severely disabled people often rely on others for basic activities of daily living. The broad range of vulnerabilities of people with chronic illness makes them dependent on family and other caregivers, medical providers and social service organizations, and government programs for economic support.

Along each dimension, if the limitations are severe enough, a person can be classified as a member of a particular vulnerable population. Although many people face a single challenge due to chronic illness, low income, or other challenges, many others face multiple challenges, often in different domains of personal well-being or social functioning.

Program Responses to Needs and Vulnerability

Policymakers, health care providers, insurers, and the public have long recognized the market failures and undesirable distributional consequences likely to arise from an unregulated private insurance market. A long history of public and private interventions has sought to address both concerns, particularly to serve specific vulnerable populations. Public programs include the creation of hospitals for the mentally ill, programs to provide medical and preventive services, and income transfer and social insurance programs. Alongside these public responses to vulnerability is a rich history of involvement by voluntary and nonprofit organizations. Nonprofit Blue Cross and Blue Shield plans were central to the development of health insurance in the 20th century. Partly for historical reasons and partly as a result of deliberate public policy, many health care providers that serve uninsured or underinsured vulnerable populations—known as the safety net—operate under nonprofit and public ownership.

In the area of health insurance coverage, the main federal and federal-state programs are Medicare, Medicaid, and the State Children's Health Insurance Programs (SCHIP). More than 80 percent of Medicare recipients are over the age of 65. However, 5 million Medicare beneficiaries are of working age, making Medicare a major source of coverage for the adult population. More than 90 percent of Medicare beneficiaries who are under 65 are eligible by virtue of disability. The remainder are eligible through the end-stage renal disease program or because they are widows or widowers of Medicare beneficiaries (U.S. Congress 2000).

Medicaid serves a range of groups, including families receiving cash welfare benefits, people with disabilities who receive federal Supplemental Security Income (SSI), and children in low-income families. Medicaid also serves certain persons with high medical expenses, some of whom live in the community and many others who are residents of nursing homes. Important expansions of Medicaid occurred during the 1980s and 1990s, extending coverage to infants, children, and pregnant women in low-income families that were not eligible for welfare. These expansions significantly increased the number of people eligible for Medicaid. For example, the mandates enacted in the Omnibus Budget Reconciliation Acts of 1989 and 1990 required that the states extend Medicaid eligibility to all children under the age of 6 with a family income below 133 percent of the federal poverty level, as well as children born after September 30, 1983, with a family income below the poverty level. In 1997, the expansions were supplemented by the creation of federal grants to fund SCHIP. These programs are aimed at children in families whose incomes are just above the limit for Medicaid eligibility. States are granted flexibility in implementing the programs and can choose upper income limits (typically around 200 percent of the poverty level), the nature of premiums and cost-sharing requirements, and the administrative form of the programs (Holahan et al. 2000; Rosenbach et al. 2001).

Finally, an important related program is welfare. In 1996, Congress enacted and President Bill Clinton signed the welfare reform law that repealed AFDC, replacing it with TANF block grants to the states. The new legislation preserved the Medicaid program as a federal-state entitlement and nominally maintained the AFDC-related eligibility rules for adults in families with dependent children, as well as the implementation schedule for the child-related expansions established in 1989–1990. Nevertheless, the implementation of welfare reform has led to large declines in both welfare and Medicaid enrollment (Kronebusch 2001a, b).

These programmatic changes influence health insurance coverage in several ways. Potential recipients must decide whether to enroll in the new welfare programs, created by the states, which emphasize work and self-sufficiency. In some cases, welfare reform may mean that recipients' behavior while enrolled affects their continued eligibility for welfare and insurance coverage. Welfare reform also changed the administrative relationships across programs. For example, cash assistance has traditionally been the main means of identifying low-income women and children and enrolling them into Medicaid programs, so the decline in TANF caseloads has complicated enrollment efforts.

A second complexity emerges from the overlapping medical and social needs of vulnerable populations. Many private and public interventions address only one of the needs, resulting in a patchwork of organizations and programs. This patchwork arose from historical accident, the dynamics of competing funding streams, and the unique political, social, and health circumstances facing particular populations. Health insurance policy is made in this environment.

Governmental programs are created and administered through political decisionmaking; therefore, the political economy of this process helps to shape the provision of health coverage. Some vulnerable populations, such as children with special health care needs, command strong constituencies that elicit sustained policy attention. Other populations are less influential. Indeed, the reasons for their health-related vulnerabilities may be associated with political disadvantage, which has its own impact on decisionmaking (Kronebusch 1997; Poterba 1998). Many programs serving the vulnerable are financed by both the federal and state governments. Thus, intergovernmental relations and the dynamics of fiscal federalism have important implications for the access of vulnerable groups to government-provided health insurance and medical services. Policy initiatives by one level of government to expand access to medical services can, perhaps unintentionally, alter incentives and resources available to address similar problems at other levels of government.

Who Are "the Vulnerable?"

With this framework in place, one can identify particular groups that exemplify these problems of vulnerability. For this analysis, vulnerable populations include:

- people with low incomes
- children
- racial or ethnic minorities and immigrants
- individuals with chronic disease
- the near elderly
- individuals with psychiatric or substance abuse disorders

Each group has a characteristic combination of the vulnerabilities discussed above. For the economically disadvantaged, job insecurity and low income hinder the purchase of private health insurance coverage. Children typically obtain insurance through a parent's employment or through public insurance. Yet parental policies do not necessarily cover children, and children are dependent on parents and guardians to make decisions for them in obtaining public and private coverage. Racial and ethnic minorities may face general economic disadvantage, as well as the barriers posed by discrimination, lack of competence in English, immigration status, and eligibility for programs. Persons with chronic disease face the general difficulties of obtaining insurance because they are less likely to be employed and face the special difficulties that come with the combination of poor health and low income. The near-elderly experience a rising incidence of acute and chronic illness, at the same time that the employment connection for insurance coverage weakens with retirement, widowhood, and divorce. Persons with mental illness or problems with substance use face potentially impaired decisionmaking and the general problem of obtaining insurance when risks are chronic and observable.

How Prevalent Is Insurance Coverage in Vulnerable Populations?

A particularly useful source for quantifying coverage of vulnerable populations is the health insurance supplement of the 1996 NHIS. The supplement is a large, nationally representative sample that provides information on the sociodemographic, economic, regional, and health factors associated with health insurance coverage. This chapter focuses on the population below age 65 because almost all Americans over that age are covered under Medicare.

The percentage of uninsured respondents in the 1996 NHIS respondents is shown in table 5.1. Hispanics and recent immigrants are the most likely groups to lack health insurance coverage. Hispanics represented one-third of uninsured adults and more than 20 percent of uninsured children in the sample. African Americans and Asian Americans are also less likely than non-Hispanic whites to have insurance coverage. As expected, low-income Americans are much more likely than affluent residents to lack insurance. Persons who are in poor health or who have a work-related health limitation are somewhat more likely to be uninsured, while adults between the ages of 55 and 64 are slightly more likely to be insured than younger adults. Men are more likely to be uninsured than women, in part because welfare-related Medicaid coverage has generally been limited to single-parent families, which are typically headed by women. As a result of the Medicaid expansions of the 1990s, children are now less likely to be uninsured than adults.

The NHIS can also be used as the basis of a multivariate statistical analysis that examines the effects of these characteristics on health insur-

Table 5.1. *Lack of Insurance Coverage in the 1996 National Health Interview Survey*

	Men 17–64 (%)	Women 17–64 (%)	Children 1–16 (%)
Native-born non-Hispanic white	13.4	10.6	8.5
African American	21.3	17.2	11.0
Hispanic/Latino	35.2	29.2	21.6
Recent immigrant	43.8	40.4	29.3
Asian	18.6	18.0	13.8
In poverty	43.5	30.8	18.4
Self-reported "poor health"	17.6	17.5	11.7
Health limitation in school or work	16.6	13.6	7.3
Age 55–64	9.1	10.9	——

ance coverage. A common multivariate approach would be to estimate a logit specification:

$$\log\left[\frac{p}{1-p}\right] = x\beta_1 + \alpha_1 Income + \gamma_1 Hours + \pi_1 Health + \varepsilon_1. \tag{1}$$

Here p is the probability of health insurance coverage. The variable x is a vector of personal characteristics, and *Income* is annual family income. *Hours* is employment status measured in hours of paid employment, and *Health* is a measure of health endowment, such as the presence or absence of chronic illness.

The results, calculated separately for children, women, and men (table 5.2) indicate that children in the South are significantly less likely to be insured than are children in other regions.[3] African-American children are slightly more likely to be insured than non-Hispanic white children, a difference that may reflect the higher public insurance coverage of African-American children. Hispanic children and recent immigrant children are much less likely to be insured than the other groups.

Poor health and health-related limitations on school or work are associated with an *increased* probability of health insurance coverage. Eligibility for public programs because of disability, along with increased demand for coverage among individuals with health difficulties, may explain this relationship.

Young men and adults between the ages of 17 and 64 in the South are less likely to have health insurance than comparable groups in other regions. Higher income and education increase the likelihood of having insurance coverage, as does marriage. Again, Hispanics and all recent immigrants face sharply lower rates of coverage.

Independent of education and income, unemployment is a strong risk factor for lack of coverage. Adult men who are not disabled are generally not eligible for public insurance, and this group is the most dependent on employer-based coverage. The near-elderly are more likely than other adults to report having insurance coverage. Whether these patterns reflect greater demand for coverage in these demographic groups is not clear. Results for women are similar.

These results highlight the role of economic factors in determining health insurance coverage. Lack of coverage is most prevalent among the near-poor, primarily young adult workers. Consistent with these results, Shi finds a striking income gradient in insurance coverage:

Table 5.2. *Probability of Uninsurance in the National Health Interview Survey, 1996 Wave, Logistic Regression Model*

	Children age 0–16 adjusted odds ratio [95% CI]	Women age 17–64 adjusted odds ratio [95% CI]	Men age 17–64 adjusted odds ratio [95% CI]
South	Referent	Referent	Referent
West	0.697	0.868	0.851
	[0.596, 0.814]	[0.762, 0.991]	[0.745, 0.971]
Northeast	0.516	0.526	0.799
	[0.428, 0.622]	[0.451, 0.614]	[0.687, 0.908]
Midwest	0.481	0.633	0.618
	[0.404, 0.574]	[0.552, 0.726]	[0.538, 0.710]
High school dropout	Referent	Referent	Referent
High school graduate	—	0.699	0.693
		[0.618, 0.789]	[0.614, 0.783]
College graduate	—	0.504	0.501
		[0.420, 0.605]	[0.425, 0.590]
African American	0.709	0.922	0.937
	[0.404, 0.574]	[0.801, 1.061]	[0.808, 1.087]
Asian	1.145	0.932	0.800
	[0.782, 1.692]	[[0.672, 1.292]	[0.574, 1.116]
Hispanic/Latino	1.588	1.497	1.611
	[1.384, 1.823]	[1.319, 1.701]	[1.420, 1.828]
Non-Hispanic white	Referent	Referent	Referent
Married	—	1.078	0.849
		[0.956, 1.215]	[0.751, 0.960]
Unmarried	—	Referent	Referent
Recent immigrant	2.04	2.818	2.281
	[1.620, 2.574]	[2.297, 3.457]	[1.875, 2.775]
Log (family income)	0.774	0.608	0.497
	[0.691, 0.866]	[0.549, 0.672]	[0.442, 0.559]
Top-coded income (over $50,000)	0.115	0.278	0.385
	[0.087, 0.150]	[0.230, 0.336]	[0.325, 0.455]
Poor health	0.533	1.037	0.821
	[0.236. 1.204]	[0.759, 1.417]	[0.571, 1.180]
Work or school health limitation	0.575	0.675	0.501
	[0.264, 1.250]	[0.538, 0.849]	[0.391, 0.642]

(*continued*)

Table 5.2. *Continued*

	Children age 0–16 adjusted odds ratio [95% CI]	Women age 17–64 adjusted odds ratio [95% CI]	Men age 17–64 adjusted odds ratio [95% CI]
Poverty	0.926 [0.746, 1.149]	0.889 [0.730, 1.083]	0.964 [0.789, 1.177]
Unemployed	—	1.899 [1.49, 2.42]	3.076 [2.444, 3.872]
Age 6 and younger	Referent	—	—
Age 7–10	1.155 [0.985, 1.355]	—	
Age 11–16	1.410 [1.223, 1.624]	—	—
Under age 25	—	1.147 [0.959, 1.372]	1.312 [1.083, 1.591]
Age 25–34	—	1.322 [1.129, 1.546]	1.873 [1.598, 2.196]
Age 35–44	—	1.109 [0.948, 1.297]	1.269 [1.078, 1.492]
Age 45–54	—	Referent	Referent
Age 55–64	—	0.859 [0.707, 1.045]	0.785 [0.632, 0.974]
Estimated population	54,791,305	71,762,297	69,657,211

39 percent of people with hourly wages below $5.00 lacked insurance coverage, as did 29 percent with hourly wages between $5.00 and $9.99. Less than 3 percent of people with wages above $20 per hour lacked insurance coverage (Shi 2000).

Based upon these findings alone, it would be hard to understand why people between the ages of 55 and 64, for example, would require special intervention. However, the social and health consequences of being uninsured vary with age and health status. Many near-elderly people experience declining health status associated with aging. Thus, even though this age group is more likely than others to be covered, it is also more likely to experience the dual challenge of poor health and lack of insurance.

One striking finding concerns the proportion of individuals with low incomes or with disabilities who obtain health coverage from public rather than private sources. Among individuals who describe their mental health as "excellent," only 7.4 percent obtained insurance from public sources, while 76 percent had private coverage. Yet among individuals who describe their mental health as "poor," 41.3 percent had public coverage, and only 27 percent had private insurance coverage. Similar results pertain among individuals whose activities of daily living (ADL) and instrumental activities of daily living (IADL) are limited and persons with cognitive limitations. Although most Americans obtain private coverage, a sizable minority of chronically ill people obtain coverage outside of the private, employer-based insurance market.

The Need for Structural Models

The analysis above is similar to a large number of studies on the demographic correlates of uninsurance. This literature identifies low income and education and marginal connection to the paid labor market as critical risk factors for lack of health insurance coverage. Univariate analysis is commonly used in reports concerning health insurance status. Health policy analysts are quite aware of the pitfalls of such descriptive statistics, however, so multivariate analysis is increasingly common. Yet multivariate analysis can also be vulnerable to bias, even when many observed characteristics of individuals and families are included in the analysis.

Because the causal pathways that link individual characteristics to health coverage, health care utilization, and health outcomes are complex and multi-directional, "structural" modeling that considers these multiple pathways is important to clarify the observed relationships in available data.

To illustrate these concerns, consider an informal model of the factors affecting the demand for medical services and health insurance.[4] Consumer demand for medical services is a function of income, the direct and indirect costs of care (such as transportation or time), health status, knowledge of medical care and health, and the relevant social and cultural norms that affect risk preferences:

$$Q^D_{Care} = \alpha_2 Income + \omega_2 Price_{Care} + \gamma_2 Health + \chi_2 Knowledge$$
$$+ \delta_2 risk\_preference + X\beta_2 + \varepsilon_2. \tag{2}$$

Demand for insurance reflects the demand for medical care, plus additional factors, including income, the price of insurance and care, the availability of alternative sources of care (including available uncompensated care), health status, knowledge of medical care and health, consumer risk preferences, and wealth:

$$Q^D_{Ins} = \lambda_3 Q^D_{Care} + \alpha_3 Income + \rho_3 Price_{Ins} + \omega_3 Price_{Care} + \gamma_3 Health$$

$$+ \chi_3 Knowledge + \delta_3 risk\_preference + \Gamma_3 wealth + X\beta_3 + \varepsilon_3. \quad (3)$$

Wealth matters in the model. Given bankruptcy constraints that restrict risk for low-wealth households, wealthier individuals may have greater incentives to purchase coverage in the event of high medical expenditure.

On the supply side, the provision of medical care services is related to input costs, reimbursement rates, and other factors such as, perhaps, provider treatment norms:

$$Q^S_{Care} = \omega_4 Cost_{Care} + \theta_4 Reimbursement + \varepsilon_4. \quad (4)$$

Finally, the price of insurance available to a given consumer reflects expected expenditure given the information available to the insurer, administrative costs, and workplace factors such as hours worked and occupation:

$$Price_{Ins} = \omega_5 E[Cost_{Care}] + \tau_5 ad\ costs + \theta_5 Hours + \kappa_5 Occupation + \varepsilon_5. \quad (5)$$

One might also consider ways in which health status influences income or employment. This suggests the specifications of equations 6 and 7 for the causal determinants of income and hours worked:

$$Income = x\beta_6 + \gamma_6 Hours + \pi_6 Health + \varepsilon_6; \quad (6)$$

$$Hours = x\beta_7 + \pi_7 Health + \varepsilon_7. \quad (7)$$

This framework suggests the difficulties that can arise from a non-structural specification such as equation 1: the logit coefficients are not derived from a causal model based on the preferences and choices available to poor households or the production technology of medical care and health insurance coverage. The results reflect a combination of supply-side and demand-side variables and thus yield no straightforward causal interpretation. People with health challenges may have greater demand for health insurance coverage, but they may also have greater difficulty obtaining coverage. The estimated logit coefficient π_1 represents the combination of these factors. For example, individuals who know that they are eligible for public insurance may wait to enroll until they are in acute medical need, thus introducing a negative correlation between health status and health insurance coverage (Davidoff, Garrett, and Makuc 2000).

Examining equations 4 and 5, one sees that health status influences insurance coverage directly, but it also influences insurance status indirectly, through its influence on work hours and earnings. Controlling for income and employment, poor health may be positively associated with health insurance coverage. Yet if these economic variables are themselves influenced by health, the univariate correlation between health and insurance coverage or the coefficient in a multivariate regression model might indicate that poor health is associated with reduced probability of coverage.

Health Insurance Decisionmaking and Vulnerable Populations

This section analyzes the reasons why many Americans in vulnerable population groups lack insurance coverage. Each group faces difficulties that affect its access to private health insurance, as well as limitations on how well public insurance programs can serve its needs. The analysis rests on a survey of the research literature and describes the background and key structural issues of health insurance and vulnerable populations.

Health Insurance and Low-Income Americans

For low-income Americans, access to health insurance hinges on their access to employer-based health coverage, their ability to purchase nongroup coverage, and their access to, and use of, government programs such as Medicaid and SCHIP. These issues apply to the general population as well, but they have special importance, and raise special concerns, for low-income populations.

People who lack employer-based coverage can purchase insurance in the nongroup market, although such policies are often very expensive (reflecting the insurer's administrative costs), exclude preexisting medical conditions, and impose waiting periods or other restrictions on coverage. Existing studies suggest that demand for health insurance is weak among low-income workers and that substantial subsidies are required if they are to buy insurance (Chernew, Frick, and McLaughlin 1997; Marquis and Long 1995; Swartz and Garnick 2000).

The increasing price (and quality) of health care services may have accelerated this trend. On some dimensions, low-income workers can contract for less expensive health care than more affluent workers, but there is no market for low-income workers to contract for 1990 medical technology at 1990 prices. As rising medical costs and stable or declining real wages increased the proportion of total compensation spent on health care, the proportion of low-wage workers willing to forgo health coverage may have increased (Gruber 2000).

Similar issues arise in the context of employer-based health insurance. Here, the decision to offer insurance is nominally made by the employer (or is shaped by collective bargaining), but the process is strongly influenced by the preferences of low-income workers. If workers do not value insurance coverage, employers will provide other forms of compensation. When coverage is offered, employees are required to pay premiums, especially for dependents, and low-wage workers are often unwilling or unable to pay those costs. As a result, workers often do not press employers for health insurance and low-wage jobs often lack coverage. Moreover, many low-income Americans are employed part-time, in positions that generally lack health insurance benefits, or have a weak, episodic connection to paid employment.

Given the transaction costs associated with providing multiple health insurance plans, many employers offer a small number of discrete plans or sometimes just a single plan. Such plans, adopted to match the demand of the "typical" employee, may not be optimal for low-income workers. Some evidence suggests that the design of company benefit packages is especially influenced by the preferences of high-income workers (Chernew et al. 1997). Because health insurance coverage is relatively more expensive for low-income workers, they feel the impacts of rising medical costs and falling real wages most keenly. Data from the 1980s and 1990s indicate that the decline of health insurance coverage was concentrated among low-income workers (Acs 1995; Kronick 1991; Rhine and Ng 1998).

The final issue concerning insurance coverage for low-income Americans is the availability and desirability of means-tested public insurance, primarily Medicaid and SCHIP, and the availability of safety net providers and uncompensated care (that is, care provided at low or no cost). While means-tested programs and safety net providers are important for low-income Americans, not all of those who are eligible for such programs actually enroll. Participation rates, or take-up rates, are frequently estimated to be 40 to 60 percent. In scrutinizing the low take-up for means-tested programs, qualitative and survey researchers have identified several barriers: burdensome enrollment processes, language barriers and fear of immigration sanctions (Ellwood and Kenney 1995; Ellwood and Ku 1998; Ku and Matani 2001), rationing of available benefits by street-level bureaucrats (Lipsky 1980), incorrect eligibility determination by officials, and recipients' ignorance about program rules and eligibility requirements (Remler, Rachlin, and Glied 2001; Stuber et al. 2000).

The social stigma of being on welfare and Medicaid has also been identified as a potential barrier to enrollment. Although several conceptual papers explore the linkage between social norms and program participation (Besley and Coate 1992), efforts to measure the prevalence and implications of welfare stigma have reached contradictory conclusions (Remler et al. 2001). State efforts to distance SCHIP from Medicaid suggest that some policymakers believe stigma is an obstacle to program participation.

Perceptions that public insurance is of low quality may also influence take-up and the perceived trade-offs between public and private coverage (Cutler and Gruber 1996). Medicaid managed-care arrangements that integrate recipients into "mainstream" health care plans may reduce such perceptions, although this effect has received limited research attention (Newacheck et al. 2001). Recent descriptions of SCHIP outreach include anecdotal accounts by potential recipients who discover that they have been enrolled in Medicaid instead. Some recipients believe that providers prefer privately insured or SCHIP recipients to those receiving Medicaid—a perception consistent with Medicaid's lower reimbursement rates relative to other payers. At the same time, evaluations of efforts to increase Medicaid reimbursement rates have brought mixed results (Mayer et al. 2000). Consumer ignorance about Medicaid provisions may reinforce such concerns.

A second issue concerns the relationship between Medicaid and other assistance programs. Historically, Medicaid coverage for low-income families with children was linked to welfare enrollment. When enacting the 1996 welfare reform, federal policymakers delinked Medicaid and welfare by not including Medicaid in the welfare-related block grants to the states and by preserving Medicaid eligibility for adults under the prereform welfare rules. The reforms also continued the phased implementation of federal mandates to cover children living in low-income families. Despite these efforts to preserve continuity of Medicaid coverage, welfare reform has resulted not only in declines in welfare caseloads, but also in declines in Medicaid receipt (Ellwood and Ku 1998; Klein and Fish-Parcham 1999;

Kronebusch 2001a). Survey data reveal that many of the families leaving welfare that are eligible for Medicaid do not receive this coverage (Garrett and Holahan 2000a, b). Specific state policies appear to affect both TANF and Medicaid enrollment adversely, despite the statutory guarantee of Medicaid coverage. These effects are most pronounced for adults, but they also extend to children (Kronebusch 2001b).

By restricting eligibility for TANF cash aid, the 1996 reforms reduced incentives for families to enroll in the most prominent means-tested program that confers automatic eligibility for Medicaid. As welfare receipt has declined among the most employable potential recipients of cash aid, health insurance coverage has declined among some poor and near-poor families headed by low-wage workers. Existing evidence suggests that although poor children have rather high coverage rates, adults who formerly received AFDC or TANF often lack coverage.

Welfare reform has created special problems for persons who incur program sanctions, who are now ineligible for public aid because of time limits on benefits; recent immigrants who are no longer eligible for benefits; and persons with mental health or substance use problems who are more likely than others to fail work requirements or receive sanctions for other reasons. The large decline in welfare receipt has created a need for new methods of outreach and enrollment for potential Medicaid recipients, including those who receive no other form of public aid.

A third cause of low take-up has received less systematic attention. People who know they are eligible for public insurance may wait to enroll until they experience specific medical concerns. Studies of children who are eligible for Medicaid indicate that those who are not enrolled are slightly healthier than their peers who are enrolled (Davidoff et al. 2000). Individuals may also assume that they will receive medical care even if they lack insurance coverage or that they could enroll in the event of an adverse health event. One study found that living near a local public hospital reduced the probability of having private insurance coverage among persons with incomes between 100 and 200 percent and between 200 and 400 percent of the federal poverty level (Rask and Rask 2000). On the other hand, another study found little evidence that the availability of safety net providers displaces Medicaid coverage (Davidoff and Garrett 2001). One complication, noted by several authors, is that safety net providers may help patients enroll in public programs, creating enrollment effects that may counteract or mask individuals' decisions to forgo private coverage in favor of access to free care.

Whether uninsured people can reliably receive free care is unclear. Some commentators suggest that cost pressures associated with managed care have reduced access to treatment, though little reliable data are available to anyone wishing to scrutinize this concern. Recent data from the Community Tracking Study suggest that regions served largely by managed care organizations experience a reduction in charity care by physicians and reduced access to care for the uninsured (Center for Studying Health System Change 1999).

Families eligible for Medicaid also face a choice between public and private coverage. The Medicaid expansions have highlighted the importance of crowd-out in shaping the impact and cost-effectiveness of expanded public programs. Although the magnitude of this effect is open to debate (Cutler and Gruber 1996; Yazici and Kaestner 2000), economic principles suggest that highly subsidized public coverage will crowd out, or reduce demand for, similar private coverage. Many uninsured persons are offered coverage by their employer or have opportunities to purchase private coverage.

Finally, the quality of public insurance may influence both take-up and the trade-off between public and private coverage. Low-income families may avoid Medicaid if they believe that such coverage will not provide access to high-quality providers or high-quality care. Both concerns are influenced by reimbursement policy.

Several studies have examined provider decisions to participate in the Medicaid program (Baldwin et al. 1996; Schlesinger and Kronebusch 1990). Expanded eligibility may have little impact if Medicaid pays providers less than the prevailing market price for services. Data collected from the 1980s and early 1990s indicate that Medicaid reimbursement rates, though lower than those of private insurance, increased in many states at the same time as expanded eligibility. One study found that the Medicaid expansions were not accompanied by increased physician participation in some states, with low reimbursement rates being a major perceived barrier to physicians' taking on Medicaid patients (Dubay et al. 1995).

Reimbursement rates also influence the quality of care. Dubay and colleagues (1995) found that publicly funded clinics and hospitals that serve a high proportion of insured patients had greater financial resources to expand the range of prenatal services. Currie, Gruber, and Fischer (1995) found that increased reimbursement rates were associated with statistically significant reductions in infant mortality. Schlesinger and Kronebusch

(1990) reported that lower reimbursement rates to physicians reduced the adequacy of prenatal care and were associated with an increase in the incidence of low birth weight, possibly because lower reimbursement rates led to reductions in the time spent with patients, thereby reducing the quality of care.

The financial effects of public insurance on family income can be large. A 1998 General Accounting Office study found that a family of four in the nongroup market would have to pay a "medium" annual premium of $7,352—the equivalent of $3.68 per hour for full-year, full-time workers—for health coverage. This is approximately the same amount that a family with an annual income below $20,000 spends on food each year (GAO 2000). Even the cheapest plans, for healthy individuals living in regions with the lowest health care costs, charge more than $3,000 per year for coverage. The financial value of Medicaid and SCHIP, which provide more comprehensive coverage than many private plans, may be even greater. During the 1990s, expanded health insurance subsidies appears to have played an important role in increasing incentives for employment among current and former recipients of AFDC or TANF (Danziger et al. 2000).

Health insurance subsidies are now the single largest category of public aid for poor and near-poor families. In fiscal year 1998, the federal government provided $277 billion in means-tested assistance to disadvantaged families. Of that amount, $72 billion was actual cash aid to disadvantaged families; $92 billion was for means-tested food, housing, education, job training, energy assistance, or other services;[5] and $113 billion was for means-tested medical benefits. (The latter figure does not include the state component of Medicaid spending or health services provided by the Department of Veterans' Affairs).

In the wake of welfare reform, health insurance subsidies are widely considered to be the most politically sustainable transfers to poor households in the United States. They are a particularly important source of economic support for politically marginal or unpopular populations that otherwise face economic need. Health insurance, whatever its impact on public health or the health status of covered individuals, is therefore a major component of public policies designed to reduce poverty and inequality.

In summary, research has identified several barriers to health insurance coverage of low-income individuals and families. First, limited income reduces low-income workers' willingness and ability to purchase insurance at the individual level and reduces the collective preferences of low-income workers for employer-based coverage. Second, health insurance options tend to be restricted to standardized benefit packages that may not match the preferences of low-income workers. Third, demand for private health coverage is reduced because many low-income Americans are potentially eligible for public coverage or for free or reduced-cost care from safety net providers. At the same time, take-up rates for public programs are often low, reflecting perceptions about programs, the stigma of participation, diverse administrative difficulties, and interactions between related programs that affect whether potentially eligible persons can successfully enroll.

Health Insurance and Children

Children depend on their parents for many things. Their characteristic vulnerabilities are associated with their developmental and health-related needs in combination with their economic dependence and limits on their ability to make decisions. This dependence is especially important for medical decisionmaking and highlights the importance of parental decisions to take up private or public health coverage. Society presumes that most parents in most situations are able to internalize the consequences of decisions for the well-being of their children and to make decisions on their behalf.

Children are economically dependent on their parents and their health insurance coverage often depends on a parent's access to employer-based coverage. Even if adults have such coverage, however, it may not be available for dependent children, or parents may not choose to buy it for them because many employer-based plans require employees to pay an additional premium for family coverage. As a result, take-up of child coverage is incomplete, although some of these children are eligible for coverage through a second parent or public insurance.

The analysis of economic decisionmaking by low-income workers presented above applies here. Low-income families face competing demands for many goods and services. Children's coverage may seem expendable because most children are relatively healthy and require few health services. The services they do use are typically inexpensive, often limited to outpatient visits that can be paid for out-of-pocket. Depending on the cost-sharing requirements of the health insurance plan, these might have been out-of-pocket expenditures even for covered children.

The availability of alternative sources of care, including free and uncompensated services from physicians, hospitals, and clinics, may also reduce incentives for child coverage.

Starting in the mid-1980s, the federal government made a major effort to provide insurance coverage for children. A series of Medicaid (and then SCHIP) initiatives created options and imposed mandates on the states to expand Medicaid eligibility for children in low-income families. The initiatives also altered incentives for parents to purchase private coverage, leading to the substitution of public insurance for private insurance. Most analysts agree that some crowd-out has taken place, but they disagree about the extent of it (Blumberg, Dubay, and Norton 2000; Cutler and Gruber 1996; Shenkman et al. 1999; Shore-Sheppard 2000; Thorpe and Florence 1998; Yazici and Kaestner 2000).

Much current research concerns administrative barriers to enrollment and reenrollment in Medicaid and SCHIP programs (Dick et al. 2002). Research on take-up has largely examined individual-level determinants of program participation, namely, knowledge of eligibility, perceptions about the program, welfare stigma, administrative procedures, and the experiences of potential recipients as they navigate the bureaucratic enrollment process (Perry et al. 2000; Stuber et al. 2000). Welfare reform has resulted in decreased enrollment in Medicaid by eligible potential recipients, including decreased enrollment of eligible children.

Another important program that covers children is SSI. The 1990 Supreme Court decision *Sullivan vs. Zebley* relaxed the eligibility criteria for children. Between 1991 and 1996, low-income children could qualify for SSI benefits by having a specific qualifying medical impairment or by having a disability determined within an individualized functional assessment (IFA) (Garrett and Glied 2000). Enrollment of children in SSI tripled, growing from 294,000 in September 1990 to more than 950,000 six years later.

Partly as a result of this rapid increase, the IFA process became increasingly controversial, particularly when used to establish eligibility based upon attention deficit-hyperactivity disorder and other behavioral disorders. Because SSI eligibility brings cash assistance in addition to insurance and social services, the possibility that benefits might create undesirable incentives or might encourage fraud is of greater concern for SSI than arises in other programs for children with special needs.

Legislation in 1996 eliminated the IFA process for children and removed behavioral disorders as a qualifying disability, leading to eligibility redetermination proceedings for all children who had been deemed eligible on the basis of an IFA or maladaptive behavior. Today, SSI applicants must have specific qualifying diagnoses or experience impairments that exceed at least one specific qualifying impairment. In part because of these changes, the number of children receiving SSI fell to 847,000 by December 1999.

While SSI reform has substantial implications for underinsurance and for child disability policy, evidence suggests that changes in SSI eligibility did not greatly affect the overall number of children receiving insurance coverage. An analysis by the Social Security Administration suggests that fewer than 100,000 children ultimately lost SSI eligibility as a result of welfare reform (Davies, Iams, and Rupp 2000). Moreover, because SSI required low family income, many children removed from the program remained eligible for public coverage. The most extensive analysis highlighted the interplay between the traditional SSI program and AFDC (Garrett and Glied 2000). In states that offer high benefits, most children who were SSI-eligible were also eligible for AFDC. Even when children are not eligible for AFDC or TANF, those who are eligible for SSI on the basis of income are eligible for Medicaid or SCHIP in most states.

In summary, lack of health coverage for children originates with many of the same factors that affect coverage of their parents. Low- and middle-income families face conflicting incentives to obtain coverage. Employer-based coverage may not be available or may require parents to pay additional premiums for dependent coverage. Public programs have expanded to cover many children in low-income families, but enrollment has also been hampered by administrative difficulties, welfare reform and other policy changes, and relatively low take-up rates. Nonetheless, children are less likely to be uninsured than nonelderly adults.

Health Insurance and Racial or Ethnic Minorities

Racial and ethnic minorities, in particular African Americans and Hispanic Americans, are less likely to be insured than non-Hispanic whites (Carrasquillo et al. 1999; Seccombe, Clarke, and Coward 1994), although the multivariate analysis presented above suggests that there are differences across minority groups. For African Americans, mean differences in coverage become statistically insignificant when one accounts for income, education, region, and other socioeconomic factors. Such findings suggest that the economic position (and perhaps geographic location) of African-American families is a critical factor in explaining low rates of health coverage.

Results for Hispanics are quite different. Rates of insurance remain low for this group, even after considering household income, education, and other factors (de la Torre et al. 1996; Valdez et al. 1993). The differences are especially large among those with low wages: according to one analysis of insurance in California, 60 percent of Hispanics earning less than $7 per hour had no health insurance in 1998. Among workers with the same wage, 26 percent of whites, 46 percent of blacks, and 41 percent of Asians were uninsured (Fronstin 2000). Much of the decline in insurance coverage during the early 1990s occurred among Hispanics (Berk, Albers, and Schur 1996; Carrasquillo et al. 1999).

One reason for the low rates of coverage among Hispanics is the large proportion of recent immigrants within this group. One-third of Hispanic Americans, and two-thirds of Asian Americans, are foreign-born (Ku and Matani 2001). Data from the 1997 National Survey of America's Families for persons with incomes below 200 percent of the poverty level show that among adults, 58 percent of noncitizens, 42 percent of naturalized citizens, and 34 percent of native-born citizens were uninsured. Contrasts among children were even more stark: 54 percent of noncitizen children, 33 percent of citizen children with noncitizen parents, and 19 percent of citizen children with parents who were citizens lacked health coverage.

Several factors contribute to these trends. Immigrants face many difficulties in obtaining jobs, insurance, and access to medical services, and those difficulties exist across the age spectrum (Angel and Angel 1996; Carrasquillo et al. 2000; Ku and Matani 2001; Siddharthan 1991; Thamer et al. 1997). Since members of minority groups have low mean incomes, they are likely to have correspondingly low rates of insurance coverage, in both the purchase of nongroup (Saver and Doescher 2000) and employer-based coverage (Hall, Collins, and Glied 1999; Schur and Feldman 2001; Seccombe et al. 1994). Such results are consistent with those found by Monheit and Vistnes (2000), who documented a dramatic decline in coverage of Hispanic male workers between 1987 and 1996.

Minority workers may have social and economic disadvantages that reduce their attractiveness to employers—and hence their wages. For example, they are more likely to suffer from inadequate education, and their first language may not be English. Because of the constraint imposed by the minimum wage, employers may be especially unlikely to offer job benefits such as health insurance to these low-wage workers.

Members of minority groups may also face systematic discrimination by employers. While discrimination may be penalized by competitive markets, recent research highlights the persistence of racial stigma in labor markets (Loury 2002). In addition to direct discrimination in job hiring and promotion, nominally nondiscriminatory sorting processes may channel members of minority groups into industries and occupations that are less likely to offer health benefits, including seasonal or part-time employment. Finally, more subtle forms of discrimination, such as redlining, may emerge in insurance markets.

The main alternative to employer-based insurance is public insurance. Three aspects of the policy and administration of public programs may have a racial component. The first concerns the administration of enrollment. Members of racial and ethnic minorities may elect not to pursue enrollment because they believe that they will be treated badly during the enrollment process or because, as members of disadvantaged groups, they are especially sensitive to welfare-related stigma. Individual caseworkers or administrative staff may discriminate against members of racial and ethnic minorities. Language is a potential barrier (Schur and Albers 1996; Weinick and Krauss 2000). Analyses of Medicaid outreach and enrollment efforts during the 1980s suggest that attention to language issues was important in increasing take-up and improving the early receipt of prenatal care.

Second, changes in the law concerning eligibility for public insurance affect recent immigrants. The 1996 welfare reform made recent immigrants ineligible for many federal entitlements that confer Medicaid coverage or facilitate Medicaid enrollment, and imposed other restrictions on eligibility (Minkoff, Bauer, and Joyce 1997). Although undocumented immigrants remained eligible for emergency Medicaid, undocumented immigrants were barred from TANF, SSI, Food Stamps, housing aid, and other important means-tested programs.

The 1996 legislation also imposed more stringent rules on immigrant sponsors in an effort to restrict immigrants' participation in federal means-tested programs. Sponsors face new responsibilities for providing financial support for immigrants, while the waiting periods before becoming eligible for specific programs such as SSI were increased (U.S. Congress 2000). States were also allowed to establish a five-year waiting period before legal immigrants admitted after August 1996 can receive non-emergency Medicaid coverage. After five years, the income of an immigrant's sponsor is included in the eligibility determination for cash aid and for Medicaid. Undocumented children are ineligible for SCHIP aid. Measures such as California's Proposition 187 may pose special access barriers, though the impact of this legislation is unknown.

Finally, responsibility for Medicaid and SCHIP policy and administration lie with state governments. Such policymaking is influenced by local public opinion, interest group activity, the availability of economic resources, and the actions and preferences of state policymakers. Racial and ethnic minorities live disproportionately in states in the South and Southwest that historically have adopted restrictive policies concerning program eligibility and low rates of insurance coverage. Although the reason is unclear, having a higher percentage of racial and ethnic minorities appears to reduce public spending at both the state and local levels (Cutler et al. 1993). Related findings on the political economy of education spending suggest similar effects (Poterba 1998).

In summary, lack of coverage among racial and ethnic minorities is often related to the general problems of economic disadvantage that limit access to employment and income and that influence the ability to purchase insurance. In addition, their history of recent immigration particularly affects the insurance status of Hispanics. Public programs do not completely fill in the resulting gaps in insurance coverage.

Health Insurance and Chronic Illness

Persons with chronic illnesses often suffer loss of income and may have difficulty obtaining or retaining employment. As a result, lack of income is an important reason for their lack of insurance coverage. Equally important, this group presents severe challenges to the insurance marketplace.

In a competitive insurance market, individuals use insurance to pool risks with others who, at the outset, share similar health risks. Later, once health risks are realized, individuals with chronic illness are charged an actuarially fair premium for health insurance coverage. Absent transaction costs and with full information about the health status of individual consumers, competitive insurance markets charge each individual his or her actuarially fair premium. Lacking sufficient information about consumer risk, fear of adverse selection may prevent insurance markets from insuring some groups at all. The presence of consumers who have high, but hidden, expected costs alters the content of insurance in other ways. Insurers face strong incentives to design cost-sharing and other plan features to be attractive to healthy consumers at the same time that they are unattractive to consumers with high expected expenditures.

When insurers know what sort of expenditures to expect, efficient pricing is possible. For modifiable risk factors, such as tobacco use, the setting of higher, actuarially fair premiums may create an incentive to reduce risky behavior. However, when used to set premiums, information about expected expenditures can also reduce consumer welfare when there are missing markets. As noted earlier, individuals cannot buy insurance against the possibility that they will be born with "uninsurable" ailments or that they will be unable to obtain coverage as high-risk persons. Competitive markets do not cross-subsidize persons with diagnosed chronic illnesses, so actuarially fair premiums for children and adults with chronic or acute illness, chronic psychiatric and substance use disorders, and other conditions are often quite high (French et al. 2000; Ireys et al. 1997; Kronick et al. 1996; Kronick et al. 2000; Kuhlthau et al. 1998; Lieu et al. 1999).

Given the possibility of public subsidy, one might address these concerns by subsidizing coverage of individuals facing high expected expenditure (Ellis 1996; Fowler and Anderson 1996; Payne et al. 2000). When the characteristics associated with high expenditure on health care are easily observed, such subsidies can be incorporated into payment policy. For example, risk contracts for health maintenance organizations within Medicare include a limited set of adjustments for several factors. Diverse risk-adjustment strategies have been proposed (Van De Ven and Ellis 2000), including subsidies to address the needs of high-expenditure individuals, and insurance "carve-outs," which are specialized plans designed to manage high-expenditure categories (Batavia and DeJong 2001; Neff and Anderson 1995; West et al. 1996).

In practice, however, many vulnerable populations pose difficult problems for risk adjustment in health insurance markets. From the payer's perspective, vulnerable populations are often unattractive customers. Existing methods for risk adjustment within the general population are at an early stage and are especially challenged when addressing specific high-risk subgroups (Ettner et al. 2000). People who are HIV-positive and people with mental or behavioral health care needs are particularly in need of coverage, and their lack of coverage has prompted efforts to develop feasible risk-adjustment strategies (Ettner et al. 2000; Van De Ven and Ellis 2000).

Costs and utilization of health care vary markedly within vulnerable populations (Ireys et al. 1997; Lamers 1999). While many public insurance programs do employ risk-adjustment algorithms, such systems capture little of the observed variance in health care expenditures. (The performance of risk-adjustment systems has not been evaluated carefully, although efforts have increased recently [Ettner et al. 2000; Kronick et al. 1996; Kronick et al. 2000; Payne et al. 2000].) Among children with special health care needs, even among those with the same diagnoses, costs vary widely. Moreover, individuals with high previous expenditures have high expected expenditures in subsequent periods (Fowler and Anderson 1996).

Some people with serious or chronic illness lack insurance coverage because they are "medically uninsurable"—that is, because they have a specific medical problem. Surprisingly, the proportion of uninsured Americans who are medically uninsurable is unknown. Reisine and Fifield (1995) found that 21 percent of people with rheumatoid arthritis reported having limited insurance because they had a preexisting condition and 11 percent reported having been denied insurance. More recently, Stroupe, Kinney, and Kniesner (2000) reported that having a chronic illness increases the probability of uninsurance by 2 to 8 percentage points; however, their sample of Indiana residents included 242 healthy persons and 215 persons drawn from a "cancer sample" that included women with breast cancer and men with testicular cancers. The sample was therefore not representative of the broad population or of the population of individuals with serious chronic illness.

The nationally representative NHIS can provide some insight here. Its data show that 0.94 percent of uninsured adult respondents, an estimated 263,000 people, reported they could not obtain insurance coverage because of a health problem. More than 60 percent of uninsured individuals reported they had no insurance coverage because coverage was too expensive or they could not afford it.

Data from the National Health and Nutrition Examination Study (NHANES) III are also useful. NHANES III features a detailed questionnaire (and medical examination) that asked respondents whether a doctor had ever told them that they have cancer, diabetes, or other serious ailments. The study also investigates respondents' insurance status and asks them the primary reason for their lack of coverage. It found that 2.2 percent of uninsured individuals had been refused insurance because of a health concern. Among those turned down, 39 percent had a specific chronic illness. Of those refused coverage because of ill health, 23 percent had been diagnosed with diabetes, 10 percent with stroke, and 9 percent with asthma.

Although the medically uninsurable are a small proportion of the uninsured, many uninsured men and women experience significant illness. NHANES III data indicate that 2 million uninsured individuals have been told by a doctor that they have arthritis, 1.8 million have asthma, and 1.3 million have chronic bronchitis. An additional 613,000 have diabetes, and 615,000 have cancer.

Practices that lead to lack of coverage or high premiums for chronically ill individuals, such as medical underwriting, are widespread in some segments of the group market and appear to be widespread in the individual insurance market (Zellers, McLaughlin, and Frick 1992). Cantor and colleagues (1995), examining data from the 1993 Robert Wood Johnson Foundation Employer Health Insurance Survey, found that medical underwriting was allowed in 35 percent of firms with fewer than 50 workers, and in 20 percent of larger firms. Yet only 5 percent of employers reported that some workers or dependent were actually excluded from coverage.

Concern about underwriting and other barriers to group coverage led to the 1996 Health Insurance Portability and Accountability Act (HIPAA). The act limits underwriting of continuously insured individuals who change group plans and prohibits insurers from imposing within-group underwriting to exclude individuals with a chronic illness. HIPAA also requires insurers who offer small-group coverage to make such policies available to all small employers.

The impact of HIPAA on insurance coverage for chronically ill individuals remains unknown. The law gives group insurers some leeway to cap lifetime payments for specific illnesses, and it does not require insurance plans to provide mental health coverage or other types of coverage that may be especially important for chronically ill individuals. On the other hand, HIPAA requires that renewal of individual policies be guaranteed, without exclusions for preexisting conditions. The act does not regulate actual premiums, does not provide public subsidies for individuals with high health care costs, and does not apply to uninsured individuals (Blumberg and Nichols 1998; Stroupe, Kinney, and Kniesner 2000).

In summary, persons with chronic illness often have high, predictable health costs. As a result, they often face difficulties when trying to buy insurance. Insurance markets are limited in their ability to protect individuals from the risk of high premiums. Chronic illness may also reduce wages and hours worked, limiting access to employer-based coverage. Although relatively few uninsured individuals report that they were denied coverage because of preexisting conditions, many Americans with chronic illness lack health insurance coverage. Government interventions that regulate private insurers to protect coverage or that provide subsidized insurance have only partially succeeded in serving the complex needs of this group.

Health Insurance and the Near-Elderly

As discussed above, Americans age 55 to 64 (who will be referred to as the near-elderly) are more likely than younger adults to hold insurance coverage. These NHIS findings are consistent with previous empirical analyses that use other data sets. Most recently, Monheit, Vistnes, and Eisenberg's (2001) analysis of 1996 data found that 87 percent of workers age 60 to 64 had some form of insurance coverage; thus, the near-elderly have the highest prevalence of coverage of any age group of adult workers. Yet Glied and Stabile (1999) noted significant declines in health insurance coverage for the near-elderly between 1989 and 1997. This adverse trend suggests that the insurance needs of the near-elderly may need to receive policy attention.

Despite their high rate of insurance coverage, individuals age 55 to 64 face several challenges that make coverage a special concern. They are five times as likely as people age 25 to 34 to report that they are in poor health, and their expected health care expenditures are twice as high (Gruber 2000). Women who are out of the workforce and in less than excellent health had especially high rates of uninsurance. Among near-elderly workers, 23 percent of women in less than excellent health reported lack of insurance coverage, compared with 16 percent of comparable men (Monheit et al. 2001).

Because many near-elderly people experience life transitions such as declining health, early retirement, or changes in household composition, several studies have suggested that they are more affected than younger workers by clauses in employer-based policies that exempt preexisting conditions from coverage and by measures that limit portability of coverage (GAO 1998). Sloan and Conover (1998) explored these concerns, using 1992 and 1994 data from the Health and Retirement Study for persons between the ages of 51 and 64. The authors found that employment (including spouse's employment), work disability, and education were the most important determinants of insurance coverage. Controlling for these factors, poor health and functional status were not associated with a higher probability of uninsurance, but were associated with receipt of public rather than private coverage.

Drawing on data from the 1996 NHIS, table 5.3 shows the prevalence of health problems among adult men and women with and without health insurance coverage. Respondents were considered to have a health problem if they reported at least one academic or work limitation due to ill health or identified their health as fair or poor. The majority of such cases involved a specific health limitation rather than self-identified fair or poor health. Particularly for women, the prevalence of health difficulties increases sharply at this age: approximately 16 percent of uninsured men, and 26 percent of uninsured women reported significant health problems. Although near-elderly individuals made up only 6 percent of the uninsured population in the NHIS sample, they accounted for 24 percent of the men and women who were both uninsured and experiencing health problems. Analysis of NHIS data, like previous research, found that women in this age group who lacked insurance coverage were substantially more likely than their insured peers to report health difficulties. A multivariate logistic regression model of health problems among all uninsured men and women indicates that for both men and women, the near-elderly are far more likely than other uninsured individuals to report serious health concerns. (See table 5.4.)

In summary, the increased likelihood of ill health and its associated costs pose particular problems for uninsured near-elderly persons. These difficulties, combined with reduced employment, early retirement, changed employment status of a spouse, and divorce or death of a spouse, can result in loss of access to group coverage. Public programs

Table 5.3. *The Prevalence of Health Limitations and Poor Health Status among Adults Who Lack Insurance Coverage*

	Insured men (%)	Insured women (%)	Uninsured men (%)	Uninsured women (%)
17–24	2.1	2.3	2.3	1.8
25–34	3.4	4.1	4.9	3.1
35–44	5.4	6.8	7.9	9.0
45–54	8.6	9.4	12.2	15.6
55–64	16.9	17.6	15.8	25.5

Table 5.4. *Probability of Poor Health Status among Uninsured Individuals in the National Health Interview Survey, 1996 Wave*

	Women age 17–64 adjusted odds ratio [95% CI]	Men age 17–64 adjusted odds ratio [95% CI][a]
South	Referent	Referent
West	0.969	0.656
	[0.621, 1.512]	[0.387, 1.113]
Northeast	0.801	0.827
	[0.458, 1.401]	[0.487, 1.405]
Midwest	0.942	0.851
	[0.572, 1.551]	[0.505, 1.434]
High school dropout	Referent	Referent
High school graduate	0.685	1.059
	[0.483, 0.971]	[0.722, 1.551]
College graduate	1.090	0.441
	[0.542, 2.190]	[0.191, 1.016]
African American	1.047	1.599
	[0.687, 1.596]	[1.033, 2.477]
Hispanic/Latino	0.728	0.461
	[0.489, 1.0851]	[0.294, 0.723]
Non-Hispanic white	Referent	Referent
Married	0.877	0.829
	[0.613, 1.256]	[0.563, 1.222]
Unmarried	Referent	Referent
Recent immigrant	0.433	0.386
	[0.233, 0.808]	[0.181, 0.8244]
Log (family income)	0.810	0.624
	[0.624, 1.051]	[0.490, 0.794]
Top-coded income (over $50,000)	1.519	0.917
	[0.747, 3.087]	[0.378, 2.225]
Poverty	1.437	1.407
	[0.899, 2.297]	[0.850, 2.329]
Unemployed	1.018	0.944
	[0.493, 2.104]	[0.458, 1.946]
Under age 25	0.471	0.388
	[0.207, 1.073]	[0.194, 0.778]
Age 25–34	Referent	Referent
Age 35–44	2.754	1.623
	[1.580, 4.799]	[1.005, 2.622]

(*continued*)

Table 5.4. *Continued*

	Women age 17–64 *adjusted odds ratio* *[95% CI]*	Men age 17–64 *adjusted odds ratio* *[95% CI]*[a]
Age 45–54	5.633	2.772
	[3.214, 9.872]	[1.664, 4.617]
Age 55–64	9.328	4.065
	[5.266, 16.523]	[2.300, 7.185]
Estimated population	9,351,929	10,744,441

a. Not shown: Asian-American subgroup.

only imperfectly expand access to insurance for those with chronic illness, including many of the near-elderly.

Health Insurance and Psychiatric Disorders

Psychiatric disorders are among the most common forms of acute and chronic illness in the U.S. population. As documented in the National Comorbidity Study, half of all noninstitutionalized adults age 15 to 54 will satisfy the standard diagnostic (DSM-IV) screening criteria for at least one psychiatric disorder during their lifetime, while 30 percent will have had at least one disorder within the previous 12 months, and 14 percent will have three or more disorders at the same time (Kessler et al. 1994). Severe psychiatric disorders are less prevalent. Regier and colleagues (1993) estimate that approximately 1 percent of the U.S. population suffers from schizophrenia or bipolar disorders. Narrow and colleagues (2000) indicate more than twice that prevalence of severe mental illness, using another definition.

Although severe mental illness is unusual, it poses distinct challenges to both research and practice concerned with health insurance coverage. First, the stigma associated with psychiatric disorders plays an important role in public policy (Domenici 1993), in providers' recognition of disorders and their referral of patients to appropriate care (Wells et al. 1996), and in individuals' willingness to seek care or to take up pertinent public services (Mechanic 1994). In the National Comorbidity Study, less than 40 percent of individuals who satisfied lifetime screening criteria for psychiatric disorders have received professional treatment, and less than 20 percent of respondents with recent disorders received treatment during the previous year. Equally striking are the patterns among severely mentally ill individuals. Among such respondents to the Healthcare for Communities survey, 59 percent obtained no outpatient care (McAlpine and Mechanic 2000). Suicidal ideation and danger to self or others from alcohol use were also negatively related to receipt of mental health services (McAlpine and Mechanic 2000). Such patterns highlight the possibility that people with psychiatric disorders may be unable to act as effective agents on their own behalf.

Second, individuals with clinically significant psychiatric disorders are often unemployed, out of the labor force, or employed in low-wage positions that may not offer health insurance coverage. Economic disadvantage is especially common among those who satisfy the criteria for severe mental illness. Although the precise criteria for severe mental illness vary (Narrow et al. 2000), persons with bipolar disorder or schizophrenia would undoubtedly be identified as experiencing significant chronic disorders that require ongoing care.

McAlpine and Mechanic (2000) have summarized health care utilization, insurance coverage, and the social circumstances of the non-institutionalized population with severe mental illness. Adults experiencing severe mental illness have significantly lower household incomes than other adults, and 69 percent of them are unmarried. Moreover, nonwhites and persons with less than a high school education are overrepresented in this population. The authors found that 20 percent of individuals with severe mental illness and 18 percent of individuals with other psychiatric disorders are uninsured; 45 percent of individuals with severe mental illness and 25 percent of those with other psychiatric disorders received some form of public insurance. Among persons with severe mental illness, insurance coverage is associated with significantly higher utilization of specialty mental health care. Given the nonexperimental nature of the available data, the causal foundation of this relationship is unclear. Individuals who seek or receive specialty care may be subsequently referred to social services and enrolled in public insurance programs.

Public insurance is especially important for individuals with the most severe psychiatric disorders, many of whom satisfy eligibility criteria for SSI or Social Security Disability Income (SSDI). Some 1.25 million Americans between the ages of 18 and 64 receive SSI benefits for psychiatric diagnoses. An additional 900,000 receive SSI because of developmental disability (U.S. Congress 2000).

Third, insurance coverage of individuals with psychiatric and substance use disorders is influenced by shifts in public policy. Until 1996, an individual could qualify for federal disability programs through a diagnosis of alcohol or illicit substance use disorders (drug addicts and alcoholics, or DA&A). At that time, approximately 209,000 persons received SSI or SSDI benefits through the drug and alcohol program. However, Public Law 104-121 eliminated eligibility for individuals whose drug addiction or alcoholism was material to the determination of disability, and between December 1996 and January 1997, 103,000 such individuals were removed from public aid. The majority of recipients who remained on the assistance rolls were recertified on the basis of psychiatric diagnoses (Davies et al. 2000). Swartz, Lurigio, and Goldstein (2000) surveyed 204 randomly selected former recipients of federal aid in the Chicago area. One year after disenrollment, 28 respondents reported monthly earnings of at least $500 and 69 requalified for public aid based upon medical or psychiatric impairment. But more than half of the former recipients—107 persons—reported monthly earnings below $500 and received no public cash aid. The health insurance status of the former recipients was not reported.

National patterns of health coverage among persons who used to receive federal aid because of a DA&A diagnosis are currently unknown. Some former recipients may be covered through general assistance and other state-level programs, but such programs vary widely and have received limited analysis (Danziger and Kossoudji 1994/1995; Schmidt, Weisner, and Wiley 1998).

Fourth, mental health services in the public sector, including substance abuse treatment, are often financed outside of the Medicaid or private insurance market, through state funds or federal programs such as the Substance Abuse Prevention and Treatment (SAPT) block grant. The impact of block grant funding on access to treatment and the interaction between block grants and health insurance coverage have received little research attention (Jacobsen and McGuire 1996; IOM 2000). The role of public mental health services in gaining access to other public health services has likewise received little systematic attention, although the analysis by Friedmann and colleagues (2001) of the link between substance abuse treatment and other forms of health care is an exception.

In summary, individuals who face psychiatric and substance use disorders may have difficulty representing themselves effectively as consumers. They also face important economic disadvantages, largely because they lack employment or have low income. Gaps in the complex array of public programs contribute to the lack of insurance coverage for this group.

Challenges for Research and Policy

In addition to problems that are specific to each vulnerable population, these groups have common concerns. Some of them concern data quality and questions for academic research. Others involve the impact of policy initiatives within a complex array of programs. Still others involve competing priorities in expanding health insurance coverage to improve health.

Inadequacy of Data

Many population-based surveys have examined health status, health insurance coverage, and health care expenditures across the U.S. population. Such surveys include the Current Population Survey, the National Health Interview Survey, the National Survey of America's Families, the Survey of Income and Program Participation, the Medical Expenditure Panel Survey, and others. Because of differences in methodology and sampling, these surveys yield somewhat different estimates of the population that lacks health insurance coverage (Fronstin 2000).

Despite the great value of such surveys, each provides limited coverage of the most vulnerable groups in the U.S. population. The Institute of Medicine (2000) notes that existing population-based surveys provide poor coverage of individuals at greatest risk of HIV infection. By excluding institutionalized populations, by using telephone surveys, and by employing sampling strategies that frequently exclude individuals in greatest need, existing data sets provide poor coverage of several vulnerable populations, including persons in inpatient psychiatric facilities and the 2 million men and women in correctional facilities. For example, prisoners are beyond the scope of such surveys as the National Comorbidity Study and the Behavioral Risk Factor Surveillance System. Each of these populations is of great public health importance and has a high prevalence of illness or injury.

Often, data regarding the insurance status of vulnerable populations are collected haphazardly, as a by-product of clinical or social services rather than as part of a concerted strategy of population-based surveillance. If health care utilization is influenced by the availability of insurance coverage, clinical data systems may be biased. In similar fashion, available data regarding chronic illness or behavioral risks are generally based upon self-reported behaviors in national surveys that do not provide adequate coverage of men and women at greatest risk. A few population-based surveys such as the National Health and Nutrition Examination Study do include medical examinations and take blood samples, but these surveys do not adequately cover the high-risk groups of greatest policy importance. As a result of these data limitations, the circumstances, and even the absolute size, of many vulnerable populations remains unknown (Kaplan and Soloschatz 1993).

Interaction Between Public Insurance and Other Funding

Many health care services for vulnerable populations are financed outside the traditional sources of public or private coverage. The interaction between health insurance coverage and other funding streams is imperfectly understood. For example, uninsured adults who require substance abuse treatment frequently receive services through the SAPT block grant. The services cost $1.5 billion in fiscal year 2000. Yet the impact of SAPT on expanding access to treatment for uninsured individuals is unknown and virtually unstudied (Jacobsen and McGuire 1996).

Safety net providers are paid by health insurance, public programs, and government subsidies. Given the complex financial arrangements that support these organizations, efforts to expand health insurance coverage may bring unanticipated effects. Duggan (forthcoming) examined the impacts of increased disproportionate share hospital (DSH) payments and found that they had little effect on the public hospitals with the largest share of indigent patients. Because public hospitals face soft budget constraints, the impact of state and federal subsidies will be on the entities that finance hospital operations. Virtually the entire benefit associated with increased DSH subsidies was captured by local governments, which reduced their subsidies to public hospitals by approximately $1 for every $1 the hospitals received in additional DSH funds. Baicker (1997) found that increased state expenditures for Medicaid were associated with reduced expenditures for AFDC and other programs targeted to poor individuals. Given the soft budget constraints faced by many safety net providers, and given the complex interplay across different levels of government, understanding the true incidence of health insurance policy initiatives is a high priority for economists and political scientists examining the political economy of expanded coverage.

Supply-Side Responses to Expanded Coverage

In addition to their budgetary effects, policies to expand insurance coverage may alter incentives to health care providers and thus produce unanticipated effects. During the 1980s and 1990s, the number of Medicaid-financed births and the proportion of pregnant women receiving Medicaid more than tripled (Singh, Gold, and Frost 1994). The health impact of such policies has been the subject of considerable debate. Many state-level studies found little impact on the adequacy of prenatal care or the incidence of low birth weight (Baldwin et al. 1996; Braveman et al. 1993; Haas et al. 1993; Long and Marquis 1998; Piper, Mitchel, and Ray 1994; Piper, Ray, and Griffin 1990). At the same time, several authors suggested that Medicaid expansion reduced infant mortality by improving access to advanced technologies such as neonatal intensive care (Braveman et al. 1991; Currie and Gruber 1996). Whatever the health impact for specific infants, Medicaid expansion greatly reduced the proportion of babies born to uninsured women (Duggan forthcoming). Thus, within five years, Medicaid payments subsidized what had traditionally been the largest single category of charity care (Norton and Staiger 1994). Expanded eligibility for Medicaid-funded prenatal care, labor and delivery, and postnatal services therefore had a substantial impact on health care providers.

More generous Medicaid policies also increased competition for the profitable classes of Medicaid patients. As Medicaid acquired a larger market share of deliveries, and as reimbursement rates converged with those of private payers in many states, providers who had not traditionally served low-income populations began to enter the Medicaid market (Langreth 1998). The resulting competition has harmed traditional safety net institutions, which have lost low-risk Medicaid patients to other providers (Gaskin, Hadley, and Freedman 2001). Because safety net providers sometimes use Medicaid funds to subsidize services for uninsured or underinsured individuals, this competition has important implications for public health. Most recently, analysts have considered Medicaid's role in providing potentially undesirable incentives for less advanced facilities to enter the market for neonatal intensive care (Baker and Phibbs forthcoming).

Priorities for Expanding Insurance Coverage

Social decisions about expanded insurance coverage can be based on many criteria. Low average cost, political feasibility, and norms of self-sufficiency are one set of pertinent criteria, and these have animated current and past efforts to expand coverage among pregnant women, infants, and poor and near-poor children. If one were to allocate resources based upon prevalence of infectious disease, the marginal impact on population health, or the consequences of poor health status, smaller but more severely disadvantaged populations such as adults with mental and behavioral disorders might receive higher priority. If one wished to focus on men and women in poor health, policies targeted towards individuals over the age of 55 would command greater attention, since 25 percent of uninsured women in this age group experience poor health or a specific health-related limitation.

Many of the analyses summarized in this chapter suggest another criterion for receiving expanded insurance coverage: populations challenged by both poverty and chronic illness. Although each of these factors is a source of vulnerability, the interplay between them creates a special vulnerability that does not arise from either factor alone. Persons with psychiatric or substance use disorders, low-income children with special health care needs, current and former welfare recipients—all of these people face economic challenges that increase the need for health insurance coverage while impeding their ability to obtain coverage and potentially limiting their ability to use available coverage to maximum advantage. Moreover, the link between low income and lack of health insurance is influenced by the economic realities of chronic illness. Poor health hinders labor market performance, thereby impeding access to health insurance and medical services.

Public health insurance seeks to accommodate the social, economic, and medical challenges facing people who have more than one source of vulnerability. Increasingly, public insurance seeks to link the health care delivery system with other components of the safety net to better serve vulnerable populations. Children with special health care needs have many medical and nonmedical needs that, in practice, are often addressed through health insurance systems. Title V care coordination services and Medicaid subsidies in school settings play an important role in securing educational services (Grossman et al. 1999; Horwitz and

Stein 1990; Liptak et al. 1998). Individuals with psychiatric disorders receive similar case management to help them secure cash assistance and social services (Bae 1997). As insurance becomes increasingly integrated with educational, rehabilitative, and social services, lack of coverage deprives individuals of a prominent entry point for receiving services to meet medical and social needs.

Conclusion

This chapter has examined the health insurance coverage of vulnerable populations. Several questions remain of social and public health concern.

For some populations, such as near-poor children who are eligible for but not receiving Medicaid or SCHIP coverage, the critical questions are concerned with take-up: How much do eligible families really value these benefits? How can public insurance programs replace traditional cash assistance programs as vehicles of outreach and enrollment? Do public programs unintentionally create barriers to enrollment and re-enrollment? For other populations, such as recent or undocumented immigrants, the critical questions concern more complex policy barriers to the receipt of health care services.

Other populations are especially vulnerable because of chronic illness. Children with special health care needs are costly for health insurance plans and have multiple medical and social needs. The ability of public payers to adequately adjust payments for risk and to monitor quality are essential questions even for children who have obtained nominal coverage. People with chronic illness are also likely to be underinsured, another cause of concern. The ability of public insurance to protect these individuals from economic hardship is unproved. Uninsured or underinsured men and women between the ages of 55 and 64 present significant concerns because of their high rates of illness.

More severely disadvantaged populations raise more difficult questions. The most widely used data and models in policy analysis concern noninstitutionalized, generally employed populations. Data regarding individuals with severe mental illness or severe substance use disorders are much less complete and of unknown quality. How large are these populations? How well do public insurance programs address their needs? If uninsured individuals receive services through the SAPT block grant, through non-Medicaid state funding for psychiatric care, or through other sources, does this ensure access to appropriate care?

Despite gaps in available data, existing research does provide useful insights for public policy. The data provide ample warning that one should not oversell the possibilities of improving health status and individual well-being through expanded health coverage. Expanded coverage is unlikely to eliminate the high rates of death and illness that arise from multiple causes and require multifaceted interventions.

At the same time, expanded coverage will provide important benefits to the intended beneficiaries and to the broader society. Expanded insurance coverage subsidizes the economically disadvantaged. It increases health care utilization by poor and near-poor children, as well as by several other important groups. Health insurance and medical providers play important roles in the delivery of social, educational, and rehabilitative services to many disadvantaged populations. Expanded coverage also provides financial support to safety net providers, which accept primary responsibility for serving the most disadvantaged segments of the U.S. population.

Health policy analysts who favor expanding coverage aspire to a comprehensive and straightforward set of interventions that will provide secure insurance coverage to Americans in the greatest need. As in the case of income support, the desire for simplicity must be balanced against the particular needs of specific populations and against the institutional complexity of existing interventions that address their social, economic, and health needs. Designing health insurance coverage that builds upon the incomplete, but essential patchwork of existing interventions remains a central challenge in serving the most vulnerable segments of the U.S. population.

NOTES

1. These estimates are from the 1987 Medical Expenditure Survey. We thank Jose Escarce for providing the figures and for suggesting this point.

2. Competitive markets also fail to address traditional externalities such as infectious disease transmission or the full social costs of substance abuse. Such public health concerns provide a second classic argument for policy intervention.

3. The NHIS is a stratified, weighted sample. In estimating these regression coefficients, the authors use the STATA 6.0 routine SVYLOGIT to accommodate the weighted and clustered nature of the NHIS sample. Following public health research practice, results are reported in the form of adjusted odds ratios, which are somewhat more easily interpreted than raw logit coefficients.

4. The authors thank Barbara Wolfe for suggesting this model.

5. All figures are from the *Overview of Entitlements,* "Green-Book" (U.S. Congress 2000).

REFERENCES

Acs, Gregory P. 1995. "Explaining Trends in Health Insurance Coverage between 1988 and 1991." *Inquiry* 32(1): 102–110.

Andrulis, Dennis P. 2000. "Community, Service, and Policy Strategies to Improve Health Care Access in the Changing Urban Environment." *American Journal of Public Health* 90(6): 858–62.

Angel, Ronald J., and Jacqueline L. Angel. 1996. "The Extent of Private and Public Health Insurance Coverage among Adult Hispanics." *Gerontologist* 36(3): 332–40.

Bae, Jay P. 1997. "Assessing the Need, Use, and Developments in Mental Health/ Substance Abuse Care." *Health Care Finance Review* 18(3): 1–4.

Baicker, Katherine. 1997. "State Decision-Making and the Incidence of Federal Mandates." Cambridge, MA: Harvard University.

Baker, Lawrence C., and Ciaran S. Phibbs. Forthcoming. "Managed Care, Technology Adoption, and Health Care: The Adoption of Neonatal Intensive Care." In *The Industrial Organization of Medical Care,* edited by David Cutler. Chicago: University of Chicago Press.

Baldwin, Laura-Mae, T. Greer, L. Gary Hart, R. Wu, and Roger A. Rosenblatt. 1996. "The Effect of Washington's Comprehensive Medicaid Expansion on Physicians' Obstetric Practices." *Journal of the American Board of Family Practice* 9(6): 418–421.

Batavia, Andrew I., and Gerben DeJong. 2001. "Disability, Chronic Illness, and Risk Selection." *Archives of Physical Medicine and Rehabilitation* 82(4): 546–52.

Berk, Marc L., Leigh Ann Albers, and Claudia L. Schur. 1996. "The Growth in the U.S. Uninsured Population: Trends in Hispanic Subgroups, 1977 to 1992." *American Journal of Public Health* 86(4): 572–6.

Besley, Timothy, and Stephen Coate. 1992. "Understanding Welfare Stigma: Taxpayer Resentment and Statistical Discrimination." *Journal of Public Economics* 48(2): 165–183.

Blumberg, Linda J., Lisa C. Dubay, and Stephen A. Norton. 2000. "Did the Medicaid Expansions for Children Displace Private Insurance? An Analysis Using the SIPP." *Journal of Health Economics* 19(1): 33–60.

Blumberg, Linda J., and Len M. Nichols. 1998. "The Health Insurance Portability and Accountability Act of 1996: Summary of Provisions and Anticipated Effects." *Journal of Medical Practice Management* 14(1): 13–18.

Braveman, Paula, Trude Bennett, Charlotte Lewis, Susan Egerter, and Jonathan Showstack. 1993. "Access To Prenatal Care following Major Medicaid Eligibility Expansions." *Journal of American Medical Association* 269(10): 1285–1289.

Braveman, Paula, Susan Egerter, Trude Bennett, and Jonathan Showstack. 1991. "Differences in Hospital Resource Allocation among Sick Newborns According to Insurance Coverage." *Journal of the American Medical Association* 266(23): 3300–3308.

Cantor, Joel C., Stephen H. Long, and M. Susan Marquis. 1995. "Private Employment-Based Health Insurance in Ten States." *Health Affairs* 14(2): 199–211.

Carrasquillo, Olveen, Angeles I. Carrasquillo, and Steven Shea. 2000. "Health Insurance Coverage of Immigrants Living in the United States: Differences by Citizenship Status and Country of Origin." *American Journal of Public Health* 90(6): 917–23.

Carrasquillo, Olveen, David U. Himmelstein, Stephanie Woolhandler, and David H. Bor. 1999. "Going Bare: Trends in Health Insurance Coverage, 1989 through 1996." *American Journal of Public Health* 89(1): 36–42.

Center for Studying Health System Change. 1999. "Managed Care Cost Pressures Threaten Access for the Uninsured." Issue Brief No. 19. Washington, DC: Center for Studying Health System Change.

Chernew, Michael E., Kevin Frick, and Catherine G. McLaughlin. 1997. "The Demand for Health Insurance Coverage by Low-Income Workers: Can Reduced Premiums Achieve Full Coverage?" *Health Services Research* 32(4): 453–70.

Currie, Janet M. 1995. *Welfare and the Well-Being of Children.* New York: Harwood Academic.

Currie, Janet M., and Jonathan Gruber. 1996. "Saving Babies: The Efficacy and Cost of Recent Medicaid Eligibility for Pregnant Women." *Journal of Political Economy* 104(6): 1263–1296.

Currie, Janet M., Jonathan Gruber, and Michael Fischer. 1995. "Physician Payments and Infant Mortality: Evidence from Medicaid Fee Policy." *American Economic Review (Papers and Proceedings)* 85(2): 106–111.

Cutler, David M., and Jonathan Gruber. 1996. "Does Public Insurance Crowd Out Private Insurance?" *Quarterly Journal of Economics* 111(2): 391–430.

Cutler, David M., and Richard J. Zeckhauser. 2000. "The Anatomy of Health Insurance." In *Handbook of Health Economics,* edited by Anthony J. Cuyler and Joseph P. Newhouse (563–643). Amsterdam: Elsevier.

Cutler, David M., Douglas W. Elmendorf, and Richard J. Zeckhauser. 1993. "Demographic Characteristics and the Public Bundle." *Public Finance/Finances Publiques* 48: 178–98.

Danziger, Sandra K., and Sherrie A. Kossoudji. 1994/1995. "What Happened to General Assistance Recipients in Michigan?" *Focus* 16(2).

Danziger, Sandra K., Mary Corcoran, Sheldon Danziger, Colleen M. Heflin, Ariel Kalil, Judith Levine, Daniel Rosen, Kristin S. Seefeldt, Kristine Siefert, and Richard M. Tolman. 2000. "Barriers to the Employment of Welfare Recipients." In *Prosperity for All? The Economic Boom and African-Americans,* edited by Robert D. Cherry and William M. Rogers, III. New York: Russell Sage Foundation.

Davidoff, Amy J., and Bowen Garrett. 2001. "Determinants of Public and Private Insurance Enrollment among Medicaid-Eligible Children." *Medical Care* 39(6): 523–35.

Davidoff, Amy J., Bowen Garrett, and Diane Makuc. 2000. "Medicaid-Eligible Children Who Don't Enroll: Health Status, Access to Care, and Implications for Medicaid Enrollment." *Inquiry* 37(2): 203–18.

Davies, Paul, Howard Iams, and Kalman Rupp. 2000. "The Effect of Welfare Reform on SSA's Disability Programs: Design of Policy Evaluation and Early Evidence." *Social Security Bulletin* 63(1): 3–11.

de la Torre, Adela, Robert Friis, Harold R. Hunter, and Lorena Garcia. 1996. "The Health Insurance Status of U.S. Latino Women." *American Journal of Public Health* 86(4): 533–7.

Dick, Andrew W., R. Andrew Allison, Susan G. Haber, Cindy Brach, and Elizabeth Shenkman. 2002. *The Consequences of States' Policies for SCHIP Disenrollment.* Washington, DC: Agency for Health Care Research and Quality.

Domenici, Pete V. 1993. "Mental Health Care Policy in the 1990s: Discrimination in Health Care Coverage of the Seriously Mentally Ill." *Journal of Clinical Psychiatry* 54(S): 5–6.

Dubay, Lisa C., Genevieve M. Kenney, Stephen A. Norton, and Barbara C. Cohen. 1995. "Local Responses to Expanded Medicaid Coverage for Pregnant Women." *The Milbank Quarterly* 73(4): 535–563.

Duggan, Mark. Forthcoming. "Hospital Market Structure and Medical Care for the Poor." In *The Industrial Organization of Medical Care,* edited by David Cutler. Chicago: University of Chicago Press.

Ellis, Randy P., Gregory C. Pope, Lisa I. Iezzoni, John Z. Ayanian, David W. Bates, Helen R. Burstin, and Arlene Ash. 1996. "Diagnosis-Based Risk Adjustment for Medicare Capitation Payments." *Health Care Financing Review* 17(3): 101–28.

Ellwood, Marilyn R., and Genevieve M. Kenney. 1995. "Medicaid and Pregnant Women: Who Is Being Enrolled and When." *Health Care Financing Review* 17(2): 7–28.

Ellwood, Marilyn R., and Leighton Ku. 1998. "Welfare and Immigration Reforms: Unintended Side Effects for Medicaid." *Health Affairs* 17(3): 137–51.

Ettner, Susan L., Richard G. Frank, Tami L. Mark, and Mark W. Smith. 2000. "Risk Adjustment of Capitation Payments to Behavioral Health Care Carve-Outs: How Well Do Existing Methodologies Account for Psychiatric Disability?" *Health Care Management Science* 3(2): 159–69.

Fowler, Elizabeth J., and Gerard F. Anderson. 1996. "Capitation Adjustment for Pediatric Populations." *Pediatrics* 98(1): 10–17.

French, Michael T., Kerry Anne McGeary, Dale D. Chitwood, and Clyde B. McCoy. 2000. "Chronic Illicit Drug Use, Health Services Utilization and the Cost of Medical Care." *Social Science and Medicine* 50(12): 1703–13.

Friedmann, Peter D., Stephenie C. Lemon, Michael D. Stein, Rose M. Etheridge, and Thomas A. D'Aunno. 2001. "Linkage to Medical Services in the Drug Abuse Treatment Outcome Study." *Medical Care* 39(3): 284–95.

Fronstin, Paul. 2000. "Counting the Uninsured: A Comparison of National Surveys." *Employee Benefit Research Institute Issue Brief* 225: 1–19.

GAO. 1998. *Private Health Insurance: Declining Employer Coverage May Affect Access for 55 to 64 Year-olds.* Washington, DC: General Accounting Office.

———. 2000. *Private Health Insurance: Potential Tax Benefit of a Health Insurance Deduction Proposed in H.R. 2990.* Washington, DC: General Accounting Office.

Garrett, Bowen, and Sherry Glied. 2000. "Does State AFDC Generosity Affect Child SSI Participation?" *Journal of Policy Analysis and Management* 19(2): 275–95.

Garrett, Bowen, and John Holahan. 2000a. "Health Insurance Coverage after Welfare." *Health Affairs* 19(1): 175–84.

———. 2000b. "Welfare Leavers, Medicaid Coverage, and Private Health Insurance." Washington, DC: The Urban Institute. *Assessing the New Federalism* Policy Brief No. B-13.

Gaskin, Darrell J., Jack Hadley, and Victor G. Freedman. 2001. "Are Urban Safety-Net Hospitals Losing Low-Risk Medicaid Maternity Patients?" *Health Services Research* 36(1 pt 1): 25–51.

General Accounting Office. See GAO.

Glied, Sherry, and Mark Stabile. 1999. "Covering Older Americans: Forecast for the Next Decade." *Health Affairs* 18(1): 208–13.

Goody, Brigid. 1993. "Sole Providers of Hospital Care in Rural Areas." *Inquiry* 30(1): 34–40.

Grossman, Lindsey K., Leslie N. Rich, S. Michelson, and G. Hagerty. 1999. "Managed Care of Children with Special Health Care Needs: The ABC Program." *Clinical Pediatrics* 38(3): 153–60.

Gruber, Jonathan. 2000. "Health Insurance and the Labor Market." In *Handbook of Health Economics,* edited by Anthony J. Cuyler and Joseph P. Newhouse (645–706). Amsterdam: Elsevier.

Haas, Jennifer S., I. Steven Udvarhelyi, Carl N. Morris and Arnold M. Epstein. 1993. "The Effect Of Providing Health Coverage to Poor Uninsured Pregnant Women In Massachusetts." *Journal of American Medical Association* 269(1): 87–91.

Hall, Allyson G., Karen Scott Collins, and Sherry Glied. 1999. "Employer-Sponsored Health Insurance: Implications for Minority Workers." New York: The Commonwealth Fund.

Hammett, Theodore M., Juarlyn L. Gaiter, and Cheryl Crawford. 1998. "Reaching Seriously At-Risk Populations: Health Interventions in Criminal Justice Settings." *Health Education and Behavior* 25(1): 99–120.

Holahan, John, Cori E. Uccello, Johnny Kim, and Judith Feder. 2000. "Children's Health Insurance: The Difference Policy Choices Make." *Inquiry* 37(1): 7–22.

Horwitz, S. M., and Ruth E. K. Stein. 1990. "Health Maintenance Organizations vs. Indemnity Insurance for Children with Chronic Illnesses." *American Journal of Diseases of Children* 144: 581–586.

Institute of Medicine. See IOM.

IOM. 2000. *No Time to Lose: Getting More from HIV Prevention.* Washington, DC: National Academy Press.

Ireys, Henry T., Gerard F. Anderson, Tom J. Shaffer, and John M. Neff. 1997. "Expenditures for Care of Children with Chronic Illnesses Enrolled in the Washington State Medicaid Program." *Pediatrics* 100(2): 197–204.

Jacobsen, Karen, and Thomas G. McGuire. 1996. "Federal Block Grants and State Spending: The Alcohol, Drug Abuse, and Mental Health Block Grant and State Agency Behavior." *Journal of Health Policy, Politics, and Law* 21(4): 753–70.

Kaplan, Edward H., and David Soloschatz. 1993. "How Many Drug Injectors Are There In New Haven? Answers From AIDS Data." *Mathematical and Computer Modelling* 17(2): 109–115.

Kessler, Ronald C., Katherine A. McGonagle, Shanyang Zhao, Christopher B. Nelson, Michael Hughes, Suzann Eshleman, Hans-Ulrich Wittchen, and Kenneth S. Kendler. 1994. "Lifetime and 12-Month Prevalence of DSM-III-R Psychiatric Disorders in the United States. Results from the National Comorbidity Survey." *Archives of General Psychiatry* 51(1): 8–19.

Klein, Rachel, and Cheryl Fish-Parcham. 1999. "Losing Health Insurance: The Unintended Consequences of Welfare Reform." Washington, DC: Families USA Foundation.

Kronebusch, Karl S. 1997. "Medicaid and the Politics of Groups: Recipients, Providers, and Policy Making." *Journal of Health Policy, Politics, and Law* 22(3): 839–78.

————. 2001a. "Children's Medicaid Enrollment: The Impacts of Mandates, Welfare Reform, and Policy Delinking." *Journal of Health Politics, Policy, and Law* 26(6): 1223–60.

————. 2001b. "Medicaid for Children: Federal Mandates, Welfare Reform, and Policy Backsliding." *Health Affairs* 20(1): 97–111.

Kronick, Richard. 1991. "Health Insurance, 1979–1989: The Frayed Connection between Employment and Insurance." *Inquiry* 28(4): 318–32.

Kronick, Richard, Tony Dreyfus, Lora Lee, and Zhiyuan Zhou. 1996. "Diagnostic Risk Adjustment for Medicaid: The Disability Payment System." *Health Care Financing Review* 17(3): 7–33.

Kronick, Richard, Todd Gilmer, Tony Dreyfus, and Lora Lee. 2000. "Improving Health-Based Payment for Medicaid Beneficiaries: CDPS." *Health Care Financing Review* 21(3): 29–64.

Ku, Leighton, and Sheetal Matani. 2001. "Left Out: Immigrants' Access to Health Care and Insurance." *Health Affairs* 20(1): 247–56.

Kuhlthau, Karen, James M. Perrin, Susan L. Ettner, Thomas J. McLaughlin, and Steven L. Gortmaker. 1998. "High-Expenditure Children with Supplemental Security Income." *Pediatrics* 102(3 Pt 1): 610–15.

Lamers, Leida M. 1999. "Risk-Adjusted Capitation Based on the Diagnostic Cost Group Model: An Empirical Evaluation with Health Survey Information." *Health Services Research* 33(6): 1727–44.

Langreth, Robert. 1998. "After Seeing Profits from the Poor, Some HMOs Abandon Them." *Wall Street Journal.* New York, April 7.

Lieu, Tracy A., G. Thomas Ray, Gail Farmer, and Gregory F. Shay. 1999. "The Cost of Medical Care for Patients with Cystic Fibrosis in a Health Maintenance Organization." *Pediatrics* 103(6): e72.

Lipsky, Michael. 1980. *Street-Level Bureaucracy : Dilemmas of the Individual in Public Services.* New York: Russell Sage Foundation.

Liptak, Gregory S., Christine M. Burns, Phillip W. Davidson, and Elizabeth R. McAnarney. 1998. "Effects of Providing Comprehensive Ambulatory Services to Children with Chronic Conditions." *Archives of Pediatric and Adolescent Medicine* 152: 1003–8.

Long, Stephen H., and M. Susan Marquis. 1998. "The Effects of Florida's Medicaid Eligibility Expansion for Pregnant Women." *American Journal of Public Health* 88: 371–76.

Loury, Glenn C. 2002. *The Anatomy of Racial Inequality.* Cambridge, MA: Harvard University Press.

Marquis, M. Susan, and Stephen H. Long. 1995. "Worker Demand for Health Insurance in the Nongroup Market." *Journal of Health Economics* 14(1): 47–63.

Mayer, Michelle L., Sally C. Stearns, Edward C. Norton, and R. Gary Rozier. 2000. "The Effects of Medicaid Expansions and Reimbursement Increases on Dentists' Participation." *Inquiry* 37(1): 33–44.

McAlpine, Donna D., and David Mechanic 2000. "Utilization of Specialty Mental Health Care among Persons with Severe Mental Illness: The Roles of Demographics, Need, Insurance, and Risk." *Health Services Research* 35(1 Pt 2): 277–92.

Mechanic, David. 1994. "Establishing Mental Health Priorities." *Milbank Quarterly* 72(3): 501–14.

Minkoff, Howard, Tamar Bauer, and Theodore Joyce. 1997. "Welfare Reform and the Obstetrical Care of Immigrants and their Newborns." *New England Journal of Medicine* 337(10): 705–707.

Monheit, Alan C., and Jessica Primoff Vistnes. 2000. "Race/Ethnicity and Health Insurance Status: 1987 and 1996." *Medical Care Research and Review* 57(S1): 11–35.

Monheit, Alan C., Jessica Primoff Vistnes, and John M. Eisenberg. 2001. "Moving to Medicare: Trends in the Health Insurance Status of Near-elderly Workers, 1987–96." *Health Affairs* 20(2): 204–13.

Narrow, William E., Darrel A. Regier, Grayson S. Norquist, Donald S. Rae, C. Kennedy, and Bernard S. Arons. 2000. "Mental Health Service Use by Americans with Severe Mental Illnesses." *Social Psychiatry and Psychiatric Epidemiology* 35(4): 147–55.

Neff, John M., and Gerard F. Anderson. 1995. "Protecting Children with Chronic Illness in a Competitive Marketplace." *Journal of the American Medical Association* 274(23): 1866–9.

Newacheck, Paul W., Tracy Lieu, Amy E. Kalkbrenner, Felicia W. Chi, G. Thomas Ray, and Joel W. Cohen. 2001. "A Comparison of Health Care Experiences for Medicaid and Commercially Enrolled Children in a Large, Nonprofit Health Maintenance Organization." *Ambulatory Pediatrics* 1(1): 28–35.

Norton, Edward C., and Douglas O. Staiger. 1994. "How Hospital Ownership Affects Access to Care for the Uninsured." *RAND Journal of Economics* 25(1): 171–85.

Nyman, John A. 2002. *The Theory of Demand for Health Insurance.* Stanford, CA: Stanford University Press.

Payne, Susan M., Randall D. Cebul, Mendel E. Singer, J. Krishnaswamy, and K. Gharrity. 2000. "Comparison of Risk-Adjustment Systems for the Medicaid-Eligible Disabled Population." *Medical Care* 38(4): 422–32.

Perry, Michael, Susan Kannel, R. Burciaga Valdez, and Christina Chang. 2000. "Medicaid and Children: Overcoming Barriers to Enrollment, Findings from a National Survey." Washington, DC: Kaiser Commission on Medicaid and the Uninsured.

Piper, Jeanna M., Edward F. Mitchel, Jr., and Wayne A. Ray. 1994. "Expanded Medicaid Coverage for Pregnant Women to 100 Percent of the Federal Poverty Level." *American Journal of Preventive Medicine* 10: 97–101.

Piper, Jeanna M., Wayne A. Ray, and Marie R. Griffin. 1990. "Effects of Medicaid Eligibility Expansion on Prenatal Care and Pregnancy Outcome in Tennessee." *Journal of the American Medical Association* 264(17): 2219–23.

Poterba, James M. 1998. "Demographic Change, Intergenerational Linkages, and Public Education." *American Economic Review* 88(2): 315–20.

Rask, Kevin N., and Kimberly J. Rask. 2000. "Public Insurance Substituting for Private Insurance: New Evidence Regarding Public Hospitals, Uncompensated Care Funds, and Medicaid." *Journal of Health Economics* 19(1): 1–31.

Regier, Darrel A., William E. Narrow, Donald S. Rae, R. W. Manderscheid, Ben Z. Locke, and F. K. Goodwin. 1993. "The De Facto U.S. Mental and Addictive Disorders Service System. Epidemiologic Catchment Area Prospective 1-Year Prevalence Rates of Disorders and Services." *Archives of General Psychiatry* 50(2): 85–94.

Reisine, Susan, and Judith Fifield. 1995. "Health Insurance Problems among Insured Rheumatoid Arthritis Patients." *Arthritis Care and Research* 8(3): 155–60.

Remler, Dahlia K., Jason E. Rachlin, and Sherry A. Glied. 2001. "What Can the Take-up of Other Programs Teach Us about How to Improve Take-up of Health Insurance Programs?" Cambridge, MA: National Bureau of Economic Research.

Rhine, Sherrie L. W., and Ying-Chu Ng. 1998. "The Effect of Employment Status on Private Health Insurance Coverage: 1977 and 1987." *Health Economics* 7(1): 63–79.

Rosenbach, Margo, Marilyn Ellwood, John L. Czajka, Carol Irvin, Wendy Coupé, and Brian Quinn. 2001. "Implementation of the State Children's Health Insurance Program: Momentum Is Increasing after a Modest Start." Washington, DC: Mathematica Policy Research.

Rothschild, Michael, and Joseph E. Stiglitz. 1976. "Equilibrium in Competitive Insurance Markets." *Quarterly Journal of Economics* 90: 629–650.

Saver, Barry G., and Mark P. Doescher. 2000. "To Buy, Or Not To Buy: Factors Associated with the Purchase of Nongroup, Private Health Insurance." *Medical Care* 38(2): 141–51.

Schelling, T. C. 1979. "Standards for Adequate Minimum Personal Health Services." *Milbank Quarterly* 57(2): 212–33.

Schlesinger, Mark, and Karl S. Kronebusch. 1990. "The Failure of Prenatal Care Policy for the Poor." *Health Affairs* 9: 91–111.

Schmidt, Laura, Constance Weisner, and James Wiley. 1998. "Substance Abuse and the Course of Welfare Dependency." *American Journal of Public Health* 88(11): 1616–22.

Schur, Claudia L., and Leigh Ann Albers. 1996. "Language, Sociodemographics, and Health Care Use of Hispanic Adults." *Journal of Health Care for the Poor and Underserved* 7(2): 140–58.

Schur, Claudia L., and Jacob Feldman. 2001. "Running in Place: How Job Characteristics, Immigrant Status, and Family Structure Keep Hispanics Uninsured." New York: The Commonwealth Fund.

Seccombe, Karen, L. L. Clarke, and R. T. Coward. 1994. "Discrepancies in Employer-Sponsored Health Insurance among Hispanics, Blacks, and Whites: The Effects of Sociodemographic and Employment Factors." *Inquiry* 31(2): 221–9.

Shah-Canning, D., J. J. Alpert, and H. Bauchner. 1996. "Care-Seeking Patterns of Inner-City Families Using an Emergency Room. A Three-Decade Comparison." *Medical Care* 34(12): 1171–9.

Shenkman, Elizabeth, Richard Bucciarelli, Donna Hope Wegener, Rose Naff, and Steve Freedman. 1999. "Crowd Out: Evidence from the Florida Healthy Kids Program." *Pediatrics* 104(3): 507–13.

Shi, Leiyu. 2000. "Vulnerable Populations and Health Insurance." *Medical Care Research and Review* 57(1): 110–34.

Shirley, Aaron. 1995. "Special Needs of Vulnerable and Underserved Populations: Models, Existing and Proposed, to Meet Them." *Pediatrics* 96(4 Pt 2): 858–63.

Shore-Sheppard, Lara D. 2000. "The Effect of Expanding Medicaid Eligibility on the Distribution of Children's Health Insurance Coverage." *Industrial and Labor Relations Review* 54(1): 59–77.

Siddharthan, Kris. 1991. "Health Insurance Coverage of the Immigrant Elderly." *Inquiry* 28(4): 403–12.

Singh, Susheela, Rachel B. Gold, and Jennifer J. Frost. 1994. "Impact of the Medicaid Eligibility Expansions on Coverage of Deliveries." *Family Planning Perspectives* 26(1): 31–33.

Sloan, Frank A., and Christopher J. Conover. 1998. "Life Transitions and Health Insurance Coverage of the Near-Elderly." *Medical Care* 36(2): 110–25.

Stroupe, Kevin T., Eleanor D. Kinney, and Thomas J. Kniesner. 2000. "Does Chronic Illness Affect the Adequacy of Health Insurance Coverage?" *Journal of Health Politics, Policy, and Law* 25(2): 309–41.

Stuber, Jennifer P., Kathleen A. Maloy, Sara Rosenbaum, and Karen C. Jones. 2000. "Beyond Stigma: What Barriers Actually Affect the Decisions of Low-Income Families to Enroll in Medicaid?" Washington, DC: George Washington University Medical Center, School of Public Health and Health Services, Center for Health Services Research and Policy.

Swartz, James A., Arthur J. Lurigio, and Paul Goldstein. 2000. "Severe Mental Illness and Substance Use Disorders among Former Supplemental Security Income Beneficiaries for Drug Addiction and Alcoholism." *Archives of General Psychiatry* 57(7): 701–7.

Swartz, Katherine, and Deborah W. Garnick. 2000. "Adverse Selection and Price Sensitivity When Low-income People Have Subsidies to Purchase Health Insurance in the Private Market." *Inquiry* 37(1): 45–60.

Thamer, Mae, Christian Richard, Adrianne Waldman Casebeer, and Nancy Fox Ray. 1997. "Health Insurance Coverage among Foreign-Born U.S. Residents: The Impact of Race, Ethnicity, and Length of Residence." *American Journal of Public Health* 87(1): 96–102.

Thorpe, Kenneth E., and Curtis Samuel Florence. 1998. "Health Insurance among Children: The Role of Expanded Medicaid Coverage." *Inquiry* 35(4): 369–79.

Tobin, James. 1970. "On Limiting the Domain of Inequality." *Journal of Law and Economics* 13(2): 263–77.

U.S. Congress. 2000. House Committee on Ways and Means. "Green-Book." *Overview of Entitlement Programs.* Washington, DC: U.S. House of Representatives.

Valdez, R. Burciaga, Hal Morgenstern, E. Richard Brown, Roberta Wyn, Wang Chao, and William Cumberland. 1993. "Insuring Latinos Against the Costs of Illness." *Journal of the American Medical Association* 269(7): 889–94.

Van De Ven, Wynand, and Randall P. Ellis. 2000. "Risk Adjustment in Competitive Health Plan Markets." In *Handbook of Health Economics,* edited by Anthony J. Cuyler and Joseph P. Newhouse (757–845). Amsterdam: Elsevier.

Weinick, Robin M., and Nancy A. Krauss. 2000. "Racial/Ethnic Differences in Children's Access to Care." *American Journal of Public Health* 90(11): 1771–4.

Weinick, Robin M., Samuel H. Zuvekas, and Joel W. Cohen. 2000. "Racial and Ethnic Differences in Access to and Use of Health Care Services, 1977 to 1996." *Medical Care Research and Review* 57(S1): 36–54.

Wells, Kenneth B., Roland Sturm, Cathy D. Sherbourne, and Lisa S. Meredith. 1996. *Caring for Depression.* Cambridge, MA: Harvard University Press.

West, D. W., M. E. Stuart, A. K. Duggan, and C. D. DeAngelis. 1996. "Evidence for Selective Health Maintenance Organization Enrollment among Children and Adolescents Covered by Medicaid." *Archives of Pediatric and Adolescent Medicine* 150(5): 503–7.

Yazici, Esel Y., and Robert J. Kaestner. 2000. "Medicaid Expansions and the Crowding Out of Private Health Insurance among Children." *Inquiry* 37(1): 23–32.

Zellers, Wendy K., Catherine G. McLaughlin, and Kevin D. Frick. 1992. "Small-Business Health Insurance: Only the Healthy Need Apply." *Health Affairs* 11(3): 270–1.

6

Challenges in Modeling
Health Insurance Coverage
Gaps in the Literature

Michael E. Chernew and Richard A. Hirth

T he decline in the percentage of Americans covered by health insurance has generated concern among policymakers and scholars
worried about the negative consequences associated with lack of coverage. Moreover, because the health care financing system is intertwined
with the labor market, policymakers are concerned about the consequences that any reforms to the system would have on labor markets
and how labor market behavior would influence the success of health
care financing reforms.

This chapter identifies gaps in our knowledge about the causes and
consequences of lack of insurance coverage. The topic is very broad, and
many studies, published and ongoing, are relevant. To identify gaps, it is
necessary first to provide a conceptual framework for thinking about
the causes and consequences of the lack of coverage and then asking
where within that framework more research is needed.

The framework is loosely based on a general equilibrium model. It
recognizes that almost all important outcome variables are determined
as part of a grand system of interactions between decentralized agents
acting to achieve their own particular objectives. Perturbations in one
part of the system will ripple through all parts of the system until a new
equilibrium is achieved. This chapter identifies important aspects of a
general equilibrium model that seem understudied and reviews studies

that raise important conceptual or empirical issues related to the general equilibrium framework.

Because of the breadth of this task, this review focuses on work that could loosely be characterized as *structural*. Structural in this context encompasses two distinct, but related ideas. First, "structural" is used in a simultaneous equations sense to refer to empirical models that include endogenous variables in the set of explanatory variables. This is in contrast to reduced-form models, which include only exogenous variables on the right hand side and measure the relationship between those variables and the dependent variable after all intervening endogenous variables have been adjusted.

Second, "structural" is used to refer to models, and associated econometric exercises, that relate the estimated parameters to underlying parameters of the primitive functions that govern behavior (e.g., utility, production, profit). Such models are *parametrically structural*. It is possible to be structural in the simultaneous equation sense but not parametrically structural. In either case, it is possible to be structural without modeling all markets or interconnections that might exist.

Structural models are important because of the many markets and actors that influence coverage decisions and subsequent consequences. The intent here is to identify areas in which current research is lacking and to highlight the methods researchers have used to address the inherent endogeneity that plagues work in this area.

Researchers, for convenience or necessity, often assume that certain theoretically endogenous variables are exogenous. The resulting estimates provide descriptive information but may not determine causality to the degree necessary to inform policy. Because almost all key variables are endogenous in the broadest sense, over the longest time frame, it is easy to take issue with almost any empirical estimate. A thoughtful critique must weigh the potential magnitude of the endogeneity bias, its qualitative importance, and the feasibility of a cure.

Existing structural research, while capturing important links among markets and actors, does not represent a full general equilibrium model. Moreover, reduced-form models are often sufficient to answer compelling theoretical and empirical questions.

The first section of the chapter provides the foundation for the research review. It summarizes each of the key classes of actors—consumers, employers, insurers, medical care providers, and the government—focusing on interrelationships among the relevant markets. The second section examines issues that appear to warrant further study.

The process used to select issues and relevant literature for this synthesis involved, in part, examining what was deemed to be structural literature through searches of Medline, Econlit, and a variety of government and nonprofit web sites. The searches focused on identifying articles related to causes of coverage (or lack of coverage), characteristics of the uninsured, and consequences of being without coverage. In total, over 800 articles were identified and categorized using a standard set of criteria regarding topic and methods. Articles were coded as structural if the authors presented an underlying model of behavior or recognized the endogeneity of key variables in their estimation. For example, articles that used instrumental variable techniques were, by definition, considered structural. Many models that one might consider structural may well have slipped through this classification system. For example, it would be desirable to include articles that use natural experiments to identify the effects of endogenous variables on outcomes of interest, but many such articles use ordinary least squares techniques and may have been mistaken for reduced-form models by abstractors. Therefore, some research was included after discussion with colleagues and after review of citations appearing in articles identified through other means. In some cases, articles that estimate reduced-form models were included if the derivation of those models reflected a structural model.

Other understudied issues certainly exist. Many of them are identified and discussed elsewhere in this book. For example, researchers have rarely treated health insurance as endogenous when modeling the effects of coverage on health status (chapter 4). The issues in this chapter were selected to complement the other discussions in this book.

Framework

Insurance status is the result of a complex set of interactions among at least five key actors: households, firms, insurers, medical care providers and the medical industry, and government. This overview of the actors, their motivations, and their interactions is intended to illustrate the general equilibrium model that determines insurance status. The discussion highlights the many dimensions that must be considered to develop a truly structural understanding of insurance status.

Households

Households' objectives are to maximize their utilities (i.e., their well-being) with respect to health insurance, health care, and nonhealth consumption. In households comprising several individuals, these decisions are generally made jointly, recognizing the preferences and opportunities of all members of the household. Demand for health insurance is a derived demand. That is, it is derived from the demand for health, the expected ability of health care to contribute to improved health, and from the fact that illness occurs randomly, placing the household's income at risk. In addition, the very high cost of health care for some illnesses implies an access motive for holding health insurance; that is, the household effectively trades a relatively small amount of income (the premium) for the ability to purchase care they otherwise could not afford in event of serious illness (Nyman 1999). Households do not know their precise health care needs before illness strikes. By choosing a plan, they will pay a lower price for medical care after illness strikes and accept a bundle of measures (e.g., network restrictions, gatekeeping, utilization review, provider capitation) designed to control the moral hazard, or greater likelihood of using services, created by the price reduction.

Household preferences with respect to health insurance depend on factors such as the degree of aversion to risk, attitudes toward health care (e.g., taste for style of care [aggressive vs. conservative], how much they value unrestricted choice of providers), family structure, health status (a function of past health insurance status), and income (a function of health and health insurance).

Because most Americans under age 65 receive their health insurance as a benefit of employment, crucial interactions occur between households and firms. The set of insurance plans available to a household depends on the decision of whether to participate in the labor force as an employee (vs. self-employment or nonemployment), whether more than one household member participates, and for which firm or set of firms the household members work. All of these decisions may themselves be a function of the health insurance offers made by firms. By determining households' incomes, these employment decisions also, in part, determine eligibility for various public programs and charity care. Given the insurance options and terms available to them through employer-sponsored plans for which they are eligible, the individual insurance market, and public programs, households then choose which employment option, if any, to take.

Firms

This overview focuses on profit-maximizing firms, although the basic points could be extended to non-profit-maximizing firms as well. Thus, understanding firms' decisions with respect to health insurance requires an understanding of how those decisions further the pursuit of profit, given the macroeconomic environment, competition in the firms' output markets, and competition for labor. Firms attempting to maximize their profits are expected to offer wage and benefit packages that attract the desired quantity and types of workers at the minimum cost in terms of total compensation. Most important, firms must decide whether to offer insurance and, if they do offer it, which plan or plans to offer. The favorable pretax treatment of employer-paid premiums and the lower load encourage employers to provide health insurance, assuming workers attach sufficient value to it.[1] Employers' decisions are expected to be based upon the value that current and prospective employees place on insurance and on particular plan attributes, relative to receiving cash compensation. Hence, employees' preferences should play a substantial role in explaining firms' choices with respect to health insurance.

What is less clear on theoretical grounds is which employees' preferences are given the most weight. There are several alternatives, such as the median employee, as in a union bargaining model (Goldstein and Pauly 1976); some set of marginal employees (e.g., the most recent hires or those most likely to be recruited away by another employer); or a broader set of workers with heterogeneous preferences (Moran, Chernew, and Hirth 2001). A firm's ability to shift the cost of health insurance onto workers via lower wages or lower wage growth also affects its incentives for providing insurance. Such wage offsets might occur at the level of the employee group as a whole (e.g., all employees within the group are effectively community rated), within specific demographic subgroups (Gruber 1994), or at the individual level. To the extent that health insurance costs cannot be shifted back onto individual workers or narrow demographic subgroups, firms would have an incentive to consider health status in their hiring decisions.

Beyond decisions about whether and what to offer, firms also must decide how to provide coverage in the most efficient manner. This decision involves issues such as whether to self-insure, whether to participate in employer coalitions, how to price plans to employees (e.g., employer pays premium in full versus employer pays a fixed amount toward any plan chosen; pricing to encourage employees to take up coverage from a spouse's job [Dranove et al. 2000]), and what information to give employees to aid or influence their choices (Scanlon et al. 2002).

Insurers

Although some health insurers are organized as nonprofit organizations, the assumption here, for simplicity's sake, is that insurers are also interested in maximizing their profits. The amount of competition in insurance markets, both within and between types of insurers—traditional, health maintenance organization (HMO), preferred provider organization, and point of service—determines strategies with respect to pricing, exclusivity of networks, efforts to control adverse selection and moral hazard, policy with respect to preventive care, new technologies, attempts to skim the cream (good risks) from the insurance pool, and actions designed to forestall the enactment of public regulations that insurers deem onerous. Less competitive markets may result in higher premiums for any given level of quality or lower quality of coverage for any given premium. However, less competition may also increase insurers' incentives to cover preventive care (as they may be more likely to view the enrollee as a long-term client) and reduce insurers' concerns about adverse selection or their ability to cream skim.

Health Care Providers and the Medical Industry

The incentives facing health care providers are a function of the insurance status of their patients. The incentives include payment amounts and methods (fee-for-service, capitation, salary), as well as other financial and nonfinancial incentives to avoid tests or specialty referrals or to steer patients to certain providers. Thus, insurance status will affect medical care utilization and, ultimately, health status. Physicians' practice patterns may reflect the insurance status of their patients; therefore, changes in overall coverage may influence all patients individually. Evidence for such a spillover exists (Baker and Corts 1996; Baker and Shankarkumar 1997) but evidence also suggests that, even when the provider is held constant, insurance type may affect utilization (Murray et al. 1992, Pearson et al. 1994).

In the long run, the structure and prevalence of insurance determine the incentives for developing new medical devices and pharmaceutical agents, along with the types of innovation most likely to be economically attractive (Weisbrod 1991). The historical fee-for-service-dominated financing system encouraged the development and diffusion of quality-enhancing technologies, even if they substantially increased the cost of care. A system dominated by managed care is more likely to encourage cost-decreasing innovations (e.g., a new pharmaceutical treatment in lieu of surgery). Similarly, managed care may encourage the development of treatments that decrease the nonfinancial (e.g., side effects) costs of seeking care (Baumgardner 1991). Because managed care has not made heavy use of patient cost sharing in the past, such plans may have a hard time controlling the use of morbidity-reducing techniques such as minimally invasive surgery (Chernew et al. 1997).

Government

Federal, state, and local governments play major roles in influencing the insurance status of the population, as direct providers of insurance, as subsidizers of private insurance, and as regulators of firms and insurers. Ascribing motives to the various agencies involved is difficult, as motivations could vary from those of a beneficent social planner attempting to discern and respond to social preferences to those of a self-interested politician beholden to special interests or a bureaucrat captured by the industry being regulated. Clearly, government influences health insurance status directly or indirectly through its interactions with each actor discussed above.

As a direct provider of insurance (e.g., Medicare, Medicaid, and CHAMPUS) and as a provider or subsidizer of charity care (e.g., public hospitals and clinics, Medicaid disproportionate share hospital payments), government can crowd out private insurance by making the alternatives of public insurance or uninsurance relatively more attractive to households (and, implicitly, to firms, which decide whether and what plans to offer based in part on their workers' preferences) (Cutler and Gruber 1996). Conversely, government encourages employers to offer, and workers to take up, private insurance by extending favorable tax treatment to premium payments and allowing employers to escape certain regulations by self-insuring under the Employee Retirement Income Security Act (ERISA). These measures are part of a general system of regulation in which various levels of government place requirements on insurers (e.g., coverage mandates, legal liability, regulation of markets for small group and individual insurance), employers (rules for benefit deductibility), providers (licensure and certification, Certificate of Need, quality regulation), and developers of new technologies (patent laws, laws with respect to substitution of generic drugs, National Institutes of Health research spending). To the extent that these various requirements, laws, and regulations affect the costs and capabilities of medical care, they will affect the rate of coverage by affecting the price and desirability of health insurance. Providers' responses to public payment policy (e.g., cost-shifting) can further affect private health care prices and utilization and, hence, insurance premiums.

Paths to Health Insurance Coverage

Because much of the discussion focuses on determinants of coverage, a more explicit outline of the various paths by which individuals may obtain coverage is useful. Such a model would reflect at least four sources of coverage: a person's own employer, a spouse's employer, a government program, and purchase of insurance in the private market. In each case, a straightforward equation can relate the probability of coverage from a given source to a variety of more detailed decisions. The equations are outlined below.

Own employer coverage (OEC):

$$P(OEC) = P(work\ for\ firm\ that\ offers) * P(eligible|offer)$$
$$* P(participate|eligible) \tag{1}$$

Spousal employer coverage (SEC):

$$P(SEC) = P(Spouse\ works\ for\ firm\ that\ offers) * P(eligible|offer)$$
$$*P(participate|eligible) \tag{2}$$

Government coverage (GOVC):

$$P(GOVC) = P(eligible\ for\ government\ coverage)$$
$$*P(participate|eligible) \tag{3}$$

Nongroup market coverage (NGC):

$$P(NGC) = P(purchase\ nongroup\ coverage) \qquad (4)$$

The nongroup coverage model would reflect the possibility of single or family coverage, and the spousal coverage model would be adjusted for children and others who might be eligible for dependent coverage from multiple sources.

Each of the terms on the right-hand side of the preceding equations reflects a more complex structural model that would recognize the discrete choice model underlying each of the probabilities. Moreover, the probabilities that appear in the equations are not independent, and sources of coverage are not mutually exclusive. The employment decisions that are embedded in the offer and eligibility terms in equations (1) and (2) are clearly jointly determined and influenced by the utility of the other branches.

Finally, the behavioral components of each of the preceding models reflect constraints emanating from the government and from the markets for medical care. For example, behavior in medical care markets determines the cost structure of insurers. Competition in insurance markets determines the markups for premiums, which influence coverage decisions, which collectively influence behavior in medical markets. Government action, whether through regulation of insurers or health care providers or through the influence exerted as a large purchaser of care, may affect behavior at many junctures in the system.

Selected Issues

Endogeneity of Workers Sorting into Firms and Firms' Decisions Regarding Benefits

A fundamental issue for empirical work in this area is the extent to which workers sort themselves into firms based on their preferences for insurance coverage. If workers sort perfectly into the labor force and into specific employment opportunities as a function of their preferences for health insurance, many of the employer decisions that are commonly considered important in models of firm behavior become unimportant. It may be prohibitively costly for all firms to provide health plan options that satisfy the preferences of all potential employees. In that case, firms might choose a niche in terms of their health plan offerings and allow workers to sort themselves into firms. The set of employers in a market area would offer benefit packages consistent with the distribution of worker preferences, and workers would select firms whose benefit offerings matched their preferences. If an exogenous shock changed workers' demand for health insurance, firm benefit offerings would change accordingly, and workers would re-sort themselves as necessary.

With perfect sorting, one would assume that lack of coverage reflected a low demand rather than an institutional barrier posed by the employer-based health care financing system (Long and Marquis 1993). The implications of sorting for policy simulations are significant. The stronger the sorting, the less responsive coverage rates would be to interventions aimed at employers (e.g., subsidies to employers, low-cost insurance pools). The ultimate impact of such interventions would depend on the extent to which they were passed on to workers. Conversely, if there is little sorting, many workers with a high demand for coverage would be employed by firms not offering it, and interventions encouraging employer-sponsored coverage would be more effective.

Strong labor market sorting on the basis of preference for health insurance also has important ramifications for studies of the demand for insurance at the firm level. With strong sorting, firm characteristics (including firm size) are endogenous. For this reason, they would not be appropriate controls in models of insurance demand. Studies of demand at the firm level (e.g., Feldman et al. 1997; Nichols et al. 2001; Hadley and Reschovsky 2002) have identified the demand equation by excluding variables thought to be related to the price of insurance but not to workers' preferences for coverage. Predominant among these variables is the size of the firm or establishment, which is related to lower prices because large employers pay insurers lower loading charges (because, in part, administrative costs and the need for costly medical underwriting efforts are presumably lower in large firms). However, if workers sort themselves into firms according to their preferences for health insurance, biased estimates can result. For example, if small employers find it more costly to provide coverage, they would simply choose to occupy the niche for workers who prefer cash compensation to health insurance. The size distribution of firms would adjust as necessary to satisfy workers' preferences.

In such an environment, models of coverage could focus only on individual and market characteristics. Estimates of demand that are identified using firm-level traits, such as models of employee take-up of insurance, which is identified using employer copremiums, would be misspecified. In addition, models of firm behavior would have to treat employee traits as endogenous. For example, if the error term in the firm-level offer equation included unobserved firm-level preferences, worker traits such as health status, gender, education, and marital status might reflect the sorting of workers with low demand for coverage into certain firms, not the impact of low-demand workers on firms' decisions. Moreover, perfect sorting would call into question the common argument that employer-based health insurance mitigates adverse selection. For these reasons, one's opinion about worker sorting has a strong impact on the interpretation of much of this work.

One would not expect perfect sorting for a variety of reasons, and empirical evidence suggests that sorting is not, in fact, perfect. From a conceptual perspective, perfect sorting requires a large number of firms willing to employ any type of worker so that heterogeneous preferences can be satisfied. Such a model must assume that firms' production functions do not present a barrier to individual sorting based on workers' tastes for health insurance coverage. For example, imagine that all office workers had a high demand for coverage and all factory workers had a low demand for coverage. If the production function required both office and factory workers, sorting across firms based on workers' tastes for coverage would not be possible.

Sorting within firms might exist, with some workers purchasing coverage and others not, but it would require incentives, such as copremiums or targeted wage offsets (Goldstein and Pauly 1976). Tax laws tend to encourage low employee copremiums, and wage offsets targeted at individuals (as opposed to groups) seem implausible. Moreover, the fixed costs of offering different health plans tend to limit the ability of firms to match workers' preferences exactly (Moran, Chernew, and Hirth 2001). Finally, models of perfect sorting become more complex in a dynamic context. Over time, workers develop firm-specific skills, but their tastes for coverage may change. Switching to another job entails costs, however, so workers may stay put, resulting in imperfect matching of preferences to benefits over time.

Many studies present descriptive statistics or reduced-form estimates consistent with implicit or explicit models of sorting. Thus, they find that workers in firms that do not offer coverage are more likely to have characteristics associated with low demand for coverage—namely, workers who are young, male, or have other sources of insurance (Long and Marquis 1993; McLaughlin 1993).[2]

Relatively few studies formally examine the extent of worker sorting. Monheit and Vistnes (1999) examined job choice as a function of preferences for insurance. Preferences were measured directly, through survey questions regarding an individual's taste for insurance.[3] The authors presented a model of job choice that recognizes the endogeneity of the wage, but they ultimately estimated a reduced-form model. The dependent variable is the probability that a worker obtains a job where coverage is offered (which does not necessarily imply that coverage was accepted by the worker). The wage differential between jobs with and without coverage is omitted from the equation because it is endogenous, and it is replaced with exogenous correlates of the wage differential. These are intended to reflect the costs of insurance (reflecting the belief that such costs are passed on to workers in the form of lower wages). The variables include occupation, state health insurance taxation rates, medical costs in the worker's county, regional variables, indicators of rural locale, and worker demographics. The findings suggest that job sorting takes place but that a substantial number of "mismatches" between workers' stated preferences and employers' decisions to offer insurance exist. Despite difficulties in fielding and interpreting surveys about preferences, additional studies that directly measure preferences for insurance and relate them to labor market outcomes would improve our understanding of the extent to which sorting takes place.

Using tax rates faced by workers to identify variations in the price of insurance, Gruber and Lettau (2000) concluded that the median tax price of a firm's workers is related to the firm's decision to offer insurance and to its total spending on insurance.[4] However, they also found evidence that the preferences of workers with the highest tax rate may receive special weight in firms' decisions, whereas under perfect sorting, all workers' preferences would be reflected in insurance decisions.

In a formal model of job sorting, Scott, Berger, and Black (1989) argued that as workers' incentives to sort themselves change over time, because of changes in marginal tax rates or changes in the importance of job benefits, employment patterns will change. For example, in industries where job benefits become more important over time, firms will substitute toward occupational groups with high demand for coverage. The authors presented evidence from several tests of job sorting, each based on longitudinal data. Although their theoretical model is relatively structural, the authors' empirical work does not address the endogeneity of key explanatory variables, such as the percent of workers' compensation paid for in the form of job benefits.

Studies of job lock also address the imperfections in sorting. This body of work investigates the hypothesis that people with insurance coverage through their employer are discouraged from switching jobs because they fear losing insurance coverage. Evidence of job lock implies some frictions in the labor market (although it may be that individuals always get their preferred benefits, even if they are not at their ideal job otherwise). If individuals could perfectly sort along all dimensions, there would be no job lock.

Currie and Madrian (1999) have provided a detailed review of this literature, including a thoughtful discussion of the important identification issues. The strategies commonly used to identify job lock rely on comparisons of job switching rates between individuals who have alternative sources of insurance and those who do not. (People with alternative sources are presumably not locked into their jobs.) The availability of alternative coverage may itself be endogenous; therefore, variables that are presumably related to the value an individual would place on insurance (e.g., family size) are often used as further sources of identification (see chapter 3). Only one study of job lock worried explicitly about the joint nature of job changes among spouses, but even this study treated the availability of spousal coverage as exogenous (Buchmueller and Valletta 1996).

In any case, the literature on job lock has reported conflicting findings. Currie and Madrian (1999) summarize the situation nicely, "the literature could benefit greatly from a systematic analysis of what constitutes a valid strategy in identifying the effect of health insurance on job turnover and how robust empirical estimates are to changes in sample composition, changes in variable definitions, and changes in estimation strategies."

On balance, there is reasonable evidence that workers sort themselves in ways consistent with preferences for insurance coverage and that the sorting is not perfect. Systems for measuring the degree of sorting or of assessing the situations in which sorting compromises statistical efforts to measure other phenomena have not been developed yet. Similarly, the policy implications of the observed degree of sorting have not been well described. For example, the stronger the sorting of workers with low preferences for health insurance into firms not offering coverage, the less responsive non-offering firms will be to premium subsidies.

Moreover, there is little indication of how long workers would take to re-sort themselves in response to policy changes. Presumably, policy changes that affected employers' incentives for providing coverage would also affect the distribution of firm size or the distribution of workers across firms, occupations, and industries, yet little is known about how long such adjustments would take or how large they would ultimately be. If such adjustments are slow, econometric strategies, such as those that rely on difference-in-difference estimators may be less subject to biases due to sorting than they would be if adjustments occurred rapidly. This is because many difference-in-difference estimation strategies assume the "treatment" does not alter the distribution of workers across firms.

With imperfect sorting, the firm's behavior and its internal decision-making rules become salient. Competition in labor markets may also become important because it determines the extent to which firms must take workers' preferences into account when making decisions about benefits. Unfortunately, these descriptive correlations leave open the question of causality: Do firms' offering decisions attract particular workers, or does the employment of particular workers determine what firms offer?

The practical significance of sorting depends on its magnitude. Sorting based on observed factors would generally not bias empirical work, but sorting based on unobserved variables could lead to erroneous conclusions. Thus the degree to which sorting influences results will depend in part on the other factors included. The importance of sorting is also likely to vary by research question.

Two studies that made different assumptions about sorting found similar results (Chernew, Frick, and McLaughlin 1997; Gruber 2001). Specifically, Chernew, Frick, and McLaughlin (1997) examined take-up rates using variation in employee copremiums to identify the price effect. They included only workers whose employers offered coverage and who did not have another source of coverage. The magnitude of the selection bias depended on the extent of sorting. The authors also controlled for worker characteristics. Thus, within this sample, the identifying assumption was that workers did not sort themselves to high or low copremium firms based on their insurance preferences. Despite its apparent weaknesses, the strategy of using copremiums to identify demand systems is not uncommon (e.g., Feldman et al. 1989). Such studies are valuable because the use of copremiums, as opposed to tax rate variation, allows one to assess the demand curve at different points, using different identifying assumptions. Although it seems clear that studies such as Chernew, Frick and McLaughlin (1997), which rely on variation in copremiums for identification, could be substantially biased by sorting, Gruber (2001) noted that his results, which relied on an arguably more exogenous source of variation (tax rates) to identify demand, are similar.

Measuring the Price of Insurance

A key variable in determining whether insurance is offered by firms and taken up by workers is price, but defining and measuring that price is not straightforward. The fundamental difficulty stems from the heterogeneity of insurance products. In a complete structural demand system, employers and employees would face a myriad of prices for a large number of potential products, among them publicly subsidized insurance. Further, the demand for health insurance coverage would be influenced by the availability of free or subsidized care, which provides "implicit" insurance. Because most people buy coverage through their employer, a complete structural demand model would recognize that employers may perceive (and act on) a different set of prices than employees do. Identifying the right set of choices for individuals would be complicated. Depending on what one assumes about the extent to which health insurance benefits influence worker sorting into firms, the set of health plans from which an individual chooses could reflect all plans in the market (assuming the individual selected the firm with his preferred plan) or only the plans offered by his employer (assuming no sorting). Moreover, if sorting is imperfect, the set from which the worker chooses should reflect options for coverage through his or her spouse.

Even if all of the health plans in a worker's set of choices were observable (including their premiums and benefit packages), the multilayered nature of health care financing would affect the price. For example, one might use the full premium, or the employee's (or employer's) share, or some combination of the two as the relevant price, depending on what one assumes about the extent to which health care premiums are shifted to groups of workers or to individual workers. Because firm decisions often apply to groups of workers, it is important to understand whether the appropriate price is that facing the median worker, marginal workers (e.g., the most recently hired or the most likely to leave the firm), or some other group of workers.

Three issues related to the measurement of price are discussed below. The first is a conceptual discussion of what the appropriate measure would be. The second is whether price should be assumed to vary at the market, firm, or individual level. The third is how the wage offset affects the measurement of price.

MEASURING PRICE CONCEPTUALLY

The dominant paradigm today, reflected in widely used health economics textbooks, defines the price of insurance as the difference between the premium and the expected payout, commonly referred to as the load (Feldstein 1999; Phelps 1997). The definition reflects a view of insurance products as primarily financial instruments: that is, individuals pay a premium in exchange for an expected payout. As Phelps states in his textbook, "If the loading fee = 0, the premium just matches the expected benefits and the insurance itself would be free." In such a setting, the price of each health plan in an individual's set of choices would be the loading fee.

Researchers seldom observe the load directly; instead, they search for correlates of the load. For example, it is generally accepted that large firms face smaller loads than small firms because sales and administrative costs do not rise in proportion to group size and larger groups can more readily avoid the costs of medical underwriting. However, the magnitude of the relationship is much more poorly understood. Tax rates are an important correlate of the load because insurance is generally purchased with pretax dollars. The ability to deduct those dollars from income tax reduces the gap between the premium and the expected payout, measured in after-tax dollars. In some cases, the tax code may generate a negative load, making the after-tax price of coverage lower than the expected after-tax cost of medical care.[5]

The subsidy for health insurance generated by the tax system has been the foundation of a substantial number of investigations of individual behavior (Gruber and Poterba 1994; Royalty 2000; Taylor and Wilensky 1983) and firm behavior (Leibowitz and Chernew 1992). Many issues arise when using tax rates as a proxy for loads—for example, variation in tax rates is correlated with variation in income. Similarly, federal tax rate changes occur simultaneously throughout the country, making it difficult to distinguish their effects from underlying time trends and unobserved factors changing contemporaneously with tax rates. Empirical issues arising from the use of taxes to identify price effects are discussed in the section on identification below.

Apart from the empirical issues raised when using proxies for the load, the wisdom of conceptualizing the price of insurance as the load should be reexamined. Insurance products are much more complicated now than when researchers first started using load as a measure of price. Even with traditional fee-for-service insurance, it was not generally recognized that the welfare loss from moral hazard should be thought of as part of the load (that is, the value of the marginal units of care consumed only because insurance reduces their price is less than their actuarial cost). Further, many insurance products provide much more than financial protection, incorporating features to control moral hazard, monitor quality of care, and negotiate favorable medical care prices. These features probably contribute to the administrative costs that constitute the load, yet they provide real value and may in fact contribute to a lower premium, despite the higher load. Essentially, good management can impart just as much value to an insurance policy as good medical care; however, using load to measure price treats management as a deadweight loss, while counting all medical care as part of the policy's value, even care induced by moral hazard.

In a simpler world, the load was positively correlated with premiums. Today, that correlation may be much weaker, or even negative. For example, if a managed care organization incurs some new administrative costs in controlling moral hazard, the load rises but the premium may fall, and enrollees may prefer the new, higher load policy to the old policy.

If one were to rely on the load as the measure of price, one might conclude that average prices rose as managed care expanded, which could explain falling coverage rates. But managed care products must be offering value for that added load; otherwise, enrollees would prefer the lower load (as traditionally measured) fee-for-service coverage. In a simple structural demand system, one would expect that the addition of extra products would increase coverage rates because some of the uninsured might prefer the new products to remaining uninsured. More complex models might yield different conclusions because the entry of managed care might influence adverse selection and the pricing of other products, potentially destabilizing equilibrium. Virtually no research has examined the impact of managed care on coverage rates from an empirical perspective. Theoretical work suggests that the impact on equilibrium is equivocal (Chernew and Frick 1999).

An alternative measure of price is the premium itself. Unlike using the load, which incorporates benefit design into the definition of price (because benefits determine the expected payout), using the premium to measure price requires controlling for benefit packages. Essentially, this is equivalent to a hedonic pricing approach, which characterizes much of the research on competition in insurance markets (Wholey et al. 1995).[6]

The tax subsidy measure of price may remain valid even if one abandons load as the conceptually correct measure. The tax subsidy measures a source of variation in premium prices that generates no value to consumers. Several factors may influence premium prices generally without influencing the tax price—for instance, competition in the health care or health insurance sectors or general inflation in health care costs. Interpretations of elasticity that are driven by variation in these factors require one to make assumptions about whether the factors generate value to consumers.[7] Consumers will be more responsive to changes in "price" if the changes in price are not associated with changes in value. If higher "priced" plans are also "better" plans consumers will be less apt to drop coverage if faced with higher "prices." Estimates of the elasticity based on variations in tax prices may not be appropriate to assess the responsiveness of individuals to rising prices in situations when the rising prices stem from increased value.

For example, reasonable evidence suggests that premiums vary because of competition in the insurance industry (Wholey et al. 1995). If tax rates are held constant, changes in insurance market competition may influence premiums and alter coverage rates. To the extent that high premiums caused by lack of competition provide no value, price elasticities may be similar to those estimated on the basis of variation in tax prices. However, if lack of competition alters product quality, price elasticities may differ.

Similarly, if variation in premium prices were caused by variation in prices or costs of medical care, elasticities would differ from those calculated using changes in tax price (because such variation would affect the adverse consequences associated with being uninsured). In fact, if the variation in medical care price were driven by variation in the quality of medical care, the elasticity would differ from that which would be observed if the variation in medical care were caused by variation in the market power of medical care providers.

Finally, health care premiums have risen over time, largely because of new technology. Very little is known about how rising premiums will affect coverage rates over time. Elasticities based on tax prices or variation in premiums will generally not provide appropriate measures of the elasticities of coverage over time. Only two studies appear to use multivariate techniques to examine the contribution of rising costs to declining coverage rates over time (Fronstin et al. 1997; Kronick and Gilmer 1999). Kronick and Gilmer (1999) relied on national measures of health care costs, relative to income, and generated most of the variance in the cost-to-income ratio from variation in income, not health care costs. Fronstin and colleagues (1997) analyzed state data from 1988 to 1992 and included only one cost proxy, the price of a hospital day. Both studies treated costs as exogenous.

PRICE AT THE MARKET, FIRM, OR INDIVIDUAL LEVEL
A separate issue related to measuring the price of health insurance in structural models is whether price should be thought of as unique to a firm or worker, or common within markets.

One approach is to treat insurance as a composite good and assume that prices vary at the market level. This approach attempts to exploit variation in the menu of prices without having to worry about the endogenous choice of plans or benefit packages made by firms or workers. It also avoids complicated issues related to the joint nature of insurance decisions within families, in which the prices of coverage for both workers are relevant.[8]

A model that uses the tax price to identify the effects of prices on coverage and that controls for worker characteristics related to tax rates is a typical example of the market-level approach. The elasticities measured relate to the probability of having or offering coverage as a function of the tax subsidy in the given area. The exact price quote or benefit package that would be chosen is treated as endogenous, and variation in worker traits are often considered endogenous as well; thus the effects of the price of insurance is identified solely from changes in the tax price, holding constant worker traits in the area. The tax subsidy serves as a price index, with the caveat that variation in the tax price may be driven largely by changes in tax rates within particular income classes. If elasticity of demand for insurance varies by income, tax price elasticities would differ from elasticities derived from variation in premiums caused by other factors, such as market structure, which would probably affect prices faced by all consumers.

Other studies measure variations in price using price lists provided by insurers, although not all firms have access to these premiums

(Leibowitz and Chernew 1992; Marquis and Long 1995; McLaughlin et al. 2002; Swartz 1988). The price quotes serve as a price index. It should not matter very much which policy is taken as the index policy, because evidence suggests that premiums for different insurance policies are highly correlated across markets (Leibowitz and Chernew 1992; McLaughlin et al. 2002). For example, Leibowitz and Chernew (1992) observed premiums of several different insurance plans in different markets and found the correlation of premiums among plans to be .99. McLaughlin and colleagues (2002) studied premiums from different insurers for different Medigap policies in different markets and found a high correlation among the premiums (although there was substantial variation in premium prices within markets). As in the tax price approach, using premiums as price indices requires one to hold benefit design constant. The exact price quote or benefit package that would be chosen is omitted from the model because it is endogenous. Moreover, because the market price approach does not use data on the relative prices of different benefits packages and plan designs, it cannot address questions related to which plan a firm or worker would purchase—but it may be a reasonable method for studying the decision to purchase coverage or not to purchase coverage.

The price index approach is imperfect because the exact premium quoted to a firm may be a function of firm or worker characteristics. In fact, a growing body of research assumes that price is firm-specific. Recent studies have attempted to estimate the prices facing firms that do not offer insurance coverage (Blumberg et al. 1999; Feldman et al. 1997; Nichols et al. 2001). These models use a structural approach to infer prices under the assumption that firms which elect not to offer coverage do so in part because they face higher prices.

Some controversy surrounds these methods. They treat the estimates as a demand equation of small firms, where the key parameter is the sensitivity of small firms to premiums. The structural model is developed primarily to address the failure to observe premiums for firms that do not offer coverage. The model uses a three-step process. In the first step, a reduced-form probit is estimated for the offer decision. The second step estimates a hedonic pricing equation based on a sample of firms that offer coverage. The sample reflects the systematic decisions of firms facing high premiums not to purchase coverage because firms facing high premiums are systematically less likely to purchase coverage and therefore not be included in the second stage of the estimation process.

Therefore, the premium equation incorporates a selection correction term generated from the reduced-form probit. Predicted premiums are generated from the premium equation. Feldman and colleagues (1997) incorporated an adjustment for selection when computing predicted premiums. The third step involves estimation of the demand equation that uses the predicted premiums from the second step as the measure of premiums (for all firms). Nichols and colleagues (2001) reported results based on imputations both with and without the selection term. Subsequent work by Marquis and Louis (2002), using Monte Carlo techniques, suggested that incorporating the selection term directly in the imputation can lead to substantial bias and that unconditional estimation leads to more accurate predictions. They recommended a third approach, based on multiple imputation, that relies on the conditional distribution of the error term. Once the imputed premiums are computed, the third step estimates the structural probit, using the predicted premiums from the second step as the measure of premiums (for all firms).

In the first two studies (Feldman et al. 1997; Nichols et al. 2001), demand was identified by excluding supply variables that appear in the premium equation but are assumed not to affect the firm's demand directly. In fact, variables may enter the premium equation either directly or via the selection term, which captures in a complex, nonlinear form the variables influencing demand. The key identifying variables for Feldman and colleagues were establishment size, the percent of employees who are permanent, years in business, whether the firm is in an urban area, employee turnover, and a binary variable indicating whether the number of temporary employees varies by season. These variables were assumed to affect premiums but not to be correlated with the error in the offering equation. Nichols and colleagues relied solely on establishment size to identify demand, including firm size variables in the structural offer equation.

A key question is whether the identifying variables reflect firm or worker tastes for coverage. For example, if workers sort themselves in the labor market, those in small firms may systematically have a lower demand for coverage. The unobserved taste variables that are correlated with observed, otherwise exogenous traits could generate a bias in the estimates of demand. For example, if establishment size is used as a variable to identify effects of price, the assumption is that the impact of establishment size on the decision to offer insurance acts exclusively through the impact of establishment size on premium prices; it does not consider any impact that may be caused by individuals with low demand for coverage choosing to work for small firms.

A third method of measuring prices is at the individual level. This approach was adopted by Pauly and Herring (2001), who estimated the load that individuals will face based on the average load in their industry, the tax subsidy appropriate for their income, and the average employer contribution in their industry. Models that use tax price as a source of variation without controlling for individual traits related to tax rates would also fit into this category. Like the market-level approach, the individual-level approach treats the specific insurance policy that an individual purchased (or would have purchased) as endogenous and does not incorporate the associated premium into the measure of price.

HOW DOES THE WAGE OFFSET AFFECT MEASUREMENT OF PRICE?

All of the methods of measuring price discussed above ignore the employer's contribution to the health insurance premium. This is appropriate for certain research topics such as for reduced-form studies of coverage rates or for investigations of firm decisions to offer coverage. In equilibrium the behaviors measured in these studies likely reflect the preferences of workers because considerable evidence suggests that the entire cost of health insurance premiums falls on workers, at least on average (Gruber 1994). In fact, some research indicates that this wage offset is group-specific. Sheiner (1999) and Pauly and Herring (1999) found that older workers, with higher expected expenditures, experience a greater wage offset, while Gruber (1994) found that the cost of mandated maternity benefits falls on women of childbearing age and their husbands.

Yet many studies use the employee's copremium as the appropriate measure of price, and workers seem more responsive to that measure than to the full premium (Chernew et al. 1997). Thus, it appears that when employees make health insurance decisions, they do not anticipate that their decisions will influence their wages. It also suggests that worker sorting based on copremiums is not perfect. If workers assume that the entire premium is ultimately paid by employers, by employees as a whole, or by large demographic subgroups of employees, then the out-of-pocket premium is the correct measure of price in determining whether to take up an employer's offer of insurance and in selecting a plan from the firm's set of offerings.

Given the role of copremiums in determining take-up rates, understanding the determinants of copremiums is important. To some extent, workers can select firms whose contribution policies match their preferences. However, competition among firms may influence copremiums. Dranove and colleagues (2000) have created a structural model of copremiums that emphasizes employers' desires to avoid covering employees' spouses. The researchers found empirical support for the model by relating rising copremiums to rising participation of women in the labor force.

Dynamic versus Static Models

The importance of understanding the dynamics of health insurance arises in part from the likelihood that short and long spells of uninsurance have different causes and consequences (Swartz 1994). Short spells may reflect situations such as transitions between jobs, whereas long spells may reflect low employability or an enduring low demand for insurance on the part of the individual. Individuals experiencing short spells without coverage are unlikely to suffer sufficient access barriers to seriously compromise long-term, preventive care, but are still at a nontrivial risk of suffering an event that would lead to hospitalization or be considered a preexisting condition when coverage is restored (Swartz 1994). It is even possible that extra care will be consumed prior to the loss of coverage (in cases where loss can be anticipated) or after coverage is resumed to make up for any reduced consumption during the short intervening spell without coverage, although Long and colleagues (1998) found little evidence of these phenomena. Conversely, those with long spells without coverage would be more likely to suffer decreased health status.

Since the causes of short and long spells are likely to be quite different, policy interventions would probably have to be prioritized and targeted to these subpopulations. Static and dynamic models can answer questions that may differ in subtle but important ways (e.g., who does not have insurance at a point in time versus who is most vulnerable to losing their coverage).

Virtually no research has created structural models of the duration of spells without insurance coverage. Monheit and Schur (1988) examined the distribution of the uninsured by spell length and described patterns of coverage gains and losses over a 32-month period. The analysis indicated that with many of the uninsured were in the midst of a short spell without coverage, whereas others represented a group who persistently lacked coverage. Swartz and McBride (1990) have examined how individual characteristics associated with lack of coverage at a point in time are related to length of time without coverage. They found, among other things, that individuals who were employed at the beginning of the spell were likely to have short spells. Swartz and colleagues (1993a, b) estimated hazard models of the duration of spells of uninsurance.[9] Their predictors were baseline characteristics measured the month before the uninsurance spell began (income, industry of employment, work status, education, demographics, and region).

Recent work has focused on particular demographic subgroups, including children (Coburn, McBride, and Ziller 2002; Czajka 1999; Czajka and Olsen 2000; Lin and Lave 1998), the near-elderly (Jensen 1992; Sloan and Conover 1998), single women (Short and Freeman 1998), the poor (McBride 1997), and Medicaid recipients (Berger and Black 1998). These articles describe the duration of spells but do not detail the relationship between duration and such outcomes as medical care utilization and health status.

Two recent studies (Czajka 1999; Czajka and Olsen 2000) have examined the dynamics of insurance and uninsurance among children, using data from the 1992–1994 Survey of Income and Program Participation. Czajka described spells of insurance and uninsurance, transitions between different types of insurance, participation in versus eligibility for Medicaid, and the relationship between coverage transitions and trigger events, such as changes in a parent's employment. Unobservable variables that could affect changes in coverage could also have affected the trigger events so we cannot say the association is causal, and no attempt was made to identify exogenous trigger events and thereby measure a causal relationship.

Jensen (1992) and Sloan and Conover (1998) studied the dynamics of insurance among the near-elderly. Both examined the effects of precipitating events such as changes in employment status, again without looking for exogenous reasons. In addition, they estimated the effects of a variety of state policies regarding health insurance regulation, cost, and availability. They did not address the endogeneity of job changes, but they did recognize that public policy may affect public attitudes toward health insurance. They used a difference-in-difference approach to account for this potential endogeneity.[10] Interpretation of longitudinal models requires a sense of whether the system is in transition or has already settled into equilibrium. The rate of positive transitions (into coverage or into better coverage) might be different if insurance-friendly policies were adopted recently, capturing a one-time transition rather than a steady state.

Rather than treating employment status as exogenous in their study of insurance dynamics among single women, Short and Freedman (1998) estimated a reduced-form model. If sufficiently powerful, exogenous predictors of employment (e.g., variations in macroeconomic conditions) could be identified. A more structural approach might be feasible in this subpopulation and others that are likely to be relatively sensitive to such conditions.

These studies provide a reasonable, descriptive understanding of the duration of uninsurance and transitions into and out of the insurance pool, and they set the stage for more detailed, structural evaluations. Such investigations could examine the effects of levels and changes in exogenous variables on insurance status and use instrumental variables to examine the effects of levels and changes in endogenous variables (e.g., changes and variations in macroeconomic conditions could proxy for employment; nonlabor income could proxy for earnings). Even determining what variables are exogenous takes on new dimensions in a dynamic context: modelers need to distinguish between exogenous baseline characteristics, exogenous time-varying characteristics, predetermined endogenous variables, and contemporaneous endogenous variables.

Identification Issues

Articles that attempt to control for the endogeneity of key explanatory variables typically use one of two methods: instrumental variables or natural experiments. Both approaches seek to identify endogenous effects by finding variables that are correlated with the endogenous variable but are statistically independent of the error term so that the measured effects are not biased by unobserved confounding variables. Despite their fundamental similarity, the approaches differ in a variety of ways.

The instrumental variables model typically relies on variables that would be considered endogenous in other settings but that are not related to the error term (i.e., not endogenous to the particular model) (e.g., cost shifters can be used to identify a demand equation). Rarely are the variables indisputably exogenous. Most such studies have a theoretical basis for considering a variable suitable for identifying and measuring endogenous effects. Testing the validity and power of instruments in explaining the endogenous explanatory variable is important and the subject of much recent research (Bound et al. 1995; Staiger and Stock 1997).

Natural experiment studies use some exogenous event generated by nature to identify the effects of endogenous explanatory variables. Rosenzweig and Wolpin (2000) distinguished between exogenous factors truly generated by nature (season of birth, twins, etc.) and factors that reflect regulatory action or public policy. Some recent studies have questioned the exogeneity of variables based on regulatory action or public policy, noting that such "experiments" are generated in a political context that may be influenced by unobserved factors related to the primary variable of interest (Besley and Case 2000; Levitt 1997; Kubik and Moran 2001). In this case the policy action would not be an appropriate tool for identifying the desired causal effects.

Another concern is the validity of the reported standard errors in much of the natural experiment work that relies on state-level policy initiatives. Bertrand, Duflo, and Mullainathan (2001) have generated "placebo" laws at the state level and tested for the effects of these randomly generated laws on women's wages. They found a statistically significant effect, at the 5 percent level, about 45 percent of the time, suggesting that the standard errors are biased downward. Several solutions exist; Arellano (1997) suggested using Huber-White standard errors.

Several types of natural experiments are commonly relied upon in studies of the causes and consequences of lack of coverage. One frequently used source of natural experiments is the cross-sectional variation and changes over time in state and federal tax rates, which are used to identify the effect of the price of insurance on coverage. (See for example, Gruber and Poterba 1994; Gruber 2001; Gruber and Lettau 2000; Leibowitz and Chernew 1992; Royalty 2000). The use of tax rate variation is attractive because tax policy is often driven by factors that are not directly related to health care. However, authors using this source of variation have often noted that cross-sectional variation in taxation may be correlated to average market-level taste for insurance, and it is possible that changes in tax rates are actually related to unobserved demand variables.

To address these concerns, Gruber (2001) and Gruber and Lettau (2000) used the National Bureau of Economic Research's TAXSIM model to simulate the extent of the tax subsidy of health insurance by state, year, and earnings. This simulated variable serves as an instrument for measuring the price of insurance. Since the model controls separately for state, year, and decile of earnings, along with a wide variety of other variables that may be related to the demand for insurance, the effect of tax price is identified by the interactions of these three factors.[11] Essentially, the variation in tax price arises from variations in the progressivity of tax schedules at any given point in time and from changes in the structure of federal and state taxation over time that have differential impacts across the income spectrum. Because some of the changes may be correlated with the demand for insurance, the authors also perform sensitivity analyses, adding year*state and year*income decile interactions. With these added interactions, identification occurs through differences across states in the progressivity of their tax schedules and changes in progressivity over time.

The range and variation in tax price are important in drawing inferences about which firms or workers the estimated elasticities reflect. The decisions of firms that would offer insurance (or workers who would take up offers) even if they faced high tax prices (low subsidies) are not reflected in the estimates. Likewise, firms (or workers) that would not offer (or take up) insurance even if they faced low tax prices are not reflected. Thus, the estimates reflect the behavior of marginal firms or workers—that is those that would offer or take up insurance at some observed tax prices but not at others (Angrist et al. 1996). Therefore, it is important to understand the range over which the observed tax prices vary.

In Gruber and Lettau (2000), the average tax price for each firm's sample of workers was 0.741, with a standard deviation of 0.058; these figures indicate that most of the firms were in a range of about 0.65 to 0.85. In Gruber (2001), the mean tax price among individuals was 0.65, with a standard deviation of 0.093, implying an approximate range of 0.50 to 0.80. However, since much of the variation can be traced back to variations in income, year, and state (the factors controlled for separately in the models because of the potential for endogeneity), the actual range and variation being used to estimate the tax price effect are less clear—even more so in specifications that include year*state and year*income decile interactions.

The additional levels of differences (or in a multivariate context, additional levels of interactions) are intended to provide greater assurance that the variation being used to identify the tax price effect is truly exogenous to the demand for insurance. However, this assurance comes at a cost. Every additional level of difference and every additional set of control variables reduces the fraction of the overall variation in tax prices that is actually used to estimate the tax price effect. This issue is often treated solely as one of statistical power, with an implicit presumption that if the coefficient of interest can nonetheless be estimated precisely, there is little reason to be concerned about the loss of variation in the tax price.

An important, often unrecognized problem also exists, however. In the extreme, much of the remaining, independent variation of the tax price measure may reflect only a few anomalous cases (e.g., states with tax policies that are very different from the national norm for certain income groups). As these potentially atypical cases make up a larger fraction of the variance actually used to identify the tax price effect in models with more levels of differences, it can become difficult to pinpoint the true source of identification and the range of tax prices to which the estimated elasticity applies.

To draw an analogy, data on twins have been used to identify the impact of education on earnings in natural experiments (Behrman and Rosenzweig 1999). Presumably, differences between identical twins in educational attainment and earnings would not reflect many of the common sources of spurious inferences: genetic ability, home environment, parental resources, and birth cohort. Thus, the studies should allow clean inferences about the relationship between education and earnings, if enough variation remains to estimate the coefficient on education precisely. Those estimates may be problematic, however. Most twins have similar educational attainment, so identification of the effect on earnings is derived primarily from the relatively few sets of twins whose educational attainments differ substantially. Those cases may themselves be unusual, reflecting a variety of unobserved anomalies such as one twin having suffered an accident or illness or substance abuse problem while the other twin did not. If the anomalies drive the variation in both education and earnings, the model would not uncover the structural coefficient on education and might well lead to a more biased estimate than a nonexperimental model would.

Despite these cautions, the tax policy natural experiment may provide the most convincing available source of exogenous variation in the price of health insurance. However, an analysis of which observations are providing the bulk of the identifying variation could clarify the range of tax subsidies to which the results pertain and provide greater assurance that the results are not being driven by a small number of atypical cases.

Impact of Labor Market Competition on Firm Behavior

What role do competitors play in firms' decisions regarding whether or not to offer health insurance? Three sophisticated studies have examined this question (Blumberg et al. 1999; Feldman et al. 1997; Nichols et al. 2001). The authors included measures of whether competitors (in product or labor market space) offer coverage, and they treated the variables as exogenous. A more structural treatment would recognize that competitors' behaviors are correlated with each other. Thus, for example, competition may drive a firm to offer coverage if competing firms do.

Alternatively, a structural model might have a niche feature, in which some firms offer coverage and others do not, facilitating worker sorting. Allowing for firms' occupying a niche is analogous to the models of the crowding out of charity care.

A third possibility would be a common market shock that caused all firms to act similarly. One possibility to adjust for this would be to use characteristics of other firms as instruments for a firm's insurance decision. This is similar to some research in the charity care literature (e.g., Frank and Salkever 1991), but this strategy requires detailed information on competitors, which might not be available.

Impact of Public Policy on Premiums and the Role of Competition

Implementation of government policies to encourage insurance coverage may influence the equilibrium value of premiums and copremiums, which may, in turn, influence the costs and impact of the government policies. For example, depending on the extent to which subsidies shift the demand for insurance (and indirectly, the demand for medical care), and depending on the extent of adverse selection in health insurance markets, policies that subsidize the cost of insurance will alter premiums. Similarly, reforms in insurance markets can influence demand for coverage and premiums.

The magnitude of the effect that a shift in demand will have on premiums depends on the nature of the policy and, often, on the degree of competitiveness in the insurance and medical care markets. If, in both markets, costs do not vary with the size of the market, and both markets are perfectly competitive, with U-shaped average cost curves, a shift in the demand curve will not influence the equilibrium level of premiums in the long run. If insurance markets or medical care markets are not perfectly competitive, the shift in demand curves induced by subsidies would tend to increase premiums in the long run.

One should expect variation in the degree of competitiveness across insurance markets. Wholey and colleagues (1995) presented a model that relates premiums to the elasticity of demand faced by HMOs. They noted that firm-level elasticity will vary with market structure. Premiums will vary with competition from non-HMO health plans and with market-level elasticity of demand for coverage. Understanding the variation in competitiveness across insurance markets is important because such variation could affect the impact of policies designed to increase coverage.

Relatively few empirical studies have investigated competitiveness in health insurance markets, and those that have, have focused on the HMO market (Feldman et al. 1993; Wholey et al. 1995). Such studies typically measure HMO competition as a function of the number of HMOs and market penetration, or the share of the health insurance market captured by HMOs (i.e., HMO penetration rate). Although competition is recognized as being endogenous, existing studies do not attempt to adjust their estimates accordingly.

Wholey and colleagues noted the endogeneity and argued that any lags in the decision to enter the market would minimize the bias and that the bias would result in an underestimate of the competitive effect. Their empirical work supports this. Premiums do respond to measures of competition. Although the theory presented by Wholey and colleagues relates explicitly to elasticity parameters, their empirical work is not tied explicitly to those parameters. Thus, one can conclude that competition can lower premiums, but one cannot ascertain the extent to which competition exists, even in the most competitive markets.

Competition in medical care markets can also affect the impact of coverage on premiums. As more individuals obtain coverage, the demand for medical care rises. The extent to which increased demand will increase premiums in the long run depends on the competitiveness of medical care markets. If medical care markets are not competitive, increased coverage will cause increased premiums, even if insurance markets are perfectly competitive.

The literature on competition in health care markets is extensive and cannot all be reviewed in this chapter. Several points are worth noting. First, conventional wisdom held that, prior to the growth of managed care, competition in medical care markets increased costs in a medical care version of the arms race (Luft et al. 1986). Moreover, Feldman and Dowd (1986) reported that hospitals in Minneapolis had substantial market power in 1981.

Since the growth of managed care, medical care markets may have become more competitive. Zwanziger and Melnick (1988) reported such a change in California, and a Dranove and colleagues (1993) reported a similar finding. Competitiveness in medical care markets depends on the hospital market structure and the insurance market structure. For example, using California data through 1994, Chernew and colleagues (2002) have reported that HMOs paid close to the marginal cost for open-heart surgery, suggesting that pricing for medical services in the HMO market is competitive; fee-for-service insurers, on the other hand, paid above costs, suggesting that hospitals had market power when serving these payers. The authors did not estimate the elasticity in the fee-for-service market—only the HMO returns were sensitive to hospital market structure. More detailed work is needed to understand variation in competition and how provider margins respond to coverage rates.

Even in a competitive medical care market, increased coverage could raise premiums because of the connection between coverage and the development of medical technology. There is widespread consensus that the development and diffusion of medical technology has been a primary cause of rising health care expenditures (Chernew et al. 1998; Cutler 1995; Cutler and McClellan 1996; Newhouse 1992; Scitovsky 1985; Scitovsky and McCall 1976).

It is likely that such technological development is related to coverage rates. Peden and Freeland (1995) have suggested that as much as 70 percent of the impact of cost-increasing technologies can be attributed indirectly to insurance coverage. Yet very little is known about the extent to which increased coverage, at the margin, affects technology development. Moreover, if the financing system becomes more dominated by managed care, incentives to develop technology are very likely to change (Gelijns and Rosenberg 1994). However, very little evidence is available concerning the extent to which managed care will alter the process and nature of medical technology developments or the ramifications new technology will have for premiums and hence coverage rates.

Apart from the effects that a shift in demand would have on premiums, subsidies may alter the average health risk of the insured. Theory is equivocal regarding whether the uninsured are healthier than the insured. Models of adverse selection suggest that the uninsured are systematically healthier, but insurers' practice of skimming the cream, plus the correlation between income, health status, and coverage, may result in an uninsured population that is systematically sicker than the insured population. Evidence supports the notion that there is great heterogeneity among the insured regarding health status, with publicly insured individuals being less healthy than privately insured. As a whole, income aside, the insured appear to be healthier than the uninsured (personal communication, Bradley Herring, 2001). Taking income into consideration may alter the conclusion. Pauly and Herring (1999) found no relationship between risk and coverage among high-income individuals. They also found that certain high-risk, low-income workers were less likely to be covered than their low-risk counterparts. The impact of selection on premiums as coverage rates rise depends more on the health of the marginal individual gaining coverage than on the average health of all uninsured persons. Very few empirical studies have examined the health status of individuals on the margin (which probably depends on the exact policy adopted). One exception is the work of Pauly and Herring (2000), which is based on a structural model of coverage, making possible simulation of such effects in the case of subsidized coverage.

A final mechanism through which expanded coverage might influence premiums is a reduction in the burden of charity care on providers. Dranove (1988) created a model of cost shifting in which hospitals increase prices to private payers as public payers decrease reimbursement. By analogy, one might assume that if reimbursement increases for currently uninsured patients, prices would fall for insured individuals, leading to lower premiums. In essence, this would be reverse cost shifting.

Whether such an effect would occur in response to increased coverage remains uncertain. Dranove's model of cost shifting is based on data from Illinois in the early 1980s. Yet, even if one accepts his evidence and assumes that evidence of cost shifting can be considered evidence of reverse cost shifting, which may not be true, the theoretical model indicates that the ability of hospitals to shift costs depends on their market power. As discussed above, it is likely that in many markets, hospitals have lost market power since the early 1980s. Thus the extent to which reverse cost shifting would hold down premiums remains unclear.

Taken together, increased coverage could affect premiums in a variety of ways. Empirical evidence of the direction and magnitudes of these effects, separately or in combination, is lacking.

Subsidies may also affect copremiums. One model has indicated that higher tax subsidies reduce copremiums (Dranove et al. 2000). Only one study has examined this issue, Gruber and McKnight (2002). They find evidence that the fall in the subsidy stemming from the favorable tax treatment of health insurance between the early 1980s to mid 1990s was associated with rise in employee copremiums.

Conclusions

The framework described in this chapter highlights the myriad of structural relationships that exist among the five key actors whose decisions and interactions determine health insurance coverage. Understanding those relationships is crucial to the development of valid policy simulations. Unfortunately, the complexity and sheer number of the relationships ensures that such simulations will always have to rely to a certain extent on assumptions and on empirical estimates that fall short of the ideal. Nonetheless, careful attention to the issues highlighted in this review can aid in both the interpretation of existing findings and the formulation of future research.

Several topics deserve more attention. First, the magnitude of employee sorting among firms on the basis of health insurance must be measured. Current evidence suggests that, although sorting exists, it is not perfect. Moreover, empirical studies are inconsistent in their consideration of sorting. Future research must determine the extent to which sorting influences econometric strategies for identifying the causes and welfare implications of lack of coverage. For example, appropriate model specification (e.g., are worker characteristics exogenous to the firm, and are firm characteristics exogenous to the worker?) and interpretation of empirical findings rely heavily on the extent to which sorting occurs. With very strong sorting, employers are primarily pass-throughs whose decisions have little impact on the prevalence and distribution of coverage in the population. With less perfect sorting, employers become active, important players.

Second, greater attention must be paid to the conceptualization of the price of insurance. Theoretical concepts of price, such as the load or the absolute premium, may not be correct in many decisionmaking contexts, particularly in a world of differentiated insurance products. In policy environments, considerable confusion may arise because of inconsistencies in the definition of normally straightforward parameters such as elasticities.

The common definition of price as the load distracts attention from important research questions. The questions include how patterns of coverage will change over time as premiums rise (largely because of medical technology) and how the development of managed care will affect coverage rates (even though it may increase loads). The first question is important because it addresses the long-term impact of policies to encourage coverage. The second question is important because the current political debate surrounding limits on managed care might be perceived in a different light if managed care prevented many individuals from losing coverage entirely.

A third area of research that deserves greater attention is the dynamic aspects of health insurance—because short- and long-term lack of coverage are quite different phenomena. Models of the dynamic patterns of coverage must be explicit about the processes that generate change in coverage status and the extent to which those triggering events are endogenous, exogenous, subject to policy manipulation, or all three.

Fourth, research is needed on the extent to which key variables such as health insurance premiums will respond to public policies designed to influence coverage rates. Theory is ambiguous in this regard, but such indirect effects may overwhelm the direct effects of policy initiatives.

Fifth, as in all empirical work, identification issues are crucial. As always, the validity of instruments in instrumental variation models is a central issue. In addition, more attention should be paid to the potential endogeneity of public policy actions that are commonly considered natural experiments and thus exogenous. Tax rate changes are perhaps the most clearly exogenous, but they may affect only a narrow set of workers (in terms of income or location) in a narrow range of price variation; other health-related regulations might be less exogenous. Moreover, the field would benefit from greater examination of the extent to which the well-known critiques leveled against instrumental techniques apply to some natural experiments. Specifically, a greater understanding of the range and source of variation in natural experiments would be valuable.

Identifying research strategies that can adequately probe these areas is a complicated matter. Clearly, there is room for novel identification strategies and data-gathering exercises (for example, no public databases are available to measure longitudinal or cross-sectional variation in premiums). As progress is made in these areas, researchers will be much better able to tell policymakers about the impact of strategies aimed at increasing rates of health insurance coverage.

NOTES

We would like to acknowledge helpful comments by Roger Feldman and John Bound and participants in the Research Agenda Setting Conference for the Research Initiative on Health Insurance held at the University of Michigan in July 2001. We also thank the Robert Wood Johnson Foundation and the Economic Research Initiative on the Uninsured.

1. Load refers to the mark-up of premiums above expected payout for medical expenses. It covers insurer administrative expenses as well as profits. Pooling is generally associated with lower loads because administrative costs decline as group size rises.

2. One potentially fruitful area in which to find evidence of sorting is models of joint household decisions regarding labor supply. Although some structural empirical models of such joint decisions do exist (Van Soest 1995), they do not incorporate the role of insurance and thus do not provide evidence of sorting. See Buchmueller and Valletta (1999) for estimates of the impact of husbands' insurance status on the labor supply of wives.

3. More generally, the issue of family decisionmaking with respect to health insurance (e.g., decisions about seeking or choosing from multiple sources of coverage, aggregating individual preferences to family-level decisions) deserves more attention.

4. "Tax price" is a function of the many taxes that might influence coverage. Higher tax rates lead to a lower "tax price," reflecting the value of pre-tax treatment of health insurance premiums relative to after-tax consumption.

5. The extent to which tax rates affect the load depends on the extent to which medical expenditures would be paid with pretax dollars. Above a certain threshold, medical expenses are tax-deductible for taxpayers who itemize their deductions. Below that threshold, higher tax rates would clearly reduce the load. Even if medical expenses were fully deductible, high tax rates would shrink the gap between premiums and expected payout when both are measured in after-tax dollars.

6. Hedonic pricing refers to efforts to adjust the premiums for plan traits (such as covered benefits), so that the variation in the measured premium does not reflect variation in benefits. Technically this is accomplished by regressing observed premiums on plan traits and using the estimated premium for a standard set of plan traits as the appropriate premium measure.

7. "Elasticity" measures the responsiveness of consumers to "price." It is computed as the percentage change in coverage for every 1 percent change in "price."

8. Shur and Taylor (1991) describe the insurance decisions of two-earner couples when both are offered coverage and when only one is offered coverage. Monheit, Schone,

and Taylor (1999) present multivariate models of coverage decisions in two-earner households when both are offered coverage. They treat the availability of the benefit as exogenous and report that copremium requirements are crucial determinants of joint insurance demand.

9. Hazard models are models used to predict the duration of spells. The "hazard rate" is defined as the likelihood a spell will end at any given point in time. Lower hazard rates lead to longer spells.

10. Difference-in-difference models refer to a set of models that use two levels of comparison to isolate the effect being studied. In some cases this would involve a before/after comparison (first difference) in a treatment and control group (second difference). The measured effect would be the difference in change between the treatment and control group.

11. In Gruber (2001), a fourth-level interaction with marital status is used.

REFERENCES

Angrist, Joshua D., Guido W. Imbens, and Donald B. Rubin. 1996. "Identification of Causal Effects Using Instrumental Variables." *Journal of the American Statistical Association* 91(434): 444–72.

Arellano, Manuel. 1997. "Computing Robust Standard Errors for Within-Groups Estimators." *Oxford Bulletin of Economics and Statistics* 49(4): 431–34.

Baker, Laurence C., and Kenneth S. Corts. 1996. "HMO Penetration and the Cost of Health Care: Market Discipline or Market Segmentation?" *Health Economics* 86(2): 389–94.

Baker, Laurence C., and Sharmila Shankarkumar. 1997. "Managed Care and Health Care Expenditures: Evidence from Medicare, 1990–1994." Working Paper No. 6187. Cambridge, MA: National Bureau of Economic Research.

Baumgardner, James R. 1991. "The Interaction between Forms of Insurance Contract and Types of Technical Change in Medical Care." *RAND Journal of Economics* 22(1): 36–53.

Behrman, Jere R., and Mark R. Rosenzweig. 1999. " 'Ability' Biases in Schooling Returns and Twins: A Test and New Estimates." *Economics of Education Review* 18(2): 159–167.

Berger, Mark C., and Dan A. Black. 1998. "The Duration of Medicaid Spells: An Analysis Using Flow and Stock Samples." *The Review of Economics and Statistics* 80(4): 667–75.

Bertrand, Marianne, Esther Duflo, and Sendhil Mullainathan. 2002. "Should We Trust Differences-in-Differences Estimates?" Working Paper No. 8841. Cambridge, MA: National Bureau of Economic Research.

Besley, Timothy, and Case Anne. 2000. "Unnatural Experiments? Estimating the Incidence of Endogenous Policies." *The Economic Journal* 110: F672–F694.

Blumberg, Linda J., Len M. Nichols, and David Liska. 1999. "Choosing Employment-Based Health Insurance Arrangements: An Application of the Health Insurance Reform Simulation Model." Report to the U.S. Department of Labor, No. 0657-001-00. Washington, DC: The Urban Institute.

Bound, John, David A. Jaeger, and Regina M. Baker. 1995. "Problems with Instrumental Variables Estimation When the Correlation between the Instruments and the Endogenous Explanatory Variable Is Weak." *Journal of the American Statistical Association* 90(430): 443–50.

Buchmueller, Thomas C., and Robert G. Valletta. 1999. "The Effect of Health Insurance on Married Female Labor Supply." *Journal of Human Resources* 34(1): 42–70

———. 1996. "The Effects of Employer-Provided Health Insurance on Worker Mobility." *Industrial and Labor Relations Review* 49(3): 439–70

Chernew, Michael E., and Kevin D. Frick. 1999. "The Impact of Managed Care on the Existence of Equilibrium in Health Insurance Markets." *Journal of Health Economics* 18: 573–92.

Chernew, Michael E., A. Mark Fendrick, and Richard A. Hirth. 1997. "Managed Care and Medical Technology: Implications for Cost Growth." *Health Affairs* 16(2): 196–206.

Chernew, Michael E., Kevin Frick, and Catherine G. McLaughlin. 1997. "The Demand for Health Insurance Coverage by Low-Income Workers: Can Reduced Premiums Achieve Full Coverage?" *Health Services Research* 32(4): 453–70.

Chernew, Michael E., Gautam Gowrisankarin, and A. Mark Fendrick. 2002. "Payer Type and the Returns to Bypass Surgery: Evidence from Hospital Entry Behavior." *Journal of Health Economics* 21(3): 451–74.

Chernew, Michael E., Richard A. Hirth, Seema S. Sonnad, Rachel Ermann, and A. Mark Fendrick. 1998. "Managed Care, Medical Technology, and Health Care Cost Growth: A Review of the Evidence." *Medical Care Research and Review* 55(3): 259–88.

Coburn, Andrew F., Timothy D. McBride, and Erika C. Ziller. 2002. "Patterns of Health Insurance Coverage among Rural and Urban Children." *Medical Care Research and Review* 59(3): 272–92.

Currie, Janet, and Brigitte C. Madrian. 1999. "Health, Health Insurance and the Labor Market." In *Handbook of Labor Economics,* vol. 3C, edited by Orley Ashenfelter and David Card (chapter 50). Amsterdam: Elsevier Science.

Cutler, David M. 1995. "The Incidence of Adverse Medical Outcomes under Prospective Payment." *Econometrica* 63(1): 29–50.

Cutler, David M., and Jonathan Gruber. 1996. "Does Public Insurance Crowd Out Private Insurance?" *Quarterly Journal of Economics* 111(2): 391–430.

Cutler, David M., and Mark McClellan. 1996. "The Determinants of Technological Change in Heart Attack Treatment." Working Paper No. 5751. Cambridge, MA: National Bureau of Economic Research.

Czajka, John L. 1999. "Analysis of Children's Health Insurance Patterns: Findings from the SIPP." Report PR99-64. Washington, DC: Mathematica Policy Research, Inc. http://aspe.hhs.gov/health/reports/sippchip/toc.htm (accessed October 31, 2003).

Czajka, John L., and Cara Olsen. 2000. "The Effects of Trigger Events on Changes in Children's Health Insurance Coverage." Washington, DC: Mathematica Policy Research, Inc. http://aspe.hhs.gov/health/reports/triggers/index.htm (accessed October 31, 2003).

Dranove, David. 1988. "Pricing by Non-Profit Institutions." *Journal of Health Economics* 7(1): 47–57.

Dranove, David, Mark Shanley, and William D. White. 1993. "Price and Concentration in Hospital Markets: The Switch from Patient-Drive to Payer-Driven Competition." *The Journal of Law and Economics* 36(1): 179–204.

Dranove, David, Kathryn E. Spier, and Laurence C. Baker. 2000. "Competition among Employers Offering Health Insurance." *Journal of Health Economics* 19(1): 121–40.

Feldman, Roger, and Bryan E. Dowd. 1986. "Is There a Competitive Market for Hospital Services?" *Journal of Health Economics* 5(3): 277–92.

Feldman, Roger, Bryan E. Dowd, and Gregory Gifford. 1993. "The Effect of HMOs on Premiums in Employment-Based Health Plans." *Health Services Research* 27(6): 779–811.

Feldman, Roger, Bryan E. Dowd, Scott Leitz, and Lynne A. Blewett. 1997. "The Effect of Premiums on the Small Firm's Decision to Offer Health Insurance." *Journal of Human Resources* 32(4): 635–58.

Feldman, Roger, Michael Finch, Bryan E. Dowd, and Steven Cassou. 1989. "The Demand for Employment-Based Health Insurance Plans." *The Journal of Human Resources* 24(1): 115–42.

Feldstein, Paul J. 1999. *Health Care Economics*. Albany, NY: Delmar Publishers.

Frank, Richard G., and David S. Salkever. 1991. "The Supply of Charity Services by Non-profit Hospitals: Motives and Market Structure." *RAND Journal of Economics* 22(3): 430–44.

Fronstin, Paul, Lawrence G. Goldberg, and Phillip K. Robins. 1997. "Differences in Private Health Insurance Coverage for Working Male Hispanics." *Inquiry* 34(2): 171–80.

Gelijns, Annetine C., and Nathan Rosenberg. 1994. "The Dynamics of Technological Change in Medicine." *Health Affairs* 13(3): 28–46.

Goldstein, Gerald S., and Mark V. Pauly. 1976. "Group Health Insurance as a Local Public Good." In *The Role of Health Insurance in the Health Services Sector,* edited by Richard H. Rosett (73–107). Cambridge, MA: National Bureau of Economic Research.

Gruber, Johnathan. 1994. "The Incidence of Mandated Maternity Benefits." *American Economic Review* 84(3): 622–41.

———. 2001. "The Impact of the Tax System on Health Insurance Decisions." Paper presented at the conference, Why Do Employers Do What They Do? Studies of Employer-Sponsored Health Insurance, Washington, DC, April 27.

Gruber, Jonathan, and Alan B. Krueger. 1991. "The Incidence of Mandated Employer-Provided Insurance: Lessons from Workers' Compensation Insurance." In *Tax Policy and the Economy,* edited by David Bradford (111–144). Cambridge, MA: MIT Press.

Gruber, Jonathan, and Michael Lettau. 2000. "How Elastic Is the Firm's Demand for Health Insurance?" Working Paper No. 8021. Cambridge, MA: National Bureau of Economic Research.

Gruber, Jonathan and Robin McKnight. 2002. "Why Did Employee Health Insurance Contributions Rise?" Working Paper No. 8878. Cambridge, MA: National Bureau of Economic Research.

Gruber, Jonathan, and James M. Poterba. 1994. "Tax Incentives and the Decision to Purchase Health Insurance: Evidence from the Self-Employed." *Quarterly Journal of Economics* 109(3): 701–33.

Hadley, Jack, and James D. Reschovsky. 2002. "Small Firms' Demand for Health Insurance: The Decision to Offer Insurance." *Inquiry* 39(2): 118–37.

Jensen, Gail A. 1992. "The Dynamics of Health Insurance among the Near Elderly." *Medical Care* 30(7): 598–614.

Kronick, Richard, and Todd Gilmer. 1999. "Explaining the Decline in Health Insurance Coverage, 1979–1995." *Health Affairs* 18(2): 30–47.

Kubik, Jeffrey D., and John R Moran. 2001. "An Instrumental Variables Approach for Estimating the Incidence of Endogenous Policies." Working paper, Syracuse University.

Leibowitz, Arleen, and Michael E. Chernew. 1992. "The Firm's Demand for Health Insurance." In *Health Benefits and the Workforce,* U.S. Department of Labor, Pension and Welfare Benefits Administration (77–83). Washington, DC: U.S. Government Printing Office.

Levitt, Steven D. 1997. "Using Electoral Cycles in Police Hiring to Estimate the Effect of Police on Crime." *American Economic Review* 87(3): 270–90.

Levy, Helen, and David Meltzer. 2001. "What Do We Really Know about How Health Insurance Affects Health?" Paper presented at Research Agenda Setting Conference, University of Michigan, July 8–10.

Lin, Chyongchiou J., and Judith R. Lave. 1998. "Duration in and Pattern of Utilization under Children's Health Insurance Programs." *Health Care Financing Review* 19(4): 101–16.

Long, Stephen H., and M. Susan Marquis. 1993. "Gaps in Employer Coverage: Lack of Supply or Lack of Demand?" *Health Affairs* 12(Supplement): 282–92.

Long, Stephen H., M. Susan Marquis, and Jack Rodgers. 1998. "Do People Shift Their Use of Health Services over Time to Take Advantage of Insurance?" *Journal of Health Economics* 17(1): 105–15.

Luft, Harold S., James C. Robinson, Deborah W. Garnick, Susan C. Maerki, and Stephen J. McPhee. 1986. "The Role of Specialized Clinical Services in Competition Among Hospitals." *Inquiry* 23(1): 83–94.

Marquis, M. Susan, and Stephen H. Long. 1995. "Worker Demand for Health Insurance in the Non-group Market." *Journal of Health Economics* 14(1): 47–63.

Marquis, M. Susan, and T. A. Louis. 2002. "On Using Sample Selection Methods in Estimating the Price Elasticity of Firms' Demand for Insurance." *Journal of Health Economics* 21(1): 137–145.

McBride, Timothy D. 1997. "Uninsured Spells for the Poor: Prevalence and Duration." *Health Care Financing Review* 19(1): 145–160.

McLaughlin, Catherine G. 1993. "The Dilemma of Affordability—Health Insurance for Small Businesses." *American Health Policy: Critical Issues for Reform,* edited by Robert B. Helms. Washington, DC: American Enterprise Institute Press.

McLaughlin, Catherine G., Michael E. Chernew, and E. F. Taylor. 2002. "Medigap Premiums and Medicare HMO Enrollment." *Health Services Research* 37(6): 1445–68.

Monheit, Alan C., and Claudia L. Schur. 1988. "The Dynamics of Health Insurance Loss: A Tale of Two Cohorts." *Inquiry* 25(3): 315–27.

Monheit, Alan C., and Jessica Primoff Vistnes. 1999. "Health Insurance Availability at the Workplace." *Journal of Human Resources* 34(4): 770–85.

Monheit, Alan C., Barbara Steonberg Schone, and Amy K. Taylor. 1999. "Health Insurance Choices in Two-Worker Households: Determinants of Double Coverage." *Inquiry* 36(1): 12–29.

Moran, John R., Michael E. Chernew, and Richard A. Hirth. 2001. "Preference Diversity and the Breadth of Employee Health Insurance Options." *Health Services Research* 36(5): 911–34.

Murray, J. P., S. Greenfield, S. H. Kaplan, and E. M. Yano. 1992. "Ambulatory Testing for Capitation and Fee-For-Service Patients in the Same Practice Setting: Relationship to Outcomes." *Medical Care* 30(3): 252–61.

Newhouse, Joseph P. 1992. "Medical Care Costs: How Much Welfare Loss?" *Journal of Economic Perspectives* 6(3): 3–21.

Nichols, Len. M., Linda J. Blumberg, Philip Cooper, and Jessica Vistnes. 2001. "Employer Demand for Health Insurance: Evidence from the Medical Expenditure Panel Survey—Insurance Component." Paper presented at the American Economic Association / ASSA Meetings, January 5–7.

Nyman, John A. 1999. "The Value of Health Insurance: The Access Motive." *Journal of Health Economics* 18(2): 141–52.

Pauly, Mark V., and Bradley Herring. 1999. *Pooling Health Insurance Risks.* Washington, DC: American Enterprise Institute Press.

———. 2000. *Cutting Taxes for Insuring: Options and Effects of Tax Credits for Health Insurance.* Washington, DC: American Enterprise Institute Press.

———. 2001. "Expanding Coverage Via Tax Credits: Trade-Offs and Outcomes." *Health Affairs* 20(1): 9–26.

Pearson, Steven D., Thomas H. Lee, Eugene Lindsey, Thomas Hawkins, E. Francis Cook, and Lee Goldman. 1994. "The Impact of Membership in a Health Maintenance Organization on Hospital Admission Rates for Acute Chest Pain." *Health Services Research* 29(1): 59–74.

Peden, Edgar A., and Mark S. Freeland. 1995. "A Historical Analysis of Medical Spending Growth, 1960–1993." *Health Affairs* 14(2): 235–47.

Phelps, Charles E. 1997. *Health Economics.* Boston, MA: Addison-Wesley.

Rosenzweig, Mark R., and Kenneth I. Wolpin. 2000. "Natural 'Natural Experiments' in Economics." *Journal of Economic Literature* 38(4): 827–74.

Royalty, Anne Beeson. 2000. "Tax Preferences for Fringe Benefits and Workers' Eligibility for Employer Health Insurance." *Public Economics* 75(2): 209–27.

Scanlon, Dennis P., Michael E. Chernew, Catherine G. McLaughlin, and Gary Solon. 2002. "The Impact of Health Plan Report Cards on Managed Care Enrollment." *Journal of Health Economics* 21(1): 19–41.

Scitovsky, Anne A. 1985. "Changes in the Costs of Treatment of Selected Illnesses, 1971–1981." *Medical Care* 23(12): 1345–57.

Scitovsky, Anne M., and Nelda McCall. 1976. "Changes in the Costs of Treatment of Selected Illnesses, 1951–1964–1971." HRA 77-3161. Washington, DC: U.S. Department of Health Education and Welfare, National Center for Health Services Research.

Scott, Frank A., Mark C. Berger, and Dan A. Black. 1989. "Effects of the Tax Treatment of Fringe Benefits on Labor Market Segmentation." *Industrial and Labor Relations Reviews* 42(2): 216–29.

Sheiner, Louise. 1999. "Health Care Costs, Wages, and Aging." Finance and Economics Discussion Series 99/19. Washington, DC: Board of Governors of the Federal Reserve System

Short, Pamela Farley, and Vicki A. Freedman. 1998. "Single Women and the Dynamics of Medicaid." *Health Services Research* 33(5): 1309–36.

Shur, Claudia L., and Amy K. Taylor. 1991. "Health Insurance in the Two Worker Household." *Health Affairs* 10(1): 155–163.

Sloan, Frank A., and Christopher J. Conover. 1998. "Life Transitions and Health Insurance Coverage of the Near Elderly." *Medical Care* 36(2): 110–125.

Staiger, Douglas, and James H. Stock. 1997. "Instrumental Variables Regressions with Weak Instruments." *Econometrica* 65: 557–86.

Swartz, Katherine. 1988. "The Demand for Self-Pay Health Insurance: An Empirical Investigation." Urban Institute Working Paper 3308-03. Washington, DC: The Urban Institute.

———. 1994. "Dynamics of People without Health Insurance. Don't Let the Numbers Fool You." *Journal of the American Medical Association* 274(1): 64–66.

Swartz, Katherine, and Timothy McBride. 1990. "Spells without Health Insurance: Distributions of Durations and their Link to Point in Time Estimates of the Uninsured." *Inquiry* 27(3): 281–88.

Swartz, Katherine, John Marcotte, and Timothy D. McBride. 1993. "Personal Characteristics and Spells without Health Insurance." *Inquiry* 30(1): 64–76.

Swartz, Katherine, Timothy McBride, and John Marcotte. 1993. "Spells without Health Insurance: The Distribution of Durations When Left-Censored Spells Are Included." *Inquiry* 30(1): 77–83.

Taylor, Amy K., and Gail R. Wilensky. 1983. "The Effect of Tax Policies on Expenditures for Private Health Insurance." In *Market Reforms in Health Care,* edited by Jack A. Meyer (163–184). Washington, DC: American Enterprise Institute Press.

Van Soest, A. 1995. "Structural Models of Family Labor Supply: A Discrete Choice Approach." *Journal of Human Resources* 30(1): 63–88.

Weisbrod, Burton A. 1991. "The Health Care Quadrilemma: An Essay on Technological Change, Insurance, Quality of Care, and Cost Containment." *Journal of Economic Literature* 29(2): 523–52.

Wholey, Douglas R., Roger Feldman, and Jon B. Christianson. 1995. "The Effect of Market Structure on HMO Premiums." *Journal of Health Economics* 14(1): 81–105.

Zwanziger, Jack, and Glenn A. Melnick. 1988. "The Effects of Hospital Competition and the Medicare PPS Program on Hospital Cost Behavior in California." *Journal of Health Economics* 7(4): 301–20.

About the Editor

Catherine McLaughlin is the director of the Economic Research Initiative on the Uninsured at the University of Michigan. She is also a professor in the Department of Health Management and Policy at the University of Michigan and a Senior Associate Editor of Health Services Research. In addition, Dr. McLaughlin is the director of the University of Michigan component of the Agency for Healthcare Research and Quality's Center of Excellence on Managed Care Markets and Quality directed by Harold Luft at the University of California–San Francisco.

Dr. McLaughlin has studied various health economics topics since joining the UM faculty in 1983. Her current research interests are focused on the uninsured, managed care, market competition, and employer and employee benefit choice. She has published numerous articles on the impact of HMOs on market competition and health care costs, the determinants of small area variation in hospital utilization and costs, and issues surrounding the working uninsured.

About the Contributors

Linda J. Blumberg is an economist and senior research associate at the Urban Institute. Her recent work includes a variety of projects related to private health insurance and health care financing, including estimating the coverage and risk pool impacts of tax credit proposals and public insurance expansions, estimating price elasticities of employers offering and workers taking up health insurance, studying the effects of insurance market reforms on the risk pool of the privately insured, and performing a series of analyses of the working uninsured. From August 1993 through October 1994, Dr. Blumberg served as health policy advisor to the Clinton administration during its initial health care reform effort.

Michael Chernew is an associate professor in the Departments of Health Management and Policy, Internal Medicine, and Economics at the University of Michigan's School of Public Health. He is coeditor of the *American Journal of Managed Care* and codirector of The Robert Wood Johnson Foundation's Scholars in Health Policy Research program at the University of Michigan. Dr. Chernew is also a faculty research fellow of the National Bureau of Economic Research, and he is on the editorial boards of *Health Services Research*, *Health Affairs*, and *Medical Care Research and Review*. In 2000, he served on a technical advisory panel for the Health Care Financing Administration that reviewed the assumptions used by the Medicare actuaries to assess the financial status of the Medicare trust funds.

Sarah Crow is an analyst with Berkeley Policy Associates, a social welfare research firm in Oakland, California. She has over five years' experience studying health policy, and was formerly a research associate at the Economic Research Initiative on the Uninsured.

Jonathan Gruber is a professor of economics at the Massachusetts Institute of Technology, where he has taught since 1992. He is also the director of the Program on Children at the National Bureau of Economic Research, where he is a research associate. Dr. Gruber's research focuses on the areas of public finance and health economics. His recent areas of particular interest include the economics of employer-provided health insurance, the efficiency of our current system of delivering health care to the indigent, the effect of the Social Security program on retirement behavior, and the economics of smoking. During the 1997–1998 academic year, Dr. Gruber served as deputy assistant secretary for economic policy at the Treasury Department.

Mary Harrington is a research investigator for the Economic Research Initiative on the Uninsured (ERIU) at the University of Michigan. Prior to joining ERIU, she was a senior researcher at Mathematica Policy Research, Inc., where her research focused primarily on Medicaid, managed care, child health, and safety net programs and providers. An expert in qualitative research methods, Ms. Harrington has designed and led numerous multisite evaluations and policy assessments. Her recent work includes lead roles in two national evaluations (for ASPE and for CMS) of the State Children's Health Insurance Program (SCHIP).

Richard Hirth is an associate professor in the Health Management and Policy department at the University of Michigan's School of Public Health. He has received several research awards, including the Kenneth Arrow Award in Health Economics from the International Health Economics Association. His research interests include the role of not-for-profit providers in health care markets, health insurance, the relationship between managed care and the adoption and utilization of medical technologies, long-term care, and the economics of end stage renal disease care. Dr. Hirth teaches courses in microeconomics and health economics.

Karl Kronebusch is an associate professor of health policy in the Department of Epidemiology and Public Health at Yale University, where his research and teaching interests focus on the politics of health and social policy. His published research has examined several aspects of participation in social programs, including the impacts of mandated Medicaid expansions, the effects of welfare reform, and the effectiveness of policies designed to improve program take-up rates. He is also examining the impacts of managed care regulation and patient protection legislation in the states. He has previously served on the faculty of the University of Wisconsin-Madison, and has been a Robert Wood Johnson Health Policy Scholar.

Hanns Kuttner is a senior research associate at the Economic Research Initiative on the Uninsured. His work focuses on making research results accessible to policy and general audiences. His research focuses on understanding coverage dynamics as well as the factors associated with changes in coverage status. Prior to joining ERIU, Mr. Kuttner served as a staff member of the Illinois Governor's Task Force on Human Services Reform and the District of Columbia's Tax Revision Commission. He also worked for the Health Care Financing Administration at the Department of Health and Human Services, and was a part of George H. W. Bush's White House policy staff working on health and social issues.

Helen G. Levy is an assistant professor in the Irving B. Harris Graduate School of Public Policy Studies. From 1998 to 2000, she was a Robert Wood Johnson Foundation Scholar in Health Policy Research at the University of California at Berkeley. She has also served as a research analyst for The Robert Wood Johnson Foundation and is a faculty research fellow of the National Bureau of Economic Research. Her research interests include the areas of health economics, public finance, and labor economics. Her most recent work explores the financial consequences of poor health for households without health insurance and the spending patterns of insured and uninsured households.

Brigitte Madrian is an associate professor of Business and Public Policy at the University of Pennsylvania Wharton School and a research associate at the National Bureau of Economic Research. She served on the faculty at Harvard University and the University of Chicago before moving to the University of Pennsylvania in 2003. Her research focuses on issues in labor and public economics, including the relationship between employer-provided health insurance and labor market outcomes, and employee savings behavior in 401(k) plans.

David O. Meltzer is an associate professor in the Department of Medicine and an associated faculty member of the Harris School and the Department of Economics at the University of Chicago. His research explores problems in health economics and public policy. A major area of Dr. Meltzer's research examines the theoretical foundations of medical cost-effectiveness analysis, including issues such as accounting for future costs due to the extension of life and the empirical validity of quality of life assessment, which he has examined in the context of diabetes and prostate cancer. Another major area of study examines the effects of managed care and medical specialization on the cost and quality of care, especially in teaching hospitals.

Len Nichols is vice president of the Center for Studying Health System Change. He provides leadership in shaping the research of the Center to inform the policy process in a timely and nonpartisan way, in addition to continuing his own research related to private health insurance and health care markets. Before joining the Center, he served as a principal research associate at the Urban Institute. During the first two years of the Clinton administration, Dr. Nichols was the senior advisor for health policy at the Office of Management and Budget (OMB). He managed and coordinated cost and revenue estimation for President Clinton's Health Security Act (HSA) and its congressional successors. Prior to his service at OMB, Dr. Nichols was a visiting Public Health Service Fellow at the Agency for Health Care Policy and Research, and served as an associate professor and Economics Department chair at Wellesley College.

Harold Pollack is associate professor at the University of Chicago School of Social Service Administration. His recent research concerns HIV and hepatitis prevention efforts for injection drug users, drug abuse and dependence among welfare recipients and pregnant women, infant mortality prevention, and child health. In addition, Dr. Pollack has been appointed to two committees of the National Academy of Sciences'

Institute of Medicine. His work appears in such journals as *Journal of the American Medical Association*, *Medical Decision Making*, *Pediatrics*, and *Social Service Review*.

Pamela Farley Short is a professor of health policy and administration at Penn State University and director of Penn State's Center for Health Care and Policy Research, specializing in the economics of health and health care. Before joining the faculty of Penn State in 1997, she was a senior economist in the Washington office of RAND and director of RAND's Center for the Study of Employee Health Benefits. For a number of years, Dr. Short was a senior manager in the intramural research program of the Agency for Health Care Policy and Research, part of the U.S. Department of Health and Human Services. She also worked in the White House for the Council of Economic Advisers as the senior staff economist for health care issues and is particularly well known for her expertise regarding the uninsured and underinsured. Dr. Short's research emphasizes the study of changes in individuals' lives over time, recently with regard to movement in and out of health insurance programs, retirement and employment transitions, and the unfolding experiences of cancer survivors.

Index